Encounters and Practices of Petty Trade in Northern Europe, 1820–1960

"This book is an exciting and welcome contribution to the study of the social and economic history of the Nordic countries. It provides a broad, yet empirically precise, interdisciplinary insight into the understudied topic of petty trade, which in turn offers a valuable entry to exploring the livelihoods, trading practices, and encounters of mobile and often marginalised social groups (e.g. Sámi, Jews, and Roma people) in Finland, Sweden and their neighbouring countries. The book is, therefore, a must-read for anyone interested in not only petty trade but also economic activities and everyday lives of ethnic, religious and/or linguistic minorities in the Nordic countries".

—Fia Sundevall, *Stockholm University, Sweden*

"The volume assembles case studies on practices of petty trade—often regarded as marginal—and highlights just how common they were throughout Europe. The book shows how such highly ambiguous and diverse activities or trades served the needs of consumption, bartering and entertainment. By reading sources against the grain, the individual chapters depict everyday routines and encounters of sellers and residents, while also reconstructing sellers' agency and tactics. Overall, this book opens up new perspectives while drawing a highly differentiated and multifaceted picture of practices often neglected by historians because they do not fit neatly into traditional categories of work or trades".

—Sigrid Wadauer, *University of Vienna, Austria*

Jutta Ahlbeck • Ann-Catrin Östman
Eija Stark
Editors

Encounters and Practices of Petty Trade in Northern Europe, 1820–1960

Forgotten Livelihoods

palgrave
macmillan

Editors
Jutta Ahlbeck
Culture, History and Philosophy
Åbo Akademi University
Turku, Finland

Ann-Catrin Östman
Culture, History and Philosophy
Åbo Akademi University
Turku, Finland

Eija Stark
The Finnish Literature Society
Helsinki, Finland

ISBN 978-3-030-98079-5 ISBN 978-3-030-98080-1 (eBook)
https://doi.org/10.1007/978-3-030-98080-1

This Palgrave Macmillan imprint is published by the registered company Springer Nature Switzerland AG.
The registered company address is: Gewerbestrasse 11, 6330 Cham, Switzerland

Acknowledgements

This collection is the result of a large project, which started in 2015, and of many engaging discussions with scholars, who have contributed to our research over the years. We are indebted to the Academy of Finland and the Kone-foundation for funding our project *Dealing with Difference: Peddlers, Consumers and Trading Encounters in Finland, 1840–1960*. Thank you for financing and believing in our research!

A great many scholars have inspired us, and we wish to thank Klara Arnberg, Åsa Bharathi Larsson, Katherine Borland, Theresa Johnsson, Pirita Frigren, Janet Gilmore, Eirinn Larsen, James Leary, Dorothy Noyes, Ariadne Schmidt, Sami Suodenjoki, Ulla Teräs, Carolina Uppenberg and Sigrid Wadauer. They have shared their thoughts and insights, giving us helpful responses to our work in progress.

We owe special thanks to colleagues from Sweden, Norway, Denmark, Austria, Iceland, the Netherlands and Finland for collaborations at conferences, workshops and seminars. These have been important platforms for us to further develop our ideas. Our colleague Hanna Lindberg deserves special words of appreciation, as her analytical mind and input pushed us to clarify our arguments and concepts. Tack Hanna!

We are also grateful to the universities that hosted us as visiting scholars, offering us an opportunity to discuss and present our research, and receive invaluable input to our ongoing work. Many thanks to the University of Madison, Wisconsin, and the Center for the Study of Upper Midwestern Cultures, Center for Folklore Studies at Ohio State University, Uppsala University and the Department of History, Stockholm University and its Department of History, and the Department of History and its Gender History Seminar at Lund University.

We have been fortunate to receive financial support previously from The Swedish Literature Society and The Swedish Cultural Foundation, and we express our warmest gratitude to the foundations.

The book has been in the making in both Turku/Åbo and Helsinki, and we wish to thank the Department of Culture, History and Philosophy at Åbo Akademi University, particularly our colleagues, who have been engaged in our work and commented upon earlier versions of chapters at seminars. Especially Johanna Ilmakunnas, Laura Hollsten and Patrik Hettula have been genuinely interested in our project and given us a constructive and inspiring critique of the manuscript. In Helsinki, The Finnish Literature Society offered us another venue and site of support, and we want to acknowledge Tuomas M. S. Lehtonen, who has been eager to test new ideas with us. Also, the seminars organized by The Society and its Research Department have very been very valuable to us.

We are also thankful to Sandra Waller and Fanny Lindroos for their professional research assistance, and for giving us important comments on our work in progress.

Finally, the editors extend their heartfelt thanks and warmest gratitude to Albion Butters, whose extraordinary language skills and professionalism were invaluable in completing this book.

Jutta Ahlbeck, Ann-Catrin Östman and Eija Stark

Turku and Helsinki, 30 September 2021

[The research for this volume was funded by the Academy of Finland (308534) and the Kone-foundation (201609155)]

Contents

Notes on Contributors

Jutta Ahlbeck PhD, Adjunct Professor (Docent), is a sociologist and historian, and researcher at Åbo Akademi University, Finland. Her research has explored health and illness, particularly the history of women's madness and psychiatry. Other research interests cover itinerant trade and materiality, childhood and modernity, power and gender, qualitative methodology.

Niklas Huldén PhD, is an ethnologist, archivist and researcher at Åbo Akademi University, Finland. Huldén has an interest in material, innovation and maritime studies. His dissertation (2018) dealt with cultural ecology in maritime environments based on probate material.

Ella Johansson PhD, is Chair Professor in European Ethnology at Uppsala University, Sweden. Her research has dealt with modernity and history in Northern Sweden. She has published extensively on Swedish national identity in relation to modern immigration. She also works in gender, heritage, and landscape studies.

Maren Jonasson MA, is a historian and researcher at Åbo Akademi University. Her scholarly interests include eighteenth- and nineteenth-century Nordic history, market entertainment, agricultural meetings and exhibitions. She is also a textual scholar and editor.

Otso Kortekangas PhD, is a postdoctoral researcher at the Division of History of Science, Technology and Environment at KTH Royal Institute of Technology, Stockholm, Sweden. Kortekangas has published books and articles on Sámi and Arctic history, and he teaches Sámi history at Stockholm University, Sweden.

Anna Kuismin is Docent of comparative literature at the University of Helsinki, Finland. Her scholarly interests include eighteenth-century Finnish self-taught writers, lay collectors of folklore, and history from below. Before her retirement, she worked as the Head of the Literature Archives of the Finnish Literature Society.

Ann-Catrin Östman PhD, Adjunct Professor (Docent), is a senior lecturer in history at Åbo Akademi University, Finland. In her research, she has focused especially on the history of gender, citizenship and work in agrarian cultures as well as in the history of consumption and trade.

Eija Stark PhD, Adjunct Professor (Docent, Folklore Studies), is a development manager in the Finnish Literature Society, Finland. Stark's research interests cover the history of social class, functions of folklore, narrative culture, critical approaches to archives and intellectual history of Finnish and Nordic folklore studies and ethnology.

Anna Sundelin PhD, is a historian and researcher at Åbo Akademi University, Finland. She has published extensively on consumption history and material culture, itinerant trade and Russian peddlers in Finland.

Kirsi Vainio-Korhonen PhD, is Professor of Finnish history at the University of Turku, Finland. In her research, she has gathered strong expertise on economic and gender history, female entrepreneurship and paid work, handicrafts relations, and household economy.

Johanna Wassholm PhD, is Adjunct Professor (Docent) of Russian and Nordic History and researcher at Åbo Akademi University, Finland. She is an expert in the field of nationalism, itinerant trade, transnational trade, consumption, Jews, Tatars, Russians and Finnish-Russian relations 1800–1930.

List of Figures

CHAPTER 1

Introduction: Encounters and Trading Practices

Jutta Ahlbeck, Ann-Catrin Östman, and Eija Stark

The long nineteenth century was a period of changing modes of labor and consumption. New livelihood opportunities opened up for the landless and poor as globalization made labor mobile. At the same time, the circulation and exchange of various goods increased considerably, which affected trade on the global, regional, and local levels. This multidisciplinary collection, *Encounters and Practices of Petty Trade in Northern Europe, 1820–1960: Forgotten Livelihoods* (henceforth *Forgotten Livelihoods*), uncovers one important yet neglected form of these emerging itinerant livelihoods—namely, petty trade—and how it was practiced in Northern Europe during the period 1820–1960 (see map in Fig. 1.1). Transnational and interregional relations characterized this sparsely

J. Ahlbeck • A.-C. Östman (✉)
Culture, History and Philosophy, Åbo Akademi University, Turku, Finland
e-mail: jutta.ahlbeck@abo.fi; aostman@abo.fi

E. Stark
The Finnish Literature Society, Helsinki, Finland
e-mail: eija.stark@finlit.fi

J. Ahlbeck et al. (eds.), *Encounters and Practices of Petty Trade in Northern Europe, 1820–1960*,
https://doi.org/10.1007/978-3-030-98080-1_1

Fig. 1.1 Map of Northern Europe. (Map by Niklas Huldén. With permission from Huldén)

populated region, where disparate groups in terms of religion, ethnicity, and language interacted.

We explore how the overall increase in consumption had wide cultural and social consequences by investigating how traders and customers interacted in different spaces. Here, ambulatory trade is considered an arena of encounters and everyday social practices. In the Nordics, as elsewhere, mobile petty traders often belonged to subjugated social groups, like ethnic minorities, migrants, and the poverty-stricken, whereas their customers belonged to the resident population. Thus, our volume asks, how were these mobile traders perceived and described? What goods did they peddle and how did these commodities enable and shape trading encounters? By approaching petty trade in terms of consumption history *and* by addressing the marginalization of particular social groups, this collection offers insights into livelihood practices at a grassroots level—an account that previous research has overlooked.

Petty trade has been, and still is, an integral part of social, cultural, and economic life in many regions of the world. As a term, *petty trade* refers to an economic activity that involves selling and buying goods—agricultural as well as consumer goods and services—on a small scale. In the nineteenth century, traditional and vernacular forms of retail, such as peddling and trade in marketplaces, continued to meet the basic needs of many customers. Petty traders, such as "peddlers," "mongers," "hucksters," "hawkers," "vendors," and "bootleggers," were all engaged in small-scale trade, and the epithets attached to these sellers were often pejorative, sometimes referring to their multiple levels of strangeness. Itinerant performers, sex workers, and professional photographers also used marketplaces and other venues to gain income from the entertainment and services they offered.

We emphasize the importance of studying how marginalized groups tried to ensure their means of support. Although there is a rich supply of fine historical works on livelihood-related struggles in the late nineteenth and early twentieth centuries, relatively few of them deal with the mixture of livelihoods, tangible everyday encounters, and ethnographies of material cultures. *Forgotten Livelihoods* undertakes a historical exploration into many aspects of mixed livelihoods that were familiar to European societies in the relatively recent past.

Petty trade has not been elaborated or studied in detail in the broad field of consumption history and the history of retail. To some extent, various forms of small-scale trade are touched upon in Ian Mitchell's impressive study *Tradition and Innovation in English Retailing, 1700 to 1850* (2014). Trading activities at fairs and urban markets in Europe have mainly been studied by scholars of early modern history, such as David Pennington in his monograph *Going to Market: Women, Trade and Social Relations in Early Modern English Towns, c. 1550–1650* (2015). Laurence Fontaine has explored peddling and petty trade in her groundbreaking *History of Pedlars in Europe* (1996).[1]

These studies suggest that petty trade engaged various groups, arguing that trading was of great importance for the lower strata in society. A few studies on labor and work practices in early-modern Sweden demonstrate that women were also largely engaged in trading activities.[2] Several studies on trading encounters and social relations draw on E. P. Thompson's concept of "moral economy." While customers are frequently presented as subordinate, neither the vulnerable position of *petty traders* nor ethnical hierarchies are adequately addressed in these studies.[3]

In his groundbreaking study *Peddlers and Princes* (1963), anthropologist Clifford Geertz demonstrates how petty traders who belonged to ethnic and/or religious minorities were indispensable to the operation of regional and national economies in periods of economic growth. Internationally, historians have analyzed itinerant trade and addressed its importance for economic development. Some scholars note that petty trade involved various groups, arguing that trading was of great importance for itinerant persons in periods of modernization.[4] However, these explorations' focus lies in governmental policies toward itinerants, not the daily practices of traders and their customers. An important study is Hasia R. Diner's *Roads Taken: The Great Jewish Migrations to the New World and the Peddlers Who Forged the Way* (2015), in which she demonstrates how peddling was often the first occupation of Jewish migrants in new countries and how their activities attracted other economically vulnerable social groups. Diner addresses the vulnerable position of petty traders and ethnic hierarchies.[5]

Arguing that hierarchies that circumscribed the lives of trading groups have been neither sufficiently studied nor problematized, we investigate the livelihoods of subjugated groups and minorities in the North. Secondly, our volume takes seriously the "material turn" in historical and social science research and we address the agency of "things" and "artifacts". We maintain that new commodities both shaped and altered social relations, thus commodities had the power not only to enable livelihoods but also at times confer higher social status to both sellers and buyers.

Encounters in the North

Northern Europe, here including the Nordic countries (Finland, Sweden, Norway, and Denmark), the Arctic and Subarctic Europe, and northern Estonia, offer an interesting case for studying petty trade during a period of economic growth and liberalization as well as nation-building. As a result of rapid economic development and the liberalization of trading regulations, there was a quick expansion and flood of goods in the Nordic region, where consumer culture was undeveloped. Especially in peripheral and mainly rural settings, peddlers and other petty traders introduced the opportunity for consumer goods to be purchased during a period, when "common people" started having the means to consume goods above the subsistence level. There was actual demand for goods among consumers, and sometimes such merchandise represented a better standard of living for rural and working-class customers, many of whom were women and young people (i.e., groups in subordinate social positions). Peddlers played an important role in providing rural and urban customers with affordable products. Still, in the nineteenth century, traditional urban marketplaces were important trading spaces in small towns. Following longstanding regulations, itinerant petty traders, and rural dealers as well as traveling performers visited towns at a certain time of the year. The marketplace was a traditional retail arena, where dealers operated from humble premises, and a place that could be used by visitors and sojourners.[6]

The Nordics comprised a large geographical, yet sparsely populated region, predominantly rural with smaller towns, the capitals of Stockholm and Helsinki, and only one metropolis, Saint Petersburg. It was situated between the West and East, and between the North and South. Finland was part of Sweden until 1809, after which it became an autonomous part of the Russian Empire as the Grand Duchy of Finland. At the turn of the century, the number of Russians increased in Finland, and strong elements of Russophobia were prevalent in all Nordic countries. Starting from 1899, Russia tightened its grip on Finland by proposing similar legislation for Finland and the rest of the Russian Empire. Finland finally gained independence in 1917, yet conflicts and tensions as to how the young nation was to be governed continued until civil war broke out in 1918.[7]

The close geographical, social, and historical relations between Finland, Sweden, Estonia, and Russia laid the foundation for diverse encounters. Petty traders often traveled across borders, and their livelihoods were transnational. In the Nordics, ethnic, linguistic, and religious minorities, like Roma, Russians, Sámi, Jews, and Tatars, often engaged in petty trade, along with vagrants, peasants, and the rural poor (see Fig. 1.2).

Petty trade thus connected and affected relations between indigenous groups and settlers. In the northern parts of Sweden, Norway, and Finland, there were many layers of entanglement between Sámi groups and the resident populations. Scandinavia's arctic and subarctic areas belonging to

Fig. 1.2 Itinerant livelihoods. Roma peddlers in Finland in 1928. (Photo by Samuli Paulaharju 1928. The Finnish Heritage Agency)

Sámi had partly been taken over by the respective states or by settlers coming from other areas. In addition to this, racist perceptions of Sámi were flourishing; they were considered less "civilized" and situated at a lower stage of cultural and evolutionary progress, but simultaneously regarded as more "authentic" and closer to nature. The Roma comprised another old minority group, which had arrived in Finland and Sweden in the sixteenth century and was generally despised in public discourses. Specific "Gypsy Laws" were passed to control and govern itinerant Roma. Similarly, as in the rest of Europe, notions of antiziganism and anti-Semitism were deeply rooted in these peripheral areas.

In addition to Russians, Sámi, and Roma, other linguistic minorities included Finnish-speaking groups in the north of Sweden and Norway, and the Swedish-speaking minority in Finland. At the turn of the century, the latter amounted to 12.9 percent of the population (about 350,000 people).[8] Although the upper class and the nobility in Finland had historically been Swedish-speaking, commoners, workers, fishermen, and farmers belonged to the Swedish-speaking population as well.

In terms of social boundaries and class hierarchies in the late nineteenth and early twentieth centuries, the vast majority were commoners not included in the old estate society. The traditional estate society consisted of the nobility, the clergy, burghers, and the landowning peasants. In Finland, for example, some 70% of the whole population in 1890 were commoners.[9] Cottagers, tenants of farms, itinerant petty traders, farm servants and rural craftsmen as well as industrial workers were tied up with hard physical labor. In terms of poverty, persons working sporadic odd jobs and small-scale hunters and fishermen were also considered commoners, since they, too, regularly knew destitution and their livelihoods were precarious.

By analyzing transnational and interregional connections in Northern Europe, this volume contributes to international research on the multilayered importance of consumption and petty trade for social relations. The chapters in *Forgotten Livelihoods* include analyses of itinerant market performers (Jonasson), stories of hidden economies (Huldén), working-class experiences of petty trade (Stark), Roma horse traders (Ahlbeck), submissive and unruly peasant traders (Östman), fictional representations of market goers (Kuismin), Sámi livelihoods (Kortekangas), Jewish and Tatar salesmen (Wassholm), women's traditional outfits as a trading strategy (Johansson), rag collectors from Russian Karelia (Sundelin and Wassholm), and Russian peddlers settling down in Finland (Sundelin). What emerges is a complex narrative of vulnerable livelihoods, often marginalized in their own time and overlooked in previous research.

Livelihoods in the Margins

The micro perspective of *Forgotten Livelihoods* enables us to uncover power relations and hierarchies that circumscribed the lives and livelihoods of petty traders—something that previous research has not sufficiently addressed. This collection contributes to broadening the scholarly fields on itinerant livelihoods and consumption history. Each chapter approaches precarious positions and relations of selling and buying, as well as addresses the specific power relations that once defined these transactions. By focusing on ethnicity, gender, class, and religion, the book provides new perspectives of itinerant trade and marketed commodities, as well as the practices, representations, and experiences of both traders and consumers.

In the middle of the nineteenth century, the growth of trade was accompanied by new laws and regulations. However, peddlers and other petty traders often operated in informal ways, sometimes illegally.[10] In Finland and Sweden, trade in the countryside was legalized in the 1840s and 1850s, which meant that shops could also be opened outside towns. As rural shops were few, however, there was still demand for the goods offered by peddlers, many of whom worked without licenses. During these years, market trade—an old and traditional form of commerce—was gradually regarded by the authorities as old-fashioned and unnecessary. After public debate in the 1860s, regulations on markets were made stricter and licenses were withdrawn. Yet, at the same time as new cultures and traditions of buying and selling emerged in the latter part of the century, older and informal forms of trade remained important in many regions. Even if local authorities tried to control urban market spaces, carnivalesque fairs took place in many towns. In a similar vein, the poor could still invoke understandings of petty trade as a form of social welfare, which permitted certain individuals—such as the widowed, elderly, and handicapped—to vend.

The chapters in this book demonstrate how small-scale traders and their customers interacted and came together in different spaces. Unlike today, when a customer goes to a grocery store or a shopping mall, or shops online, traders in the past visited and operated in both private (homes) and public outdoor spaces (town markets, fairs, door to door). Thus, the chapters explore the nexus of practices and how traders appropriated places and created multilayered spaces. The open-air market represented a traditional retail arena, where vendors operated from relatively simple premises and according to customary practices. Some peddlers remained in one fixed location, using a market stall that was locked up and left under the supervision of a watchman when not in use. Others used horse carts, mobile stalls, or rucksacks. Itinerant peddlers carried their merchandise on a horse cart or on their back in a rucksack (see Fig. 1.3). Some sold their items to passengers-by, while some made door-to-door deliveries.[11]

This volume takes its point of departure in a broad intersectional approach, but gendered aspects of petty trade are pivotal. By studying how trading encounters as well as commodities were gendered, the authors open up new perspectives. Through the concept of space, we address questions of how hierarchies and differences were manifested and changed. The chapters demonstrate gender as a central part of the using and taking of spaces, and the gendered dichotomy of the private and the public that

Fig. 1.3 The peddler Juho Monthan on his 80th birthday in 1929. (Photographer unknown. The Finnish Heritage Agency)

was created and reconstructed in everyday practices. Both women and men were involved in trading spaces, in marketplaces, and in domestic spaces in homes. By scrutinizing everyday social practices and laypeople, the book makes the repertoires of women and men visible and thereby studies the intertwined making of gender and space.[12]

The relatively homogeneous and quickly developed North provides an interesting case to investigate social relations not only across borders, but also across social class, ethnicity, and language relations. Nowadays, the Nordics are famous for their social democracies, gender equality, welfare benefits, and low level of corruption. Up until the mid-twentieth century, most countries in the North were predominantly agrarian, as industrialization began only in the late 1800s. The majority of the population were peasants (farmers or farmhands) or employed by town industries that were dramatically increasing.

Peddling was often the first occupation of migrants in their new countries, and these activities often attracted other economically vulnerable social groups. However, as an effect of the overall increase in consumption, peddling and the growth in trade decreased the hierarchical gap between social groups. Selling food became increasingly important to feed the burgeoning town populations in this era of industrial expansion. Hence, sellers belonging to subjugated groups started appealing to the middle and upper classes with much-needed products, services, and food. For example, food was sold in local food markets or by vendors selling their wares door to door in ways that connected the upper class with traders.[13] Moreover, encounters with distinctive ethnicities became more frequent in the contexts of marketplaces and street vending in towns. Just like ethnic minorities, women took part in petty trade as capable actors, creating a gendered niche of economic opportunity through the capitalization of their cooking and vending skills.[14]

Trading Practices: Creative Uses of the Social Order

Theoretically, the collection follows Michel de Certeau's (1984) notion of *practices* in emphasizing the potential significance of seemingly trivial and routine everyday activities, such as walking, talking, reading, or selling and buying commodities. We argue that there is a need to think in a more nuanced way about daily encounters between mobile groups and the resident population.

These encounters were physical and tangible. As social relations and subjectivities were constructed in a constantly ongoing process of performance, interactions between traders and consumers were mutually constitutive. In their selling and buying practices, subjects were "making" and performing ethnicity, gender, and class. Inspired by de Certeau, we approach petty trade as sets of heterogeneous and changing practices, shaped and used in particular spaces. In his plea for the study of the political aspects of everyday practices, de Certeau sheds light on ordinary rituals and the utilization of urban spaces.[15] All the chapters investigate practices, rituals, and forms of interactions that over time became attached to the daily routines of buying and selling. In addition to this, the chapters point to the ways in which traders and customers made use of various geographical places, transforming them into economic spaces of trading (see Fig. 1.4).

The concept of practice thus relates to *space*, which we understand as "a practiced place," in which subjugated ("the weak") and ruling ("the strong") groups come together.[16] De Certeau opens up questions about how informal practices and material encounters in the marketplace can be understood. Rejecting dichotomies, de Certeau describes the tangible and momentary tactics people develop to pursue their goals and adapt to their surroundings. These tactics were embodied as well as mental, being inscribed in posture, manners, clothing, and modes of speaking.

Fig. 1.4 Jewish traders selling clothes at the *Narinkka*, a market square in central Helsinki, Finland, in 1929. Jewish and Russian traders were given the right to trade only in this place. The name of the market square is derived from the Russian expression на рынке (na rynke), which means "at the marketplace". (Photo by Rafael Roos. Helsinki City Museum)

In our volume, we look at how customary and informal as well as formal practices were enacted, enunciated, transformed, and invented. Despite local government authorities' efforts to control the market space and selling encounters, in addition to their general hostility toward mobile peddlers, residents continued to buy goods and foods from petty traders.[17] The majority of these peddlers worked without licenses, thus bending regulations and laws. Although local and state authorities regulated—and even withdrew—permissions and authorizations for market trade in Nordic towns in the late nineteenth century, peasants and other traders defied strictures and continued selling and bartering various commodities at annual or quarterly fairs in small towns.

Making use of the dominant social order and displaying forms of resistance, or what de Certeau calls tactics, "ordinary people" are not to be understood as passive and submissive but rather as active, capable of manipulating and (re)shaping the environments around them through everyday actions. De Certeau approaches situated practices as examples of how "the weak make use of the strong," which "lends a political dimension to everyday practices."[18] Despite repressive societal structures (that always exist in a society), ordinary people enact elements of creative tactics to make use of the very same structures—an account echoing Foucault's notions of power and resistance.[19] The task is to scrutinize uncountable and small transformations of and within dominant systems.[20]

Following the trajectory outlined by de Certeau, *Forgotten Livelihoods* makes visible the countless, seemingly insignificant practices by means of which both sellers and customers leverage specific circumstances and positions.[21] Our volume discloses how petty trade could be practiced in a myriad of ways, both informally and illegally, as well as based on creative understandings of the legal order and formal restrictions.

Encounters between sellers and buyers consisted of marketing tactics that included performance and interaction; for example, sellers would holler and cry their wares, and they would dress up in a certain way. The appearance of a seller was adjusted to meet the expectations of buyers and, more broadly, city culture. Similarly, petty traders could provide entertainment by singing, dancing, fortune telling, storytelling, or exhibiting their "extraordinary" and "exotic" bodies, sometimes exaggerating their ethnic difference, or playing with their exoticism and mythological appearance to attract the audience and ultimately get money (see Jonasson; Johansson; Wassholm in this volume).

On Things and Materiality

Scholarship on the history of things has pointed to their capacity to mediate human relationships among social groups across space and time.[22] We are thus interested in the meanings given to the actual items (i.e., the consumer goods) and, following theories of material cultures, we understand artifacts, objects, and things not as passive, but rather as social agents, or "actans," actively shaping the social.[23] We are further informed by anthropologist Daniel Miller, who maintains that to go beyond a dualistic approach means "recognizing that the continual process by which meaning is given to things is the same process by which meaning is given to [human] lives."[24] In his pioneering work, Arjun Appadurai talks about "the social life of things,"[25] giving an apt description of how things circulate and are redefined: "… today's gift is tomorrow's commodity. Yesterday's commodity is tomorrow's found art object. Today's art object is tomorrow's junk. And yesterday's junk is tomorrow's heirloom."[26] Moreover, "things" are commodified as they travel and are given new meanings in different contexts. Rags, for instance, usually worthless to the individual, could be redefined as valuable materials and pivotal economic goods, because they were needed and used in paper production in the early 1800s (see Sundelin and Wassholm in this volume).

Commodities undeniably played an important role in enabling encounters between petty traders and their customers, not only as things for sale (see Fig. 1.5). Goods also embodied, shaped, and altered social relations, thereby representing a sort of materialization of such relations. Commodities were also gendered, classed, and ethnicized, as were economic activities, spheres, and practices. Postcolonial studies have drawn attention to the potential empowerment for subjugated social groups by means of artifacts.[27] Yet, petty trade could also have an oppressive force, in that it was often an enforced form of livelihood for poor and vulnerable social groups. Feminist scholars have demonstrated how gendered relations are among the social relations that artifacts clearly embody, convey, and shape.[28] Gender can be imprinted onto objects through associations with gendered divisions of labor, and through associations with gender symbols and myths. These aspects were visible in petty trade, in which gendered artifacts contributed to the maintenance of gendered social relations, especially relations of power (particularly in relation to the sedentary community), but also reciprocal relations.

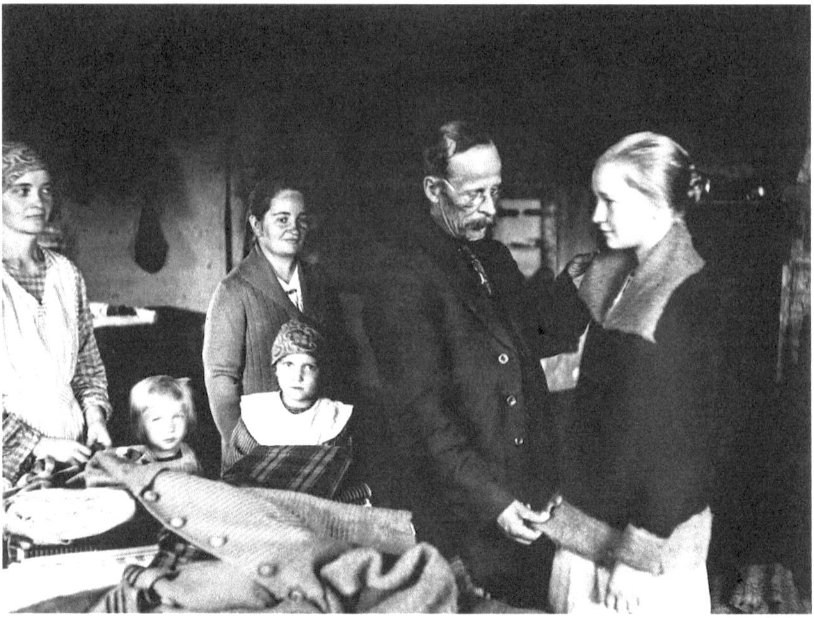

Fig. 1.5 The Karelian peddler Stepan Stepanoff fitting on clothes for his customers in Northern Karelia in 1926. (Photo by H. Tarkkonen 1926. The Finnish Heritage Agency)

For instance, Roma men became associated with horses, whereas Roma women were seen in relation to handicrafts, particularly laces (see Ahlbeck in this volume). Commodities carried meanings and strategies. Laces and textiles were not only coveted commodities; they also served as a means to establish trust and respectability and to strengthen social relations between petty traders and peasants. By donating or exchanging laces (for food and shelter), Roma women could establish close contact with the matrons and other women of the house, thus ensuring entry the next time the family came to the village.

What do we mean when we say that practices or materials were ethnicized? Not only gender but also ethnicity was imprinted onto both livelihoods and artifacts. For example, "Gypsy horse trading," "Rucksack-Russian peddling," and "Sámi reindeer herding" were ethnicized in the sense that they were identified exclusively through particular practices (see chapters by Ahlbeck; Sundelin; Kortekangas in this volume). Consequently, their commodities were ethnicized; for instance, laces and horses were strongly associated with "gypsies," and textiles with Russian peddlers. The way traders were regarded by their customers, or how they were portrayed in the public discourse, affected how their goods were looked upon. The racist stereotypes of Roma peddlers and Afro-American entertainers, for example, meant that "Gypsy things" and "indecent Negro shows" were, like the traders themselves, presented as undesirable and worthless: Roma's horses were in bad shape and not suitable for proper farm work, their handicrafts and other commodities were of poor quality, the entertainment provided by Afro-American women was lousy, and so forth.

Not only nonhuman things, but also human bodies were commodified, traded, and consumed similarly as goods. Female bodies, in particular, became visible at fairs and in marketplaces, some as prostitutes or sellers of sex (Vainio-Korhonen in this volume), others exhibiting their "exotic" bodies—in this case, black bodies[29]—as entertainment to be gazed at (Jonasson in this volume). Female traders also displayed their bodies through specific clothes and costumes, which enabled them to establish themselves as sellers or workers specialized in certain trades (Johansson in this volume). These cases illustrate practices of selling and consumption of female bodies in different ways. While commodification is often understood as oppressive in that it regulates female bodies in an objectifying way, the chapters in our volume look at how female traders *used* their bodies to their own advantage, employing performative "tactics," recognizing that their bodies were marketable commodities.

Although these female traders' activities may be regarded as subversive, the women were nevertheless responding to poverty, vulnerability, and marginalization, often lacking other livelihood options, which reflects the importance not only of gender but also social class and race. In addition, we do not know how the women themselves experienced their livelihoods, as we do not have personal (first-person) accounts, only sources written by authorities and the public.

Trapped in Traditions: On Sources, Methods, and Ethics

The manifold materials and sources used in this volume consist of public writings (e.g., newspapers), ethnological questionnaires, popular descriptions, oral history interviews, fiscal and legal sources, police archives, reminiscences, illustrations, photographs, fiction, and memoirs. Given the visible nature of petty trade and materiality regarding vending, surprisingly little is known about the social encounters and practices of small-scale trade. Certainly, due to taxation and legislation on trade, there are several extant historical documents on petty trade in various Nordic national and provincial archives. In official archival sources, however, traders were often depicted from the perspectives of the resident groups or from the top-down view of the authorities, whereas the "voices" of the subordinate groups remained silent. Our volume discloses examples of both life writings (see Stark in this volume) and attempts to outline biographies of traders, insofar as the sources allow (see chapters by Vainio-Korhonen and Sundelin in this volume).

In exploring the vulnerable livelihoods often pursued by marginalized social and ethnic groups in the late nineteenth and early twentieth centuries, we need to address the problematic power asymmetries concerning historical sources. Public documents, newspapers, and ethnographic sources, like folklore collections, unmistakably illustrate the hierarchical nature of cultural knowledge, that is, how cultural memory was produced, collected, and shaped by ideological and political motives, such as nation-building forces. Albeit official records and writings may reveal how petty trade was practiced and (re)presented in public discourses, more personal accounts—such as how traders looked upon their work, why some ended up as full- or part-time petty traders, how they created social networks, and the consumption patterns of the lower social classes—are difficult to trace.

Ethnographic and cultural archives in the Nordic countries were long seen only as a means of promoting the representative characteristics of the national (majority) and of serving the nation-state project. As organizations endowed with institutional power, therefore, archives have not only been depositories of collectibles but active agents of inclusion and exclusion.[30] One obvious reason for the absence of folksy types of petty trade, consumer goods and entertainment, is the modern nature of the phenomenon. From the nineteenth century onwards, European scholars interpreted mainly rural people as possessing oral as well as material traditions, which were considered to have been handed down from previous generations. Among scholars, the commoners have usually been called "the folk" (Swedish: *allmoge*, *bonde*; Finnish: *kansa*, *rahvas*).

Scholars and ethnographers, who dealt with the culture they themselves were not part of, objectified the rural, non-educated people and their vernacular culture, thereby removing these people's own possibility to act as protagonists and to make their own interpretations of their culture. Often this top-down relationship was stated in the letters, questionnaires, and instructions of the archives sent to lay collectors.[31] When discussing the concept "ordinary people," Michel de Certeau points at the marginality of the majority, emphasizing that most people can be considered "unseen" and "un-read." Depicting marginality as universal, he nevertheless pays attention to how various groups are positioned hierarchically within the dominant cultural economy.[32] Thus, the majority is by no means homogeneous; the possibilities of deployments of practices and utilization of space are related to power relations and different relationships of force.

Since many of the traditional minorities resorted to street vending or ambulatory petty trade, their livelihoods were seen as marginal and not fitting the grand narrative based on sedentary peasant ideals. Thus, petty trade as a specific livelihood of ethnic minorities was long neglected. For example, the Archives of the Finnish Literature Society organized dozens of ethnographic questionnaires in 1936–1968, but none focused on marketplaces or the petty trade of consumer goods. Contrary to the Finnish Literature Society, however, Swedish-speaking cultural heritage archives in Finland organized questionnaires on Russian itinerant peddlers in 1957 and 1968.[33]

Many of the chapters in this volume deal with social groups that were not in power but rather in marginal and vulnerable positions, due to their ethnicity and lack of resources—that is, poverty. By taking seriously the subjugated voices that do exist and the ones we are able to trace, *Forgotten Livelihoods* sheds more light on social and cultural encounters, tense or peaceful, and experiences concerning petty trade and economic change. Ethical sensitivity and source criticism are part of our methodological awareness. By taking seriously subordinate experience, insofar as it is possible, we aim at producing ethically sustainable research.

Presentation of Chapters

Each chapter delves into different forms of itinerant livelihoods and consumption in Northern Europe, during a time of increasing modernization and globalization, suggesting how these phenomena can be analyzed and understood. Collectively, the contributions develop novel approaches to such important themes as marginalization, ethnic relations, poverty, and possibilities of social mobility, namely, large social phenomena over time and space.

Otso Kortekangas investigates trade, a forgotten Sámi livelihood, as portrayed in the journals of two nineteenth-century Nordic clergymen, Jacob Fellman (Finland) and Petrus Læstadius (Sweden). Kortekangas argues that studying trade involves an *unearthing* of forgotten Sámi livelihoods in two ways. First, detaching Sámi livelihoods from a strong connection to land enables us to see livelihoods and practices beyond the somewhat limiting stereotype of indigenous peoples as innately attached to landscape or the environment. Secondly, following the more conventional connotation of the verb 'to *unearth*,' indicating that the traditional Sámi way of life was not a monoculture of reindeer, paints a more complex and richer understanding of the history of Scandinavia's arctic and subarctic expanses.

In her chapter, **Ella Johansson** examines late nineteenth-century Swedish female peddlers, the *Dalkullor* from the district of Dalarna (or Dalecarlia), and more specifically how these women used traditional clothing as "marketing strategies." During this period, this county located in central Sweden came to symbolize the most representative region of "Swedishness." Seen as a link to a glorious past, this region was admired for its archaic and authentic material culture. Johansson suggests that this "ethnification" was a livelihood strategy for the poor.

Anna Sundelin and **Johanna Wassholm** trace a forgotten, yet important itinerant means of livelihood, namely, rag collecting. Rags played an essential role as raw material for the paper and textile industries in the nineteenth century. The chapter identifies a business logic based on the idea that material perceived by one individual as worthless could be turned into something of economic value. As rags were commodified, they acquired new value in a different context. By analyzing newspapers, periodical articles, and responses to ethnographic questionnaires, the authors follow a group of rag collectors from the Karelian Isthmus, who utilized their favorable geographic location to gain a livelihood from a circular flow of goods. Sundelin and Wassholm demonstrate how an earthenware pot could be bartered for a discarded garment, which in turn became a piece of the puzzle in the process that kept industry and economic growth going.

Ann-Catrin Östman investigates informal market gatherings in Western Finnish towns, where traders operated from humble premises and according to customary rules. Peasant traders marketed food, firewood, and other agricultural products, as well as animals and handicrafts, in towns. When economic regulations were liberalized in the middle of the nineteenth century, market trade—a vernacular form of commerce—was increasingly viewed as disruptive and immoral, as well as old-fashioned and unnecessary. Influenced by Michel de Certeau's understanding of practices, Östman focuses on the complex relationships between regulations, practices, cultural environment, and social hierarchies.

In a similar vein, **Niklas Huldén** looks at the long tradition of barter trade between peasants, fishermen, and other inhabitants of Estonia and Finland. This commerce established encounters over the Gulf of Finland that were mutually beneficial, as the parties could trade their surplus means, exporting mainly salted herring from Finland and receiving grain products, mainly rye, from Estonia. Trade strongly depended on developing personal acquaintances with traders from the other side of the gulf, forming a sort of partnership called *sepra* that could last for a season or even years and decades. Huldén's analysis includes the diverse goods that were traded and the practices of the gift-giving tradition.

Jutta Ahlbeck explores Roma livelihoods, particularly horse trading. Until the mid-twentieth century, the Finnish Roma (Kaale) supported themselves by means of small-scale itinerant trade, such as peddling and market trade. The chapter traces the Roma's strategies of survival in the first half of the twentieth century by analyzing interviews with members of this group. The Roma narratives emphasize respectability, inclusion, and belonging in terms of livelihood, thus defying the majority's persistent view of "Gypsies" as beggars and swindlers. Respectable horse trading was constructed in relation to Roma masculinity and, concomitantly, respectability was gendered as masculine. Ahlbeck suggests that these performative accounts are critical for understanding subjugated groups, with particular significance for Roma, marginalized within dominant discourses.

Following the theme of gendered livelihoods, **Kirsi Vainio-Korhonen** investigates women's sex trade in early nineteenth-century Finland. In addition to doing cleaning work or laboring as tavern maids, petty traders, or servants for families, sex work was one way for poor women to earn a living. Vainio-Korhonen demonstrates how sex trade in early modern towns seldom had its own separate space or place. It was practiced indoors and outdoors, in taverns, in the streets and marketplaces, at dances, and on excursions and picnics. The selling of sex spread across the town and beyond its borders.

Sex and female bodies could hence be employed as means of livelihood, as "entertainment" for customers and viewers. **Maren Jonasson** examines the livelihoods of six itinerant artists with "extraordinary" bodies who performed, and were exhibited, in the Nordic countries in 1860–1910. They traveled extensively and were put on display to varied audiences in Denmark, Norway, Sweden, and Finland at town markets, in restaurants, and at other locations and events where large crowds were expected to gather. These performing artists made their living and supported their families by exhibiting their "deviant" or "exotic" bodies to a paying audience. Jonasson discusses the agency of these artists, their marketing strategies and merchandise, and the ways in which they framed their bodies.

Entertainment as merchandise is additionally elaborated in the chapter by **Anna Kuismin**. She investigates representations of popular amusements in Finnish newspapers, periodicals, and fiction from the 1870s to the 1910s. The focus is on broadside ballads and on how these texts portrayed sellers of songs more generally, but the chapter also explores how these traders were seen by the people who bought their commodities. The period has been called "the golden age of broadside ballads," during which the culture of creating, selling, and consuming (singing and reading) these texts belonged to the unschooled common people, while educated writers repeatedly attacked such activities. Kuismin argues that fairs represented a space in which carnivalesque elements disrupted the monotonous daily life. Again, the lower classes enjoyed the amusements, while newspapers and fictional texts complained about the noise, excess drinking, and the petty crimes found at fairs.

Johanna Wassholm explores how "Rucksack Russians," Tatars, Eastern Jews, and saw grinders were portrayed as a threat in the late nineteenth- and early twentieth-century Nordic countries. By analyzing newspaper writings, Wassholm demonstrates how itinerant traders coming from outside local communities stirred ambivalent emotions among the majority population. Theoretically speaking, such newspapers' depictions are analyzed through the concept of enemy image, defined as a stereotypical and negative evaluation of the "Other." The enemy image emanates in a perception of the unfamiliar or strange and is utilized with an aim to evoke negative emotions toward outsiders. Wassholm offers a multifaceted picture of the specific contexts in which mobile traders from the outside were welcomed and rejected, respectively.

Experiences of petty trade are also examined by **Eija Stark**, who analyzes written autobiographies of working-class rural Finns and stresses the strategies of petty trade for coping with poverty, as well as its social consequences, during the rise and formation of the modern welfare state. The chapter approaches petty trade as a form of livelihood among the rural working class and as a visible sign of consumerism represented in personal narratives. Moreover, Stark examines what kind of class conflicts as well as cultural clashes petty trade comprised.

The individual chapters end with an exploration of the shift from itinerant to sedentary life. **Anna Sundelin** analyzes mobile traders from Russian Karelia who abandoned their itinerant livelihood and settled down in Finland in the late nineteenth and early twentieth centuries. Many of these former peddlers opened up stores in the Finnish countryside, making use of their skills as traders and previously formed networks to keep their stores well supplied. Sundelin combines a multitude of sources, such as business licenses, photographs, and advertisements, and offers new insights into the transition from itinerant peddling to storekeeping, as well as the experiences of migrant entrepreneurs.

In the conclusions, editors **Jutta Ahlbeck**, **Eija Stark**, and **Ann-Catrin Östman** discuss how both trading encounters and commodities were charged with meaning, and intimately connected to gendered, ethnicized, and classed practices. The editors ask whether, in an ambiguous way, communities aimed at securing the flow of goods by keeping the trading groups in the margins and by accentuating their otherness. On the other hand, traders themselves sometimes *emphasized* their difference as a strategy to secure their own livelihood. Thus, traders were forced to deal with difference, whether they tried to escape the norms that defined them or chose to stay in the margins.

Forgotten Livelihoods demonstrates how open flows of goods and adjacent trading encounters changed the position of peripheral and/or marginal groups, including traders as well as customers. In the nineteenth century, new livelihood opportunities emerged for itinerant traders, who distributed the increasing supply of colonial and industrial commodities, handicrafts, and drapery. These traders not only gained their livelihoods from petty trade, but they also acted as important intermediaries in providing rural and urban customers, often from lower social strata, with reasonably priced merchandise. More importantly, people from different backgrounds, cultures, and ethnicities came together in new ways, with petty trade functioning as a significant social arena for such encounters.

How did the customers regard petty traders who belonged to other social, ethnic, or religious groups? How and where did encounters between sellers and buyers take place? How did traders and consumers interact? Where did they meet? Were economic practices, individual products, and encounters gendered, ethnicized, classed, or racialized—and, if so, how? To what extent were these relations based on reciprocity and inclusionary practices, or, conversely, on subordination and discrimination?

Forgotten Livelihoods uncovers the ambiguous and forgotten histories of petty trade and demonstrates how some of the peddlers became visible figures, sometimes despised "Others" and at other times familiar guests, or even spouses, in both textual discourses and public spaces. It addresses the asymmetry of narratives and how the stories of peddlers and itinerant trade belong to the cultural domain of the resident population. Public documents, folklore, popular imagination, and archival institutions concerning peddling reflect the views of the majority. By attempting to trace the voices of the traders themselves, we offer an ethically sound and more complex understanding of what it meant to be a peddler, and thereby contribute to the history of subordinate groups.

Notes

1. To some extent, market trade and other forms of petty trade in nineteenth- and early twentieth-century Europe are touched upon in Jon Stobart and Ilja Van Damme's (eds.) *Modernity and the Second-Hand Trade. European Consumption Cultures and Practices, 1700–1900* (2010) and in Michael K. Goodman, David Goodman & Michael Redclift's (eds.) *Consuming Space. Placing Consumption in Perspective* (2010).
2. E.g., Maria Ågren. 2016. *Making a Living, Making a Difference: Gender and Work in Early Modern European Society.*
3. See, David Pennington. 2015. *Going to Market. Women, Trade and Social Relations in Early Modern English Towns, c. 1550–1650*; Adrian Randall and Andrew Charlesworth (eds.). 2000. *The Moral Economy and Popular Protest*; Norbert Götz. 2015. "Moral Economy: Its Conceptual History and Analytical Prospects." See also Graham, 2010, pp. 4–7.
4. See, e.g., Leo Lucassen, Wim Willems, and Annemarie Cottaar. 1998. *Gypsies and Other Itinerant Groups. A Socio-Historical Approach.*
5. See, e.g., Fontaine 2011, pp. 37–40; Wassholm and Sundelin 2018b, pp. 191–197; Wadauer 2012, pp. 225–230.
6. Wassholm and Sundelin 2018b, pp. 191–197; Wassholm 2020, pp. 11–14.
7. The Finnish Civil War was a fight for the leadership and control of *Finland* between White *Finland* and the *Finnish* Socialist Workers' Republic (Red

Finland) during the country's transition from being a Grand Duchy of the Russian Empire to an independent state.

8. SÅF 1916 [*The Yearbook of Finland's Statistics*, 2016].
9. Alapuro 1988, p. 33.
10. Johanna Wassholm and Anna Sundelin. 2018a. "Emotions, Trading Practices and Communication in Transnational Itinerant Trade"; Sigrid Wadauer. 2011. "Mobility and Irregularities: Itinerant Sales in Vienna in the 1920s and 1930s."
11. Bromley 2000, p. 2.
12. Michel De Certeau. 1984. *Practices of Everyday Life*; Doreen Massey. 1994. *Space, Place, and Gender*; Heuvel 2018, pp. 694–696.
13. See, Teubner 2019, p. 240; Graham 2010, pp. 33–42.
14. See, Teubner 2019, p. 232.
15. De Certeau 1984, pp. xiv–xvi.
16. De Certeau 1984, pp. xix, 117–118.
17. E.g., Pekka Nevalainen. 2016. *Kulkukauppiaista kauppaneuvoksiin. Itäkarjalaisten liiketoiminta Suomessa.*
18. De Certeau 1984, p. xvii.
19. Foucault 1978, p. 95.
20. De Certeau 1984, pp. xii–xiv.
21. De Certeau 1984, p. xv.
22. See, e.g., historian Ivan Gaskell in his extensive studies, especially 2018, p. 218. See also Ulrich et al. (eds.) 2015. *Tangible Things. Making History through Objects.*
23. E.g., Bruno Latour. 2005. *Reassembling the Social. An Introduction to Actor-Network-Theory.* The fields of material cultures, actor-network-theory, science and technology studies, "thing theory," posthumanism, new materialism, and so forth are extensive and cannot be elaborated within the scope of this chapter. Given the broad remit of these studies, it is not surprising that there is no strict consensus as to what precisely is meant by "materiality" or to what extent things can be regarded as "having" agency; see, e.g., Gaskell 2018, pp. 217–218.
24. Miller 2002, p. 417.
25. Arjun Appadurai. 1986. "The Social Life of Things. Commodities" in *Commodities in Cultural Perspective.*
26. Appadurai 2006, p. 15.
27. E.g., Mihesuah. 2010. *Repatriation Reader. Who Owns American Indian Remains?*; de Witte and Meyer 2012, pp. 47–48; Harlin 2019, pp. 258–259.
28. Anne-Jorunn Berg and Merere Lie. 1995. "Feminism and Constructivism. Do Artifacts Have Gender?"; Maureen Daly Goggin and Tobin Fowkes. 2009. *Women and Things, 1750–1950. Gendered Material Strategies*; Carla

Bittel, Elaine Leong, and Christine von Oertzen. 2019. *Working with Paper. Gendered Practices in the History of Knowledge.*

29. There is a long tradition of feminist postcolonial thought that problematizes the commodification of black female bodies. bell hooks (1992) argues that western culture produces, promotes, and perpetuates what she calls the "commodification of Otherness" (p. 21) through the exploitation of the black female body. This commodification has included the sexualization of black women.
30. Anttonen 2012, p. 328.
31. Lilja 1996, pp. 189–191; Mikkola et al. 2019, p. 62.
32. De Certeau 1984, pp. xvi–xvii.
33. See, Wassholm and Sundelin 2018b, p. 135.

Bibliography

Ågren, Maria (ed.). *Making a Living, Making a Difference. Gender and Work in Early Modern European Society.* Oxford: Oxford University Press, 2016.

Alapuro, Risto. *State and Revolution in Finland.* Berkeley: University of California Press, 1988.

Anttonen, Pertti. "Oral Traditions and the Making of the Finnish Nation." In *Folklore and Nationalism in Europe during the Long Nineteenth Century*, edited by Timothy Baycroft and David Hopkin, 325–350. Leiden & Boston: E.J. Brill, 2012.

Appadurai, Arjun. "Introduction. Commodities and the Politics of Value." In *The Social Life of Things. Commodities in Cultural Perspective*, edited by Arjun Appadurai, 3–63. Cambridge, UK: Cambridge University Press, 1986.

Appadurai, Arjun (ed.). *The Social Life of Things. Commodities in Cultural Perspective.* Cambridge, UK: Cambridge University Press, 1986.

Appadurai, Arjun. "The Thing Itself." *Public Culture* 18, no. 1 (2006): 15–22.

Berg, Anne-Jorunn, and Merete Lie. "Feminism and Constructivism. Do Artifacts Have Gender?" *Science, Technology, and Human Values* 20, no. 3 (1995): 332–351.

Bittel, Carla, Elaine Leong, and Christine von Oertzen. *Working with Paper. Gendered Practices in the History of Knowledge.* Pittsburgh: University of Pittsburgh Press, 2019.

Bromley, Ray. "Street Vending and Public Policy. A Global Review." *International Journal of Sociology and Social Policy* 20 (2000), 1–29.

De Certeau, Michel. *The Practice of Everyday Life.* Berkeley: University of California Press, 1984.

Diner, Hasia R. *Roads Taken. The Great Jewish Migrations to the New World and the Peddlers Who Forged the Way.* New Haven: Yale University Press, 2015.

Fontaine, Laurence. *History of Pedlars in Europe.* Durham: Duke University Press, 1996.

Fontaine, Laurence. "Märkte als Chance für die Armen in der Frühen Neuzeit." *Zeitschrift für Agrargeschichte und Agrarsoziologie* 59, no. 2 (2011): 37–53.

Foucault, Michel. *The History of Sexuality: An Introduction, Vol. I.* New York: Vintage Books, 1978.

Gaskell, Ivan. "History of Things." In *Debating New Approaches in History*, edited by Marek Tamm and Peter Burke, 217–246. Bloomsbury: Bloomsbury Academic, 2018.

Geertz, Clifford. *Peddlers and Princes. Social Development and Economic Change in Two Indonesian Towns.* Chicago: University of Chicago Press, 1963.

Goggin, Maureen Daly, and Beth Fowkes Tobin. *Women and Things, 1750–1950: Gendered Material Strategies.* Farnham: Ashgate Publishing, 2009.

Goodman, Michael K., David Goodman, and Michael Redclift (eds.). *Consuming Space. Placing Consumption in Perspective.* London: Routledge, 2010.

Graham, Richard. *Feeding the City. From Street Market to Liberal Reform in Salvador, Brazil, 1780–1860.* Austin: University of Texas, 2010.

Götz, Norbert. "Moral Economy. Its Conceptual History and Analytical prospects." *Journal of Global Ethics* 11 (2015): 147–162.

Harlin, Eeva-Kristiina. "Sámi Archaeology and the Fear of Political Involvement. Finnish Archaeologists' Perspectives on Ethnicity and the Repatriation of Sámi Cultural Heritage." *Archaeologies* 15, no. 2 (2019): 254–284.

van den Heuvel, Danielle. "Gender in the Streets of the Premodern City." *Journal of Urban History* 45, no. 4 (2018): 693–710.

hooks, bell. *Black Looks. Race and Representation.* Boston: South End, 1992.

Latour, Bruno. *Reassembling the Social—An Introduction to Actor-Network-Theory.* New York: Oxford University Press, 2005.

Lilja, Agneta. *Föreställningen om den ideala uppteckningen. En studie av idé och praktik vid traditionssamlande arkiv. Ett exempel från Uppsala 1914–1945.* Skrifter utgivna genom Dialekt- och folkminnesarkivet i Uppsala B:22. Uppsala: Dialekt- och folkminnesarkivet i Uppsala, 1996.

Lucassen, Leo, Wim Willems, and Anne-Marie Cottaar (eds.). *Gypsies and Other Itinerant Groups. A Socio-Historical Approach.* London: Palgrave Macmillan, 1998.

Massey, Doreen. *Space, Place, and Gender.* Minneapolis: University of Minnesota Press, 1994.

Mihesuah, Devon A. (ed.). *Repatriation Reader. Who Owns American Indian Remains?* Lincoln and London: University of Nebraska Press, 2010.

Mikkola, Kati, Pia Olsson, and Eija Stark. "Minority Cultures and the Making of Cultural Heritage Archives in Finland." *Ethnologia Europaea* 49, no. 1 (2019): 58–73.

Miller, Daniel. "Artefacts and the meaning of things." In *Companion Encyclopedia of Anthropology*, edited by Tim Ingold, 396–419. London: Routledge, 2002.
Mitchell, Ian. *Tradition and Innovation in English Retailing, 1700 to 1850.* Farnham: Routledge, 2014.
Nevalainen, Pekka. *Kulkukauppiaista kauppaneuvoksiin. Itäkarjalaisten liiketoiminta Suomessa.* Helsinki: SKS, 2016.
Pennington, David. *Going to Market. Women, Trade and Social Relations in Early Modern English Towns, c. 1550–1650.* Farnham: Ashgate, 2015.
Randall, Adrian, and Andrew Charlesworth (eds.). *Moral Economy and Popular Protest. Crowds, Conflict and Authority.* London: Palgrave, 2000.
Stobart, Jon, and Ilja Van Damme (eds.). *Modernity and the Second-Hand Trade. European Consumption Cultures and Practices, 1700–1900.* London: Palgrave Macmillan, 2010.
SÅF 1916 [The Statistical Yearbook of Finland]. Helsingfors: Statistikcentralen, 1917.
Teubner, Melina. "Street food, Urban space, and Gender. Working on the Streets of Nineteenth-century Rio de Janeiro (1830–1870)." *International Review of Social History* 64 (2019): 229–254.
Ulrich, Laurel Thatcher et al. (eds.). *Tangible Things. Making History through Objects.* Oxford: Oxford University Press, 2015.
Wadauer, Sigrid. "Mobility and Irregularities: Itinerant Sales in Vienna in the 1920s and 1930s." In *Shadow economies and irregular work in urban Europe (16th to early 20th centuries)*, edited by Thomas Buchner, and Philip R. Hoffmann-Rehnit, 197–216. Münster, New York: Lit Verlag Dr. W. Hopf, 2011.
Wadauer, Sigrid. "Asking for the Privilege to work: Applications for a Peddling Licence (Austria in the 1920s and 1930s)." In *Poverty and Sickness in Modern Europe. Narratives of the Sick Poor, 1780–1938,* edited by Andreas Gestrich, Elizabeth Hurren, and Steven King, 225–246. London and New York: Continuum, 2012.
Wassholm, Johanna. "Tatar Pedlars in the Grand Duchy of Finland in the Late Nineteenth Century." *Studia Orientalia Electronica* 8, no. 2 (2020): 8–24.
Wassholm, Johanna, and Anna Sundelin. "Emotions, Trading Practices and Communication in Transnational Itinerant Trade. Encounters between 'Rucksack Russians' and their Customers in the late Nineteenth- and early Twentieth-century Finland." *Scandinavian Economic History Review* 66, no. 2 (2018a): 132–152.
Wassholm, Johanna, and Anna Sundelin. "Småskalig handel på glidande skalor. Försörjning och konsumtion i Finland 1800–1940." *Historisk Tidskrift för Finland* 103, no. 2 (2018b): 191–204.
de Witte, Marleen, and Birgit Meyer. "African Heritage Design." *Civilisations. Revue internationale d'anthropologie et de sciences humaines* 61, no. 1 (2012): 43–65.

CHAPTER 2

Un*earthing* Livelihoods: Sámi Trade as an Active Livelihood

Otso Kortekangas

This chapter argues that Sámi trade is a "forgotten livelihood," a part of Sámi history ignored at the cost of generalizing narratives of the Sámi as nomadic hunter-gatherers and, later, as semi-nomadic reindeer herders. For this reason, studying Sámi trade entails an un*earthing* of disregarded Sámi history in two ways. First, detaching Sámi livelihoods from a strong connection to land enables us to see livelihoods and practices beyond the limiting stereotype of indigenous peoples as innately attached to the landscape or the environment. Secondly, the chapter pursues the more conventional connotation of the verb "to *un*earth," that is, "to discover." Indicating that the traditional Sámi way of life was no monoculture of reindeer but included many different sources of sustenance paints a more complex, and richer, image of the history of Scandinavia's arctic and subarctic expanses.

Following these two definitions of unearthing, the chapter explores what status Sámi trade had among other livelihoods described in the

O. Kortekangas (✉)
The Division of History of Science, Technology and Environment,
KTH Royal Institute of Technology, Stockholm, Sweden
e-mail: otso@kth.se

J. Ahlbeck et al. (eds.), *Encounters and Practices of Petty Trade in Northern Europe, 1820–1960*,
https://doi.org/10.1007/978-3-030-98080-1_2

journals of two nineteenth-century Nordic clergymen, Jacob Fellman (Finland) and Petrus Læstadius (Sweden). It also lays bare some of the functions that Sámi traders had in nineteenth-century arctic and subarctic Europe. The focus of the chapter is on (1) Sámi trade at the various annual or seasonal fairs that formed the only fully legally sanctioned context and space for trade outside towns and (2) everyday trade practices among the Sámi, and between Sámi and other Nordic individuals.

Methodological Considerations

This chapter aims to diversify the historical imagery of Sámi livelihoods and ways of life. This means avoiding reproduction of the strong, existing stereotypes of Sámi as reindeer herders or being somehow more innately connected to the environment than other Nordic populations. In this regard, the chapter continues the program laid out by the archeologist Ingela Bergman and the ecologist Greger Hörnberg. Bergman and Hörnberg point out that the generally accepted notion of Sámi people mainly being sustained by large-scale reindeer herding is inaccurate. To be sure, many Sámi have been reindeer herders for centuries, yet the repetition of this stereotypical notion silences other histories of Sámi livelihoods and ways of life, such as agriculture or, in the case of this chapter, trade.[1] As Bergman and Hörnberg show, from a historical perspective, agriculture is as typical a Sámi livelihood as reindeer herding. Their article postulates that age-old Sámi agriculture has become a forgotten livelihood, since scholarly and popular narratives of the Swedish and Finnish settlers have presupposed an exclusively nomadic and primitive Sámi presence in the colonized land. The existence of such a narrative in its turn reveals an age-old structure, where the Nordic majority populations have for a long time had the power to define how and in what ways the Sámi are viewed and understood. This chapter challenges earlier popular and scholarly narratives by aiming to bring forth active Sámi history through introducing several Sámi individuals, men and women, practicing different forms of trade. The chapter frames these individuals as agents who made active and conscious choices instead of merely living under circumstances and rules created by others. This is not to deny that there existed and still exist real power structures that benefit Nordic populations other than the Sámi, but rather to offer a more balanced, nuanced, and broad picture of life in the Nordic subarctic and arctic regions in the early nineteenth century.

Trade always entails power structures and an asymmetric distribution of power: "whoever controls the [consumption] circuits, enjoys an exceptionally favorable position," as historian Daniel Roche reminds us.[2] In the two cases of trade at fairs and everyday trade, the types of control of the circuit of consumption and trade were rather different. Analysis of the journals of Fellman and Læstadius turns a specific focus toward the roles the two clergymen ascribed to the Sámi at the fairs and in everyday trade practices. From the outset it is clear that Sámi trade was diverse: the roles that Sámi individuals had within the circuits of consumption ranged from consumers to traders and suppliers. When exploring both fair trade and everyday trade practices, the general theoretical framework of this collection adheres to Michel de Certeau's notion that even the smallest, and at first glance insignificant, practices carry meaning. De Certeau maintains that larger societal structures, such as the circuits of consumption studied in this chapter, are *strategically* constructed to benefit the powerful. Combining the theory of de Certeau and Roche, those in control of the circuits of consumption define the strategies and the choreography of trade relations and transactions. De Certeau's crucial addition to this structuralist notion is that individuals within the structures can act *tactically*, avoiding or subverting the rules, or, so to speak, "playing the system." By actively using the strategy and the loopholes and inconsistencies in it, individuals and groups can use their own tactics to cope with, circumvent, or even subvert the strategies.[3] At fairs, the forms and practices of trade were regulated with certain trading rights, trading times and spaces. The fairs, normally organized in connection with important Church holidays, were in general an important component of the strictly regulated trade in the Swedish and Finnish countryside.[4] Under these regulations, Sámi traders could still be *tactical* about their trade. As this chapter reveals, Sámi traders could plan and choose which fairs to trade at, based on their knowledge of favorable points of time and the shortest distance to larger towns and the Swedish capital, Stockholm. In the case of everyday trade practices where trade regulations did not apply, many Sámi commodities had very strong status within the circuits of consumption.

Furthermore, in many instances, the simple everyday trade practices of the Sámi taking place under the radar of what was officially regulated trade turn out upon closer investigation to be conveyances of important commodities. One such case is Fellman's note on the "fishing Sámi" supplying "shoe-hay" (a natural insulation against freezing temperatures) to the reindeer herders of northernmost Finland and Norway. This seemingly simple commodity was collected and carefully prepared by the fishing Sámi, and then sold to the reindeer herders in exchange for reindeer meat, demonstrating a high degree of specialization and differentiation in both production and supply.[5]

The examination of Jacob Fellman's and Petrus Læstadius' depictions of Sámi trade requires excavation of actual trade practices buried beneath a substantial layer of centuries-old stereotypes of Sámi traders as unprofessional and often intoxicated individuals, in a sense stripped of credible agency. On the other hand, these stereotypes become important objects of study in themselves, as prejudices generally abounded around traders from different cultural backgrounds.

Background and Earlier Research

Earlier studies on Sámi trade have in most cases concentrated on the role of traders from the majority cultures, and how these traders established networks and structures that disrupted older patterns of Sámi livelihoods. Swedish historians Gunlög Fur and Daniel Lindmark situate merchants trading with Sámi in a pattern of intensified contacts between Swedes and Sámi (to use modern ethnic terms) beginning in the sixteenth century and intensifying throughout the seventeenth and eighteenth centuries.[6] Besides trade, these intensified contacts also included agricultural colonization, more strictly regulated taxation of the Sámi, and Lutheran missions.

Several studies allocate to the Sámi a more active role as traders than Fur and Lindmark have done. Roger Kvist and Lars-Ivar Hansen show that the yearly mobility of the reindeer-herding Sámi of the mountain areas, following the grazing patterns of their reindeer herds, entailed that they had a crucial role in tying together the North Atlantic and the Baltic spheres of trade.[7] They traded with Norwegians on the coast of the Arctic Ocean, and when they followed their reindeer herds to the lowlands in Sweden and Finland in the winter, they connected with the tradesmen from the Bothnian coastline. Even if Sámi trade was strictly regulated in the nineteenth century and officially only allowed at fairs, many Sámi commodities such as handicrafts and fish made their way into the trade records of merchants in the towns of the Bothnian coastline, such as Piteå.[8] These Bothnian tradesmen, in their turn, had frequent connections with Stockholm. This traditional pattern was already shifting in the early nineteenth century, as the different states started regulating and policing their borders more strictly, and reindeer herders could not cross them as freely as before. Maria Lähteenmäki has also commented on the traditional cross-border character of the Sámi areas. Discussing the famous and large Skibotn fair in northernmost Norway that attracted people from around the North Calotte area, Lähteenmäki points out that the trade routes of the Sámi in Finland to this and other fairs were already hundreds of years old by the turn of the nineteenth century.[9]

Most Nordic scholars on Sámi history tend to write Sámi history in nation-state chunks, treating the history of Norwegian, Swedish, or Finnish Sámi and largely ignoring the important cross-border history of the population. As pointed out by Veli-Pekka Lehtola, the Sámi in what is now northernmost Finland traditionally had a yearly cycle of movement and life that was oriented toward the shores of the Arctic Ocean rather than south toward what was to become independent Finland. The fairs of the Norwegian coastline were a paramount part of this yearly cycle. Only after the infrastructure and mental imagery of independent Finland as a unified country reached these areas did age-old patterns start to change and the southern direction become more interesting.[10] The scholarly state of the art still reflects this nationalization of Sámi ways of life, as most studies on the Sámi continue to portray them as a minority population in one of the nation-states they inhabit.[11]

Between Ethnography, Physiocracy, and Mission: Fellman's and Læstadius' Journals

Jacob Fellman and Petrus Læstadius were both clergymen educated in the university towns of Turku (Fellman) and Uppsala (Læstadius). They were typical nineteenth-century Lapland clergymen; like many of their colleagues, they both had ancestors who had served as clerics in the northern areas of Sweden and Finland. Accordingly, their two journals are part of a genre characteristic of nineteenth-century Nordic Lutheran clergymen that blended accounts of missions and religious life with descriptions of the local people and their livelihoods. Judging by the journals, Fellman and Læstadius saw it as one of their main duties to improve God's creation through ameliorating agriculture, the livelihood they perceived as critical for the national economy. This mix of physiocratic and Lutheran ideas, dubbed "the Godly economy" by the historian Tore Frängsmyr, was widespread among the Nordic clergy in the eighteenth and early nineteenth centuries.[12] Fellman and Læstadius, however, made an important exception for the large-scale reindeer herding practiced by the Sámi. Their notion of reindeer herding as the most sustainable livelihood in the mountainous areas unsuitable for cereal cultivation deviated from the general argument highlighting the primacy of agriculture among other livelihoods.[13] Fellman's and Læstadius' journals show great and detailed knowledge and expertise regarding the various Sámi livelihoods. The authors were well acquainted with the geographical, social, and economic circumstances of the Sámi areas. Differently from most people traveling in northern Fennoscandia in the nineteenth century and writing descriptions of the Sámi, Fellman and Læstadius lived and worked in the area for years, forming relationships with the locals and familiarizing themselves with the environment. Læstadius was himself partly of Sámi origin, a fact he openly discusses in his journal although generally distancing himself from the Sámi populations.[14]

Læstadius' journal (first published in 1831) is rather directly related to his activities as a missionary in the Sámi areas. In addition to surveying the religious life of the Sámi, the journal includes depictions of the nature and livelihoods of his area of activity. Fellman's texts resemble more a traditional journal, written as a record of his daily life. Fellman also observed the plants and animals of his parish: he was an enthusiastic botanist, and the journal includes one of the first catalogues of the flora of northernmost Finland. *Helsingfors Tidningar*, a Helsinki-based semiweekly, published the first part of Fellman's journal in 1830. Jacob's son Isak Fellman edited and published the whole journal in 1906.[15]

Læstadius' and Fellman's reports of the Sámi traders attending the fairs are often quite impressionistic, highlighting the "exotic behavior" that the two men observed during the fairs. It is both relevant and difficult to discover actual trade practices in these descriptions, ranging from the modality of parody (comparing the Sámi to Classical Roman literary figures) to exotifying and judgmental comments. This aligns well with Seppo Knuuttila's studies on how elites depicted common people, and especially minorities. Lacking alternative means to cope with the otherness of minorities in literary terms, educated elites often used the trope of classic literature, for instance, to describe the "strangeness" and "alienness" of the people described.[16]

When studying the journals' accounts of everyday practices of trade, the difficulty lies in detecting the short and seemingly insignificant text passages on Sámi trade both within the Sámi community and with other populations. Whereas descriptions of Finnish, Swedish, and Norwegian merchants run over several pages, the everyday trade practices of the Sámi are treated rather nonchalantly, often as evidence of the fact that the Sámi had to resort to trade when their *actual* way of life (e.g., reindeer herding or fishing) was not strong enough or healthy enough to sustain them.

Fairs and Everyday Trade Practices Among the Sámi

The fairs (North Sámi: *márkan*) in the Sámi area traditionally had a close connection with Church holidays. Large gatherings in central church villages during important holidays meant a great opportunity for trade, and combining different social events was reasonable given the vast distances that some Sámi individuals had to travel to reach the nearest church village (see Fig. 2.1). The connection between Christianity and trade is epitomized in the place name of the first church built in the Eanodat-Gárasavvon area on the northernmost Swedish-Finnish border. Constructed in the early seventeenth century, the church was simply called *Márkan*—both

Fig. 2.1 String of reindeer on its way to the market in the northernmost part of Finland in the 1920s. (Photo by Juhani Ahola. The Finnish Heritage Agency)

"church village" and "the Fair." During important Church holidays, local Sámi and other locals would gather around the church to attend services but also—in many cases more importantly—to participate in the fair with its trade and social practices. The name Márkan is an unusually straightforward indication of the close connection between the practices of church-going and trade in the Sámi areas in particular and in Europe in general. In all parts of the Swedish (and later also Finnish) Sámi areas, churches emerged in places that the Sámi had earlier used as more or less sedentary winter villages. Márkan was also a typical location for church and fair activities, since, according to oral tradition, it was used as a *sieidi* (traditional Sámi sacred place) possibly long before the arrival of Christianity in this area.[17] Combining mission work with trade, these places became some of the most important arenas of cultural contacts between the Sámi and other Nordic populations.[18] Both Fellman and Læstadius include lengthy descriptions of the spectacle of the fair, in all its social, ecclesial, and trade-related activity. Fellman describes the fair in Inari, whereas Læstadius includes accounts of several fairs at different locations in the Swedish Sámi areas.

Only to later depart from the stereotypes attached to Sámi at the fairs, I will begin with what I judge to be the most heavily biased account, Petrus Læstadius' farce-like sequence on the Sámi at the last day of the fair of Arjeplog, where he makes intertextual references to classic Greco-Roman mythology. According to Læstadius, on this final day many Sámi spent on alcohol most of what they had earned earlier at the fair. The "Saturnalian" scenes of drunken friendship and love among the Sámi were occasionally interrupted by more aggressive acts of quarreling and fighting, as if the god Aeolus had broken an opening in the cliff for the winds. Here Læstadius paraphrases Virgil's account of Aeolus, King of the Winds, in the first book of the *Aeneid*.[19] The drunken aggression of the Sámi was let out like the winds that Aeolus set free at the behest of the goddess Juno, almost destroying the fleet of Aeneas en route to Italy. Adding to the impressionistic confusion of the scene, Læstadius gives no other clues to the readers as to why he compared the Sámi in Arjeplog to the Trojans on the Mediterranean. As discussed by Seppo Knuuttila, however, using classic literature as a model to describe the Other, whether common people or minorities, has been a traditional literary trope in European majority depictions of common people and minority populations.[20]

Læstadius' bizarre and farce-like depiction in any case offers a picture of the Sámi as individuals without any larger capacity of rational planning—they sold all their goods only to spend the money on drinks on the final day of the fair. The widespread alcohol consumption in northern Scandinavia has been documented by many others than Petrus Læstadius, and it was typical for journals and periodicals to highlight drinking and other morally questionable behavior at the fairs. Drinking was also something that the lay (yet intra-church) religious movement established by Petrus' brother Lars Levi Læstadius forcefully turned against. Nevertheless, Petrus Læstadius' description of the Sámi at the last day of the Arjeplog fair is hardly an appropriate account of their actual transactions and practices. On the other hand, selling goods only to afford drinks when enjoying a rare social occasion, meeting with family, relatives, and friends, can also be interpreted as highly intentional and rational behavior, rather than a result of drunken stupor and fervor. This interpretation is supported by the work of Jouko Heinonen, who has studied fairs in the southern Finnish province of Päijät-Häme in the nineteenth and twentieth centuries. Heinonen postulates that the fairs have always had as much a function of amusement than trade. Alcohol has been an integral part of the culture of the fairs also elsewhere than in the Sámi areas. Moreover, moralizing depictions of the alcohol use of fairgoers are not specific to the Sámi context.[21]

Læstadius painted a more sober picture of Sámi behavior in his depictions of the fairs in Åsele and Arvidsjaur. Læstadius divided fair commodities into two categories: *lantmannavaror* (farmers' goods) and *lappmannavaror* (Sámi goods). The most important article among the Sámi goods was reindeer skins. According to Læstadius, the Åsele fair was an economically productive fair for the Sámi, as it was frequented by merchants who immediately after the market continued to Stockholm to sell the goods. The supply of Sámi goods was still scarce in the capital, as the Åsele fair was held early in the season, in early January; thus, the Sámi received the best price for their reindeer skins and other Sámi goods at this fair.[22] This is also in line with Kvist's and Hansen's conclusions that Sámi traders had a rather independent position and traded, through proxies if not otherwise, with both Stockholm merchants and Arctic Ocean merchants.

Jacob Fellman's accounts of fair practices are more neutral in tone and style, compared to Læstadius' narrative embellished with parody and intertextual references to classical literature. Recounting his first visit to the Inari fair held at Christmas, Fellman still makes the point that drinking was a problem. Everything passed in a good manner, according to Fellman, apart from the drinking, which was "excessive." Fellman's account also confirms that northern Scandinavia, Finland, and northwestern Russia in the early nineteenth century were still very much a part of the trade sphere of the Arctic Ocean coastline. Participants at the Inari fair, Fellman describes, included "Russians from Kola, Russian and Norwegian Lapps, liquor traders from Sodankylä, Kemijärvi and Enontekiö as well as Norwegians from the Varangerfjord [a close-by inlet of the Arctic Ocean]."[23]

Fellman wrote a longer account of the fair in Inari upon his next visit to that event, during his second year in Lapland. The days were short, and the nights were long, with "20 hours of night and 4 hours of twilight."[24] Nevertheless, the transactions were busy. Fellman mentions that a few merchants from the town of Tornio at the far end of the Gulf of Bothnia had arrived at the fair. Of all the townspeople, the Tornio merchants had the exclusive right of trade at the fair, but they did not show up every year. The Tornio merchants brought with them, for instance, lead, gunpowder, hemp, rope, and kettles. These were traded with the Sámi for reindeer skins, as well as other skins and furs and dried fish, which the Sámi had caught, among other places, in the Arctic Ocean. Like Læstadius' account, Fellman's notes of the Inari fair also confirm the intermediary role that the Sámi had in connecting the Baltic and the Arctic Ocean trade spheres.

Fellman commented briefly on the fair transactions between the reindeer-herding Sámi from Utsjoki in Finland and Finnmark in Norway: these reindeer herders stayed with local Sámi in Inari during the fair. For this hospitality, combined with shoe-hay and cloudberries from the Inari Sámi, the reindeer herders paid "several loads of reindeer meat," which the Inari Sámi received after the fair when the Church holidays were over.[25] Shoe-hay may seem like a petty commodity at first sight, but in light of de Certeau's framework highlighting the importance of even the most seemingly trivial and insignificant practices, its production demonstrates a high degree of specialization among the Inari Sámi. This natural insulation against freezing and potentially fatal temperatures was crucial for the reindeer herders of Utsjoki and Finnmark. In a passage where Fellman describes Sámi clothing, he elaborates on the practices of producing shoe-hay. Fellman noted that the fishermen of Inari could gain a whole reindeer (for food) in exchange for "one or a couple of tufts of this hay." The production of shoe-hay was a highly specialized process. The raw material was a specific species of sedge, the bladder sedge (*Carex vesicaria*), that was collected in August, then bundled and beaten until it "disintegrated into fine threads, like hemp or flax." The shoe-hay bundles were then stored away for the winter season. A bundle of hay in the shoe was much warmer than even several layers of socks, and it could be dried and reused up to eight times (see Fig. 2.2).[26]

Fellman's description of the practices of shoe-hay production, from collecting bladder sedge to selling it to the reindeer-herding Sámi, suggests the existence of a high level of expertise and specialization behind a seemingly trivial commodity. The quality of Sámi shoe-hay was such that the 1910–1913 British Antarctic Expedition (the Terra Nova Expedition) included in their equipment "Lapp shoes," which were stuffed with hay for insulation.[27] Although *stricto sensu* outside of the scope of the current chapter, this example further confirms the high level of differentiation and technology that the shoe-hay making of the Sámi showcased, as well as the fact that the technology, use, and trade value of this specific commodity was also known to outsiders, not only the Sámi.

Fig. 2.2 An Inari Sámi boy making shoe-hay in 1925. Shoe-hay processing and dog breeding were important Inari Sámi livelihoods, and children would sometimes participate in the crafting of shoe-hay. (Photo by Samuli Paulaharju. The Finnish Heritage Agency)

Another example of an intra-Sámi trade practice and specialization that Fellman mentions is the selling of herding dogs. Being more sedentary than the nomadic reindeer herders, the fishing Sámi bred, trained, and sold dogs to the reindeer herders for a substantial income. A dog pup was worth a *slaktren* (a reindeer to be butchered for consumption rather than kept alive for a long time) and a trained dog sold for even more, depending on its skills in herding.[28] Again, the investment in time and resources needed to breed dogs that were specifically trained for reindeer herding shows that the Sámi trade practices were complex, highly specialized, and demonstrated apparent differentiation and optimization of skills, trade, and economic practices. This trade between the different Sámi groups was, of course, a part of larger circuits of consumption in northernmost Finland and Scandinavia, where Sámi reindeer skins played an important role. As reindeer skins were arguably the most important Sámi commodities, the breeding of herding dogs and providing shoe-hay for managing the herds in freezing temperatures were crucial auxiliary functions to this trade. If not in control of the whole circuit of consumption in Roche's terms, the Sámi reindeer herders as well as the Sámi individuals providing them with necessities for their livelihood nevertheless had a firm grip on that specific part of the circuit of consumption.

Not all trade practices that occurred outside of the fairs took place in an intra-Sámi setting, however. Læstadius briefly mentions reindeer cheese being traded by the reindeer-herding mountain Sámi of Sweden when they visited Norway during the summer. In exchange for the cheese, they acquired woolen and sheepskin blankets from Norwegian farmers.[29] It is, once again evident that the Sámi possessed goods that were in demand among the majority populations.

The Arctic Ocean fishing of the Inari Sámi is another example of differentiation of trade and everyday practices noted in Fellman's journal. Lake Inari and surrounding smaller bodies of water provided the Sámi of the area with fish for everyday consumption, but this local practice of fishing did not generate any substantial surplus. For this reason, the Inari Sámi complemented their economy with fishing in the Arctic Ocean during the spring and the summer. This may have constituted a problem, given that juridically speaking, the Inari Sámi came from across the Finnish border and exploited the resources of a foreign country, Norway. However, as Fellman notes, the Inari Sámi paid tax on their Arctic Ocean fish at the same rate as the Norwegians did, based on an old agreement preceding the contemporaneous state borders in the area. This reflects the traditional reality of mobility and trade of the Sámi, where the area up to a few hundred kilometers south of the Arctic Ocean coastline formed a natural area for reindeer herding, trade, and mobility. Only when the borders of the modern nation states became controlled and policed more closely did these age-old patterns of mobility start to change, making it more difficult for the Sámi to carry out and develop their traditional livelihoods.

Fellman's journal includes yet other instances of everyday trade that are mentioned only in passing but nevertheless support the argument of Sámi trade as an active and independent livelihood. For instance, pearl fishing was a seasonal livelihood for some Inari Sámi. Fellman mentions that the rivers of Inari and Lutto were exploited for this purpose, and he also speaks of handicrafts, and especially sleighs drawn by reindeer, as items that the Inari Sámi sold to the reindeer herders.[30] An interesting example of a Sámi tradeswoman is Anna Aikio, introduced in Fellman's journal. After Aikio's spouse passed away, she made a living by breeding foxes and selling the furs at the fair in Inari.[31] This again highlights the role of Sámi trade as an active livelihood and that this livelihood was at least at times also available to women.

Conclusions

This chapter studies Sámi trade as an active livelihood rather than a side story or a "last resort" when other livelihoods had failed. As pointed out by Bergman and Hörnberg, bringing forward other Sámi livelihoods than the conventionally highlighted Sámi reindeer herding helps us see and frame the Sámi livelihoods and economy in a more diverse and accurate light.[32] Based on the journals of the two nineteenth-century Lutheran clergymen Petrus Læstadius and Jacob Fellman, this chapter demonstrates several instances of trade as a livelihood that was chosen deliberately as a source of income. The specialization of both production and commerce is one indication of such activity. The highly specialized livelihoods of shoe-hay production and breeding of herding dogs among the Sámi of the Inari area in Finland, and the selling and trading of these goods with other Sámi groups, clearly illuminate the various ways in which the Sámi could make a living through trade. Other examples include the making of reindeer cheese, which the Swedish Sámi sold to Norwegian farmers in exchange for wool and sheep blankets. The fishermen of the Lake Inari area also practiced seasonal fishing in the Arctic Ocean, generating a surplus that was difficult to obtain through lake fishing alone. All these cases go to show that trade was indeed an active livelihood. On top of that, trade was also an independent livelihood, and not always a mere auxiliary of other livelihoods. Sámi individuals trading at the various fairs in the Sámi area were often *tactical* about their choices, to use the wording of Michel de Certeau; when their trade rights were heavily restricted by laws and regulations concentrating on legal trade at the fairs, the Sámi could, for instance, choose which fairs to attend and sell their goods at. As an elucidating example, attending the fair in Åsele was beneficial to Sámi traders since the fair took place early in the season, and the demand for Sámi goods, most importantly reindeer skin, was still high; the supply was low compared to later points of time, when several other fairs took place. The location of Åsele was also favorable, as it was one of the southernmost marketplaces in the Sámi area, and for this reason accessible to merchants practicing trade in Stockholm.

The Sámi traders played a crucial role in tying together the trade spheres of the Arctic Ocean and the Baltic Sea, as Kvist and Hansen have demonstrated.[33] This is confirmed by the chapter at hand. The integration of the two markets also connects the findings to Daniel Roche's notion of the power involved in controlling the circuits of consumption. While the Sámi traders were in many instances subordinate to the merchants of the majority populations that had legally better rights at the fairs, their crucial role in connecting the Baltic and Arctic Ocean trade spheres gave them a strong and secure position within trade in the whole northern Nordic area.

The findings of this chapter entail an unearthing of Sámi livelihoods in two ways, as outlined in the introduction of this chapter. On the one hand, the mere action of discovering, discussing, studying, and presenting Sámi livelihoods that are not directly connected to reindeer herding broadens our conception of Sámi livelihoods and life. This broadening of perspective is necessary, since both popular and scholarly narratives of Sámi life historically and today often presuppose a strong connection between Sámi individuals and reindeer herding. On the other hand, unearthing also means disconnecting the Sámi from a stereotypical connection to nature or the environment. To avoid walking into old pitfalls of othering and exotifying, we should not label the livelihoods and lifestyles of indigenous populations a priori as essentially different from those of the so-called industrialized, modern or Western world. Conceptually detaching indigenous peoples from an axiomatic relationship to nature is a step in the right direction in this regard. Through showing that the Sámi were as active and skillful traders as any other Nordic tradesmen, this chapter goes toward understanding the Sámi as not essentially different from other

Nordic populations, but as individuals and groups having access to various kinds of livelihoods that partly overlapped with those of the other Nordic populations.

Notes

1. Bergman and Hörnberg 2015, pp. 57–59.
2. Roche 2000, p. 15.
3. De Certeau 1984, pp. xix, 29–30.
4. E.g., Heinonen 2003, pp. 24–25.
5. Fellman 1978, p. 54.
6. Daniel Lindmark. 2002. "Diaspora, Integration, and Cantonization. Swedish Colonial Education from a Theoretical, Comparative, and Concluding Perspective."; Gunlög Fur. 2006. *Colonialism in the Margins. Cultural Encounters in New Sweden and Lapland.*
7. Kvist 1986, pp. 19–40; Kvist 1989; Hansen 1987, pp. 216–243.
8. Marklund 2008, pp. 352–357.
9. Maria Lähteenmäki. 2006. *The peoples of Lapland. Boundary Demarcations and Interaction in the North Calotte from 1808 to 1889.*
10. Lehtola 2012, p. 71.
11. E.g., Kortekangas 2017, p. 15; Minde et al. 2008, pp. 1–4.
12. Henrysson 1989, p. 4; Frängsmyr 1971/1972, pp. 217–244; Adolfsson 2000.
13. Kortekangas 2020, pp. 520–525.
14. See, Sörlin 2002, p. 86 and Ahlström 1966; for a discussion on Læstadius' origins; Otso Kortekangas. 2020.
15. Panelius 1978, pp. 5–15; Väre 2011, pp. 1–3, 18.
16. Seppo Knuuttila. 1994. *Tyhmän kansan teoria: näkökulmia menneestä tulevaan.*
17. Paulaharju 1932, 44.
18. Anderzén 1996, p. 9.
19. Læstadius 1836, pp. 126–127.
20. Seppo Knuuttila. 1994. *Tyhmän kansan teoria: näkökulmia menneestä tulevaan.*
21. Heinonen 2003, pp. 7, 34–35.
22. Læstadius 1836, pp. 44–45, 80.
23. Fellman 1906a, p. 13.
24. Fellman 1906a, p. 82.
25. Fellman 1906a, p. 83.
26. Fellman 1906a, p. 28.
27. Lyons 1924, p. 35.

28. Fellman 1978, p. 51.
29. Læstadius 1836, p. 218.
30. Fellman 1906b, pp. 342–346.
31. Fellman 1978, p. 136.
32. Bergman and Hörnberg 2015, pp. 57–59.
33. Kvist 1986, pp. 19–40; Kvist 1989; Hansen 1987, pp. 216–243.

Bibliography

Adolfsson, Maria. *Fäderneslandets kännedom. Om svenska ortsbeskrivningsprojekt och ämbetsmäns folklivsskildringar under 1700- och 1800-talet.* Stockholm: Stockholm University, 2000.

Ahlström, Gunnar. *De mörka bergen. En krönika om de lappländska malmfälten.* Stockholm: Norstedt, 1966.

Anderzén, Sölve. *Teaching and church tradition in the Kemi and Torne Laplands, northern Scandinavia, in the 1700s.* Umeå: Umeå University, 1996.

Bergman, Ingela, and Greger Hörnberg. "Early Cereal Cultivation at Sámi Settlements. Challenging the Hunter-Herder Paradigm?" *Arctic Anthropology* 52, no. 2 (2015): 57–66.

De Certeau, Michel. *The Practice of Everyday Life.* Berkeley: University of California Press, 1984.

Fellman, Jacob. *Anteckningar under min vistelse i Lappmarken vol. 1.* Helsinki: Finnish Literature Society, 1906a.

Fellman, Jacob. *Anteckningar under min vistelse i Lappmarken vol. 3.* Helsinki: Finnish Literature Society, 1906b.

Fellman, Jacob. *Anteckningar under min vistelse i Lappmarken. Första och andra året.* Stockholm: Rabén & Sjögren, 1978.

Frängsmyr, Tore. "Den gudomliga ekonomin. Religion och hushållning i 1700-talets Sverige." *Lychnos* (1971/72): 217–244.

Fur, Gunlög. *Colonialism in the Margins. Cultural Encounters in New Sweden and Lapland.* Leiden: Brill, 2006.

Hansen, Lars-Ivar. "Handel på Nordkalotten." In *Nordkalotten i en skiftande värld. Kulturer utan gränser och stater över gränser*, edited by Kyösti Julku, 216–243. Rovaniemi: Pohjois-Suomen historiallinen yhdistys, 1987.

Heinonen, Jouko. *Markkinat ja toripäivät. Päijät-Hämeen markkinat ja torikauppa.* Lahti: Päijät-Hämeen liitto, 2003.

Henrysson, Sten. *Prästerna i Lappmarken före 1850. Ursprung och arbetsuppgifter.* Umeå: Umeå University, 1989.

Knuuttila, Seppo. *Tyhmän kansan teoria: näkökulmia menneestä tulevaan.* Helsinki: Finnish Literature Society, 1994.

Kortekangas, Otso. "Whose History is Sámi History? Utility, Nation-State and the Indigenous Studies Paradigm: A Historiographical Comment." In *The Barents and the Baltic Sea Region: Contacts, Influences and Social Change*, edited by Kari Alenius and Matti Enbuske, 101–108. Rovaniemi: Pohjois-Suomen historiallinen yhdistys, 2017.

Kortekangas, Otso. "The Nomads, the Settlers and the In-betweens. Nordic Clergymen on Sámi livelihoods in the early Nineteenth century." *History and Anthropology* 31, no. 4 (2020): 510–525.

Kvist, Roger. "Den samiska handeln och dess roll som social differentieringsfaktor: Lule lappmark 1760–1860." *Acta Borealia* 3, no. 2 (1986): 19–40.

Kvist, Roger. *Rennomadismens dilemma. Det rennomadiska samhällets förändring i Tuorpon och Sirkas 1760–1860.* Umeå: Umeå University, 1989.

Læstadius, Petrus. *Journal af Petrus Læstadius, för första året af hans tjenstgöring såsom missionaire i Lappmarken.* Stockholm: Hæggström, 1836.

Lehtola, Veli-Pekka. *Saamelaiset suomalaiset. Kohtaamisia 1896–1953.* Helsinki: Finnish Literature Society, 2012.

Lindmark, Daniel. "Diaspora, Integration, and Cantonization. Swedish Colonial Education from a Theoretical, Comparative, and Concluding Perspective." In *Education and Colonialism. Swedish Schooling Projects in Colonial Areas, 1638–1878*, edited by Daniel Lindmark, 15–40. Umeå: Umeå University, 2000.

Lyons, Henry George. *Miscellaneous Data (British Terra Nova Antarctic Expedition 1910–1913).* London: Harrison and Sons, 1924.

Lähteenmäki, Maria. *The peoples of Lapland. Boundary Demarcations and Interaction in the North Calotte from 1808 to 1889.* Helsinki: Finnish Academy of Science and Letters, 2006.

Marklund, Bertil. "Skogssamernas ekonomiska rum." In *Människor i Norr. Samisk forskning på nya vägar*, edited by Peter Sköld, 343–448. Umeå: Umeå University, 2008.

Minde, Henry et al. "Introduction." In *Indigenous Peoples. Self-determination, Knowledge, Indigeneity*, edited by Henry Minde et al., 1–26. Delft: Eburon Publishers, 2008.

Panelius, Olav. "Inledning." In *Introduction to Anteckningar under min vistelse i Lappmarken. Första och andra året*, edited by Jacob Fellman, 5–15. Stockholm: Rabén & Sjögren, 1978.

Paulaharju, Samuli. *Seitoja ja seidan palvontaa.* Helsinki: Finnish Literature Society, 1932.

Roche, Daniel. *A History of Everyday Things. The Birth of Consumption in France, 1600–1800.* Cambridge, UK: Cambridge University Press, 2000.

Sörlin, Sverker. "Rituals and Resources of Natural History." In *Narrating the Arctic. A Cultural History of Nordic Scientific Practices*, edited by Michael Bravo and Sverker Sörlin, 73–122. Canton, MA: Science History Publications, 2002.

Väre, Henry. "Jacob Fellman. The Botanising Priest." *Memoranda Societatis pro Fauna et Flora Fennica* 87 (2011): 1–20.

CHAPTER 3

Dressed for Peddling: Dalkullor, Marketing and Practices of Tradition

Ella Johansson

An old photo from the archive of the Kulturen museum in Lund in southern Sweden shows a day of celebration sometime in the early 1890s (see Fig. 3.1). Two Swedish museums of cultural history, Kulturen in Lund and Skansen in the capital of Stockholm, were the world's first open-air museums. These museums were constructed as small-scale versions of the nation, presenting an educational project about the Swedish people, the "folk" and their heritage. At the open-air museum of Skansen,[1] the idea was to represent "all" of Sweden through buildings representing the different regions, all collected in a limited and strollable area. Both Kulturen and Skansen organized parties or festivals where people both benefited from and contributed to the atmosphere of the environment as they dressed up in "suitable" outfits. It was a way to engage the public, raise money and give life to the "walk about Sweden" that was the open-air museum's idea.[2] The founder of the Kulturen museum, Georg Karlin, arranged ticketed events, which included markets and bazaars, as well as

E. Johansson (✉)
Department of Cultural Anthropology and Ethnology, Uppsala University, Uppsala, Sweden
e-mail: ella.johansson@etnologi.uu.se

J. Ahlbeck et al. (eds.), *Encounters and Practices of Petty Trade in Northern Europe, 1820–1960*,
https://doi.org/10.1007/978-3-030-98080-1_3

Fig. 3.1 A playful folklore setting and a day of celebration at one of the world's first open-air museums, Kulturen, in Lund, Sweden, in the early 1890s. The museum was constructed as a small-scale version of the nation, and in the photograph, people are dressed up as immigrants, different minorities, and some are wearing regional costumes. (Photo by Lina Jonn. The Archive of the Kulturen Museum in Lund, Sweden)

what he called "purely ethnographical festivals" with attractions like "a Scanian peasant wedding" or "Gypsy camp," featuring theatrical folklore pieces enacted by students.[3]

The women in this photo are all wearing what were called "national costumes,"[4] in this case mainly local southern Swedish costumes with their characteristic white headscarves. The sixth person from the left in the front row, with a dark peaked hood and a striped apron, is wearing a Rättvik costume from *Dalarna*, also known as Dalecarlia. This costume embodied more than anything else the national image of Swedish women. Although the costume originally was a local dress, it became popular among upper- and middle-class women in the late nineteenth century in the cities, and it could be bought ready-made. The Rättvik costume also became a common motif in popular culture, appearing on countless postcards, brands, advertisements, and packages of products.[5]

In a way, the photo with individuals wearing different "traditional" or "national" costumes in a masquerade-like manner seems to mix notions of "otherness" and "sameness." Hence, the question of who is impersonating "the Other" and who is impersonating the "national ancestors" is not clear-cut and needs further discussion. If this is a celebration of the Swedish nation, it does not at first glance seem to be about an exclusion of groups that in those days were seen as strange or socially ambivalent in relation to the nationalist ideology of distinctiveness and internal homogeneity. This is a playful folklore setting, where immigrants and minorities are given space in some odd ways.[6] For instance, the woman dressed as a "Sámi woman" is wearing a "national costume"; however, this so-called "Lapp costume," in white or blue, was also worn by non-Sámi women. The dress was seen as a suitable outfit for ladies who went skiing. Like everyone else in the photo, this woman has given herself the right to dress up as a representative of a minority, secure in the claim it still embodies Swedish identity and solidarity. Similarly, several men are dressed as representatives of ethnic groups or otherwise "alien" people. For instance, the man in the center of the photo is probably dressed as an Italian organ grinder, part of a poor group who peddled around Sweden—and Europe more generally—at that time. This chapter exemplifies the relation between the fascination with the dangerous and alien and its part in the Swedish nation-building.[7]

My starting point involves the costumes from the Swedish region of Dalarna and the women who wore these dresses under different circumstances. The Rättvik costume, with its high, black hood and horizontally striped apron, will be a focus of the study. I will focus mainly on the women from Rättvik and Dalarna, who wore the traditional costume in modern and urban settings. This practice will be located in relation to contemporary notions of femininity and respectability and in terms of the making of identity and tradition for the Swedish nation and, to some extent, for the Dalecarlians themselves. Additionally, I will touch upon another group of women from Dalarna, that is, the hair-crafters from Mora.

Dressed in their costumes, Dalarna women were also mobile, and they were in fact seen in great parts of the country, above all in Stockholm, where they comprised a big and visible group of migrant workers from the district. The mobility and visibility in metropolitan life of the Dalarna people are, of course, an important reason for their fame.

The Dalarna mobile livelihoods were certainly not at the margins of how national identities were constructed. I will here look further into how heritage and concepts of national ethnicity were shaped by encounters between rural and urban, work and leisure, and markets and market strategies. I will argue that both poverty and the precarious, mobile livelihoods of the Dalecarlians were pivotal in the construction of the modern Swedish nation-state and national identities. The migrant work of the *Dalkarlar* (men) and *Dalkullor* (women) is well studied in literature and in ethnographic notes in folklife archives, and it has been published on in several texts, for example, by Lars Levander and Göran Rosander, and more recently by historian Anna Götlind.[8]

Picturesque Heritage Production

The Rättvik dress has a black skirt, on the front of which an apron-like, horizontally striped piece of cloth is sewn. It is the only example of horizontal stripes in Swedish traditional dress.[9] It is remarkable that the costume allows for public appearance without an apron, a garment that was as important for female decency as covered hair was for married women.

The most distinct feature is the peaky, dark hood. The hood was only to be worn by unmarried women (i.e., those women who also went to work in Stockholm). The hood seems to have gotten higher and pointier during the nineteenth century, especially when worn as a national costume, where the hood was used by both the married and unmarried, but also among the proper Dalkullor from Dalarna.

In the "authentication process" of the Dalkullor, cultural representations such as art and fiction were also used to depict a romantic and idealized notion of the "national maid."

There was thus a movement from the visibility of exotic and colorful dress in the urban landscape to paintings and the picturesque rural, folklife genre in the mid nineteenth-century Düsseldorf School, to the tableaus or living paintings of the museum. Early national Romantic-period ethnographical or folkloristic texts often had titles such as *Folklivsbilder*, *Taflor ur folklifvet*, or *Dalmålningar*, comprising pictures, paintings, and tableaus from folklife.[10]

The folklife genre painting by Amalia Lindegren *Lillans sista bädd* ("The last bed of the little one") from 1858 shows a cottage interior. A woman in a Rättvik costume, reserved for unmarried women, is crying while kneeling over a cradle. A small girl and two men are surrounding the crying mother. This painting came to represent the origin of the Nordic Museum, which focuses on cultural history, and the open-air museum of Skansen. At the Scandinavian Etnographica collection housed in the vivid downtown shopping street Drottningatan in 1873, Arthur Hazelius built a tableau of this interior with Rättvik-dress mannequins impersonating the mourning figures. The following year, the painting was published in the widely disseminated magazine *Hemmets familjejournal*. The interior tableau also appeared at the World Expo in Paris in 1878. There, as well as in Drottninggatan, a "live" *kulla*, known as *Pariser Anna* ("Parisian Anna"), flanked the exhibit as a kind of hostess.[11]

In the late nineteenth century, Dalecarlian dresses were commonly worn by non-Dalecarlian women—namely, by upper- and middle-class women—but also as a uniform for the saleswomen in the capital's leading department store, as well as by serving staff in many restaurants and cafés. It seems as if the Dalecarlian female costume granted women of all social classes and backgrounds some sort of social status and sign of virtues, such as trustworthiness, diligence, and respectability.[12]

Dalarna and Representations of Swedishness

The fascination with Dalarna in the nineteenth-century nation-building processes, here represented and "exaggerated" in both material and visual artefacts, is in many respects coherent with mainstream theories about nationalism and concerns about origin, purity, and authenticity. A utopia or model for the nation may be found or invented in a mythical past and at the same time appear in a contemporary *topos*. Many scholars have pointed out that in the case of Sweden, the district of Dalecarlia—and more precisely the parishes around Lake Siljan—has come to stand for the most representative region of "Swedishness," with the area being interpreted as a link to a glorious past.[13]

Levander has documented the traditional language and culture of this region, as well as the heroic travels of the women hair peddlers from Våmhus.[14] In other publications, apart from the ones on Dalarna, he also revealed his interest in the "illegitimate" sides of traditional society such as outcast groups, vagrancy, crime, begging, and peddling.[15] There are, of course, a lot of oral history and folklore collections about the migrant Dalecarlians. Rosander discussed factors that made Dalarna a national ideal, even though the lifestyle of its inhabitants was very "atypical."[16]

Dalarna was admired for its archaic and authentic material culture. Long church boats, as well as the collaborative social system that went with them, were believed to carry traces of Viking ships and Ledung organization, understood as the first expression of Swedish state formation.[17] The Dalecarlian use of a runic alphabet up until the twentieth century, ancient types of low timber houses with dragon ornaments inside and outside, and, not least, the traditional costumes of the peasants were all important material elements that contributed to interpretations of the Dalarna culture as archaic and essentially Swedish.

Above all, Dalarna represented a social utopia. The egalitarian group of smallholding yet still landowning peasants, with elaborate systems of cooperation, was idealized. Ethnologist Göran Rosander has pointed out, however, that this was not at all typical for the rest of Sweden but instead limited to this geographical-cultural district.

Northern or Upper Dalarna had a heritage system based on "real estate," dividing property in the form of *realia*, that is, dividing up the land and matters in their actual form. It was *not* customary, as in other parts of Sweden that one brother got the farm, and the other brothers and sisters were compensated with money or an equal value of mobile goods. The land around Lake Siljan was gradually divided up into extremely small farms with extremely small plots, and extensive villages grew in all directions, crammed with very small farmhouses.[18] There seems to have been few attempts to limit the number of children, and all siblings ended up as landed farmers. This was important, since it meant that they all had shares in extensive forested commons, which could be exploited, for example, by grazing, forestry, and tar, charcoal, and iron production. Many other supplementary sources of income were also necessary. This was arranged through domestic craftsmanship and seasonal migration. The latter included more or less organized begging and, later in the early modern era, trading in the form of house-to-house peddling, as well as migrant wage work outside the area.

The migrant work was called *herrarbete* ("gentry work"), meaning labor for people who paid others to work for them, a system that supposedly did not exist within their own communities. Men had been regularly leaving Dalarna for migrant work since the sixteenth century or late medieval era. Earlier, it is believed that, they supplemented meager agriculture by breaking ore and processing and trading iron. Men's trading was combined with their own manual craftsmanship, for example, working in metal, wood, or painting for export to other, mainly rural parts of Sweden.

There was a developed internal division of specialties and products between parishes and villages. In Stockholm, construction work and woodwork, such as sawing firewood for the wealthier families and institutions, were ways of making money.

People from Dalarna thus spent a lot of time away or on the road, mainly in neighboring provinces or in Stockholm. Some men and women also traveled to other countries, such as Finland, Russia, Germany, and Britain. Widely known and identified as a group, they were recognized through their dress. The term *dalkarlar* or *dalfolk* (literally, "the people of Dalarna") was used for men and women together, although *dalkarlar* means Dalecarlian men; alternatively, *kulla* (pl. *kullor*) has become the common Swedish word for women from Dalarna, although specifically referring to unmarried women.

Labor Migrants and Utilization of the Costume

Peddling, in particular, was part of the trade that made the dress, figure, and silhouette of the women from Rättvik a national symbol. Let us start with their migrant wage work. Women are said to have started doing *herrarbete* around 1770, yet it is very possible that they worked in the surrounding agricultural areas even earlier.[19] Their visibility in Stockholm was partly due to the outdoor work they did, with gardening being both the first and the most recent type.[20] The *Årstafruns dagbok*, an extensive diary of the lady of the Årsta estate in the county of Stockholm, reports the annual arrival and leaving of her garden *kullor* as early as the late eighteenth century.

Another occupation that definitely contributed to the "image-building" of the *kullor* was their involvement as *roddarmadamer* ("rowing madams") during the period of 1822–1862. They maintained a kind of "boat cab" or small-scale ferry enterprise between the many islands in the archipelago and the bays of Stockholm. It was hard physical work, consisting of either rowing or manually operating a paddle-wheel boat, but the women are reported to have entertained their passengers by telling melancholy stories or by singing and blowing their horns. The boats were sometimes decorated with green branches. The first *roddarkullor* were hired by wealthy Stockholmers to row their private boats, for example, between their town houses and their nearby rural homes, or for outings. These private boats soon came to be put into use in regular business, with *kullor* rowing them for full-time employment, being free to make as much as they could if they worked overtime after ten in the evening.

There was often conflict between *kullorna* and poor Stockholm women, who had originally enjoyed the privilege of rowing to support themselves. Late popular sources describe—but falsely, it seems—that the *kullor* thoroughly outcompeted the old rowing madams, whose practice of the trade had long been permitted. There are striking parallels with modern-day taxi organizations and controversies in multicultural metropolitan areas in relation to ethnicity and newly arrived groups. In 1853, *kullor* controlled 67 registered boats, around which time they were gradually replaced by steamboat lines.

It is likely that the rowing business gave a pastoral and romantic aura to the women (see Fig. 3.2). Very hard work that seems to have little to do with national romanticism, however, was building labor, where they did the heaviest of tasks, carrying mortar and brick up to the male construction workers. Dalecarlian groups of men played significant roles as

Fig. 3.2 A *Dalkulla* from the parish of Floda blowing a horn. The mobile livelihoods of the Dalecarlians were pivotal in the construction of Swedish national identities. (Photographer unknown. Nordiska museet)

subcontractors in the industrial growth of housing and infrastructure in Stockholm and Sweden overall. Related and neighboring women joined them as wage- or pieceworkers at these as well as at other building sites.[21] The work of Dalkullor as stevedores, another break from gender norms, seems to have been predominant in small harbors on northern Swedish coasts, where they also worked at sawmills.[22]

The first factory to hire men and women from Dalarna was the Liljeholmens candle factory, founded in 1839. The factory operated on a seasonal basis. A xylography from 1861 shows all the workers in the factory hall being women from Rättvik. Breweries, dairies, and water factories also specialized in hiring *kullor*. They washed and labeled the bottles; this was perhaps the most heavy, damp, and unhealthy work that they did but also the best paid job work female workers could have. Paintings and pictures show them transporting, loading, and unloading very large and heavy milk containers.

In the early era of mass reproductions, the Rättvik costume benefited from its graphic qualities, being strikingly clear and easily identifiable, even in simple black-and-white print. Thus, *kullorna* are often seen in otherwise "trivial" and mundane pictures of cities and factories, as well as in advertisements and packaging.

Apart from private gardens, a big group of around a hundred women worked at Stockholm's Northern Cemetery in Solna. In gardening work, the picturesque, staffage quality of their dress was obvious. Yet, it is striking how "uniform-like" and professional the dress looks in the mass photos from the barrack of the *kullor* by the Northern Cemetery. One can note that they were not as popular in Solna among the lower strata of society as among the bourgeoisie. Housewives from the shanty town of Hagalund threw stones through the windows of their barracks during the economic crisis and food shortages in 1920. This was because *kullorna* were thought of as having the money to buy the food the Hagalund people needed. Possibly involved in the animosity were other feelings of rivalry and contempt for the group of single women. Even the local Mayday demonstration that year was directed against them.[23]

A type of work that *kullorna* seem to have very consistently avoided was household work. As laborers, they were as badly paid as other women were in their time. That meant half the payment of what men got for the same kind of work, as is evident in the documents from the mixed workplace of the Liljeholmen candle factory. Yet, it seems that their strategy was to maximize income in pure money, in order to bring cash back to Dalarna after their migrant season. They did not compromise in this by conforming to norms about femininity, frailty, or security. It is also possible that their avoidance of household work was part of an ideology of not mixing with non-Dalecarlian people, reflecting a kind of endogamous identification based on ethnicity. This is not to say that their endogamy was very strict in practice, however, as a lot of anecdotal material speaks to the contrary.

Dalecarlians from Rättvik coming to the capital for seasonal work housed themselves—men and women together—in the stable of an inn on Hornsgatan Street. There they rented one big room and two smaller ones, where they slept and teamed up for simple and low-cost cooking. In some cases, the Stockholm upper-class ladies who visited the slums were very worried about the living conditions of the working class, as they imagined the confined housing conditions could cause sexual immorality and other moral problems.[24] Still, the moral standards of *kullorna* in their mixed quarters were never questioned. It is said somewhere that the costume was worn to mark oneself as not being a prostitute, in order to be able move freely in the urban environs at all hours without being solicited by men.[25] This would have been in contrast to other unmarried female workers, who could not survive without some kind of economically based relationship with one or several men.

Since the young women who came from Dalarna were wearing their costumes in the streets of Stockholm, one could ask how their visibility was connected to the possibility of making a living, as well as how they were looked upon by their employers, customers, and people who encountered them in the streets. According to all types of text and evidence around this well-publicized and popular group, Dalecarlian people had an overwhelming good reputation as being completely honest, extremely hardworking, and very trustworthy. When it came to sexuality and chastity, the women were known for marrying into their own community and having an extremely low rate of birth out of wedlock. This was in an era where the illegitimacy rate was very high in other settings, especially in Stockholm and the regions surrounding Dalarna.

Rural Vagrants and Female Peddlers

In the early modern era, one Dalecarlian complementary means of subsistence—which was not in any obvious way the case among the *kullor*, who went to Stockholm later in the nineteenth century—was begging. In the early modern period, Dalecarlian begging was organized through established routes, with assigned districts for different parishes or villages. This especially involved children. During "normal years," beggars were given food through culturally defined rules of generosity: two spoons or ladles of flour should be poured in the beggars' bags by each host. In "folk memory" recordings, the neighboring district of Hälsingland is described as "the Eldorado of the begging Dalecarlians."[26] According to interviews with people from Älvdalen, the farmers in Hälsingland were made to believe that begging people from Dalarna would ruin the fertility of the fields with magic if they were not fed. They would be "happy to get us back" for that reason.[27]

How organized and "profitable" the mendicant begging actually was, is, of course, a matter of relativity and interpretation. Just like the *herrarbete*, it was a way of fighting hunger and starvation. Begging could also be more subtle and combined with peddling—sometimes with "symbolic" merchandise of very low value that people would buy as part of a moral economy—or searching for work, as well as getting food and lodging for small services when traveling on the way to work somewhere else. This all comprised part of the migrant work conditions in rural communities.

In his solid and empirically very detailed—but perhaps not so easily accessible—doctoral dissertation, Rosander also presents several examples of negative stereotypes about the Dalecarlians. The examples mainly originate from rural and/or lower social strata, not from the wealthy citizens of Stockholm of the nineteenth and early twentieth centuries. In contrast to the examples given above, in these anecdotes the Dalecarlians are described as lazy and sly. Thus, it seems that the Dalecarlians managed to increase their status considerably during this period. The aura of trust combined with exoticism around *kullorna* was also used in advertisements by the emerging industrialists. The Victoria (later Mazzetti) chocolate factory and Alfa Laval-Separator used Rättvikskullor in their advertisements. Rättvikskullor also wrapped parcels at the department stores Nordiska Kompaniet and Leja. Rättvik-clad women were one of the most common images in Swedish advertisements of the time. Another commodity branded with Dalkullor was tobacco. Many sources report that Dalkullor were often chain-smokers who used iron pipes. The simple black-and-white pictures from tobacco emballage or matchboxes show, for example, a pipe-smoking Dalkulla carrying a pipe-smoking baby on her back in a bag, or majestically looking out over a wild landscape, pipe in her hand and surrounded by a herd of cattle.[28]

Pipe-smoking women can represent a focal point of exotism and orientalist odalisque romanticism, with water pipes, hashish, and opium. Smoking tobacco in an iron pipe was also seen as a habit of Sámi, Roma, and traveler women. It is one of the visual stereotypes that surrounded them and in later stages was reproduced, for example, in the imagery of "Tinkermovies," a popular film genre. There is, however, cause to assume that many women in the mainstream, core culture all over rural northern Sweden smoked a pipe in the eighteenth and nineteenth centuries. It is important to note that nations and nationalism are not entirely constructed out of sources of imagined purity and heroism. The authenticity of the nation seems to also need a heritage that includes pollution, ambivalence, and sexuality, in the same way that this is ascribed to subaltern groups.

Managing Cultural Pollution

I will continue the description of *kullorna* in the contexts that stressed their factual and symbolic connection with groups that were poor, marginal, vagrant, and excluded. Such classifications go back to premodern society, with its concepts of domiciliary rights, vagrancy, infamy, and dishonesty.

One of the oldest images of *kullor* is a painting representing women from Mora or Våmhus, peddlers and craftswomen selling rings and other jewelry made from horsehair. Made in the 1830–1840s, this was when journeys possibly began to extend across Europe (see below). Horsehair was an ideal material for poor and marginalized peddlers and travelers. It could be obtained at little or no cost, had little weight and volume, and could be processed to increase its value with a reasonable margin of profit. Horsehair was not a problematic material in itself; it was used for upholstering and furnishing fabrics. Yet, in the symbolic world of premodern Europe, the handling of dead horses' bodies was a strong taboo, being a task for hangmen. These two tasks of handling deaths and the remains from humans and horses were central in the classification of a social pariah group considered "dishonest," a categorization that is connected to the domiciled population's classification of excluded and vagrant groups, including travelers, tinkers, and gypsies.[29] Presumably, the Våmhus *kullor* got the small amounts of horsehair they needed from living horses. This was problematic, however, in terms of symbolic pollution and purity. Not only horses themselves—being both holy and yet inedible, potentially polluting animals—but also hair can be ambivalently regarded as somewhere between purity and danger. Hair has an ambiguous relation to the body; it is a part of the body but also something that can leave the body in cleaning and grooming, and in this respect, it is both powerful and polluting, like bodily fluids. Thus, hair is culturally problematic and carries various social stigmas. While this was not the case for the *kullor* themselves, who were involved in the hair trade, it was likely involved in the fascination they evoked.[30]

Pieces of horsehair were laced with contrasting colors to produce patterns. Similar crafts can be seen in present times, for example, as bracelets crafted and sold in the streets by so-called "New Age travelers." The rings could often be laced with inscriptions. The latter would refer to love and friendship, but there were also rings with naughty inscriptions.

The Swedish novel classic *Det går an* from 1839 is a radical advocacy for conscientious marriage or even free love, in the name of women's freedom and self-rule.[31] The protagonist Albert buys a pair of horsehair rings from a group of Dalkullor during the beginning of the steamboat journey stage of the novel. He gives one to the other protagonist, Sara, who was the one to first take interest in and negotiate the purchase. At the end of the journey, she will decline his formal proposal, yet suggests to him a life together "in free love," which allows her to maintain her glaziery and legal adulthood. The rings from the Dalkullor are paradigmatic of the theme of the novel, in which illegitimate liaisons are represented as more authentic and virtuous than the established and corrupt version, legal marriage. In a similar way, the incident reflects the ambiguous role of the Dalecarlian women combining illegitimacy, primitivism, and simpleness with cultivation, decency, and virtue.

The next step in the evolution of the Våmhus peddling tradition was to abandon horsehair for works in human hair. This development did not reduce the problematic symbolism concerning bodies, pollution, and borders. According to oral tradition, the craft was learned by young women in England in the 1830s, which would indicate that they were transnational migrants already before the crafting of human hair.

The heroic history-writing of the hair-crafting Våmhuskullorna presents the women's journeys to metropolitan cities like Helsinki, St. Petersburg, Copenhagen, London, Hamburg, and Berlin. Such business occupied 200–300 women every year, half of them abroad.[32] The women's spirit and ability to conduct business are in present times stressed as role models of entrepreneurship, as exemplified by the fact that the founder of the Greyhound bus company, Carl Eric Wickman, and one of the most famous Swedish building contractors, Anders Diös, had mothers who were hair *kullor*.

Different types of dress were used very strategically. Fashion dress was worn when selling in Britain and Russia, whereas traditional costumes helped business in Denmark and Germany. A group of five *kullor* all married in Berlin, meeting their future husbands when wearing fashion dress, and a famous *kulla* married to become Countess Kalling in Sweden. Others are said to have married high officers, industrialists, and noblemen, and an "almost prince" in Norway, Scotland, Finland, and Russia.

Levander reports that a peddling Dalkulla—interestingly, probably before 1840, when peddling among the wealthy homes of Stockholm—was embraced by a lady who felt and examined her skull through the hair "for lumps." She was enthusiastic over her findings and exclaimed that the young *kulla* should come and live with them, to become educated and take her rightful position "amongst us."[33]

There is a notion in these stories that people from Dalarna stood outside or above the social hierarchy and rank, either by not understanding or ignoring it, or by possessing some kind of intrinsic aristocracy themselves. In teaching of standard history, this was reinforced by their direct negotiations with, and assistance to, the future King Gustav Vasa to free the nation from the Danes. It was promoted by the common proverb in which Dalecarlian soldiers answer the orders of an officer: "Orsa company will not make firm promises." In the nationalist narrative genre of popular memory collected in the folklife archives, Dalkullor have been in direct contact with the kings of Denmark, the United Kingdom and Sweden, either being invited to show their goods or themselves contacting the royalty to negotiate their terms of working in the country. These stories speak of an identity, network, and social capital that stands above all forms of social hierarchy.[34]

Paradoxes of Authenticity: The "Folk" as "Inventors of Tradition"

Dress did, of course, have a function in identifying this certain group as a category, allowing them to profit from the reputation as honest and hard-working people to hire as workers, to buy merchandise from, or to help or at least respect. Traditional dress from other local districts and parishes around Stockholm filled the same role in branding certain quality products, mainly food produced in the hinterland, shipped to Stockholm by the producers and marketed on a daily basis. The Dalecarlian women's costumes were also a signal of chastity and unsociability to men from other groups, and they served to establish and maintain the group's endogamy in urban and even metropolitan environments. They also let the members of the group identify each other in a complex environment for mutual support.

When comparing older and newer pictures, the uniformity of the actual dress increased over time. Simultaneously, contemporary hairstyles and blouses were mingled with the dress of the proper *kullor*, who still kept their most distinguishing garments, the skirt and the hood.[35] Overall there is a strong cause to reinterpret such "traditionalism" not only in terms of an invented tradition by "nationalist" actors, but as an aspect of the group's own involvement in the outside world, including mobility, the market, and modernity, as well as their active use of, and invention of, tradition.

The dialects of Northern Dalarna are very ancient and can be seen as survivals of older strata in time. To an outsider, they are incomprehensible, as if they were languages of their own. The Älvdalen tongue is, in fact, classified as its own proper language. Yet, the *herrarbete* meant that everybody was "bilingual." This bilingualism possibly explains the traditionalism in the "insider" language. A constructed secret language is also known from the male painters from Rättvik and the tanners and furriers from Malung, as well as the peddlers from Västergötland and the chimney sweepers, the latter being a profession associated with the old "dishonest" social groups or guilds, such as hangmen and knackers. Secret—and sometimes invented or constructed—languages are indeed one of the features of vagrancy and marginality.

One thing that the Dalarna people had in common with other mobile, more obviously ethnic or ethnicized groups in different parts of history was that they were not merely a result of traditionalism, but of intensive encounters with cities and urbanity, mobility, market involvement, and so forth. Many Swiss so-called traditional areas, such as Lötchentaal, with cultural "relics" and "survivals," had the male population on the move as mercenaries for many centuries. The Swiss mercenaries were the group in which *nostalgia* was first diagnosed as a disease. The Dalecarlians share this form of melancholy and could also be compared with the Polish Gorals and their very similar lifestyle. Known for their colorful traditional dress and seen as national icons as well, they still work as seasonal migrants at building sites in Europe and North America. These groups shared a similar strategy in that they carefully guarded and divided their property, and thus remain landed peasants or farmers.

It is likely that the awareness and interest for one's own tradition—and the nostalgia, emotional intensity, and even sentimentality toward one's own cultural forms that can be distinguished when coming back home, for example—are based in "modern-like" experiences of mobility, market behavior, and urbanity. History might help us see a more complex interrelationship between poverty and ethnicity. Ethnification can be a strategy from the poor themselves, as well as a way of the state and the elite to demarcate and identify the poor.[36]

The invention of tradition should not only be understood as strategic marketing and branding of oneself. We should consider the people from Dalarna as discovering themselves in the same sense and under similar conditions as the romantic elites who invented the idea of the nation. Also, the romantic nationalism had strong roots in a "diasporic" situation, namely, the culture young students developed in their local communities' "nations" at centrally located universities, away from their homes. "Nostalgia," as an emotional structure, represents a genesis of identity politics, with similarities between high-brow nationalism and the business culture away from home developed by people from the peripheries in Europe.

This probably also spills over in a strategic use and invention of tradition. Accordingly, perhaps the Stockholm bourgeoisie had cause to identify with the Dalecarlians. The latter already knew a lot about the disenchantment and re-enchantment of the tradition that the elite in the capital were trying to encompass.

Notes

1. Skansen was conceived on the basis of the world exhibitions, and especially the Parc Étranger in Paris in 1867. For example, at the exhibition of the peasant village of Austria-Hungary, Arthur Hazelius got the idea of exhibiting life-sized, costume-clad wax dolls of peasants from the work of the Swedish artist Karl August Söderman. Bringéus 1972, pp. 7–10; Bjarne Stocklund. 2001. "Idéen om ett friluftsmuseum."
2. Johansson 2007, pp. 81–85.
3. Mark 2001, pp. 52–55.

4. Lundström 2005, p. 181.
5. Michel Pastoreau. 2001. *The Devil's Clothes. A History of Stripes and Striped Fabric.*
6. Norma Montesono-Parra. 2002. *Zigenarfrågan. Intervention och romantik.*
7. This chapter was originally a presentation at the German conference "Faszination des Illegitimen" with sub-sessions such as "Illegitimate lineages in the family tree of the nation building," see Constanze Gestrich, and Thomas Mohnike. 2002. *Faszination des Illegitimen. Alterität in Konstruktionen von Genealogie, Herkunft und Ursprünglichkeit in den skandinavischen Literaturen seit 1800.* This has made me look closer at how surprisingly in some aspects the Dalarna could be idealized, while the thing they encountered (i.e., the migrant peddlers and laborers) represented the same kind of phenomenon that would cause condemnation and exclusion, both from the point of view of the classificatory systems of a traditional society and from the modern nineteenth century, middle-class "Victorian" or "Oscarian" ideology.
8. Lars Levander. 1935a. "Hårarbete i Dalarna"; Barbara Kirschenblatt-Gimblett. 1998. *Destination Culture.*
9. Michel Pastoreau. 2001. *The Devil's Clothes.*
10. Mark 2001, pp. 52–55.
11. Bjarne Stoklund. 2001. "Idéen om ett friluftsmuseum."
12. Lars Levander. 1935b. "Hårarbete i Dalarna"; Lars Levander. 1944. *Våmhusfjärdingen.*
13. The social and material cultures of Dalarna have triggered the idea of the area being the most authentic and ancient district in Sweden. Göran Rosander. 1976b. "Turismen och den folkliga kulturen."; Ella Johansson. 1987. "Vår stolta särprägel. Nationalism och svenskhet i etnologin."; Ralph Tuchtenhagen. 2005. "Aus dem Tälern zu Nationalen Högen."
14. Lars Levander. 1943–1953. *Övre Dalarnes bondekultur under 1800-talets förra hälft.*
15. Lars Levander. 1933. *Brottsling och bödel*; Lars Levander. 1934. *Fattigt folk och tiggare*; Lars Levander. 1935a. *Landsväg, krog och marknad.*
16. Lars Levander has documented the traditional language and culture of Dalarna. Göran Rosander has published on migrant labor and the early tourist industry and the brand images of the Dalkullor. Historian Anna Götlind has written about the special types of migrant labor the women from Dalecarlia engaged in. My points are informed by theoretical perspectives that did not exist in the time of Levander or Rosander, before constructivist theories on nation-building and the invention of tradition, as well as the perspectives of Orientalism, postcolonialism, and queer theory on exclusion and inclusion, exoticism, mimesis, masquerade, imitation,

and desire. Still, many aspects of their material, especially the anecdotal notes, add a great deal to what I see as an unconscious or anticipatory "Faszination des Illegitimen" in Rosander's and Levander's research.

17. Ella Johansson. 1987. "Vår stolta särprägel. Nationalism och svenskhet i etnologin."
18. Elisabeth Wennersten. 1971. "Realarvets sociala regelverk"; Ulf Sporrong and Elisabeth Wennersten. 1995. "Leksands sockenbeskrivning."
19. Supporting this, historian Maria Wallenberg Bondesson, who studied on witch crazes and revivalist movements (2002). "Rum, väckelse och gemenskap. Om väckelserna i Delsbo, Forsa och Enånger i Hälsingland under 1700-talets sista decennier" and in 2003. *Religiösa konflikter i norra Hälsingland 1630–1800*), finds Dalkullor earlier in the surrounding districts, where they worked on farms. Some took a prominent position in the revivalist movement as preachers and ecstatic mediums, thereby transcending their low status as extra workers.
20. Christine, Lindquist. 1984. *Rapport över Dalkullor vid Göta kanal år 1813.*
21. Christine, Lindquist. 1984. *Rapport över Dalkullor vid Göta kanal år 1813.*
22. Anders Björklund. 1977. *Splitvedsjäntor och andra arbeterskor vid de norrländska lastageplatserna.*
23. Göran Rosander. 1967. *Herrarbete.*
24. Jonas Frykman. 1977. *Horan i bondesamhället.*
25. Oral communication with Prof. Nils Arvid Bringeus.
26. Göran Rosander. 1967. *Herrarbete. Dalfolkets säsongvisa arbetsvandringar i jämförande belysning.*
27. Lars Levander. 1914. *Livet i en älvdalsby före 1870-talet*; Lars Levander. 1953. *Älvdalskt arbetsliv under årtiondena omkring 1800-talets mitt.*
28. Göran Rosander. 1989. "Dalkullor i reklamen."
29. Brita Egardt. 1962. *Hästslakt och rackarskam*; Adam Heymowski. 1969. *Swedish 'travellers' and their ancestry*; Birgitta Svensson. 1993. *Bortom alla ära och redlighet;* Norma Montesino. 2002. *Zigenarfrågan*; Judith Okeley. 1996. *Own or Other Culture.*
30. Mary Douglas. 1966. *Purity and Danger. An analysis of Concepts of Pollution and Taboo;* Jonas Frykman. 1977. *Horan i bondesamhället.*
31. Almqvist 1838. Translated as "Sara Videbeck and the Chapel" by Adolph B Benson in 1919.
32. Levander 1944a, p. 183.
33. Levander 1944a, p. 183.
34. In the case of the Swedish king, this seems to be derived from the story of "the beautifull *dalkulla*," who in some sources is said to have met the crown prince. Anna Götlind. 2013. *Förbindelser.*
35. These signal professionalization; see Trevor-Roper 2008, pp. 195–215.

36. Birgitta Svensson. 1993. *Bortom alla ära och redlighet*; Norma Montesino. 2002. *Zigenarfrågan*. I am indebted to discussions with Norma Montesino-Parra for the conception of this chapter.

Bibliography

Almqvist, Carl Jonas Love. *Det går an. Hvarför reser du?* Stockholm: Hörberg, 1838.

Almqvist, Carl Jonas Love. *Sara Videbeck and The Chapel*, translated by Adolph B. Benson. New York: Twayne, [1919] 1972.

Björklund, Anders. *Splitvedjäntor och andra arbeterskor vid de norrländska lastage-platserna*. Stockholm: Liber Förlag, 1977.

Bringéus, Nils-Arvid. "Artur Hazelius och Nordiska museet." *Fataburen. Nordiska museets och Skansens årsbok*, 7–32. Stockholm, 1972.

Douglas, Mary. *Purity and Danger. An Analysis of Concepts of Pollution and Taboo*. London: Routledge & Paul, 1966.

Egardt, Brita. *Hästslakt och rackarskam. En etnologisk undersökning av folkliga fördomar*. Nordiska museet, PhD dissertation. Lund: University of Stockholm, 1962.

Frykman, Jonas. *Horan i bondesamhället* [Whores in peasant society], LiberLäromedel, PhD dissertation. Lund: University of Lund, 1977.

Frykman, Jonas, and Orvar Löfgren. *Culture Builders. A Historical Anthropology of Middle-class Life*. New Brunswick: Rutgers University Press, 1987.

Gestrich, Constanze, and Thomas Mohnike (eds.). *Faszination des Illegitimen. Alterität in Konstruktionen von Genealogie, Herkunft und Ursprünglichkeit in den skandinavischen Literaturen seit 1800*. Würzburg: Ergon, 2007.

Götlind, Anna. *Förbindelser. Fem Leksandskvinnor i Gamla stan—plats, arbete och resande under 200 år*. Stockholm: Stockholmia förlag, 2013.

Heymowski, Adam. *Swedish 'travellers' and their ancestry. A social isolate or an ethnic minority?* Acta Universitatis Upsaliensis. PhD dissertation. Uppsala: University of Uppsala, 1969.

Houltz, Anders (ed.). *Arbete pågår. I tankens mönster och kroppens miljöer*. Acta Universitatis Upsaliensis. PhD dissertation. Uppsala: University of Uppsala, 2008.

Johansson, Ella. "Mägde der Nation. Dalkullor in der nationalen Ikonologie und sozialen Praxis." In *Faszination des Illegitimen. Alterität in Konstruktionen von Genealogie, Herkunft und Ursprünglichkeit in den skandinavischen Literaturen seit 1800*, edited by Constanze Gestrich and Thomas Mohnike, 81–102. Würzburg: Ergon, 2007.

Johansson, Ella. "Vår stolta särprägel. Nationalism och svenskhet i etnologin." *Nord-nytt. Nordisk tidsskrift for folkelivsforskning* 30 (1987): 43–49.

Kirshenblatt-Gimblett, Barbara. *Destination Culture: Tourism, Museums, and Heritage*. Berkeley: University of California Press, 1998.

Levander, Lars. *Livet i en älvdalsby före 1870-talet*. Reprint [Elfdalens hembygds-fören.], [Älvdalen], [1914] 1979.

Levander, Lars. *Brottsling och bödel*. Stockholm: Gidlund, [1933] 1975.

Levander, Lars. *Fattigt folk och tiggare*. Stockholm: Åhlén & Söner, 1934.

Levander, Lars. *Landsväg, krog och marknad*. Stockholm: Gidlunds and Institutet för folklivsforskning vid Nordiska museet och Stockholms universitet, [1935a] 1976.

Levander, Lars. "Hårarbete i Dalarna." *Svenska kulturbilder* 4, no. 7/8 (1935): 135–154.

Levander, Lars. *Övre Dalarnes bondekultur under 1800-talets förra hälft 2 Förvärvsarbete*. Stockholm: Jonson & Winter i distribution, 1944a.

Levander, Lars. *Övre Dalarnes bondekultur under 1800-talets förra hälft*. Stockholm: Jonson & Winter i distribution, 1943–1953.

Levander, Lars. *Våmhusfjärdingen. Den nya tidens genombrott i en Dalabygd*, edited by Olof Köpmans, Hed Olof Anderssons, Filip Rombos et al. Serie: Folklivsskildringar. Stockholm, 1944b.

Levander, Lars. *Älvdalskt arbetsliv under årtiondena omkring 1800-talets mitt*, Reprint, Mora. Utg. av Stig Björklund. [1953] 2002.

Lindquist, Christine. *Rapport över dalkullor vid Göta kanal år 1813*. Göteborg: Göteborgs universitet, Historiska institutionen, 1984.

Lundström, Catarina. *Fruars makt och omakt. Kön, klass och kulturarv 1900–1940*. Umeå: Umeå universitetet, 2005.

Mark, Jan. "I begynnelsen var teatern eller resan till landet längesen." *Friluftsmuseet*. Kulturen i Lund: Kulturhistoriska föreningen för södra Sverige (2001): 152–161.

Montesino Parra, Norma. *Zigenarfrågan. Intervention och romantik*. Lund: University of Lund, 2002.

Okely, Judith. *Own or Other Culture*. London: Routledge, 1996.

Pastoureau, Michel. *The Devil's Cloth. A History of Stripes and Striped Fabric*. New York: Columbia University Press, 2001.

Rosander, Göran. *Herrarbete. Dalfolkets säsongvisa arbetsvandringar i jämförande belysning*. Lundequistska bokhandeln. PhD dissertation. Uppsala: University of Uppsala, 1967.

Rosander, Göran. *En Leksandssågare i Stockholm: ur en kassabok från 1840-talet*. Falun: Dalarnas Museum, 1972.

Rosander, Göran. *Dalska arbetsvandringar före nya tidens genombrott*. Stockholm: Institutet för folklivsforskning, 1976a.

Rosander, Göran. "Turismen och den folkliga kulturen." *Dalarnas hembygdsbok*. Årsbok Dalarnas hembygds och fornminnesförbund (1976b): 213–225.

Rosander, Göran. *Gårdfarihandel i Norden. En översikt av en gammal handelsform*. Stockholm: LT and Institutet för folklivsforskning, 1980.

Rosander, Göran. "Bryggerikullorna. Några anteckningar om säsongmässiga arbetsvandringar." *Svensk bryggeritidskrift* 10 (1962): 225–240.
Rosander, Göran. "'Industriens vaktparad'. Varuexpositioner i Sverige före första världskriget." *Saga och sed. Kungl. Gustav Adolfs akademiens årsbok* (1983): 105–159.
Rosander, Göran. "The 'nationalisation' of Dalecarlia. How a Special Province became a National Symbol for Sweden." *Arv. Scandinavian Yearbook of Folklore* 42 (1986): 93–142.
Rosander, Göran. "Hur Dalarna blev svenskt ideal." *Saga och sed Kungl. Gustav Adolfs akademiens årsbok* 1993 (1994): 7–73.
Rosander, Göran, "Dalkullor i reklamen." *Företagsminnen*. Bromma: Föreningen Stockholms företagsminnen (1989): 22–33.
Sporrong, Ulf, and Elisabeth Wennersten. *Leksands sockenbeskrivning D. 10 Marken, gården, släkten och arvet. Om jordägandet och dess konsekvenser för människor, landskap och bebyggelse i Tibble och Ullvi byar, Leksands socken 1734–1820*. Leksand: Kommunen, 1995.
Stoklund, Bjarne. "Idén om ett friluftsmuseum." *Friluftsmuseet* edited by Ella Johansson. Lund: Kulturhistoriska föreningen för södra Sverige. (2001): 10–27.
Svensson, Birgitta. *Bortom all ära och redlighet. Tattarnas spel med rättvisan*, Nordiska museet, PhD dissertation. Lund: University of Stockholm, 1993.
Trevor-Roper, Hugh Redwald. *The Invention of Scotland. Myth and History*. New Haven: Yale University Press, 2008.
Tuchtenhagen, Ralph. "Aus dem Tälern zu nationalen Höhen." *NordEuropaForum* Heft 1 2005. 2005 DOI10.18452/7850.
Wallenberg Bondesson, Maria. "Rum, väckelse och gemenskap. Om väckelserna i Delsbo, Forsa och Enånger i Hälsingland under 1700-talets sista decennier." In *Periferins landskap: historiska spår och nutida blickfält i svensk glesbygd*, edited by Ella Johansson, 163–180. Lund: Nordic Academic Press, 2002.
Wallenberg Bondesson, Maria. *Religiösa konflikter i norra Hälsingland 1630–1800*. Acta Universitatis Stockholmiensis. PhD dissertation. Stockholm: University of Stockholm, 2003.
Wennersten, Elisabeth. "Realarvets sociala regelverk: om släkten, gården och jorden i Ullvi by." *Leksands sockenbeskrivning* 10 (1971): 73–331.

CHAPTER 4

Rag Collectors: Mobility and Barter in a Circular Flow of Goods

Johanna Wassholm and Anna Sundelin

"Bring out all your old stuff!" This is how a rag collector greets his prospective customers in *Bilder ur Folkets lif i Östra Finland*, the book by Finnish writer and folklore collector Johannes Häyhä published in 1898.[1] The rag collector featured in Häyhä's depiction has much in common with the itinerant traders who form the focal point of this chapter. They came from a small number of parishes close to the border between the Grand Duchy of Finland and Russia in Vyborg County and maintained a circular flow of goods in which principally earthenware was exchanged for cloth waste, which was then sold in turn as a raw material to the paper industry. Men from the parish of Muolaa in particular were associated with this type of trade in the public consciousness. The trade in earthenware and rags was so closely linked that it seems appropriate to consider it under one heading, something that is also emphasized by Greta Karste-Liikkanen in her 1968 book *Pietari-suuntaus kannakselaisessa elämänkentässä 1800-luvun loppupuolelta vuoteen 1918* about livelihoods on the Karelian Isthmus.[2]

J. Wassholm (✉) • A. Sundelin
Culture, History and Philosophy, Åbo Akademi University, Turku, Finland
e-mail: johanna.wassholm@abo.fi; anna.sundelin@abo.fi

J. Ahlbeck et al. (eds.), *Encounters and Practices of Petty Trade in Northern Europe, 1820–1960*,
https://doi.org/10.1007/978-3-030-98080-1_4

The overall aim of the chapter is to provide an insight into an itinerant means of livelihood which had a business logic based on the idea that material perceived by one individual as worthless can be turned into something of economic value. We examine this topic from three perspectives. In the first part of the chapter, we analyze why the trade in earthenware and rags became such an important source of livelihood for peasants in a specific area of Vyborg County. In the second section, we consider the practices that formed part of the circular flow of trade and were deployed in the encounter between the traders and their customers in Finnish rural settlements. Finally, in the third part we look at what happened to the rags once they had been collected by the traders and at the economic valuations associated with the rag trade as a form of livelihood.

From a theoretical viewpoint, the perspectives we have adopted have been influenced by two approaches used in research on the history of consumption. First, we are interested in commodification, starting from the definition by sociologist Arjun Appadurai of a commodity as an article of economic value.[3] We focus specifically on the circular flow of goods that led to rags becoming commodified, that is, acquiring a value that provided itinerant rag collectors with a livelihood. Like Frank Trentmann, who emphasizes that the commodification of waste presupposes a level of mobility that went beyond the local area, we also stress the significance of distance and mobility.[4] During the nineteenth century, waste materials such as rags, scrap metal, and waste paper were shipped from Europe as far as the USA to satisfy the demand of American industry for raw materials.[5] In this study, we are able to show how a group of traders who journeyed all over Finland, with a trading network that also straddled the border with Russia, maintained a corresponding flow of goods on a smaller scale. Our second theoretical approach is based on the premise that barter was an important practice in the encounter between traveling vendors and their stationary customers. During the 1800s, barter played an important role in both rural trading and peddling as well as other types of petty trade. Bartering offered peasants a practical means of obtaining desired consumer goods in a society where access to cash was limited.[6]

As with the collection of other types of "waste," rag collection has primarily come to be noticed in earlier research as a form of livelihood associated with poor people on the margins of society in urban settings.[7] In a Nordic context, rag collection is chiefly mentioned in passing as a subsidiary occupation of peddlers or Roma people.[8] Where Finland is concerned, the rag trade is cited as a secondary occupation of Russian-Karelian peddlers, while Antti Häkkinen states that Jewish hawkers in the towns and Tatar peddlers also bought or bartered for rags and other goods from time to time alongside their main trading activity.[9] The rag collectors from the Karelian Isthmus that we study here differ from these groups with regard to certain key aspects. The first is that they traded in a more organized manner and in goods which, by virtue of their volume, necessitated a developed transport system and mobility over long distances, including across the border between Finland and Russia. Mobility was a prerequisite for business profitability in an agrarian and sparsely populated Finland. The second key factor is that they specialized in a specific type of trade consisting chiefly of earthenware and rags, while the third is that the rag trade was their principal form of livelihood.

References to the circular trade in which we are specifically interested are found primarily in works covering the unique economic conditions in Southeast Finland. The most detailed analysis of this features in the work by Greta Karste-Liikkanen already mentioned, in which she starts out from the circular goods flow when dealing with the rag trade.[10] The rag trade is also covered in local historical works about the parishes of Muolaa and Valkjärvi, where this form of livelihood was most prevalent.[11] The significance of rags as a raw material for the paper industry is alluded to in the history of papermaking and in historical accounts about individual paper mills, but the focus in these cases is usually on the function of the rags in the actual production process, while their journey to the mill is rarely considered.[12] One exception to this is Vilho Annala, who devotes a number of pages in his history of the Tervakoski paper mill near Hämeenlinna to how the raw material was procured.[13] The use of rags in the paper industry in Sweden starting in the seventeenth century has been studied by Helene Sjunneson and Ylva Sjöstrand.[14]

Relatively few sources of information survive relating to petty trade plied on the margins of society, and this is true also of the circular goods trade that we are studying.[15] We draw mainly on newspapers and responses to ethnographic questionnaires to find answers to the questions we pose. We primarily analyze newspaper and periodical articles that we have found by doing searches for Swedish and Finnish words linked to the rag trade in the newspaper database of the National Library of Finland. Digitalization and the ability to search the database have made it possible, based on isolated references in the press, to gather enough basic source material to create an overall picture of the encounters, locations, and practices that formed part of the circular trade in earthenware and rags and the value judgments reached in relation to the activity.

The material obtained from newspapers is complemented by responses to the questionnaire *Kringvandrande ryska handelsmän* ("Russian itinerant peddlers") in the cultural studies archive Cultura at Åbo Akademi University in Finland. The questionnaire was sent out by the Institute of Cultural History (KIVA) in 1957 and 1968. The trade in rags was not specifically asked about in either version, but ten or so respondents mention rag traders in their answer to the question "Were there different types of Russian peddlers?" in the version sent out in 1968. Since the question was absent from the previous version, its addition indicates that Professor Helmer Tegengren, who compiled the questions, had noticed that the respondents had mentioned rag traders in their answers to the first questionnaire. The references are also of interest insofar as the rag collectors were Finns from Vyborg County, but were associated in these responses with other groups of peddlers originating in Russia.

A Distinctive Spatial Economy

"As is already known, a number of country folk in our eastern parishes, especially in Walkjärwi and Muolaa, made a living from cloth waste for a long time. To purchase or barter for their goods, these folks traveled around the entire southern region of the country, especially in winter."[16]

The trade in rags is described as an important form of livelihood for peasants in some parishes on the Karelian Isthmus close to the border between Finland and Russia. The settlement most closely associated with the trade was Muolaa, which is mentioned in several contexts as a place that became known throughout Finland thanks to the itinerant rag collectors.[17] In one response to a questionnaire, a respondent calls the rag collectors simply "the men from Muolaa" (Finnish: *Muolaan miehet*).[18] The rag trade was also an important way of making a living in Muolaa's neighboring parish Valkjärvi, which was known primarily, however, for its artisans, who made carts for the Finnish and Russian markets.[19] Other places on the Karelian Isthmus, such as Hiitola and Antrea, were also occasionally associated with the trade in cloth waste.[20] In some cases, the regional affiliations of the rag traders are alluded to in more general terms, and they are described as "traders from the Karelian Isthmus," "Vyborg folk" or "Vyborg rag collectors."[21]

The fact that the trade in earthenware and rags became such an important form of livelihood for peasants in Muolaa and neighboring parishes is explained by several concurrent factors derived from the distinctive historical and geopolitical development of the region. One important factor was the founding of the city of St. Petersburg at the far end of the Gulf of Finland in 1703, which had far-reaching consequences for the economic development of Southeast Finland. The city grew rapidly: by 1810 it was home to over 330,000 inhabitants and at the turn of the century in 1900 its population numbered more than 1.2 million.[22] This contrasted with the population of Finland, which was around 800,000 at the beginning of the nineteenth century and rose to 2.7 million a century later. The growing metropolis became important for Finland's economy as a whole and dominated that of Southeast Finland. For the peasant farmers on the Karelian Isthmus, the agricultural trade, which provided the city with timber and food, and freight carriage, which ensured that the goods were transported to it, were important ancillary occupations.[23] Within this unique economy, the itinerant traders in earthenware and rags constituted a specialized group that maintained a flow of goods that extended geographically between St. Petersburg and large areas of Finland (see Fig. 4.1).

Another factor that affected the development of the Karelian Isthmus was that it was incorporated into the Russian Empire as the Vyborg Governorate during the period from 1721 to 1812, following Sweden's defeat in the Great Northern War (1700–1721). As a result of this, a significant share of the land in the region was given to Russian estate owners. The peasants in the region were tied to the land in a way that hampered the development of agriculture and contributed to a shift by the population toward other forms of livelihood, something that was made possible by the proximity of St. Petersburg. After Finland in its entirety became part of the Russian Empire in 1809, the area was incorporated with the Grand Duchy in 1812 as Vyborg County. A customs frontier was established between the Grand Duchy and Russia, meaning that the region's trade with St. Petersburg officially became a form of foreign trade. The incorporation with Finland did not solve the problems of the ceded lands, however. Even if a kind of resolution of the issue was achieved in 1867, when the Finnish state began to buy up the lands that the tenants could redeem against favorable loans, the development of agriculture in Vyborg County lagged behind the rest of the Grand Duchy in practice well into the twentieth century.[24] The view that the ceded lands had made living conditions in the region uncertain and had driven the population to seek

Fig. 4.1 The rag collectors carefully packed the earthenware and other fragile goods in hay. The hay also provided food for the horses in the winter and was useful if the need arose to conceal any illegal goods. (Photo by Matti Poutvaara. The Finnish Heritage Agency)

alternative mobile forms of livelihood was a perception that even the press of the time explicitly made known.[25]

At the national level, the expansion of the rag trade at the end of the nineteenth century is explained by two parallel trends affecting the economy. First, there was growing demand for cloth waste, an important raw material for the burgeoning paper industry and in part also for the textile industry. Up to the 1840s, paper was manufactured exclusively from textile fibers; rag collection was thus a necessity to keep paper production going and the raw material was often in short supply.[26] From the 1840s onwards, mechanization of the paper industry was introduced, and pulp produced from wood began to replace textile and cloth waste fibers to some extent. The methods were used in parallel going into the twentieth century, however, or alternatively a mix of textile fibers and wood pulp was used; for better-quality paper in particular, rags continued to be the most important raw material. The rapid growth in the consumption of paper and the establishment of an increasing number of paper mills therefore ensured a rising demand for rags, even though they accounted for a dwindling share of the raw material input for the paper industry.[27] The requirement for wool rags in the textile industry remained high throughout the 1800s.[28]

The second factor was that the liberalization of trade laws affected opportunities for making a living from collecting rags. Until the 1860s, rag trade in Finland was regulated by a royal ordinance dating from 1738, which reflected the desire of the authorities to safeguard the access of paper mills to rags. Paper mills were granted the privilege of collecting cloth waste within a limited area, while an obligation was imposed on peasants to supply rags to the paper mills in the form of a "rag tax." It was the duty of every head of a household to keep linen and wool waste along with wastepaper, a task that could be delegated in practice to a maid, for example.[29] When the trade laws began to be liberalized in the mid-1800s, regulation of this kind based on privileges was regarded as obsolete. At the 1867 Diet, the peasantry submitted a petition aimed at liberalizing the rag trade. The ordinance on trade and industry issued by the Diet in 1868 prescribed that the collection and purchase of rags, tree seeds, horsehair, bristles, hair, cattle bones, horn, and other "waste of such kind" was permitted to every inhabitant of the Grand Duchy.[30] In other words, collecting and trading in rags was now "free and handed over to private consideration and venture," as an article in the newspaper *Wiborgs Tidning* expressed.[31] At the same time, the formulation "waste of such kind" emphasized that households produced material that was viewed from their perspective as scrap, but which had economic value.[32]

Aulis J. Alanen maintains that rag collectors from the Karelian Isthmus had journeyed around western and central Finland already before 1868, although without proper permits.[33] However, more men engaged in the trade with the liberalized regulation. The main barter goods of the rag traders, earthenware, was likewise mentioned in the ordinance of 1868, which permitted peddling only to persons with citizens' rights in the Grand Duchy who were allowed to trade in glassware and ceramic objects, faience, and local handicraft products. The fact that the rag collectors were Finnish citizens and traded in permitted merchandise meant that they could make a living in a lawful manner, which made their legal status more secure than was the case with many other itinerant groups engaged in trade. As "foreign nationals," Russian Karelians and Tatars, for example, could not formally obtain the right to engage in peddling in Finland. Even if both the customers and the authorities commonly turned a blind eye to the situation when it came to peddling, they were at constant risk of getting into trouble with the law enforcers.[34]

Geographical factors also explain why earthenware in particular became the principal barter goods of the rag collectors. Situated in the Muolaa parish was the village of Kyyrölä, which was mostly inhabited by ethnic Russians. These were descendants of Russian serfs who had been moved to the ceded estates from the region of Yaroslavl after the area was incorporated into Russia in 1721, bringing with them the production of earthenware, which continued to be an important sideline for the inhabitants of the village and to a lesser extent for those in neighboring villages also. At the end of the nineteenth century, the village's output of earthenware pots was so great that they could not all be sold locally, and thus itinerant traders were commissioned to distribute the goods to consumers around Finland. The absence of any developed ceramic handicrafts in the rest of the Grand Duchy increased demand for the pots.[35] In 1882, a contributor to the *Åbo Underrättelser* laments the general state of artisan skills in Finland, for example, saying that the country's potters had failed to move forward in the design of their products and especially with their oddly shaped clay cuckoos.[36]

Although the Karelian rag collectors were Finns, the distinctive historical development of the Karelian Isthmus and its proximity to Russia meant that a geographical, cultural, and mental barrier existed between their place of origin and the rest of Finland. This is reflected in the kind of language used in the press, where it can be read how the "Muolaa dweller recognizes that he is a Finn, but not even he himself can guarantee that he follows Finnish custom,"[37] about what "the Finns" thought of the men from Muolaa or how the men saw themselves as going "to Finland" when they set off on their trading trips.[38] It can thus be said that when the Karelian rag collectors journeyed around Finland, they were perceived to some extent as outsiders, albeit probably to a lesser degree than other groups of itinerant traders who originated in Russia. The level of mobility that was a condition of maintaining the flow of goods covered large parts of Finland. In the source material, mobility is often referred to at the county level—for example, that the rag traders moved around in Mikkeli, Kuopio, Vaasa, and Oulu counties.[39] In other cases, a particular direction is emphasized (e.g., "the southern part of the country"), but there is a lot to suggest that the rag traders from the Karelian Isthmus traveled "around the whole of Finland."[40]

Encounters and Practices in the Circular Flow of Goods

Accounts of the rag traders' encounters with customers note that they were often prefaced by a "jingle," with which the traders alerted the customers to their arrival. By the time they arrived at a village or farm, the men had traveled over long distances and were recognizable from a long way off by their large load, which consisted of goods that would be bartered for cloth waste.[41] Filling the cart or sledge with goods to barter was an important part of the advance preparations for trading trips. The traders procured merchandise from a variety of locations, Kyyrölä being the most important of these: a journey there to obtain earthenware pots naturally formed part of the preparations. Apart from crockery, the rag traders also carried sundry items which were sometimes purchased collectively in St. Petersburg. The trader who visited the city could procure cheap items such as plates, spoons, knives, cups, combs, soap, needles, buttons, and rings on behalf of a group of rag collectors.[42] Before they departed, the tradesmen also procured goods for the journey in Vyborg, including the well-known Vyborg pretzels and other biscuits and pastries that they took with them, according to sources. Products mentioned in this context included small, star-shaped honey cakes, and other baked goods with east-Finnish- or Russian-sounding names such as *kauriska*, *orehki* and *preniki* (biscuits made from a syrupy dough).[43]

It is also claimed in the newspapers that the rag collectors distributed contraband, a practice that has often been associated with itinerant trade. Above all, the contraband comprised intoxicating substances such as so-called "Hoffmann's drops," a medicament that was often used for the purpose of inebriation at the end of the 1800s. It is likely that the Karelian rag collectors had easy access to illegal intoxicants since their home parish lay close to the Finnish-Russian border and that traders from Southeast Finland were often suspected of distributing alcohol smuggled into the Grand Duchy from Russia. A report by Finnish pharmacists dating from 1899 in connection with a petition to the estates to stop the abuse of medicinal products containing alcohol confirmed that "itinerant peddlers, rag collectors, etc.," supplied smuggled Russian goods to their customers.[44] In another article in the newspaper *Wiipurin Sanomat*, the writer claims that the rag collectors made big profits from purchasing cheap Hoffmann's drops in St. Petersburg and transporting them across the border without paying any duty.[45]

Packing the goods in the horse-drawn sledge or cart was an important practice prior to departure.[46] Both the pots that the traders took with them and the cloth waste to be bought were bulky items that took up a lot of space, and it was therefore essential to have a large and sturdy cart or sledge. The merchandise also had to be packed in such a way that it did not break when traveling on the bumpy roads; careless handling or poor packing could have devastating consequences for the outcome of the trip. Earthenware pots in particular were fragile in this regard and were carefully packed in hay.[47] The hay provided food for the horses in the winter and was also useful if the need arose to conceal any illegal goods. In 1896, for instance, a report featured in the press about a rag collector who had hidden a hundred bottles of punch and several bottles of Hoffman's drops in his load.[48] Rag traders placed the smaller items, baked goods, and cash in a lockable box that also served as a seat on the cart.[49]

When all the preparations had been completed, it was time to get on the road. The seasons influenced the journey insofar as the traders usually set off at the approach of winter, more precisely at the time when the snow made it possible to travel with a horse and sledge.[50] It was customary for the rag traders to set off from a particular location all together in a long caravan and then separate after a time to head to different regions of Finland.

In their encounter with the customers, the rag collectors sought to acquire cloth waste of a value that exceeded the value of the goods they handed over. They looked mainly to acquire linen and cotton waste, but also wool waste, which the textile industry used to weave new wool fabric.[51] Apart from various types of textile waste, the rag collectors also collected other goods on a smaller scale from time to time, according to sources. These items included dead cats, the fur of which had a resale value, and ant eggs, which were used as food for cagebirds and other animals as well as a raw material for the pharmaceutical industry. In Ristiina parish in Savonia, a rag collector in 1893 tells, for example, of buying ant eggs, which he says he could get a good price for in Vyborg or St. Petersburg.[52]

On arrival at a farm, the itinerant vendors encountered primarily women, who oversaw clothing in the household. Someone in the household would be tasked with collecting cloth waste, and the rag collectors would entice prospective customers by marketing the merchandise they offered in exchange. The enterprise thus revolved around barter, a practice that was characteristic of petty trade.[53] The relative significance of barter should be considered on a sliding scale, however; while it was an alternative to payment in cash for peddlers and other petty traders, for the rag collectors it was the actual reason for their trading activities.[54] This difference of degree is also expressed in one answer to a questionnaire, in which the respondent states that fabrics were purchased for cash from peddlers, while folk received various goods from the rag collectors in exchange for rags.[55] Another respondent says that cash certainly featured in transactions, but only in cases where the customer did not have enough cloth waste to cover the total cost of the goods they desired.[56] Barter also featured as a practice explicitly in the familiar "jingle" that in many contexts came to represent the encounter between rag collector and customer: "No money required for items large or small/Rags and scraps gladly accepted."[57]

Women were a prime client group for the rag collectors, as they were responsible for both textiles and managing food in the household. Thanks to a change in eating habits, there was a growing demand at the end of the nineteenth century for the pots, or so-called stoneware, that the rag collectors carried in their loads. In farming households, meals had previously been consumed from large communal pots, but at this time people were beginning to use individual items of crockery, glassware, and porcelain.[58] The recognition by the authorities of this change in the everyday consumption patterns of the lower classes of society was noticeable in a 1868 trade and industry ordinance, when crockery was included among the products that peddlers were permitted to trade. With the Kyyrölä ceramics, which had a good reputation with the customers, the Karelian rag collectors had thus opened up a useful niche market. Many of the questionnaire respondents emphasize the good quality of the pots; they are described as having been carefully produced and skillfully shaped. The glazed inside and attractive decoration using flower motifs, for example, are highlighted, as is the fact that the quality of the pots improved over time.[59] The rag collectors can thus be seen as suppliers of a utility article of high quality which the consumers associated with a specific place of production.

Another customer group that the rag collectors encountered were children. The collectors attempted to entice children to seek out cloth waste for them by promising Russian *preniki* cookies and other sweets in exchange for rags.[60] According to the cultural historian Lauri Kuusanmäki, the visit of the rag collectors was one of the few occasions when children living in the countryside got to taste delicacies of this kind; they only received such items otherwise as gifts in connection with journeys made

Fig. 4.2 The rag collectors also brought with them items intended specifically for children. Clay cuckoos made in Kyyrölä were popular toys that were also used as musical instruments. (Unknown photographer. The Finnish Heritage Agency)

by farm folk to the towns and markets.[61] The rag collectors also brought with them items directed specifically at these young consumers. In particular, clay cuckoos made in Kyyrölä were popular toys that were also used as instruments (see Fig. 4.2).[62]

While the encounter with women and children is described in relatively neutral terms, the liquor-trading encounters gave rise to a more negative choice of words.[63] With their illicit trade the rag collectors were accused of spreading depravity among their clientele, which probably consisted chiefly but not exclusively of men. From Suonenjoki, it was reported in 1888, for example, in an ironic tone that a rag trader's liquor had sold well among the working men of the town, while the women claimed they needed medicine for "stomach pains" or a "headache." It was assumed that the rag collector in question had continued to ply his successful trade elsewhere unless the rural police had apprehended him for the illicit activity.[64] At the same time, writers in the press indicate that the trade in alcohol fulfilled a daily need in the encounter between the rag collectors and their customers. The collectors were dependent on finding accommodation during their travels and the offer of liquor is described as an easy way of securing a welcome among their customers.[65]

The bartering that took place in the encounter between the rag collectors and their customers was both practical and worthwhile for both parties. The customer received utility goods delivered directly to the home and in the transaction got rid of material that no longer had any functional role. A single household was rarely able to collect so much cloth waste that it would have had any resale value, but rags could nevertheless become an economic resource, especially in times of need. In their book *Lumppappersbruken i Finland* ("Rag Paper Mills in Finland"), Gabriel Nikander and Ingwald Sourander show that the interest in selling rags increased during hard times, such as in the famine years of the 1860s or the depression of the 1890s, while it declined in times of prosperity.[66] For their part, the rag collectors exploited the niche that was facilitated by their habit of traveling long distances and by the growing demand for both cloth waste and utility goods.

From Waste to Processed Product

Once the rag collectors had bartered the goods they had brought with them, they were left with a sledge or cart filled with rags, a load that could be considered a "harvest," which in the next stage of the cycle would be turned into cash. Cotton and linen waste were sold to paper factories and wool waste to textile mills. A portion crossed the border and was sold to Russian factories; newspaper articles from the 1860s and 1870s tell of wandering rag collectors who conveyed their loads "directly to a paper mill situated close by in Russia."[67] One important market was the rapidly expanding industry in St. Petersburg, which with its rising demand for raw materials also helped to maintain a flow of goods in Finland.[68]

The expanding paper industry in Finland simultaneously gave rise to a sharp increase in demand for rags in the Grand Duchy, too, which created a competitive advantage for the rag collectors. They were free to supply goods to the highest bidder and transported rags directly to the large paper mills in Tampere and Valkeakoski, for example.[69] The increasingly tough struggle for raw materials also prompted factories to start engaging intermediaries to buy up rags locally on their behalf.[70] In Vyborg, the trading company Clouberg & Co. acted as an agent for the paper mills in both Tervakoski and Tampere. To keep up in competition with both domestic and Russian factories and to secure access to raw materials, F. B. Frenckell, for example, the owner of the big paper mill in Tampere, ordered Clouberg to pay whatever price was demanded to ensure that traders would deliver their cloth waste to his factory.[71]

The economic value of rags is also reflected in dishonest attempts to make money at times. In 1893, thieves got their hands on a quantity of cloth waste of unknown value when they broke into the rag warehouse of the Clouberg trading firm in the Kolikkomäki area of Vyborg.[72] Two years later, an attempt at forgery was reported at the same warehouse. A rag collector was given a receipt showing that he had delivered 12 kg of rags at a value of 1 mk 17 p, which he could redeem at the offices of the trading firm. The man passed the receipt to his brother, however, who in turn gave it to a woman who altered it to show that the delivery had consisted of 352 kg of cloth waste at a value of 34 mk 32 p.[73] This latter case also highlights the importance of the cash economy in the circular flow of goods. While the encounter with their customers was characterized by bartering, the rag collectors were paid in cash for the goods they supplied directly to the mills or to intermediaries. With the cash they could pay any debts they had incurred in advance of their trip and procure new merchandise for the next trading trip.

The rag traders played an important role in providing industries with essential raw materials, which meant that their activity was rated as mainly positive from an economic perspective. A certain value was attached to their role in taking charge of materials regarded by people as waste on behalf of industry. In a processed form, the cloth waste had value for the national economy, and in a figurative sense for the development of society as a whole. This aspect was emphasized in 1883 by a contributor to the periodical *Suomen Teollisuuslehti*, which was a mouthpiece for industry in Finland: "It could be said that our current society is dependent to a certain extent on the rag collectors." The rag collectors ensured that paper production could be kept going, and the paper mills were a guarantee in turn of the publication and dissemination of literature, which spread knowledge that contributed to the creation and maintenance of an educated and civilized society.[74]

The significance of the paper industry to the Finnish economy meant that a shortage of raw materials was a constant source of concern for the authorities and for the industry. Although pressure had been brought to bear in various ways, such as through edicts and a rag tax, it had proved difficult over the years to induce folk to provide rags and other waste material.[75] At the end of the 1800s, the press regularly drew attention to the importance of waste to industry. In *Åbo Underrättelser*, a writer remarked in 1886, for example, that it was lamented with good reason that Finland was poor, and that the situation would not improve while "so much wastefulness with all manner of small stuff prevails." The author compared Finland with rich countries where even material that could appear worthless to the individual was systematically kept and utilized. In addition to rags, he cited cotton reels, phosphorus sticks, empty tins, broken glass, ash, worn-out leather and rubber footwear, broken sewing needles, and medicine bottles, among other things. In Finland, as elsewhere, people should heed the saying *många bäckar små, gör en stor å* ("from little acorns, mighty oaks grow").[76] The industry's need for rags and the fear that usable material would be lost are also reflected in the notices and articles in the newspapers exhorting the public to keep their discarded textiles instead of throwing them away.[77] The point was made at the same time that access to waste textiles should be safeguarded by adequately remunerating those who handed them over. The value of the goods or the sum of money offered for rags was described as so poor that it did not encourage households to practice thrift.[78]

In parallel with the economic discourse that put a positive value on rag collection, another view is presented that judges this form of livelihood in a more negative light. The opinion representing this perspective presents the itinerant lifestyle of the rag trade as demoralizing and as a factor that hampered the development of agriculture and the handicrafts in Vyborg County. The absence of a significant proportion of the male population from parishes such as Muolaa and Valkjärvi for long periods in the winter had a detrimental effect in many respects. The men were prevented from making the agricultural implements needed for improving the efficiency of the region's neglected agriculture and they did not have time to get involved to the necessary extent in agricultural work, repairs, and planting new crops. Several critics saw an explicit connection between the nomadic life and the neglected state of agriculture in Muolaa and Valkjärvi; the region where rag trading was a particularly important form of livelihood was also the region where the farms were in the worst state.[79]

An even more serious problem was the indolence that critics believed that the rag trade gave rise to. The young men of the district marked time until they were old enough to set out on the road and thus grew up with a mentality that alienated them from artisan crafts and agriculture. Who would want to put in the effort to cultivate the soil when "easy money" was to be made in St. Petersburg, asked one contributor to the *Maakansa* newspaper in 1913.[80] In Muolaa in particular, this type of "speculative trading" appeared to be especially deeply rooted in the population. The general trend in Karelia, where the lifestyle was beginning to take on more civilized forms thanks to work to educate and inform the public, did not extend to Muolaa.[81] Such views represent typical conceptions of mobile groups in society and itinerant trade, and can in addition be linked to the stereotypical images of the Karelian, for which not least Zacharias Topelius laid the foundations in his description of the Finnish peoples in the school reading book *Boken om vårt land* ("Book of our Land"). In this, the Karelians appear as an ethnic group that is mobile and enterprising by nature and "likes travel and trade, making long journeys in its own country and to Russia for its merchandise."[82] A contributor to the *Laatokka* newspaper noted in 1892 that the alleged aptitude of the Karelians for trade, underpinned by historical development, had been preserved in its purest form in precisely the home districts of the rag collectors.[83]

Conclusions

In this chapter, we have looked at how itinerant rag traders, chiefly from the parishes of Muolaa and Valkjärvi in Southeast Finland, made their living from trading in earthenware and rags at the end of the 1800s and the start of the 1900s. We were interested in the factors that contributed to this form of livelihood becoming common in a specific area of Southeast Finland, in the encounters and practices that characterized the trade and the economic value judgments associated with the trade in rags.

The rag traders were a specialized group of traders on the Karelian Isthmus, the unique geographical and historical features of which resulted in a significant proportion of the region's population making its living from freight carriage and mobile trade of various forms. The conditions for gaining a livelihood from the circular flow of goods improved at the end of the nineteenth century due to the growth in consumption, liberalization of the laws on trade and industry, and the increasing demand of expanding industries for raw materials such as cloth waste. The rag traders exploited their geographical location by buying sundry merchandise in St. Petersburg on favorable terms and procuring ceramic objects in Kyyrölä. Some of the purchasing was carried out collectively, showing that the rag collectors were also organized among themselves. In addition, they had the ability to utilize the mobility over long distances that was necessary for the commodification of cloth waste in the sparsely populated territory of Finland, and they maintained networks through which they could sell the rags they collected. To keep the circular flow of goods in operation thus called for wide-ranging knowledge as well as an idea of how the activity could be made profitable.

In the encounter with customers, the sources describe how the traders greeted the customers with a familiar "jingle" and tried to induce them to surrender cloth waste, which they took in exchange for the goods they had brought with them. The encounter normally took place between male rag traders and female customers, who were usually at home and were responsible for the pots that the rag collectors wanted to exchange for the fabric waste they coveted. Children also featured in the encounter and were encouraged by the rag collectors to seek out rags with inducements of pastries and sweets. Men were probably the principal group of customers in the trade in the illegal liquor that the rag collectors were said to carry with them, but this encounter is not described in greater detail in the sources we studied. Alcohol was a way of making the money last longer, but at the same time it was an illicit form of trade that could potentially create problems with the authorities.

The most important practice in the flow of goods was barter, which offered the customer a practical means of disposing of material perceived as scrap. Even if the customer had realized that the waste had economic value, a single household would scarcely have been able to amass such a large quantity of rags and transport it over such long distances that the goods could have been turned into a resource. In exchange, the customer received utility goods, primarily ceramic objects from Kyyrölä, which had a good reputation as quality merchandise and for which there was a use in the daily life of the household. Cash only entered the picture when the traders sold the rags, either directly to factories in Russia and Finland or to intermediaries who acted as agents for the paper industry. With the cash they could pay off any debts that had arisen in advance of their trading journey and buy goods ahead of the next trip. Although the circular trade was based on barter, it is worth noting that the names given to the itinerant traders derived from the rags they collected and not from the earthenware that they principally gave in exchange. They thus belong to a subcategory of migrant traders whose primary function was to collect items that they passed on to industry as raw material.

The public had an ambivalent attitude to the activity of the rag traders. From the perspective of the local and national economy, it was an important occupation, as it guaranteed expanding industries access to essential raw materials. Industry representatives underlined this fact in appeals in the press, in which they urged households to keep materials that had a reuse value in another context. In this regard the activity of the rag collectors was evaluated positively in a manner that was seldom or never applied to other itinerant groups of traders. In parallel, however, the press adopts a patronizing attitude to the rag traders. In this discourse, their mobile form of livelihood is associated in a stereotypical manner with fraudsters and idlers chasing "easy money." An itinerant lifestyle was thought to alienate the rural population from agriculture, which was seen as a more honorable way of earning a living.

By studying the practices and places that had significance for the circular trade in earthenware and rags, we shine a light on a mobile form of livelihood that previous research has largely overlooked. We aim to highlight how material which lacked value from the viewpoint of the individual could be commodified, meaning that it acquired new value in a different context. The growing pace of industrialization in the late 1800s ensured that the demand for both old and new types of raw materials increased. The simultaneous liberalization of the laws on trade and industry gave rise to new possibilities of making a living for people who were prepared to move around and had the ability to build up a functional flow of merchandise. In a circular flow of goods such as this, an earthenware pot could be bartered for a discarded garment, which in turn became a piece of the puzzle in the process that kept industry and economic growth going.

Notes

1. Häyhä 1898, p. 41.
2. Karste-Liikkanen 1968, p. 197.
3. Appadurai 1986, p. 3.
4. Trentmann 2016, p. 628.
5. Zimring 2005, pp. 12–13. Trade was mainly on a national scale up to the Second World War, but particularly valuable merchandise, such as cotton and tropical foodstuffs, was transported over long distances at an early stage to satisfy demand in Europe. Topik and Wells 2012, p. 597.
6. Haapala 2007, pp. 46–49; Alanen 1957, p. 333; Rosander 1980, p. 84.
7. See, e.g., Faure 1996, pp. 60–61; Wynne 2015, pp. 1, 34–49; Strasser 1999, p. 8.
8. See, e.g., Rosander 1980, p. 78; Rekola 2015, p. 59.
9. Nevalainen 2016, p. 22; Naakka-Korhonen 1988, p. 146; Häkkinen 2005, p. 249.

10. Karste-Liikkanen 1968, pp. 197–204.
11. Sarkanen and Repo 2002, pp. 62–64; Seppänen 1953, pp. 361–366, 373–377.
12. See, e.g., Gabriel Nikander and Ingwald Sourander. 1955. *Lumppappersbruken i Finland*; Panu Pulma, 2012. "Lumpputampilta paperikoneelle: Paperin tekijät ja paperinteon koneellistuminen 1800-luvun Suomessa"; Markku Kuisma. 1993. *Metsäteollisuuden maa. Suomi, metsät ja kansainvälinen järjestelmä 1620–1920.*
13. Annala 1950, pp. 177–181.
14. Helene Sjunneson. 2012. *Papper och lump. Studier av kontinuitet och förändring i nordisk pappersindustri från 1600-tal till 1900-tal*; Ylva Sjöstrand, 2020. "Lump. Textil återvinning under det långa 1800-talet."
15. Strasser 1999, p. 8; Mikkola and Stark 2009, pp. 4–6.
16. *Folkwännen* 10/15/1879, p. 3.
17. E.g., *Folkwännen* 7/24/1867, p. 2; *Wiborgs Tidning* 10/9/1879, p. 1; *Maakansa* 5/1/1913, p. 4; Karste-Liikkanen 1968, p. 199; Sarkanen and Repo 2002, p. 62; Naakka-Korhonen 1988, p. 6.
18. KIVA FM 1064:7; *Laatokka* 5/4/1892, p. 3; *Savo-Karjala* 12/14/1892, p. 2; *Wiipurin Sanomat* 10/18/1894, p. 2. Sometimes the reference is negative, like when the newspaper *Päivälehti* (9.8.1894, p. 4) highlights that Muolaa is known for its "brawling rag collectors."
19. *Karjalan Ääni* 1/22/1927, p. 3; Ahlqvist 1859, pp. 23–24; Karste-Liikkanen 1968, p. 200.
20. *Laatokka* 11/16/1886, p. 2; *Wiipurin Sanomat* 10/18/1894, p. 2; *Maakansa* 1/29/1921, p. 1; 3/19/1927, p. 4; KIVA FM 960:3–4; Hämynen et al. 1997, p. 181; Alanen 1957, p. 189.
21. Naakka-Korhonen 1988, p. 146; Kuusanmäki 1936, p. 116; KIVÅ FM 918:3.
22. Engman 2003, p. 101.
23. Engman 2003, pp. 111–130.
24. Regarding the ceded lands, see Jyrki Paaskoski. 1997. *Vanhan Suomen lahjoitusmaat 1710–1826.*
25. See, e.g., *Wiipurin Uutiset* 2/24/1888, p. 2; *Wiipurin Sanomat* 9/30/1892, p. 2.
26. See, e.g., Nikander and Sourander 1955, p. 28; Kuisma 1993, pp. 308–310; Pulma 2012, pp. 100–106. The growing demand is also discussed in the newspapers. See, e.g., the advertisement for Oravais Woolen Mill in *Suomalainen* 3/30/1893, p. 4.
27. Rudin 1995, p. 205; Nikander and Sourander 1955, pp. 10, 190–191.
28. Sjöstrand 2020, pp. 16–17.
29. Alanen 1957, p. 188. See also Sjöstrand 2020, pp. 17–19.

30. Annala 1950, p. 178; Wassholm 2020, p. 122.
31. *Wiborgs Tidning* 5/23/1868, p. 1. See also *Suomalainen Wirallinen Lehti* 5/23/1868, p. 1.
32. Other residues that acquired value during industrialization were, for example, scrap metal, bones, ash and grease. Zimring and Rathje 2012, p. 357.
33. Alanen 1957, p. 189.
34. See e.g., Wassholm and Sundelin 2018a, pp. 139–140.
35. Regarding earthenware production in Kyyrölä. See, e.g., Karste-Liikkanen 1968, pp. 197–200; Virrankoski 1963, pp. 430–431; Kaukiainen 1982, pp. 178–179.
36. *Åbo Underrättelser* 9/24/1882, p. 2.
37. *Laatokka* 5/4/1892, p. 3.
38. *Päivälehti* 5/2/1895, p. 3.
39. Sarkanen and Repo 2002, p. 62.
40. *Folkwännen* 10/15/1879, p. 3; 7/24/1867, p. 2.
41. KIVA M 2068; FM 941:2–3; 960:3–4; 1064:7.
42. Sarkanen and Repo 2002, p. 62; Karste-Liikkanen 1968, pp. 197, 200.
43. *Ilmarinen* 6/11/1881, p. 1; *Keski-Suomen Sanomat* 1/12/1911, p. 2; KIVA FM 941:2–3; 960:3–4.9; 1064:7.
44. *Farmaceutisk Tidskrift* 4/29/1901. The extent of the smuggling is demonstrated by the fact that in 1899, county sheriffs in the Valkjärvi district confiscated over 100 kg of Hoffmann's drops.
45. *Wiipurin Sanomat* 10/23/1894, p. 3.
46. KIVA FM 1064:7.
47. Sarkanen and Repo 2002, p. 62.
48. *Päivälehti* 3/22/1886; *Wiipuri* 3/28/1896.
49. Ahlqvist 1859, pp. 23–24; Sarkanen and Repo 2002, p. 62.
50. KIVA FM 941:2–3.
51. Answers to the questionnaires mention *villa- ja kangaslumppu* ("wool and fabric rags") (KIVA FM 960:3–4), *pellava ja villa* ("linen and wool") (KIVA FM 1064:7) and *pellava- ja hamppurätit* ("linen and hemp rags"). In the last case, it is said that wool was not accepted (KIVA FM 941:2–3). A number of rag collectors also specialized in sacks. Seppänen 1953, pp. 373–377.
52. KIVA FM 960:3–4; *Wiipurin Uutiset* 7/11/1888, p. 2; *Mikkeli* 7/29/1893, p. 3; 8/5/1893, p. 3. For the trade in ant eggs, see Karjalainen 1979, pp. 71–78; Nevalainen 2016, p. 165.
53. We have previously looked at barter in petty trade in Finland during the 1800s in the following studies: Wassholm and Sundelin 2020, p. 121. Wassholm and Sundelin 2018a, p. 138, b, pp. 246–247.

54. KIVA FM 941:2–3.
55. KIVA FM 960:7.
56. KIVA FM 941:2–3.
57. Häyhä 1898, p. 41.
58. Sillanpää 1999, p. 43.
59. KIVA M 2068; FM 941:2–3; 960:3–4, 7; 1064:7.
60. KIVA FM 1064:7.
61. Kuusanmäki 1936, p. 116.
62. KIVA FM 960:3–4; 1064:7. Regarding the clay cuckoos, see Vuorela 1975, p. 669.
63. Regarding liquor trading in questionnaires, see KIVA FM 918:3; 941:2–3.
64. *Tapio* 2/25/1888, p. 2.
65. *Päivälehti* 5/2/1895, p. 3.
66. Nikander and Sourander 1955, p. 28.
67. *Wiborgs Tidning* 10/9/1879, p. 1; *Folkwännen* 7/24/1867, p. 2.
68. Karste-Liikkanen 1968, pp. 197, 200; Hämynen 1993, p. 181; Naakka-Korhonen 1988, p. 6.
69. *Folkwännen* 7/24/1867, p. 2; *Laatokka* 5/4/1892, p. 3.
70. Karste-Liikkanen 1968, pp. 197, 200; *Wiborgs Tidning* 10/9/1879, p. 1.
71. Annala 1950, pp. 177–178.
72. *Wiborgsbladet* 10/26/1893, p. 3.
73. *Fredrikshamns Tidning* 6/29/1895, p. 3. The Clouberg trading company also featured in the press in 1890 when the public health committee in Vyborg ordered it to "remove its rag warehouse" in one of the town's suburbs. The reason was that the rags were "of such a nature that contagious diseases are spread easily by them and epidemics mostly occur in said suburb." *Östra Finland* 10/8/1890. p. 2; *Wiborgsbladet* 10/8/1890, p. 2.
74. *Suomen Teollisuuslehti* 5/23/1883, p. 9. Original Finnish: "Woisi sanoa, että nykyinen yhteiskuntamme johonkin määrin riippuu – lumppukauppiaista."
75. Nikander and Sourander 1955, p. 28.
76. *Åbo Underrättelser* 3/30/1886, p. 1.
77. See, e.g., *Wiborgs Tidning* 10/23/1867, p. 2; *Wasabladet* 11/2/1867, p. 3–4; *Borgåbladet* 3/6/1875, p. 2; *Suomen Teollisuuslehti* 2/28/1883, p. 51; *Hämäläinen* 4/29/1891, p. 2.
78. *Åbo Underrättelser* 3/30/1886, p. 1.
79. *Ilmarinen* 6/11/1881, p. 1; *Maakansa* 5/1/1913, p. 4.
80. *Ilmarinen* 6/11/1881, p. 1; *Maakansa* 5/1/1913, p. 4.
81. *Laatokka* 5/4/1892, p. 3.
82. Topelius 2017, p. 227.
83. *Laatokka* 5/4/1892, p. 3.

Bibliography

Archival Sources

Cultural studies archive Cultura at Åbo Akademi University, Turku.
Questionnaire KIVA 9: Kringvandrande ryska handelsmän [Itinerant Russian Peddlers], 1957.
Questionnaire KIVA 9B: Kringvandrande ryska handelsmän [Itinerant Russian Peddlers], 1968.

Published Sources

Periodicals

Borgåbladet, 1875.
Farmaceutisk Tidskrift, 1901.
Folkwännen, 1867, 1879.
Fredrikshamns Tidning, 1895.
Hämäläinen, 1891.
Ilmarinen, 1881.
Karjalan Lehti, 1913.
Karjalan Ääni, 1927.
Keski-Suomen Sanomat, 1911.
Laatokka, 1886, 1892.
Maakansa, 1913, 1921, 1927.
Mikkeli, 1893, 1894.
Päivälehti, 1886, 1894, 1895.
Savo-Karjala, 1889, 1892.
Savonlinna, 1894.
Suomalainen, 1893.
Suomalainen Wirallinen Lehti, 1868.
Suomen Teollisuuslehti, 1883.
Tapio, 1888.
Wasabladet, 1867.
Wiborgsbladet, 1890, 1893.
Wiborgs Tidning 1867, 1868, 1879.
Wiipuri, 1896.
Wiipurin Sanomat, 1892, 1893, 1894.
Wiipurin Uutiset, 1888.
Åbo Underrättelser, 1882, 1886.
Östra Finland, 1890.

Literature

Ahlqvist, August. *Muistelmia matkoilta Wenäjällä wuosina 1854–1858*. Helsinki: Suomalaisen Kirjallisuuden Seura, 1859.

Alanen, Aulis J. *Suomen maakaupan historia*. Helsinki: Kauppiaitten kustannus, 1957.

Annala, Vilho. *Tervakosken paperitehtaan historia*. Helsinki: Tervakoski Oy, 1950.

Appadurai, Arjun. "Introduction. Commodities and the Politics of Value." In *The Social Life of Things. Commodities in Cultural Perspective*, edited by Arjun Appadurai, 3–63. Cambridge, UK: Cambridge University Press, 1986.

Engman, Max. *S:t Petersburg och Finland. Migration och influens 1703–1917*. Bidrag till kännedom av Finlands natur och folk 130. Helsingfors: Finska Vetenskaps-Societeten, 2003.

Faure, Alain. "Sordid Class, Dangerous Class? Observations on Parisian Ragpickers and Their Cités During the Nineteenth Century." In *"Peripheral" Labour? Studies in the History of Partial Proletarianization*, edited by Samir Amir and Marcel van den Linden, 157–176. International Review of Social History Supplement 41. Cambridge, UK: Cambridge University Press, 1996.

Haapala, Pertti. "Kun kaikki alkoi liikkua." In *Suomalaisen arjen historia. Modernin Suomen synty*, 47–64. Helsinki: Weilin + Göös, 2007.

Häkkinen, Antti. "Kiertäminen, kulkeminen ja muukalaisuuden kohtaaminen 1800-luvun lopun ja 1900-luvun alun maalaisyhteisössä." In *Vieraat kulkijat—tutut talot. Näkökulmia etnisyyden ja köyhyyden historiaan Suomessa*, edited by Antti Häkkinen, Panu Pulma and Miika Tervonen, 225–262. Historiallinen Arkisto 120. Helsinki: Suomalaisen Kirjallisuuden Seura, 2005.

Hämynen, Tapio. *Liikkeellä leivän tähden. Raja-Karjalan väestö ja sen toimeentulo 1880–1940*. Historiallisia Tutkimuksia 170. Helsinki: SHS 1993.

Hämynen, Tapio, Kimmo Katajala, and Pekka Kauppinen. *Itä-Suomi ja Pietari. Kirjoituksia toimeentulosta suurkaupungin vaikutuspiirissä*. Studia Carelica Humanistica 9. Joensuu: Joensuun yliopiston humanistinen tiedekunta, 1997.

Häyhä, Johannes. *Bilder ur folkets lif i Östra Finland: Wintersysslor*. Helsingfors: Finska litteratursällskapet, 1898.

Karjalainen, Sirpa. *Muurahaisten munittaminen*. Helsingin yliopiston kansatieteen laitoksen tutkimuksia 7. Helsinki: Helsingin yliopiston kansatieteen laitos, 1979.

Karste-Liikkanen, Greta. *Pietari-suuntaus kannakselaisessa elämänkentässä 1800-luvun loppupuolelta vuoteen 1918*. Kansatieteellinen Arkisto 20. Helsinki: Suomen muinaismuistoyhdistys, 1968.

Kaukiainen, Yrjö. "Perinteinen kotiteollisuus." In *Karjala 3: Karjalan yhteiskunta ja talous*, edited by Yrjö-Pekka Mäkinen and Ilmari Lehumusvaara, 173–183. Hämeenlinna: Karisto, 1982.

Kuisma, Markku. *Metsäteollisuuden maa. Suomi, metsät ja kansainvälinen järjestelmä 1620–1920*. SKST 1055:1. Helsinki: Suomalaisen Kirjallisuuden Seura, 1993.
Kuusanmäki, Lauri. "Kulutustavarain leviäminen maalaisväestön keskuuteen." In *Suomen kulttuurihistoria* IV: *Industrialismin ja kansallisen nousun aika*, edited by Gunnar Suolahti et al., 96–119. Jyväskylä and Helsinki: K.J Gummerus Osakeyhtiö, 1936.
Mikkola, Kati, and Laura Stark. "Himotut ja halveksitut kulutustarvikkeet: uusien kulutustottumusten vaikutukset suomalaisiin maalaisyhteisöihin 1800-luvun loppupuolella ja 1900-luvun alkupuolella." *Historiallinen Aikakauskirja* 107, no. 1 (2009): 4–17.
Naakka-Korhonen, Mervi. *Halpa hinta, pitkä mitta. Vienankarjalainen laukkukauppa*. SKST 491. Helsinki: Suomalaisen Kirjallisuuden Seura, 1988.
Nevalainen, Pekka. *Kulkukauppiaista kauppaneuvoksiin. Itäkarjalaisten liiketoimintaa Suomessa*. Helsinki: Suomalaisen Kirjallisuuden Seura, 2016.
Nikander, Gabriel, and Ingwald Sourander. *Lumppappersbruken i Finland*. Helsingfors: Suomen Paperi-insinöörien yhdistys, 1955.
Paaskoski, Jyrki. *Vanhan Suomen lahjoitusmaat 1710–1826*. Bibliotheca Historica 24. Helsinki: Suomen Historiallinen Seura, 1997.
Pulma, Panu. "Lumpputampilta paperikoneelle: Paperin tekijät ja paperinteon koneellistuminen 1800-luvun Suomessa." In *Kansallinen kapitalismi, kansainvälinen talous*, edited by Niklas Jensen-Eriksen, Mirkka Lappalainen, Jouko Nurmiainen and Sakari Siltala, 100–123. Helsinki: Kustannusosakeyhtiö Siltala, 2012.
Rekola, Tuula. "Romernas tidiga skeden i Finland—från 1500-talet till mitten av 1800-talet." In *De finska romernas historia från svenska tiden till 2000-talet*, edited by Panu Pulma, 20–82. SSLS 800. Helsingfors: Svenska litteratursällskapet i Finland, 2015.
Rosander, Göran. *Gårdfarihandel i Norden. En översikt av en gammal handelsform*. Stockholm: LTs Förlag, 1980.
Rudin, Bo. *Pappersmakeri. Ett klassiskt hantverks historia och teknik*. Hässelby: Rudin, 1995.
Sarkanen, Jaakko, and Kaino Repo (eds.). *Muolaa ja Äyräpää vv. 1870–1944*. [Toijala]: Muolaalaisten seura, 2002.
Seppänen, Unto. *Valkjärvi. Pitäjä kohtaloitten kannaksella*. Lahti: Valkjärven historiatoimikunta, 1953.
Sillanpää, Merja. *Happamasta makeaan. Suomalainen ruoka- ja tapakulttuurin kehitys*. Vantaa: Finfood, 1999.
Sjunneson, Helene. *Papper av lump. Studier av kontinuitet och förändring i nordisk pappersindustri från 1600-tal till 1900-tal*. Stockholm: Kungl. Tekniska Högskolan, 2006.

Sjöstrand, Ylva. "Lump. Textil återvinning under det långa 1800-talet." *Scandia* 86, no. 1 (2020): 11–34.

Strasser, Susan. *Waste and Want: A Social History of Trash.* New York: Metropolitan Books, 1999.

Topelius, Zacharias. *Naturens Bok och Boken om Vårt Land*, edited by Magnus Nylund. ZTS XVII. Helsingfors: Svenska litteratursällskapet i Finland, 2017.

Topik, Steven C., and Allen Wells. "Commodity Chains in Global Economy." In *A World Connecting 1870–1945*, edited by Emily S. Rosenberg, 593–813. Cambridge, MA: Belknap Press of Harvard University Press, 2012.

Trentmann, Frank. *Empire of Things. How we Became a World of Consumers from the Fifteenth Century to the Twenty-first.* London: Allen Lane, 2016.

Virrankoski, Pentti. *Myyntiä varten harjoitettu kotiteollisuus Suomessa autonomian ajan alkupuolella (1809–noin 1865).* Helsinki: Suomen Historiallinen Seura, 1963.

Vuorela, Toivo. *Suomalainen kansankulttuuri.* Porvoo, Helsinki and Juva: Werner Söderström Osakeyhtiö, 1975.

Wassholm, Johanna, and Anna Sundelin. "Emotions, trading practices and communication in transnational itinerant trade: encounters between 'Rucksack Russians' and their customers in late nineteenth- and early twentieth-century Finland." *Scandinavian Economic History Review* 66, no. 2 (2018a): 132–152. https://doi.org/10.1080/03585522.2018.1466725.

Wassholm, Johanna, and Anna Sundelin. "'Det hänger på ett hår.' Praktiker, moral och varuflöden i handeln med människohår i Finland 1870–1900." *Historisk Tidskrift för Finland* 103, no. 2 (2018b): 231–261.

Wassholm, Johanna, and Anna Sundelin. "Gendered Encounters in Mobile Trade: Human Hair as a Commodity in the Nordics, 1870–1914." *History of Retailing and Consumption 6*, no. 2 (2020): 118–136. https://doi.org/10.1080/2373518X.2020.1859927.

Wynne, Deborah. "Reading Victorian Rags. Recycling, Redemption, and Dicken's Ragged Children." *Journal of Victorian* Culture 20, no. 1 (2015): 34–49.

Zimring, Carl A. *Cash for Your Trash. Scrap Recycling in America.* New Brunswick, NJ: Rutgers University Press, 2005.

Zimring, Carl A., and William L. Rathje (eds.). *Encyclopedia of Consumption and Waste: The Social Science of Garbage.* Thousand Oaks, CA: SAGE Publications, 2012.

CHAPTER 5

Unruly and Submissive Marketgoers: Peasants Practicing Trade and Forming Markets

Ann-Catrin Östman

In mid-nineteenth-century Finland, quarterly markets were held in towns around the country. On these occasions, various groups of traders met customers from different social strata. In the coastal towns of Ostrobothnia in western Finland, peasant households sold agricultural produce and handicrafts (see Fig. 5.1). Town dwellers purchased food and other agricultural produce from farms in the surroundings as well as from peasant households in the interior parts of the region. Moreover, town burghers retailed their commodities and poorer sellers traded clothing, food, or beverages. For instance, commoners could buy clothes and clothing, minor manufactured goods, pottery, and metalware.[1]

At that time, the marketplace represented an established and traditional trading space, where dealers sold goods from simple stalls according to customary rules and regulations. As economic regulations were liberalized, market trade—a vernacular form of trade—was regarded as

A.-C. Östman (✉)
Culture, History and Philosophy, Åbo Akademi University, Turku, Finland
e-mail: aostman@abo.fi

J. Ahlbeck et al. (eds.), *Encounters and Practices of Petty Trade in Northern Europe, 1820–1960*,
https://doi.org/10.1007/978-3-030-98080-1_5

Fig. 5.1 At the turn of the twentieth century, market days were arranged three times a year in the Finnish coastal town of Kristinestad/Kristiinankaupunki. (Photo by Matti Poutavaara. The Finnish Heritage Agency)

old-fashioned and unnecessary, as well as disorderly and degenerate. In previous decades, the county governor had annulled some of the quarterly markets in this region. In 1866, the Finnish diet withdrew all the licenses of the markets in these towns on the Bothnian coast.[2]

Despite the regulations, peasants, other traders, and marketgoers continued their practice of gathering at markets in several locations, despite their informal and illegal nature. In this chapter, I will explore these types of markets mainly by using newspaper material. When and where did individuals and groups meet for unlicensed markets? Who visited these markets as traders, consumers, or visitors? How can we understand these informal practices and trading activities?

The elements that made up these markets were often the same as those of sanctioned ones: trading goods, making contacts, exchanging ideas, and enjoying entertainment. Anthropologist Börje Hanssen defined the market as a disorderly gathering of persons from different regions. In general, these markets had fixed end and start dates.[3] However, earlier studies show that commoners have used the very concept of "market" in various ways. For example, women who sold food and beer used the term more broadly when accused of illegal transactions. Moreover, in summertime, trading on boats or in the harbor was common. Thus, there was no sharp, unambiguous boundary between everyday trading encounters and publicly organized market trade. Also in other places, various groups gathered informally at markets.[4]

Sociologist Patrik Aspers defines the broad concept of the market as a social structure for exchange. Hence, we can interpret the market as an institution as well as an event. In both meanings, the market is formed by common understandings of social practices and of shared cognitive frameworks. Differentiating between trade and the market, Aspers emphasizes that the latter is public, and that the principle of competition is essential to its function. However, power relations as well as networks can circumscribe trade and trading activities.[5] The distinction made by Aspers can shed light on informal markets and trading encounters shaped by hierarchical as well as reciprocal relations.

Social hierarchies were embedded in the trading encounters at the marketplace. For instance, cultural distance characterized the relations between the urban middle and upper classes, on the one hand, and commoners, on the other. Regardless of the legacy of the relatively free peasants, the cultural representations of the peasantry were also contradictory and ambiguous in a Nordic context.[6]

According to Michel de Certeau, "ordinary people" can manipulate their environments through everyday actions. In discussing trajectories in studies of marginalized groups, de Certeau stresses that the aim of this project is not to give voice to the silent or collective masses. Instead, the goal is to make visible the uncountable practices by means of which people make use of specific regulations and places.[7] For instance, he is interested in how commoners or marginal groups used traditions.[8] De Certeau defines space as "a practiced place," thus opening up questions about how informal practices can be interpreted. These regular activities in the towns are part of a process of appropriation of space.[9]

Influenced by de Certeau's understandings of practices and re-employments, I will focus on the complex relationships between regulations, practices, social hierarchies, and economic development. Divided into three sections, the analysis observes the uses of former regulations, the utilization of urban space, and the trading activities of rural persons at informal markets. By using newspaper materials as well as questionnaires and studies on local history, I examine the maintenance of market traditions.

Regulations and Elite Understandings of Market Trade

In the middle of the nineteenth century, new laws and regulations accompanied the growth of trade. According to newspaper commentators, the markets had turned into fan fairs, as the events were characterized as a general opportunity for people to hang around. For those in power, some marketgoers proved to be troublesome: the markets were seen as degenerate and potentially dangerous places in the eyes of officials and the elite. In addition to this, some newspapers presented a critical view of the commodities offered for sale in market squares (see also Kuismin in this volume).[10]

In 1859, trade in the countryside was legalized, and subsequently rural stores were opened. In 1865, when the Finnish Parliament carried out an investigation on the importance and future of traditional markets, the issue was referred to counties, magistrates, and other authorities for consideration.[11] Magistrates in Ostrobothnia regarded traditional market trade as unnecessary. When towns in this region considered the matter, merchants and artisans could take part in the meetings. Most likely, the local merchants wanted to keep competitive outsiders away, while municipal officials simultaneously wanted to control and tax local trading. In these discussions, the practices and habits of the lower classes were heavily criticized.[12]

As a result, the government decided to close all the regular markets in the coastal towns of Swedish-speaking Ostrobothnia. In other parts of the country, the regional and local authorities conversely suggested that some of the traditional markets still be licensed. Thus, societal progress, economic development, and moral arguments were key aspects that framed the discussions.[13]

Commenting on this question, the clergy—who interfaced with the commoners daily and knew their ways of life—foresaw that withdrawing the licenses would only make matters worse, as prohibitions did not stop commoners from holding a market.[14] Interestingly, to defend markets, some members of the Diet underlined the charitable nature of petty trade.[15] Traditionally, town authorities had allowed vending as a form of social welfare and permitted poor individuals, such as widows, the elderly, and disabled people, to engage in street vending.[16]

However, the arguments for licensing markets were mainly economic: the commentators regarded markets as necessary in an undeveloped country. In a sparsely populated area, regular markets would make it easier to define fair prices. The authorities considered it important to bring sellers and consumers together at the same time, as this would inspire competition among sellers. In addition, several persons stressed the value of interregional exchanges and depicted how special products of various regions were continually exchanged with those of others. Therefore, arranging markets was a way to protect the common good, as often interpreted from an urban bourgeoisie perspective.[17] In the end, however, fewer markets per annum were allowed, and thereafter the markets would be arranged in the middle of the week, not during weekends.[18]

Depictions of Markets and Some Remarks on the Sources

There is a limited amount of archive materials, such as fiscal and legal sources, concerning these informal forms of exchange. As the historical records are relatively sparse, I mainly, although not only, make use of newspapers for this study. The digitalized Finnish Historical Newspaper Library offers opportunities to search for writings about informal market gatherings. When utilizing this database, I searched for *qwasimarknader/kwasimarknad*, the contemporary Swedish term used for these markets.[19] Moreover, I also studied early ethnological questionnaires focusing on trade. The tradition of local history-writing can also shed light on market gatherings; for instance, scholarly work has been done on the history of Vasa (Finnish: Vaasa), Nykarleby (Finnish: Uusikaarlepyy), and Gamlakarleby (Finnish: Kokkola).[20]

The towns under study were small. In the middle of the nineteenth century, the biggest one, Vasa, had 15,000 inhabitants. This region of Finland was primarily populated by Swedish speakers (see map in Fig. 5.2). Nevertheless, these markets attracted both Swedish- and Finnish-speaking peasants from wider regions. During the market days, Finnish-speaking people from other towns or nearby rural areas in the interior parts of the region traveled there. In contemporary sources, the Finnish speakers were often depicted as peasants from the interior parts of the country (*upplandet, inlandet*).[21]

I analyze newspapers published in Swedish in Finland between 1850 and 1900. With great frequency, mention of markets—that is, *qwasimarknad/kwasimarknad*—appeared in newspapers. Articles repeatedly depicted market gatherings and market trade in derogatory terms, and

Fig. 5.2 The southern and central parts of Finland with coastal towns. (Map by Niklas Huldén)

moralistic attitudes toward vernacular consumption and lower-class behavior were articulated. Newspapers often focused on disorder, unrest, and idleness, and usually they offered pejorative views of the laboring classes.[22] Thus, when it comes to gaining an understanding of trade in the marketplace, these writings—and other texts that circulated during this period—can be misleading.

I contrast these texts against ethnographical material collected much later, in the 1960s and 1970s, when two institutions circulated questionnaires to collect information about traditional forms of trade and encounters between country folk and urban dwellers. These were directed at both Swedish- and Finnish-speaking respondents who regularly answered questionnaires with different themes. This empirical material consists of over fifty answers to two questionnaires: "Travels for trade" ("Handelsresorna" MV/K12) and "Countryside and town" (SLS 1185 "Stad och land"). In their responses, persons with rural backgrounds depict customary practices and oral traditions. Occasionally, the respondents also refer to oft-told narratives concerning markets. To some extent, these descriptions are experience-based.[23] Thus, the texts show us how different writers perceived, named, and described a shared tradition.[24]

Markets on the Cycles of the Year: Re-employments of Traditions

In 1863, a newspaper wrote about the summer market in Vasa. In depicting fish cargoes, the author underlined the importance of the exchange between the fishing areas on the coast and the peasantry in the interior. In summertime, the fishermen in the archipelago delivered fish (in this case, Baltic herring). Even if the peasant households suffered from a lack money during this time of year, they could still purchase herring. As these persons built their exchange on trust and traditions, the customers from parishes further from the sea would pay these suppliers at the market in December, which usually took place before Christmas. The peasants in the farmlands would then deliver cereals in exchange. In passing, the writer revealed that the latter market was not formally licensed. Although the authorities had withdrawn the licenses for the December market, people still came together to trade on the old St. Thomas' Day (December 21).[25]

Newspapers reveal that buyers and traders effectively continued to carry on trade after 1866. For instance, there is an entry on a market that took place in 1867 in Vasa.[26] In the 1870s, after the great famine in 1868, markets were regularly held in this town.[27]

Newspaper articles reported when and where bigger markets took place. In the years to come, old-fashioned small-town markets were arranged on a semi-regular basis in several of the coastal towns in Ostrobothnia: Gamlakarleby,[28] Nykarleby,[29] and Kristinestad (Finnish: Kristiinankaupunki).[30] Generally, events seem to have taken place twice a year in each town. However, the coverage is far from even, and these texts are but examples of when people took part in markets.[31]

The great number of notices about “informal markets” (Swedish: *qwasimarknad/kwasimarknad*) in the searchable database containing digitalized newspapers reveals the importance of occasions when individuals and groups held markets without permission. The term used to depict these gatherings is itself first found in newspapers from 1867, and it seems to have been coined around that time. To an increasing degree, the term *kwasimarknad* was used in the 1880s and 1890s. Initially, the newspapers applied it to depict market trade in Ostrobothnia, but later they also alluded to informal market gatherings in other areas of the country.

In the questionnaires, writers who usually had a rural background often used the traditional names of these markets. The terms related to old church holidays, such as St. Thomas’ Day mentioned earlier. Michaelmas (*Mikaelsmässan*)—that is, the Feast of Saint Michael—is mentioned in newspapers as well as questionnaires.[32] Apparently, the autumn markets in the beginning of October were still characterized by the free week traditionally given to the servants. Moreover, respondents to questionnaires also mentioned markets called Candlemas (*Kyndelsmäss*) in the beginning of February.[33]

Earlier market laws stipulated physical and temporal boundaries for trading encounters. Among other regulations, there were prohibitions against forestalling and engrossing (i.e., buying up goods in advance to sell later at a higher profit). Interestingly, people often gathered at these informal markets on Fridays and Saturdays. But according to the ordinance of 1866, the markets would be held on Wednesday and Thursday, which would protect the towns from markets during the weekend. In the Diet, the clergy had been suggesting this solution.[34]

It was not always easy to know when these informal gatherings took place, as an ironic short paragraph shows in a paper published for a broad audience, depicting a market in Nykarleby. Since marketgoers entered the town on separate days, the informal market lasted a week. In the beginning of the week, visitors from the neighboring parishes north of the town are said to have arrived. According to this slightly paternalistic author, rural groups from the villages south of town entered the marketplace on the second day. On the following days, Finnish speakers from other parts of the region made their way to this tiny coastal town inhabited by about 1500 persons.[35]

According to the questionnaires, some of the visitors stayed the night in town. Burghers and merchants commonly offered simple lodging to their rural customers during markets. These guests were expected to buy commodities from their stalls and shops, or to exchange their own goods with the merchant. The peasants could buy commodities in springtime and pay with agricultural produce in the autumn. Another alternative was to pay for rooms provided by urban house owners, often widows trying to eke out a living.[36]

While varying in size and duration, the markets largely followed patterns and rules that had been in existence earlier. Re-employing traditions and bending earlier regulations,[37] various groups visited the coastal towns at certain times. Moreover, newspapers played a central role in shaping and maintaining these traditions. The very fact that newspapers reported about these markets undoubtedly increased their popularity. In some cases, the newspapers referred to them as customary.[38]

To a certain extent, the authorities of these towns tried to control the markets. A short text notes the attempts to empty the small town of Kristinestad after five days of market celebrations in 1876: "the marketgoers were literally drummed out by our skillful fingerless extra fireman, on an old cracked drum, with the consequence that peace and quiet was brought back."[39] The magistrates in several towns attempted to gain control of the attendees by forbidding the sale of alcohol during these markets. Moreover, police and other guards patrolled the towns. Interestingly, these informal gatherings were made formal by means of restrictions and the mechanisms created for controlling the masses.

The Use of Urban Space

From time to time, the commentators stressed the influx of people from the countryside and complained about commercialized amusements and drunkards invading the streets and alleys. Local newspapers regularly described how the laboring classes—that is, farm masters, farm hands, urban servants, and low-status workers—gathered in the streets. In some papers, the term "a motley mass" is used.[40] The newspapers often underlined the rural character of the market. However, when commoners from remote communities visited a market in Gamlakarleby, they behaved well:

> Horse trading was probably the main concern for most market visitors. Sober and decent, however, these market visitors came along. I met long transports of market people, both at my arrival and on the return journey, without seeing a drinker among them.[41]

In this case, it happened that newspaper stressed the calmness of the markets. However, newspapers often circulated negative depictions. In these portrayals of market life, drunken persons played pivotal roles. As underlined in newspaper portrayals, these markets—or fairs—included popular recreation (see Kuismin in this volume). Besides entertainment and consumerism regarded as unnecessary, the newspapers complained about violence, murders, thefts, and pickpockets.

The portrayals of country folk were contradictory. On one hand, the editors often depicted the misbehaviors of rural youth and laboring classes as well as of farmers. The upper classes may have expected subordination from these groups. On the other hand, in some of the texts small-scale consumers were depicted as passive and stupid. In some of the newspaper articles, the peasants and other rural visitors were depicted as uneducated victims easily cheated by dishonest traders or artists.[42] This reveals a paternalistic attitude toward the rural commoner, often depicted collectively, without any reference to class differences.

Even the term "orgy" was used in a portrayal of fairs in Vaasa in 1871. Similar concerns about noisy masses were often voiced. For instance, young people were said to have celebrated on the streets of Gamlakarleby in 1889. In this regard, the newspapers seldom made distinctions between Swedish- and Finnish-speaking commoners. The common denominator was thus class, not language. In several towns, the court records were full of cases concerning drunkenness and violation of the peace in the city. However, a newspaper commentator later depicted these men as obedient to the law, who always showed up at court when prosecuted.[43]

Several observations can be made from the questionnaire responses. There was a shared view among older informants (born in the countryside) that "in the past" it was common to go to the market.[44] There are some depictions of what it was like to be part of a mass of people walking, talking, laughing, and having fun. Some of these narratives give us insight into the feelings and practices of marketgoers, albeit in a nostalgic way.

> There were vendors in abundance with useful goods, but others with a lot of knick-knacks. People crowded between the market stalls—you would see if you could afford to buy something. The girls saw the beautiful hair combs, hair nets, brooches and fragrant soaps and of course they bought something from the market. The family back home and acquaintances wanted to hear news from the market and what we bought and if we met some acquaintances people.[45]

The respondents recount the journeys made by their parents and tell stories about how they first visited towns during markets. Questionnaires representing the voices of the lower classes that once regularly went to markets thus differ greatly from the newspaper depictions. Following tradition, the fairgoers from different households often continued to travel together from distant villages in rows of carriages.

> In the past, it has been said how horse-drawn carriages in long trains went to the market. It was farmers, crofters, cottars, and servants who, after the hard-working term, had finally hoarded everything.[46]

Various groups of itinerant traders and artists wandering around the country visited these informal markets. Newspapers indicate that the sellers had different social, linguistic, and ethnic backgrounds. It was regularly mentioned that peddlers from Russian Karelia were trading their goods at these informal markets. These small-scale dealers were often peasants. While trade in rural areas was forbidden in Finland and Sweden until the middle of the nineteenth century, the traditions and opportunities of rural traders were stronger in Russia proper. Traders from Russia proper had the right to take part in the licensed markets.[47]

Other mobile traders or persons for whom the entertainment provided an income were also aware of these informal market traditions. From time to time, the newspapers turned their attention to Roma market visitors, almost constantly in a negative way.[48] Occasionally, the newspapers also focused on Jewish peddlers. In addition, persons who offered various forms of entertainment were mentioned.[49] Following traditional regulations, various groups visited towns at certain times of the year, and the marketplace was frequented by peddlers and sojourners. Thus, a well-known periodicity seems to have facilitated these encounters and informal gatherings.

Looking for popular procedures that manipulated the mechanisms of discipline and cultural order, Michel de Certeau underlines that marginal groups turned the actual order of things to their own end– however, without any illusion that this hierarchical system would be changed.[50] Re-employing older regulations, rural dealers, consumers, and itinerant petty traders visited these coastal towns at certain times. In an informal manner, numerous groups of marketgoers continued to use urban space for trade and gatherings during traditional market days. These traders probably knew that these informal market gatherings offered large numbers of consumers.

Temporarily, various groups used the market squares as a common ground. When simple stalls were set up in the marketplace, older cultures of retail seem to have been followed there. Even if the commerce was unregulated, older traditions of assigning spaces and stalls were re-employed: some depictions show that the marketplace in the town square was divided: rural sellers used one part of the square, while merchants and artisans had their places in other rows.[51]

According to previous regulations, horse trading was not allowed in the marketplace.[52] Typically, horse trading was done on the outskirts of the small towns, and during the winter on the ice. These places were called *plassi* (in both Swedish and Finnish texts), and according to the newspapers' depictions, they were noisy, full of drunks, and where fraud and animal cruelty took place.[53] Roma vendors, in particular, became a target of blame. As men were responsible for horse trading, they were the ones mostly found at the *plassis*.[54]

Trading women appeared in the newspaper material, but only to a lesser extent (see Fig. 5.3).[55] Women were defamed if they were drunk, which was noticed a couple of times. According to the questionnaires, it was usually the master of the house and young adults who traveled to the markets. However, these texts reveal that married women also attended the markets.[56] There was female attendance at the fairs, and women were involved in trading activities, too:

> Many women also traveled to the market and in the square, they offered what they had worked on for many months of the year. There was homespun woolen yarn, knitted socks and mittens, linen cloths, and other women's handicrafts. There were no fixed prices on what was then marketed, but those who had good goods also got a better price for their products.[57]

The order of the market space was more likely to be associated with status and poverty than gender. Many individuals had a need for extra income. In the questionnaires and in other historical descriptions, we can find depictions of the poor who lived in the surrounding countryside offering goods on the fringe of the marketplace.[58] Making use of the market space and taking advantage of understandings of informal rights, persons with little or no means traded wooden dishes, spoons, or simple brooms. The poor, especially women, sought to earn a meager living by

Fig. 5.3 A vending woman in Ostrobothnia in 1923. Many commoners, especially women, needed an extra income, and selling wheat bread in the marketplace, food coveted by many, was one way of securing a living. (Photo by Samuli Paulaharju 1923. The Finnish Heritage Agency)

selling simpler items, handcrafted goods, or beer during these informal market periods. In part, this can be seen as a replacement for begging. Yet, poverty-stricken individuals made use of older traditions that granted the poor—especially the "deserving poor"—the right to sell.

Traveling to fairs, peasants could sell their goods before reaching the marketplace, even if the sale of food was forbidden beyond the legal boundaries of the market, according to the regulations on weekly markets.[59] Whereas some persons sold directly to customers in the homes of the buyers and outside the marketplaces, others chose to retail their commodities on the outskirts of town.[60]

Peasants as Consumers and Sellers

In an informal manner, various groups of marketgoers continued to use urban space for trade and gatherings during traditional market periods. Being located by the coast, these towns were connected by seaways. In the late nineteenth century, the railways in Finland made both long- and short-distance travel more feasible, and the questionnaires show that marketgoers did use trains for short journeys. At that time, visitors could travel by train and also ship their goods by rail.[61]

The interests of traders and consumers seem to have coincided. Even if the markets were associated with rural groups, various groups of traders made use of the public spaces of the towns. At the same time that merchants offered goods and bought rural produce, peddlers and other petty traders used these markets for trading. For instance, newspaper articles depict a variety of artisans and craftsmen, including bookbinders, tinsmiths, hat makers, and goldsmiths. Shoes were offered by so-called *marketents* (i.e., contractors of the Russian army).[62]

Women and men from peasant households acted as both consumers and traders. To a growing degree, rural households acquired goods, as they now had the income to consume goods above the subsistence level. Commoners could acquire products in urban rural shops, from peddlers and from stalls in the marketplace. The number of available commodities increased, among them fabrics and clothing, porcelain, agricultural implements, lighting, and various foodstuffs such as sugar, coffee, and wheat bread.[63] The consumers at the marketplace belonged to non-elite groups, rural as well as urban.[64] However, the consumption patterns of the commoners were, as the above discussion reflects, often depicted in negative ways.

In contrast to the ambivalence or even hostility toward market commodities found in newspapers, one finds a much more positive attitude toward such goods in the answers to the questionnaires. The respondents mentioned a range of utilities bought at the markets, comprising handmade products from various regions as well as factory-made goods. In these depictions, there is a consensus about the importance of the markets held in this region in the past. Besides clothing, respondents mentioned purchases of leather items, furniture, dishes, and tableware. Also within the range of possibility were sleighs and saddles, and some of the respondents underlined that utilities were obtained:

> Craftsmen of various kinds came to the market with their products. There were tinsmiths from Lillkyrö, who marketed milk kegs, jugs, mugs, toy spinners, petroleum cannisters and liquor bottles. There were potters selling stone dishes, pots and clay cuckoos, and tanners and saddlers selling slings, straps, and bridles.[65]

This example is typical, and most of these commodities can be considered useful in daily life. In several cases, the respondents of the questionnaires present long lists of commodities, reflecting their ambition to depict the past in a thorough way. One respondent reported that her mother, born in 1866, underlined that purchases were accompanied with laughter and conversation.[66]

Mostly, the respondents portray wares of domestic origin, such as leather items and clothes offered by commissioners from factories. However, foreign-made fabrics, clocks, and guns are also mentioned. Recalling the markets, the respondents also mention that men and youngsters bought suits—one elderly man wrote that his mother used to buy factory-made cloth from Karelian peddlers. Out of these she made dresses, which she, for her part, offered at the markets. This woman used older traditions of trading and developed new selling practices.[67] This example shows that a variety of traders made use of informal patterns of trade.

Wheat bread was another oft-mentioned item of market consumption. Petty traders from the southern part of Karelia were known for selling pastries called *viborgskringlor* ("pretzels from Viipuri").[68] In the nineteenth century, due to undeveloped agricultural techniques and the long winter, wheat was seldom cultivated in these regions of Finland.

Some observations can be made from the responses to the questionnaires. Persons from rural households seemed to have become, by a large majority, the main buyers. Markets offered an opportunity for consumer goods to be purchased and for forms of consumption regarded as important. At the turn of the century, commoners bought a considerable portion of commodities in the market square. In fact, this old form of petty trade was probably strengthened during a period of modernization and economic growth.

Besides enabling purchases, the markets also provided income for the rural population. Several respondents in the aforementioned questionnaires, born in the late nineteenth century, pointed out how important and "normal" it was to sell at markets. Peasant households traded food, hay and firewood, animals, and handcrafted goods:

> Of many kinds were the goods and products that were to be sold in the market square, where there was both meat and butter, homemade cheeses and much else that belonged to life's necessities and nourishment. Of the handicraft products there was also much and many different kinds—there were vessels, both buckets and milk pails with carved wooden ladles and spoons, and boxes of wood.[69]

When it came to food, the consumers also belonged to well-off groups. Sellers implicitly knew their repertoires. In the questionnaires one finds depictions of how rural small-scale traders circulated information about the prices that might be accepted that day. More experienced sellers helped a novice when it came to trading.[70] Early on, the newspaper started to publish information about the prices of foodstuffs and other commodities offered by peasants. As result, the settings of trade at the markets changed.

The local newspapers seldom depicted patterns of ordinary trading encounters. Nevertheless, newspaper reports on the markets frequently described commodities from various parishes: for instance, metalware from one Finnish community and smoked ham from another. A coastal community was associated with furniture.[71] In some questionnaires, the Finnish speakers note the traditional costumes worn by Swedish-speaking women in the coastal areas.[72] In a similar vein, the newspapers occasionally described the traditional or old-fashioned clothing of peasant women, or the clothes worn by peasant men.[73] Thus, social groups could be identified by their clothing, their marketed goods, and regional specialties.

Conclusions

This chapter has offered an exploration of practices of traditional and informal markets during an era of modernization. Although local and governmental authorities completely withdrew permissions for market trade in towns in western Finland, peasants and other traders defied laws and continued selling and bartering various commodities at annual or quarterly markets. The activities of the peasant groups did not change in reaction to the new formal rules. In Ostrobothnia, new regulations and restrictions, enacted during a period of rapid change, were ineffectual. At the end of the nineteenth century, these markets still had important commercial functions. Undoubtedly, newspapers played a central role in maintaining these traditions.

Re-employing traditions and regulations, various groups continued to meet during the markets, imitating earlier practices. Constructed through these practices, these informal markets can be interpreted as conscious uses of space; such regular activities in the towns were part of a process of appropriation. Transgressing limits imposed by regional and governmental authorities, commoners and petty traders collectively and regularly appropriated urban environs. Newspapers shed light on the market practices very differently than ethnographic questionnaires, which reflect the commoners' and marketgoers' own voices.

These customary and vernacular forms of trade continued to meet the basic needs of various groups, and the markets seem to have been important for the rural producers as well as urban residents and itinerant traders. It is obvious that shared assumptions about trade laid the foundation for these market encounters, enabling rural groups in particular to draw on, re-employ, and practice earlier traditions. As a result, these groups collectively created and upheld economic and cultural spaces by following and bending customary rules and regulations.

Notes

1. Jouko Heinonen. 2003. *Markkinat ja toripäivät. Päijät-Hämeen markkinat ja torikauppa*; Martti Varsta. 1946. *Mikkelin kaupungin markkinat loistokautenaan 1838–1867.* Birgitta Skarin Frykman. 1993. *Larsmässemarknaden. En folklig karneval i 1800-talets Göteborg.*
2. Heinonen 2003, pp. 55–60. This goes for the following towns in the region inhabited by Swedish speakers: Kristinestad, Kaskö, Vasa, Nykarleby, Jakobstad, and Gamlakarleby (Finnish: Kristiinankapupunki, Kaskinen, Vaasa, Uusikaarleby, Pietarsaari, Kokkola).
3. Hanssen 1952, p. 272; Storå 1997, pp. 5–8; Heinonen 2003, pp. 19–22.
4. See, for example, Levander 1935, p. 140; Luukko 1981, p. 275; Skarin Frykman 1993, pp. 16–17.
5. Aspers 2011, pp. 20–27. See also Kortekangas in this volume.
6. Högnäs 1995, pp. 7–11; Östman 2010, pp. 250–252; 2012, pp. 126–128.
7. De Certeau 1984, pp. xxiii, 29–42; Stark 2011, pp. 31–34; Koivunen and Syrjämaa 2011, pp. 47–51; Skarin Frykman 1993, pp. 14–17.

8. De Certeau 1984, p. xvx.
9. De Certeau 1984, pp. xii–xiii; Skarin Frykman 1993, pp. 14–17; Tooftgard 2015, pp. 1–6; van den Heuvel 2018, pp. 693–965.
10. Varsta 1946, pp. 119–124; Heinonen 2003, pp. 13–15, 53–54; Mats Berglund. 2009. *Massans röst. Upplopp och gatubråk i Stockholm 1719–1848.* Aino Suomaa. 2018. *Lantdagsdebatt om marknader 1863–1864.*
11. Heinonen 2003, pp. 55–57. See also Varsta 1946, pp. 138–144.
12. Ea:2791 Register of Correspondence, Economic Division, Senate of Finland; Möller 1973, pp. 189–190.
13. Varsta 1946, pp. 145–147; Heinonen 2003, pp. 55–58; Suomaa 2018, pp. 27–28.
14. Ea:2791 Register of Correspondence, Economic Division, Senate of Finland.
15. Suomaa 2018, p. 18.
16. Bladh 1991, pp. 190–192.
17. Ea:2791 Register of Correspondence, Economic Division, Senate of Finland.
18. Heinonen 2003, pp. 58.
19. Also *qvasimarknad/qwasimarknader/kvasimarknader.*
20. Anneli Mäkelä. 1987. *Vasa stads historia III;* Erik Birck. 1980. *Nykarleby stads historia del* II. Sylvi Möller. 1973. *Gamlakarleby stads historia* I.
21. Högnäs 1995, pp. 8–9.
22. Heinonen 2003, pp. 12–15; Östman 2020, pp. 82–83; Stark 2011, pp. 80–84.
23. In 1968, Hanna Granskog-Ekman sent a text about the history of trade in the parish of Närpes to the Society of Swedish Literature in Finland (SLS 906 Anteckningar om folklivet i Närpes, Hanna Granskog-Ekman).
24. Lönnqvist 2016, pp. 52–53; Pia Olsson. 2014. "Good Factual Knowledge for Future Generations. Questionnaire Activity Defining Traditional Culture." See also Nils Storå. 1997. "Kommers och karneval. Fiskmarknaden som mötesplats"; Anna-Maria Åström, 2001. "Strömmingsmarknaden som identitetssymbol."
25. *Wasabladet* 7/4/1863.
26. *Wasabladet* 2/2/1867, 7/71867.
27. *Wasabladet* 1/30/1878, 7/1/1871; *Åbo Underrättelser* 2/15/1870, 7/6/1871; *Hufvudstadsbladet* 2/20/1872.
28. Möller 1973, p. 190. *Hufvudstadsbladet* 11/19/1879; *Åbo Posten* 11/20/1897.
29. *Dagens Nyheter* 1/13/1877; *Åbo Underrättelser* 1/11/1877.
30. *Finlands Allmänna Tidning* 2/20/1879.
31. In the towns of Kaskö (Kaskinen) and Jakobstad (Pietarsaari), however, no markets seem to have been arranged during this period.

32. SLS 1185, pp. 273, 425.
33. See, for example, *Wasa Nyheter* 11/26/1897; *Dagens Nyheter* 1/13/1877. SLS 11985, pp. 276, 371, 420, 426, 432, 439, 443.
34. Heinonen 2003, p. 58.
35. *Folkwännen* 11/14/1890.
36. Möller 1973, p. 189.
37. See de Certeau 1984, p. xiv.
38. *Åbo Posten* 11/20/1889; *Österbottningen* 3/23/1902; *Wasa Posten* 3/12/1901.
39. *Wasabladet* 2/23/1876.
40. *Westra Finland* 9/3/1898.
41. See *Hufvudstadsbladet* 11/19/1879; *Åbo Posten* 11/20/1897.
42. For instance, see *Wasabladet* 4/16/1881; *Wasa Tidning* 2/20/1885; *Wasa Nyheter* 7/12/1897; *Wasa Posten* 3/12/1897.
43. Mäkelä 1987, pp. 163–165; Birck 1980, pp. 308–316.
44. SLS 1185, pp. 64, 189, 284.
45. SLS 1185, p. 151.
46. SLS 906, pp. 45–46.
47. Wassholm 2017, pp. 666–667; Björkman 1980, pp. 61–62.
48. For instance, see *Nya Pressen* 1/24/1883; *Westra Finland* 10/15/1892; *Wasabladet* 2/12/1887.
49. *Wasa Framåt* 10/25/1881; *Wasabladet* 2/16/1878. See Jonasson in this volume.
50. De Certeau 1984, p. 26.
51. *Jakobstad* 5/22/1907.
52. Birck 1980, pp. 313–316.
53. Cannelin 1855, pp. 17–19. *Åbo Posten* 10/13/1877, 2/10/1880.
54. *Westra Finland* 3/9/1898.
55. Skarin Frykman 1993, pp. 20–22.
56. SLS 1185, pp. 134, 155, 439. MV K12/109 and K12/455.
57. SLS 1185, pp. 7–8.
58. SLS 1185, p. 329; MV K12/455.
59. Birck 1980, pp. 653–656.
60. MV/K12/15; Östman 2020b, pp. 202–206.
61. Storå 1979, pp. 421–422; SLS 1185, pp. 152–153, 273.
62. *Jakobstad* 5/22/1907; Björkman 1980, pp. 61–62.
63. Ulväng 2012, pp. 63–64. See also Sundelin in this volume.
64. Heinonen 2003, pp. 127–129.
65. SLS 1185, p. 457. See also SLS 1185, p. 284.
66. SLS 1185, p. 458.
67. SLS 1185, p. 177.
68. SLS 1185, pp. 164, 444.

69. SLS, 1185, p. 7.
70. SLS 1185, pp. 7–8.
71. *Wasa Nyheter* 11/26/1897, 3/30/1899; *Österbottningen* 3/23/1902.
72. MV K12/466 and K12/257.
73. *Jakobstad* 5/22/1907.

Bibliography

Archival Sources

The National Archives of Finland, Helsinki.
Economic Division, Senate of Finland, Ea:2791 Register of Correspondence.
Finnish Heritage Agency, Helsinki.
Questionnaire K12 Handelsresorna 1965.
The Society of Swedish Literature in Finland, Helsinki.
SLS 906 Anteckningar om folklivet i Närpes, Hanna Granskog-Ekman 1968. ("Depictions of folk culture in Närpes").
SLS 1185, Land och stad ("Countryside and town") 1976.

Published Sources

Newspapers

Dagens Nyheter, 1877.
Finlands Allmänna Tidning, 1879.
Folkwännen, 1890.
Jakobstad, 1907.
Hufvudstadsbladet, 1872, 1879.
Wasa Nyheter, 1897.
Wasa Posten, 1897, 1901.
Wasabladet, 1863, 1867, 1871, 1876, 1878, 1881, 1887.
Westra Finland, 1892, 1898.
Åbo Posten, 1877, 1880, 1897, 1901.
Åbo Underrättelser, 1870, 1871, 1877.
Österbottningen, 1902.

Literature

Aspers, Patrik. "Markets, Evaluations and Rankings." *Historical Social Research/Historische Sozialforschung*36, no. 3 (2011): 19–33.
Berglund, Mats. *Massans röst. Upplopp och gatubråk i Stockholm 1719–1848*. Stockholm: Stads- och kommunhistoriska institutet, 2009.

Birck, Erik. *Nykarleby stads historia. Del 2: 1810–1875.* Nykarleby: Nykarleby stads historia, 1980.

Björkman, Hjalmar. *Bidrag till Jakobstads historia III.* Vasa: Fram, [1924] 1980.

Bladh, Christine. *Månglerskor. Att säja från korg och bod i Stockholm 1819–1846.* Stockholm: Kommitten för Stockholmsforskning, 1991.

Cannelin, Gustaf. *Maunulan Matti ja hänen viimeinen markkinaretkensä.* Helsinki: Raittiuden ystävien kirjasia 1. Raittiuden ystävät, 1855.

De Certeau, Michel. *The Practice of Everyday Life.* Berkeley: University of California, 1984.

Hanssen, Börje. *Österlen. En studie över social-antropologiska sammanhang under 1600- och 1700-talen.* Hälsingborg: LT förlag, 1952.

Heinonen, Jouko. *Markkinat ja toripäivät. Päijät-Hämeen markkinat ja torikauppa.* Lahti: Lahden kaupunginmuseo, 2003.

Heuvel, Danielle van den. "Gender in the Streets of the Premodern City." *Journal of Urban History* 45, vol. 4 (2018): 693–710.

Högnäs, Hugo. *Kusten och skogarnas folk. Om synen på svenskt och finskt lynne.* Stockholm: Atlantis, 1995.

Koivunen, Leila, and Taina Syrjämaa. "Tekijöiden ja yleisöjen valta näyttelyissä. Antonio Gramscin ja Michel de Certeaun teoriat epävirallisen vallan tutkimuksessa." In *Vallan teoriat historiantutkimuksessa*, edited by Ilana Aalto, Laura Boxberg, Ulla Ijäs and Heli Paalumäki, 40–49. Turku: Turun historiallinen yhdistys, 2011.

Levander, Lars. *Landsväg, krog och marknad. Ur samhällsdjupen i forna tider.* Stockholm: LTs förlag, 1935.

Luukko, Armas. *Vasa stads historia I: 1608–1721.* Vasa: Vasa stad, 1981.

Lönnqvist, Bo. "Kansallismuseon ja Seurasaarisäätiön varhainen perinnekyselytoiminta." In *Kirjoittamalla kerrotut. Kansatieteelliset kyselyt tiedon lähteinä*, edited by Pirjo Korkiakangas, Pia Olsson, Helena Ruotsala and Anna-Maria Åström, 40–54. Helsinki: Ethnos 2016.

Mäkelä, Anneli. *Vasa stads historia III, 1809–1852.* Vasa: Vasa stad 1987.

Möller, Sylvi. *Gamlakarleby stads historia III.* Gamlakarleby: Gamlakarleby stad, 1973.

Olsson, Pia. "'Good, Factual Knowledge' for Future Generations: Questionnaire Activity Defining Traditional Culture." *Journal of Finnish Studies* 18, no. 1 (2014): 65–90.

Pennington, David. *Going to the Market. Women, Trade and Social Relations in Early Modern English Towns, c. 1550–1650.* London: Ashgate, 2015.

Skarin Frykman, Birgitta. *Larsmässemarknaden. En folklig karneval i 1800-talets Göteborg.* Göteborg: Göteborgs universitet, 1993.

Stark, Laura. *The Limits of Patriarchy. How Female Networks of Pilfering and Gossip Sparked the First Debates on Rural Gender Rights in the 19th-Century Finnish-Language Press.* Helsinki: Suomalaisen Kirjallisuuden Seura, 2011.

Storå, Nils. "Kommers och karneval. Fiskmarknaden som mötesplats." *Budkavlen* 76 (1997): 5–16.

Storå, Nils. *Kronoby kommuns historia 1865–1968*. Kronoby: Kronoby kommun, 1979.

Suomaa, Aino. *Lantdagsdebatt om marknader 1863–1864*. Kandidatavhandling i historia. Åbo: Åbo Akademi, 2018.

Tooftgard, Jens. "Marketplaces and Central Spaces. Markets and the Rise of Competing Spatial Ideals in Danish City Centres, c. 1850–1900." *Urban History* 43, no. 3 (2015): 1–19.

Ulväng, Marie. *Klädekonomi och klädkultur. Böndernas kläder i Härjedalen under 1800-talet*. Möklinta: Gidlunds förslag, 2012.

Wassholm, Johanna. "Handel i marginalen. Den judiska småhandeln och lokalsamhället i Åbo i slutet av 1800-talet." *Historisk Tidskrift för Finland* 102, no. 4 (2017): 589–617.

Varsta, Martti. *Mikkelin kaupungin markkinat loistokautenaan 1838–1867*. Mikkeli: Mikkelin kaupunki, 1946.

Åström, Anna-Maria. "Strömmingsmarknaden som identitetssymbol." *Gränsfolkets barn. Finlandssvensk marginalitet och självhävdelse i kulturanalytiskt perspektiv*, edited by Anna-Maria Åström, Bo Lönnqvist and Yrsa Lindqvist, 290–312. Helsingfors: Svenska litteratursällskapet i Finland 2001.

Östman, Ann-Catrin. "Gendered Understandings of Agrarian Population in early Finnish Social Studies." In *In Experts We Trust: Knowledge, Politics and Bureaucracy in Nordic Welfare States*, edited by Åsa Lundqvist and Klaus Petersen, 249–268. Odense: University of Southern Denmark Press, 2010.

Östman, Ann-Catrin. "Civilising and Mobilising the Peasantry: Co-operative Organization and Understandings of Progress and Gender c. 1899–1918." In *Co-operatives and the Social Question: The Co-operative Movement in Northern & Eastern Europe 1880 to 1950*, edited by Mary Hilson, Pirjo Markkola and Ann-Catrin Östman, 121–136. Cardiff: Welsh Academic Press 2012.

Östman, Ann-Catrin. "Att synliggöra det nedvärderade. Om skildringar av småhandel i frågelistsvar och tidningstexter." *Saga och Sed*. Kungl. Gustav Adolfs Akademiens årsbok 2019 (2020): 73–87.

Östman, Ann-Catrin. "Smör och känslor i kristid. Torgförsäljning och livsmedelsdistribution i österbottniska städer 1915–1918." In *Köpa salt i Cádiz och andra berättelser*, edited by Henrika Tandefelt, Julia Dahlberg, Aapo Roselius and Oula Silvennoinen, 199–209. Helsinki: Siltala, 2020b.

CHAPTER 6

Gifts, Feasts, and the Surplus of Friendship: Practices in a Remembered Economy of Petty Trading

Niklas Huldén

The long tradition of trade between the areas of the contemporary states of Estonia and Finland has its roots in prehistoric times. This includes the freight trade of merchants of Tallinn (Reval) with Hanseatic connections and the trade of both Finnish and Baltic (Estonian-Livonian) nobles, who claimed the right to trade in the Gulf of Finland. However, such trade was not without conflicts, which show up in historical sources from the fourteenth century onwards.[1] Throughout the centuries, the whole region and parts of it had been ruled by different emerging countries, monarchies, and rulers, including Denmark, The Livonian Order of the Brothers of the Sword, the Teutonic Order, Novgorod, bishoprics and the city of Riga in Livonia, Poland-Lithuania, Russia, Sweden, and Livonia.[2] After the Second World War, Estonia was joined to the Soviet Union, until it again gained independence in 1991. From 1812 until the First World War, both Estonia

N. Huldén (✉)
Culture, History and Philosophy, Åbo Akademi University, Turku, Finland
e-mail: niklas.hulden@abo.fi

J. Ahlbeck et al. (eds.), *Encounters and Practices of Petty Trade in Northern Europe, 1820–1960*,
https://doi.org/10.1007/978-3-030-98080-1_6

and Finland were part of the Russian Empire, Finland being a Grand Duchy with separate laws.

In the nineteenth century, trade heavily depended on developing personal acquaintances with traders from the other side of the gulf. Petty trade across the Gulf of Finland was predominantly based on barter. The Gulf of Finland is about 40–80 miles (70–140 km) wide between its northern and southern shores. With good winds, crossing the gulf would take about one day of travel for a nineteenth-century sailing vessel. In bad weather, people could need to wait for good wind for days or even weeks. The Finnish coast in general has more archipelago islands than the Estonian side, but they are also smaller (see map in Fig. 6.1).

In the eastern parts of the gulf, peasants and fishermen from both areas traded directly with each other, crossing in small sailing boats. This was also helped by the Finnish and Estonian languages being almost mutually intelligible. Together people formed a sort of trade partnership called *sepra* (Estonian: *sõbra*), which could last for a season or even for years and decades.[3] As a practice, the *sepra* included the giving of mutual gifts, social

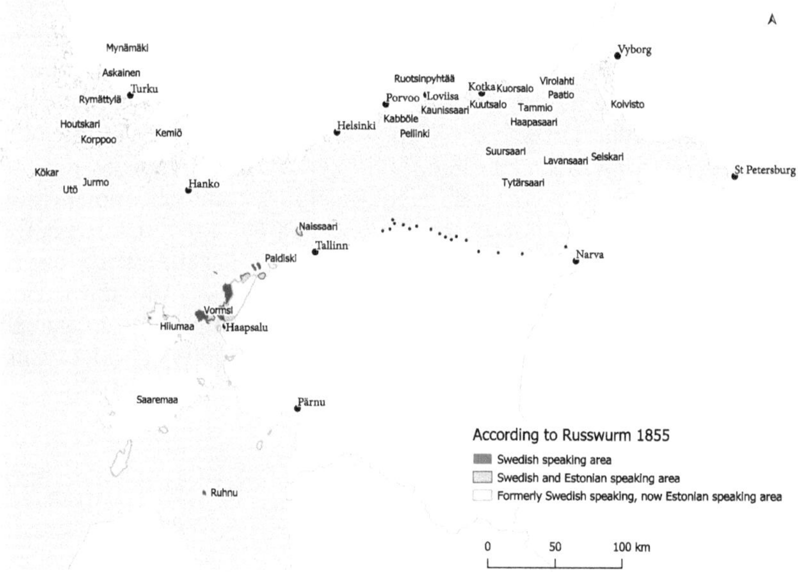

Fig. 6.1 Map of the Gulf of Finland. (Map by Niklas Huldén)

meetings, and even feasting and dancing. Moreover, family members of the trade partners often participated in the seasonal expeditions. Finnish traders mostly visited special fairs or marketplaces on the Estonian coast during specific seasons, mostly just before midsummer and during autumn. Most Finnish villages had their own Estonian target harbor. In turn, Estonians often went fishing along the Finnish coast, either on their own, paying some rent to the owners of the local water rights, or as hands for the Finnish fishermen. Living in small sheds erected by themselves or by Finns, the Estonians still participated in the local community life, sometimes arranging dances or other festivities. The giving of gifts was also included on these fishing expeditions.

This chapter concentrates on small-scale trade through the practice of *sepra* among the peasants, fishermen, and other coastal inhabitants of the area (see map in Fig. 6.1). Having a long tradition, the trade could have its origins in the settling of the coastline by the Finno-Ugric-speaking peoples in prehistoric times. Although such petty trade was declared illegal and the different rulers tried to direct all commerce to the cities, in practice it could not be prohibited.[4] The aim here is to examine the practices that the ordinary traders engaged in to establish and maintain contact with each other in the different locales in the area. To this end, the chapter stresses the actual practices in actual trading encounters described through writings and answers to ethnographic questionnaires, as well as the previous literature. The descriptions include some of the diverse goods that were traded and the gift-giving tradition in the eastern part of the Gulf of Finland, compared to the somewhat differing customs in the western part.

Reciprocal Trade, Authentic Friendship, and Ethnographic Questionnaires

From the western parts of the Gulf of Finland, peasants and fishermen mainly traveled to Tallinn and other well-known trading centers to sell or trade their salted herring for grain, which local merchants had traded from peasants and manors in the Estonian inland. This resulted in complex networks and dependencies between merchants and peasants, which also were incorporated in the cultural heritage of the *sepra* trade. In these situations, the traders also anticipated and received some gifts from the merchants, who in turn expected the traders to be loyal and trade their goods with the same merchants in the future.[5] In the first half of the nineteenth century in Estonia, only the gentry had possibilities to trade in any substantial way, and they also used bigger vessels for their sea traffic. When the system of serfdom was abolished in Estonia in 1858, commoners among the coastal dwellers could also participate in some trading. This usually started off with sales of their own products and crops, and then slowly developed into getting items from the interior of Estonia for transport and trade.

In the first decades of the twentieth century, the trade became much more diverse, incorporating exports of lumber, firewood, potatoes, apples, and sometimes entirely new concepts, such as fish-canning industries. The area of trade could include the coastline down to Poland and westward to Sweden. The sizes of boats and vessels used in the trade grew larger during the late nineteenth century, but even in the 1920s they were still not usually motorized.[6]

The First World War struck this trading tradition hard. The independent new nation-states, Estonia, and Finland naturally tried to bind the market to bigger established merchants, and the small-scale (almost hidden) economy was not tolerated any more. By the Second World War, it had almost vanished, and after the war it would take until the 1990s before commerce picked up again to any significant extent.

Both Finnish and Estonian researchers, usually historians and ethnologists, have regarded *sepra* trade as positive, indicating an authentic friendship between the "peoples" involved. It has been described as mutually beneficial, since the parties could exchange their surplus stocks, exporting mainly salted herring from Finland and receiving grain products, mainly rye, from Estonia.[7] Furthermore, *sepra* trade has also been used ideologically to bolster the idea of Finland and Estonia as brotherly nations. After Estonia gained independence for the second time in 1991, the *sepra* markets were revived in the form of trade festivals that alternated between the two countries.

I base my analysis on two ethnographic questionnaires. I mostly rely on a questionnaire sent out by Professor Helmer Tegengren from Åbo Akademi University in 1969–1970.[8] The questionnaire received 176 answers from inhabitants in both Swedish- and Finnish-speaking areas along the southern Finnish coastline. The material has also partly been used in Tegengren's own article.[9] In the easternmost part of the Swedish-speaking area in Finland, the word *sepra* was also used in Swedish, but in western Finland the word was not generally known. The second questionnaire that I use is from the Institutet för språk och folkminnen (then called

Dialekt- och folkminnesarkivet) in Uppsala, Sweden. It was directed toward the Swedish-speaking Estonians with experience in petty trade, who had relocated to Sweden after the Second World War in 1946. Only two answers were received, but they include very long and thorough descriptions of the trade in northwestern Estonia.

The use of ethnographic questionnaires for ethnological investigations has been common since the 1950s, but the method developed throughout the twentieth century. In Finland, it was generally used to describe the past in a way that the "nation" wanted it to be. One has to consider that in the developing new nation, ethnology and folkloristics belonged to the cluster called "national sciences." These had a mission in building the society, which incorporated the idea of a worthy past. Even when misery and defiance were found, they could be elevated into a representation of a common struggle for a better present. In short, ethnographical questionnaires often functioned as rescue operations, striving for a folk culture in the making. This continued well into the 1980s and to some extent is true even today. That said, making a questionnaire required great knowledge and investigation before it could be sent out. This made the dialogue between the responsible archive or scientist and the respondents somewhat skewed. The interest of the questions was clearly defined, which pointed the respondents toward giving the right answers. However, one frequently finds answers opposing the questions: "No it was not like that at all, it was like this." Subsequently, the questionnaires became less leading and sought to give alternatives, to achieve greater variance and capture the respondents' own words. Yet, it is inevitably the case that questionnaires are captives of their own time and should be studied in context, which in its turn demands education. This is something often discussed in contemporary literature regarding their use.[10]

An Anthropological Excursion

When investigating how the trading practices in the research area were established, varied, and evolved through time, it is necessary to define the terms in anthropological research concerning exchange economies regarding trade. Economic transactions in ethnographic records are often described in a simplistic way as consisting of two general types. The "vice versa" movement or transaction between two parties can be described as *reciprocity*. In our case, this includes the direct bartering between Finns and Estonians—as in *sepra* trade—but in some ways it also concerns trading with various merchants in the cities.

The centralized movement or collection and redistribution of goods within members of a group is called *pooling*. The two types do merge, as pooling can be seen as a system of reciprocity but within relations.[11] Here, it would be represented by *sepra* or peasant traders that accumulated supplies and trade goods in their local community by means of pooling, sometimes stretching the local boundaries quite far. The goods would usually be transported and traded by a head trader and the providers would be paid according to their share, either in goods or in money. The pooling trader was required to have a good reputation and status in the community. Sometimes the traded goods were bought from the providers, and this can be seen as a step toward the freight trade that dominated the area in the late 1800s and early twentieth century.

The giving of gifts as an incentive to building trust is something that has received a great deal of attention in previous anthropological research. The complex practices of gift-giving as a whole have been studied by Marcel Mauss, for example, who pointed out that gifts are seldom purely altruistic by nature, and that they almost always demand a counter type of payback of some sort. He based his arguments on several complex institutional practices where the giving of gifts—in a broad sense—was crucial, from inherited belongings through the potlatch tradition to issues of early law in the West.[12] Unlike Mauss, Sahlins formulated his view on the basis of trading encounters in particular. He considered that the giving of gifts had a strong role as a startup practice for establishing a trade friendship or trade partnership. In a broad sense, one has to include the feast in this activity for building trust and barter, as it often represented a sort of payback for received gifts.[13]

Regarding reciprocity, one must distinguish some different categories that sometimes seem to blend in practice. While *generalized reciprocity* could be described as the solidary extreme, sometimes called the putatively altruistic "pure gift," this type of gift or assistance always demands some sort of payback, although its actual expression is vague, varied, and can be postponed. In material form, it is sustained by prevailing social relations; it is especially common in close kin relationships but can also be seen in some forms in trade practices. Most trade practices, however, tend to follow the device of *balanced reciprocity*, which is a midpoint with ethnographic visions of trade, with gift-exchange, buying and selling, and payment involving "primitive-money." Social relations hinge on material flow, which has to be reciprocated within a set period of time. On the other side, we find *negative reciprocity* as the unsociable extreme. This is the attempt to get something for nothing, often with impunity. It comprises several forms of appropriation and transactions opened and conducted toward one's net utilitarian advantage. Inductive ethnographic terms include "haggling" or "barter," "gambling," "chicanery," "theft," and other varieties of seizure.[14]

These must be seen as a continuum, and some of the aspects will also be found in this material. Usually, one can see some combinations relating to kinship distance and rank, but trade between strangers needs to be constructed by different practices and means. All participants in trade, of course, are interested in gaining as much as possible in the exchange of goods. But to avoid negative reciprocity and strive toward balanced trade, some checks and balances have to be established. These consist of special and delicate institutional means regarding the exchange.

Common means are "trade-partnerships" and "trade-friendships," which can be initiated by "gift-giving." This may lead to a delay in reciprocity, as getting a direct return may be seen as unseemly. Hospitality is given by both parties on different occasions, and it seems to be a mentality of the marketplace. For example, food offered in a generalized way as a type of hospitality tends to lead to good relations.[15]

Therefore, most trading and exchanging of goods fall under the scheme of balanced reciprocity, following customs of formal friendship or kinship, that is, *trade partnerships*. The instigating mechanism for these, sometimes very long-lasting partnerships can be found in *gift-giving*. The friendships or alliances are then affirmed through various feasts and entertainments that the partners dispense to each other in turn for pleasure and amusement. Mechanisms for peacemaking and further affirmation through marital alliances, for instance, can also be coupled with these festivities. It is not uncommon, however, for a certain amount of imbalance to be embedded in the exchange of goods. This sustains the trade partnership by compelling another meeting. Of course, this imbalance can open up the trade to elements of negative reciprocity, as evidenced in the source material.[16] In the following, I will mostly concentrate on the reciprocal practices through citations of the ethnographic questionnaires, while the larger concept of *sepra* and peasant trade are dealt with in more general terms.

Real *sepra* Trade and "Peasant Trade"

People living on the different islands in the eastern part of the gulf participated in *sepra* trade at least from the seventeenth century onward.[17] The word *sepra* (or *sõpra, sõbra*), which can be found in different forms in the Baltic, Estonian, and Finnish languages (and as a loanword also in Russian), could have originally been translated as "team" or "teamwork," but ultimately it became associated with "friendship." According to ethnologist Kustaa Vilkuna, the Finnish word *seura* ("company") is close to the original meaning. The historian Seppo Zetterberg remarks that sources regarding merchants in Tallinn mention the so-called *söbrerei* (German: *sepraing*) in Estonia/Livonia already in the fifteenth century. The city merchants tried to stress the point that this trading between peasants and common people in the countryside was in fact illegal. But in this regard, they had to fight with the Estonian/Livonian noblesse, who were also intertwined in massive trading in the countryside, leaving the official network of city traders aside. As the nobles had significant ruling power into the twentieth century, this kind of trade continued for hundreds of years.[18]

It is in this eastern area of the Gulf of Finland that one can still find a genuinely "positive" attitude toward the term and its use for trading between Finns and Estonians. The term was also used in the whole of Estonia and other Baltic countries as a description of the not always frictionless relationship between merchants and peasants/producers. The latter often fell into a lifelong reliance on the former, sometimes even with a vulnerable position due to debts, reflecting a situation that can be found in most societies that engage in this kind of trade.[19]

Many early ethnographers or lay collectors of folk traditions depicted the importance of having a *sepra* partner and how this relationship benefited both trading partners. One of them, Eljas Raussi, described the *sepra* as follows:

> In a decent barter trade, both partners will win because they give away what they have too much of and take what they need, both at home and when traveling and peddling the goods.[20]

This also emerges quite unprovoked in some answers to the questionnaire (Swedish-speaking 15 A) that did not even mention the word *sepra*. Such answers expressed that you do better trade if you have a *sepra*. That said, one must reflect on what barter trading really involved. The anthropologist David Graeber argued that there is no society that locally depends on barter trade. He refuted the common idea of barter trade as the foundation of all economic transactions, and indeed he found amusing earlier anthropologists' fascination with everything containing reciprocity. According to Graeber, barter was linked to trade with strangers, and mostly in societies that already had monetary institutions or where people had developed the idea of financial value regarding traded goods.[21] Anthropologists such as Marshal Sahlins prefer talking about exchange trade and reserve the word "barter" for more negative aspects of this trading.[22]

In the case of Estonian-Finnish barter, most of the goods had a price that was valued in terms of money, which was recognized also in the actual barter event (see Fig. 6.2). The trade partners were strangers to one another, but they did bridge that fact by using, among other things, the means and practices of making gifts and affirming festivities, thereby building mutual trust in the form of a friendship that supported a continuing partnership. This partnership could also depend on debt, however, in

Products from Finland	**Products from Estonia**
Fish (mainly herring)	Grain (mainly rye)
Salt (due to custom charges contraband)	Potatoes
Matches	Apples
Tobacco	Salt
Butter	Hemp, linen
Firewood and woodwork	Smoke-cured meats
Cobblestones (for streets, mostly to St. Petersburg)	Spirits & liqueur
	Fish
Innovations (shoes with heels, often called Finnish shoes in Estonia)	Horses, piglets, sometimes cattle
	Wooden rowboats
The trade evolved through pooling practices into regular freight trade in the latter half of the 1800s.	Innovations (fish-smoking and canning industries)

Fig. 6.2 Products of trade in the Gulf of Finland ca. 1850–1930

which case delayed payments comprised a driving force in persistent business.

I am using relevant factors in the huge mutual relationship where almost any movement of people to one side of the gulf was mirrored by an equivalent but never identical movement to the other side.

Barter as Reciprocal Trust

The Estonian temporary marketplaces of *sepra* trade were well known. Ships and vessels from certain Finnish areas used to dock in certain Estonian harbors (see map in Fig. 6.3). In the older tradition, it seems like the Estonian traders also had similar bases on the Finnish coast.[23] It appears that these steady base camps in Finland later became less steady and the Estonians fished and traded where they could, often shifting their selling of goods to the coastal areas in the countryside a bit further from the coast.[24]

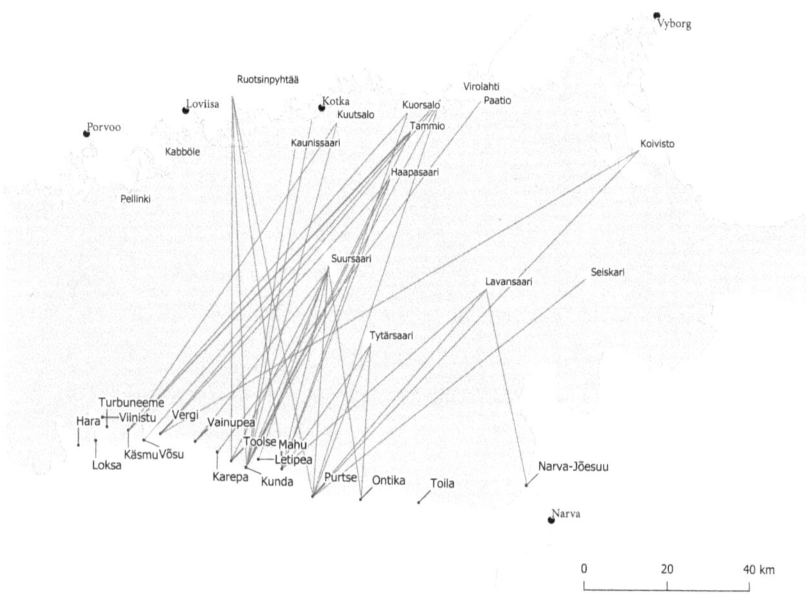

Fig. 6.3 Map of temporary marketplaces on the Estonian coast and the main places in Finland where the *sepra* traders came from. (Map by Niklas Huldén)

Answers to the questionnaire (KIVA 15a) describe the situation when Finns visited Estonia in the eastern part of the gulf. Two longer answers shed some light on the trade as a whole:

> The sea trade to Estonia was carried out with small sailing vessels and was barter trade by nature. They traded salted herring to the Estonians. Due to the open coastline, the Estonians had difficulties catching [their own] herring with the fishing equipment of that time. The Finns brought back rye and potatoes. It was mostly the islanders [e.g., the inhabitants of the islands in the eastern part of the Gulf of Finland] that participated in this trade, but they in turn sold the [Estonian] products to other Finns. After the year 1866, when the law changed, they began bringing spirits from Estonia, too. Spirits were even brought over the ice with horse sleighs during winter. There were few usable harbors on the Estonian side; most used were the mouth of Narva River, Kunda (herring trade), and Loksa, whence the Finns also imported bricks.[25]

A well-informed answer picks up the subject of trade a little further on in time, when it already involved bigger two-masted boats called *jaala*. These vessels would then get even larger, with multiple decks, after the 1880s. They were often built by the skippers themselves, sailed for about ten years, and then sold to Estonians. In this case, we can already see the freight trade taking shape. The following example tells the story of a relatively successful individual, traveling on a two-masted *jaala* as a freight trader doing business with merchants in the cities, but still maintaining a *sepra* network with 20–30 families in Estonia, with whom he traded at very special and joyful happenings two to three times a year:

> All the *saarelaiset* [the inhabitants of the islands in the eastern part of the Gulf of Finland] had so-called *tepras* or trading partners in Estonia. They were treated almost like relatives, and the relationships could exist for generations. One family from the islands (in Finland) could have 10–30 *sepra* families in Estonia, who received salted herring twice a year from the Finnish fishermen. These transactions were always made as barter. The Estonian *sepras* gave 2 to 2.5 times rye to 1 measure of salted herring ... During these travels one always brought gifts to the *sepras* ... On these travels there were usually a lot more people aboard the ship. Usually, the women of the skipper's family and sometimes also neighbors that didn't have boats of their own. There could be 20–30 persons aboard. Especially on the midsummer travels, people used to camp in big tents made of the sails. They slept near the tent walls and in the middle was a big table with benches around. On the

> outside was a fireplace where you made food and coffee. The *sepras* were invited into the tent and offered food and tastings of herring and the coffee was fortified with something stronger. People talked about news and gossiped in mixed language. The *sepras* also had their wives and often a couple of children with them. The *sepras* arrived at the harbor with horse carts and often had foals running alongside, to the children's delight … They also brought with them grain as payment for the fish received last season, as they were always in debt to the islanders … There was no actual marketplace, but the beach was wide and open, and you could see as many as 300 horses with chariots at one time.[26]

Many answers in the questionnaire mention 10–20 *sepras* as a usual number, while some mention up to 40. The network size seems to have some correlation to how long each family had been in business. Some answers name three to four generations of trade partnerships.[27] Others had less experience.

> We used to make these *sepra* travels three times a year from Tytärsaari. We went to Moksa and Purtse harbors. We traveled in June, September, and November.
>
> We didn't have more than four *sepras*, as we were beginners in the business. These *sepras* were living about 40 km inland from the shore, and the older men [in the Finnish group] never bothered to walk all that way to tell [the *sepras*] that the herring had arrived. Other people could have tens of *sepras*.
>
> The barter went as follows: when we brought a small barrel of herring in June, the *sepra* would give two small barrels of rye to us. The same procedure every time. If they did not have any rye, the payment would have to be postponed until the next journey.[28]

Was *sepra* trade in any way biased in favor of any of the trading partners, such as to reflect the negative reciprocity in anthropological terms? The questionnaire does not explicitly bring up this theme, but some answers appear to refer to these aspects in a subtle way. The quite common reply "The Estonians were always in debt" seems to indicate that the Estonian *sepras* always had to compensate for earlier trade. Moreover, the fact that the Finnish traders could have so many *sepra* families per trader seemed biased. Additionally, Estonian farmers had a less independent position regarding their ownership and rights to their land; only in the 1860s did they at last have the possibility to purchase land.[29] Indeed, *sepra* trade seems to have partially depended on the fact that the manors in Estonia also had a need to trade with anyone they wanted to without having to depend on the city merchant houses. But most answers in the questionnaire—which consist of Finnish informants—seem to point to the equality and good terms in the trade: "The Estonians admired the Finns and were therefore very hospitable."[30] "The spring-herring was often given to the *sepras* on credit [...] Then in August we started fishing again, and made the same trip as in spring, but now the *sepras* [Estonians] could give back what they had received on credit. Neither I or anybody else has ever found someone cheating in this matter."[31] "The spring herring was exchanged as one barrel herring for two barrels of rye or barley or three barrels of potatoes; the autumn herring was a little more expensive in price [...] The Estonians seldom haggled but if it sometimes happened, some fellow Estonian would quickly say 'Kust tema Soome *sepra* leipä saap, kuita kive päällä elap?'" which can be interpreted as "How should this Finnish friend get his bread [otherwise], when he lives on a rock?"[32]

The only negative comments concerning reciprocity in the Finnish answers seem to concentrate on the conditions when the wars started in 1914 and 1939. The border closed abruptly and the Finnish *sepras* could not get their remuneration, as it was always the Estonians who were in debt.[33] All the positive attitudes in the questionnaire responses can probably in some ways be attributed to the timing of the questionnaire (1969–1971). In the middle of the Cold War, with Estonia trapped behind the Iron Curtain, the past experiences being asked about may have been described in a shimmer of nostalgia. One also has to consider that all islands in the gulf's eastern outer archipelago, inhabited by most of the people remembering the *sepra* trade, also were lost after the Second World War, thus forcing the inhabitants to migrate to mainland Finland.

In their answers, the islanders do stress that these *sepra* trading fairs often functioned as a type of family gathering, and they were in fact the only business travels in which the wives and younger children of the traders did participate. Other answers by people from the Finnish coast confirm this: "We did not take any family with us on the *sepra* travels. Only the islanders did that."[34]

Some details in the questionnaire responses stressed that the practices were not ideal all the time. The same answer as above continues: "The women mostly contributed to the trade by begging. Not all of the islanders had their own vessels, but they could still participate by traveling in other people's boats. [...] We always picked up a fisherman's family from

Suursaari on our travels."[35] The wandering hordes of begging women were not particularly popular on the Estonian coast, and sometimes they traveled on foot to the Estonian villages inland. They were called "crows" by the Estonians.[36] But we also find examples of Finnish women trading with Estonian *sepras* on their own: "My father went to Estonia to trade salted herring for rye [and] they had companions there called *sepras*. When my father drowned when I was six years old, my mother went on the same trade when I was eight. It was the same barter trade with the Estonians. The yacht was called 'Emigrant.' We also sold firewood to Estonia."[37]

In the End, It Was Business

Keeping count of all the transactions made on credit could be a problem, and there are some surviving "*sepra* books" from Haapasari in Finland which seem to have been kept in order to address this matter. There is some debate if they were only retained as a way of remembering how much herring the Estonian *sepras* wanted in the autumn, or if they were indeed books tracking debt. The fact that there is no evidence of such books existing in Estonia may indicate the latter.[38]

Overall, we can sum up the *sepra* trade in the eastern part of the Gulf of Finland as being an old tradition, which gave the fishermen from the Finnish coast and the outer islands a market for sometimes quite meager catches of spring herring. This product was harder to sell in Finland and in the Estonian city markets. Barter trade on credit—herring in spring for grain in the autumn—was in a way a good deal for both partners. By the second half of the nineteenth century, *sepra* trade was already mixing with more regular freight trade in bigger vessels. But many of the *sepras* from both sides of the gulf held these trading meetings in high regard well into the twentieth century.

Farther westwards of the Gulf of Finland, the form of trade was usually called "peasant trade" (Swedish: *allmogeseglation*, *bondeseglation*). The trading goods were much the same as in the *sepra* trade to the east. The main cargo the Finns brought to Estonia was salted herring in wooden barrels. The trade also evolved from personal trade journeys into pooling practices, where some trusted fisherman or trader collected fish from other fishermen in the area and paid them in cash after the journey. This evolution was also common in areas of *sepra* trade outside of the traditional *sepra* market seasons.

The main differences between *sepra* trade and the trade conducted with merchants in the cities, mainly in Tallinn but to some extent also in Paldiski and Hapsal, were that the bartering was less pronounced, and the fishermen usually got paid in cash. It was not uncommon, however, for the same merchant who bought the fish to pay in grain and flour from the firm's own supplies. Wives and children did not generally participate in these trade journeys, but there were exceptions. In particular, younger men could travel across the gulf as helping hands, and sometimes also wives or daughters came as cooks and maids, as the crew always slept in the boats during the trip. Due to the fire hazard, the actual cooking had to be done on shore in special cooking houses.

The cargo taken home back to Finland could be very varied: "We took back home flour, potatoes, horses, carriages, smoked ham, small amounts of Riga balsam and cheap butter for use at home."[39] But often only some homecoming gifts were purchased.

The practices that these journeys entailed can be seen in a longer response:

> In the spring we sailed over to Estonia to Reval (Tallinn). One used all kinds of vessels, from smaller fishing boats to yachts and galleys, and went from Korpo, Nagu Hitis and Dragsfjärd parishes. In general, we had salted herring as cargo and went straight to the harbor in Tallinn. We sold the herring to different firms; one of them was called Roterman. The cargo was taken to the *vrakgård* [storage yard] where it was measured, packed again in bigger containers and sent away. We were paid in cash and in flour. People spoke Russian, German, Estonian and some Swedish, so you got by. One stayed in Tallinn until the business was finished, could be a couple of days. The skipper usually had some helping hand with him on the travel and people usually slept on the boat in Tallinn.
>
> You couldn't really afford to buy that much in Tallinn. Usually it was some *saijas* [wheat buns] that you could take as treats for the people at home. These travels lasted from the middle of the 1800s. When the First World War broke out, it was the end of it all.[40]

If family members sometimes had the opportunity to travel with the skipper, it was seen as somewhat of a luxury experience, although they seldom took part in any of the cities' cultural life. Some responses remark that the common Estonians in Tallinn seemed poor, and that the city was shabby:

> Some other family members could join the travels to Tallinn and Paldiski to make some small purchases. It was no tourist attraction, so to say; in fact, it was the opposite [...] The common people were badly clad and dwelled in sheds.[41]

In general, the respondents stressed in a positive manner the fact that people traded with the same merchant. It was a safe bet, and people could always rely on the same trading firm. But the herring sellers had to live with the general avarice that seems to have marked the trading partners. Especially the repackaging of the salted herring seems to have gotten on the nerves of the sellers.

> However thoroughly you packed the herring in the containers, you had to have extra containers with herring and brine [as the traveling packed the herring still more]. The skipper had to open the wooden barrels, fill them up and then seal them again. A controller made tests of the goods and sometimes the herring was rejected or considered inferior. The price went from bad to worse and you also got a name of selling bad fish.[42]

Another fisherman tells, "Any positive stories from these travels are few and mostly forgotten, as this herring trade was an emergency solution needed for the existence of the fishermen." He goes on to rant about the scrupulous rejection of fish and the bad prices.[43] Some of the negative reciprocity in the trade can also be seen in responses that mention the possibility of getting in a debt cycle with the city merchants, so most preferred not to take any cargo back home on credit.[44] However, some of the trading practices did resemble the act of giving of gifts, which I discuss next.

The Custom of Treating and the Feast

Before we consider the gifts described in the questionnaire responses, it makes sense to briefly look at some of the practices suggested as predecessors of those appearing in *sepra* trade. The ethnologist Sven Andersson suggested in 1953 that shared practices of the *sepra* "institution" could have their roots in the tradition of "treating," which was common in temporary "fishing camps" along the Swedish coast of the northern Baltic Sea from medieval times onward. Simply put, this meant that people, mostly from more densely populated areas, traveled to fishing grounds where a multitude of fishermen had gathered for a specific seasonally recurring catch. The "treaters" brought with them alcoholic beverages, which they offered to the fishermen in exchange for some fish. This often led to problems, as the drunken fishermen could fall into debt to the treaters, in the end losing the whole lot of their seasonal catch. This was a problem discussed in high societal institutions for hundreds of years, but the tradition never really got under control. Treating also spread to the east, along with the expansion of Sweden's reign. According to Andersson, this could have triggered the practices of *sepra* trade.[45]

Without doubt, treating with gifts in *sepra* trade was common. Ethnographer Elias Raussi (b. 1800) described such meetings in the 1840s in Virolahti, Eastern Finland. Reflecting how the Estonians were received on their arrival at the Finnish coast, he depicts how the old men from the village would rush down to the harbor to greet the Estonians with blessings and handshakes, and also to get tastings of the gifts and "freebies" the Estonians had brought with them. The women and children in their turn got wheat bread (*sarvisaija*) as gifts. In this situation, it was the Estonians who traveled to their *sepras* in Finland, but later the situation more or less reversed.[46]

Almost all the questionnaire responses from the area of the eastern Gulf of Finland mention this kind of gift-giving half a decade later. From the viewpoint of the Finnish traders, we have a similar description:

> During these travels the *sepra* were always at first treated with seasoned fish, so-called *parkkikalaa*, which was made of uncleansed, lightly salted [herring] baked on pieces of pine bark [cortex]. It was brown to the color and very tasty. The *sepras* [Estonians] responded with eggs, butter, and wool. [...] Outside of the tent [that the Finns made from sails] they had a stove where they made coffee and food. In the tent the *sepras* [Estonians] were offered food and herring and some stronger beverages put in the coffee, which was called *norri*. There was a lively discussion on all kinds of news and subjects, *rääkittiin* (Estonian: "we spoke"). [...] The *sepras* brought with them the flour [rye] to pay for the fish received on the previous visit.[47]

The questionnaires also include questions about festivities and marriages between Finns and Estonians. The festivities were common but sometimes the question of marriages is dealt with: "it was common among the islanders," who were often defined as "from the other islands."

> The social meetings were usually spiked with liquor in the boat cabin. Of course, young couples sometimes fell in love and then youngsters brought

home a wife from Estonia. From Tytärsaari I can remember four couples. But these *sepra* travels had to be made on a tight time schedule. We had big boats and the Estonian harbors were bad if the wind started to grow stormy. But youths also went to Estonia just for fun and then they used smaller motorboats. They could be there for weeks. Sometimes we performed some [theater] play. Oh, that joy! Sometimes we went and fetched youths from Estonia and had a feast on Tytärsaari.[48]

Some similar practices appeared in the western peasant trade, too, although those seemed to be a bit more private. Almost all the responses dealing with the western peasant trade depict dealings with city merchants and firms, of which Roterman is mentioned most often. But some answers also disclose Estonian farmers coming to the harbor in Tallinn to sell their products directly to the Finnish herring traders. The language used in these transactions could be mixed; the responses mention Estonian, Finnish, Swedish, Russian, and German.[49] Some responses also mention women as traders, but in general they did not often travel for the western trade.

Sometimes women also participated in the trading travels to Tallinn. My grandmother went several times. She had families whom she knew and traded with. She had with her smoke-cured mutton and cheese to keep up the relationships. Also, some salted herring, but most of those goods were in the main cargo.[50]

The peasant traders' practices in dealing with the city merchants also sometimes included gifts, but it was selectively the merchant who made the offers, which often represented payback for a trusted delivery of fish, coupled with purchasing from the same merchant the trade goods to be taken back home.

If one bought the whole cargo from the same merchant, the skipper was invited to the merchant's home for some drinks with snacks. He could also get some porcelain plates or coffee cups "on the trade" as gifts.[51]

Father told us that our grandfather on the evening before the departure [back to Finland] always went to the merchant's home dressed in his best clothes from his youth. He had knee-short trousers and a vest of homemade lambskin with brass buttons, white stockings, and shoes with brass buckles.

> With that he wore a short, blue coat. It was always very late when he came back to the boat.[52]

> The use of alcohol in the peasant trading business was common, and both buyers and sellers thought it benefited the trade.
>
> The people I spoke to never told of any other amusements than drinking. Especially Boberg said that the trading was much better if you drank alcohol with the other trader. [...] And there was the art form of stacking up the firewood in the measure, so that you filled it with as little wood as possible.[53]

> If the measuring of firewood was performed by the buyer, the people doing it had to be "greased" with alcohol. Otherwise, they would stack the firewood too tightly.[54]

Here we do find some mention of the negative reciprocity that one would expect to be present in trading with strangers. But we also see the tactics that compel the forming of trade partnerships and friendships.

Some responses also mention Estonian traders visiting the Finnish archipelago and coast. The responses deal with practices in the end of the 1800s and in the beginning of the twentieth century. Estonians regularly bought living fish from fishermen in the Archipelago Sea in western Finland. They then sold the fish in Riga.[55] The inhabitants in western Estonia also started regular freight trade in the latter half of the nineteenth century, often visiting the Baltic countries and Finland and Sweden.[56]

Questionnaire 15 A also mentions the movement of people from Finland to Estonia and vice versa, sometimes in connection to trading and fishing. Several responses from the Åland Islands describe a legendary "Russian" trader who established himself in Enklinge in the beginning of the twentieth century. "Jesmin" (or Jasmin) was probably a trader from Vormsi in Estonia. He traded grain and flour that he brought to Enklinge with his own ship, exchanging the grain directly for salted herring from fishermen. He had to leave some of his grain in storage in Enklinge and asked one of the local fishermen to keep it over the winter. The fisherman said he could not afford to buy that much, but Jesmin replied, "Trust is as good as money." They shared companionship for many years, but after 1909 he was never seen again.[57]

Conclusions

The ethnographic questionnaire material used in this chapter provides a colorful depiction of the clearly extensive petty trade engaged in about a hundred years ago, as remembered by the people involved in it. Barter trade was especially persistent in the *sepra* trade area in the eastern part of the Gulf of Finland. To some extent, the responses from the Finnish inhabitants idealize the trade as very friendly and an even exchange that benefited both trading partners in a long-term relationship. While the questionnaire directs the responses, in my opinion the questions asked in this case were quite skillfully formed and did lead to nuanced and reflective responses. The *sepra* trade may be a bit romanticized from the Finnish point of view at the time the questionnaire was sent out, yet I still think that the people involved in it were far more closely knit than those engaged in the peasant trade in the western part of the gulf. The responses regarding this latter form of trade also bring up more negative aspects of the different practices. Thus, one can say that balanced reciprocity, as described by Sahlins, functioned as the common field for the business transactions in *sepra* trade as well as in the eastern peasant trade.

The evolution of pooling practices also seems to have been concurrent in the whole area. According to the questionnaire responses, gift-giving and festivities functioned in a motivating and formative manner for trading partnerships. Friendships can also be seen in both variants of trade, although they played a greater social, collective role in the *sepra* tradition. The intertwined coherence of debt and trust to some extent also reveal constellations of negative reciprocity, as the business transactions show tendencies of inequality and cheating. But again, these seem to be indicated less in the responses from the *sepra* area.

It is, therefore, not so surprising that in the 1990s, when Estonia again became independent, the *sepra* trading contacts were once again celebrated in a symbolic way. Old fairgrounds and marketplaces were revived, and still-living tradesmen from before the Second World War met once again. This has now evolved to an annually arranged happening that still involves petty trade but more clearly celebrates the friendship of the two countries (see Fig. 6.4).

Trade between the countries is now massive, including tourism, working migration, mutual industries, and a planned tunnel or two. But the planned *sepra* festival in 2020 had to be canceled due to the COVID-19 pandemic, and symbolically this perhaps illustrates the changing status of

Fig. 6.4 Advertisement for a *sepra* festival. (Artist: Nina Halmetoja. Pro Kelkkaniemi & Municipality of Virolahti)

state borders. Crossing them once again has proven difficult, prohibiting much of the interaction that has characterized the development during the last decennia, but for an altogether different reason.

Notes

1. Kerkkonen 1959, pp. 12–17.
2. Zetterberg 2017, pp. 37–42.
3. Kustaa Vilkuna. 1964a. *Kihlakunta ja häävuode. Tutkielmia suomalaisen yhteiskunnan järjestymisen vaiheilta.*
4. See Orrman 2003, p. 112.
5. Helmer Tegengren. 1974. "Bondeseglationen mellan Finland och Estland."
6. Stahl 1964, pp. 196, 208.
7. See e.g., Arved Luts. 1960. "Rändpüügist Eesti merekalastuses"; Kustaa Vilkuna. 1964a. *Kihlakunta ja häävuode. Tutkielmia suomalaisen yhteiskunnan järjestymisen vaiheilta*; Yrjö Kaukiainen. 1970. *Suomen talonpoikaispurjehdus 1800-luvun alkupuoliskolla (1810–1853)*; Helmer Tegengren. 1974. "Bondeseglationen mellan Finland och Estland"; David Papp. 1977. *Åländsk allmogeseglation. Med särskild hänsyn till sjöfarten på Stockholm. Sjöfarten i Lemlands socken 1800–1940*; Arved Luts, Elle Vunder, and Ilmari Vesterinen. 1994. *Kaksi virolaista tutkielmaa*; Raimo Päiviö. 2009. *Mikä Tappoi Seprakaupan? Suomalaisten ja virolaisten harjoittamasta vaihto- eli seprakaupasta, sen siipumisesta 1800-luvun lopulta ensimmäiseen maailmansotaan ja sen loppumisesta 1920- ja 1930-luvuilla.*
8. Nr 15a "Allmogeseglation på Estland."
9. Helmer Tegengren. 1974. "Bondeseglationen mellan Finland och Estland."
10. See Pia Olsson. 2014. "'Good Factual Knowledge" for Future Generations. Questionnaire Activity Defining Traditional Culture"; Pia Olsson and Eija Stark. 2014. "Making Cultural Heritage in Finland. The Production of and Challenge to Tradition"; Pirjo Korkiakangas, Pia Olsson, Helena Ruotsala, and Anna-Maria Åström. 2016. *Kirjoittamalla kerrotut. Kansatieteelliset kyselyt tiedon lähteinä.*
11. E.g., Sahlins 1974, p. 188.
12. Mauss 1999, pp. 28–34.
13. Sahlins 1974, pp. 200–216.
14. Sahlins 1974, pp. 192–195.
15. Sahlins 1974, pp. 200–216.
16. Sahlins 1974, pp. 220–222.
17. Vilkuna 1964a, p. 155.

18. Zetterberg 2017, pp. 101–104.
19. Johan Ludvig Birck. 1961. *Bondeförplägningen och böndernas skuldsättning hos handelsmännen*; Graeber 2011, p. 107.
20. Päiviö 2009, p. 33, author's translation.
21. See discussion in Graeber 2011, pp. 21–36.
22. Sahlins 1974, p. 195.
23. Vilkuna 1964a, p. 153.
24. Vendell, SLS 182 c 1881.
25. KIVA FM 4709, Virolahti.
26. KIVA FM 4702, Suursaari/Strömfors.
27. KIVA FM 4718, Vehkalahti; FM 4719, Tytärsaari.
28. KIVA FM 4711, Tytärsaari.
29. Zetterberg 2017, pp. 158–162.
30. KIVA FM 4718, Vehkalahti/Hamina.
31. KIVA FM 4727, Tytärsaari/Loviisa.
32. KIVA FM 4730, Virolahti. This phrase in some sort of pidgin Estonian/Finnish (the phrase in Estonian being something like "Kust tema Soome sõbra leiba saab, kui ta kive peal elab") alludes to the fact that the Finns from the outer islands in the Gulf of Finland hardly had any possibilities to grow their own crops. It also illustrates the language use in the *sepra* trade. Almost all Finnish language answers in the questionnaire say that trade was done in Estonian, "which was easy to learn," and "everybody from the islands understood Estonian" (KIVA FM 4727, 4737, 4739). According to Raimo Päiviö, the Estonians in turn said that they used many Finnish words when they traded (Päiviö 2009, p. 46). In the end, many words from each language were probably recognized as dialectal on both sides of the gulf.
33. KIVA FM 4713, Vehkalahti.
34. KIVA M2886, Pyhtää.
35. KIVA M2886, Pyhtää.
36. Päiviö 2009, pp. 71–73; Vilkuna 1964a, p. 72.
37. KIVA M2876, Pyhtää.
38. Päiviö 2009, pp. 43–45.
39. KIVA M 2897, Nagu.
40. KIVA M 2542.
41. KIVA M 2566, Helsinki.
42. KIVA M 2564, Vänö.
43. KIVA M 2557, Kökar.
44. E.g., KIVA FM 4635.
45. Andersson 1953, pp. 30–35.
46. Vilkuna 1964a, p. 153.
47. KIVA FM 4702, Suursaari/Strömfors.

48. FM 4711, Tytärsaari.
49. KIVA M 4109, Nagu.
50. KIVA M 2567, Kökar.
51. KIVA M 2549, Kökar.
52. KIVA M 2541, Snappertuna.
53. KIVA M 2553, Snappertuna.
54. KIVA M 2984, Nagu.
55. See David Papp. 1979. *Åländsk allmogeseglation. Med särskild hänsyn till sjöfarten på Stockholm. Sjöfarten i Lemlands socken 1800–1940*; KIVA M 2091, Hitis.
56. ISF Acc.nr 17927:1.
57. KIVA M 2892, Kumlinge, M 3004, Enklinge.

Bibliography

Archival Sources

Helsinki

Svenska Litteratursällskapet i Finland r.f. Arkiv.
Vendell, H. A. SLS 182 c Reseberättelse (1881).

Turku

Cultural Studies Archive Cultura at Åbo Akademi University.
Questionnaire 15a (1969–70) Allmogeseglation på Estland.
Acc.nr FM 4635, Taivassalo, Farmer Santeri Kleemola b. 1901.
Acc.nr FM 4702, Suursaari/Strömfors, Fisherman Eino Ranta b. –
Acc.nr FM 4709, Virolahti, Häradsdom. Eino Raunio b. 1895.
Acc.nr FM 4711, Tytärsaari/Lovisa, Ilmari Niemelä b. –
Acc.nr FM 4713, Vehkalahti/Hamina, Verneri Saarinen b. 1891.
Acc.nr FM 4718, Vehkalahti, Skipper Nestori Lommi b. –
Acc.nr FM 4719, Tytärsaari/Helsinki, Skipper Olavi Kiiski, b. –
Acc.nr FM 4727, Tytärsaari/Loviisa, Timberman Eevald Kurki b. –
Acc.nr FM 4730, Virolahti, Annikki Markkula b. –
Acc.nr FM 4737, Hamina, Ms Saima Niemelä b. –
Acc.nr FM 4739, Hamina, Ms Naimi Vanhala b. –
Acc.nr M 2541, Snappertuna, Teacher Einar Öhman b. 1892.
Acc.nr M 2542, Korpo, Mrs Axa Österlund b. 1897.
Acc.nr M 2549, Kökar, Mr Daniel Carlberg b. 1889.
Acc.nr M 2557, Kökar, Farmer Anton Hellström b. 1898.

Acc.nr M 2564, Vänö/Hitis Farmers wife Anna Clemets b. 1892.
Acc.nr M 2566, Helsinki, Helmsman N. Carlsson b. 1895.
Acc.nr M 2567, Kökar, Fiskarhustru Berta Karlberg b. 1900.
Acc.nr M 2553, Snappertuna, Smith Hjalmar Blomqvist b. 1897.
Acc.nr M2876, Pyttis, Landlord Axel Sjöberg b. 1882.
Acc.nr M 2886, Pyttis, Mr Emil Malm b. 1880.
Acc.nr M 2892, Kumlinge, Teacher Kurt Lindh b. –
Acc.nr M 2897, Nagu, MA Dido Björkblad b. 1936.
Acc.nr M 2091, Hitis, Farmer Ture Eriksson b. 1894.
Acc.nr M 2984, Nagu, Fisher Karl Lindblom b. 1896.
Acc.nr M 3004, Kumlinge, Mr Valdemar Engblom b. –
Acc.nr M 4109, Nagu, Elsa Storgård b. 1898.

Uppsala

Institutet för språk och folkminnen (ISF).
Frågelista om estlandssvenskarnas handel (1946).
Acc.nr 17927:1. Andreas Stahl, Rickul, Estland.
I wish to thank Heidi Granqvist and Tõnu Uuskyla for their help with the translations from Estonian.

Literature

Andersson, Sven. "Primitiv byteshandel på forna fiskelägen." *Budkavlen* (1953): 1–96.

Birck, Johan Ludvig. *Bondeförplägningen: Och Böndernas Skuldsättning Hos Handelsmännen*. Jakobstad: Jakobstads tryckeri och tidning, 1961.

Graeber, David. Debt. *The First 5,000 Years*. New York: Melville House, 2011.

Kaukiainen, Yrjö. *Suomen talonpoikaispurjehdus 1800-luvun alkupuoliskolla (1810–1853)*, Loviisa: Painoyhtymä Oy, 1970.

Kaukiainen, Yrjö. "Suomenlahden seprakaupan juuret." In *Viipurin läänin historia II. Viipurin linnaläänin synty*, edited by Jukka Korpela, Yrjö Kaukianen, Jouko Nurmiainen, and Otto-Iivari Meurman. Lappeenranta: Karjalan Kirjapaino, 2014.

Kerkkonen, Gunvor. *Bondesegel på Finska viken. Kustbors handel och sjöfart under medeltid och äldsta Wasatid*. Helsingfors: Svenska litteratursällskapet i Finland, 1959.

Korkiakangas, Pirjo, Pia Olsson, Helena Ruotsala, and Anna-Maria Åström (eds.). *Kirjoittamalla kerrotut. Kansatieteelliset kyselyt tiedon lähteinä*. Helsinki: Ethnos, 2016.

Luts, Arved. "Rändpüügist Eesti merekalastuses." *Eesti Rahva Muuseumi aastaraamat XVII* (1960): pp. 129–168.

Luts, Arved, Elle Vunder, and Ilmari Vesterinen (eds.). *Kaksi virolaista tutkielmaa*. Jyväskylä: Jyväskylän yliopisto, 1994.

Mauss, Marcel. *Lahja.Vaihdannan muodot ja periaatteet arkaaisissa yhteiskunnissa*. Helsinki: Tutkijaliitto, 1999.

Olsson, Pia. "'Good Factual Knowledge' for Future Generations: Questionnaire Activity Defining Traditional Culture." *Journal of Finnish Studies* 18, no. 1 (2014): 65–90.

Olsson, Pia, and Eija Stark. "Making Cultural Heritage in Finland. The Production of and Challenge to Tradition." *Journal of Finnish Studies* 18, no. 1 (2014): 3–10.

Orrman, Eljas. "Keskiajan maatalous." In *Suomen maatalouden historia 1. Perinteisen maatalouden aika esihistoriasta 1870-luvulle*, edited by Viljo Rasila, Eino Jutikkala, and Anneli Mäkelä-Alitalo, 87–114. Helsinki: Suomalaisen Kirjallisuuden Seura, 2003.

Päiviö, Raimo. *Mikä tappoi seprakaupan? Suomalaisten - ja virolaisten harjoittamasta vaihto- eli seprakaupasta, sen siipumisesta 1800-luvun lopulta ensimmäiseen maailmansotaan ja sen loppumisesta 1920- ja 1930-luvuilla*. Turku: Turun yliopisto, 2009.

Papp, David. *Åländsk allmogeseglation. Med särskild hänsyn till sjöfarten på Stockholm. Sjöfarten i Lemlands socken 1800–1940*. Stockholm: Stockholm University, Institutet för folklivsforskning vid Nordiska museet och Stockholms universitet, 1977.

Papp, David. "Mjöl mot strömming. Estländska jalor i Ålands skärgård." *Budkavlen* (1979): 5–23.

Rasila, Viljo, Eino Jutikkala, and Anneli Mäkelä-Alitalo (eds.). *Suomen maatalouden historia 1. Perinteisen maatalouden aika esihistoriasta 1870-luvulle*. Helsinki: Suomalaisen Kirjallisuuden Seura, 2003.

Russwurm, Karl. *Eibofolke oder die Schweden an der Küste Esthlands und auf Runö, eine ethnographische Untersuchung mit Urkunden, Tabellen und lithographirten Beilagen, Zweiter Theil*. Reval: In Commission bei Fr. Fleischer, 1855.

Sahlins, Marshall. *Stone Age Economics*. New York: Aldine De Gruyter, [1972] 1974.

Stahl, Andreas. "Sjöfart och fiske hos Estlands svenskar." In *En bok om Estlands svenskar 2*, edited by Edvin Lagman, 191–230. Stockholm: Svenska Odlingens Vänner, 1964.

Tegengren, Helmer. "Bondeseglationen mellan Finland och Estland." *Budkavlen* (1974): 8–42.

Vilkuna, Kustaa. *Kihlakunta ja häävuode.Tutkielmia suomalaisen yhteiskunnan järjestymisen vaiheilta*. Helsinki: Otava, 1964a.

Vilkuna, Kustaa. "Suikiminen ja saaliin vaihtokauppa." *Kalevalaseuran vuosikirja* 44, 117–149. Helsinki: WSOY, 1964b.

Zetterberg, Seppo. *Uusi Viron historia*. Helsinki: Suomalaisen Kirjallisuuden Seura, 2017.

CHAPTER 7

Mobile Sex Trade: Fairs and the Livelihoods of Female Itinerant Sex Workers in Early Nineteenth-Century Finland

Kirsi Vainio-Korhonen

The topic of this chapter is early nineteenth-century fairs and marketplaces as possible locations for sex work. The people of the time knew that visitors to fairs were susceptible to sexually transmitted diseases. They were particularly afraid of syphilis, an insidious and painful disease which, besides being contracted by those of a sexually active age, also brought suffering to children and the elderly. As well as being transmitted through sexual contact, syphilis could be passed on through pox, warts, and ulcers around the mouth during the rash stage of the disease. An imperial decree of 1811 required that Finnish male merchants, servants of the bourgeoisie, and female hawkers traveling to fairs were free from venereal disease. They had to show a "certificate of health" from a doctor before they could be granted the required travel pass. In Sweden, an equivalent decree was issued a year later in 1812, enforcing the medical examination of tavern maids, traveling salesmen, and journeymen. As far as women were

K. Vainio-Korhonen (✉)
Finnish History, University of Turku, Turku, Finland
e-mail: kirvai@utu.fi

J. Ahlbeck et al. (eds.), *Encounters and Practices of Petty Trade in Northern Europe, 1820–1960*,
https://doi.org/10.1007/978-3-030-98080-1_7

concerned, this decree named various kinds of female market traders: sellers of spirits, coffee brewers, and sellers of trinkets. In Finland, other groups obliged to undergo medical examination for venereal disease were the urban "fornicating" female population, sailors returning home, and prisoners.[1]

Correspondingly, the spaces and locations in which sex work took place changed over time from taverns and fairs to streets and brothels. During the eighteenth century, sex workers in European towns did not yet generally stand out socially or geographically from other members of the urban poor. They lived in the same blocks and plots of land where the poor customarily lived.[2] Historian Tony Henderson, who has researched London's prostitutes in 1730–1830, found that these women walked on the same streets and in the same parks, drank in the same public houses, and lived in the same buildings as other impoverished Londoners.[3] In research on sex trade, street prostitution and "streets of sin" are first cited as a common form of prostitution only from the late nineteenth century and the early twentieth century onwards. As far as Finland is concerned, this describes ways in which late nineteenth-century "street walkers" in the cities of Helsinki or Turku tried to attract male attention through their movements, calls, or clothing. In the Swedish capital of Stockholm, only a few prostitutes lived in and received clients in their own homes. A quarter of prostitutes were housed in brothels, while the remainder plied their trade on the streets and in hotels that rented rooms by the hour.[4]

Prostitution has been described as "the world's oldest profession," but as a historical phenomenon it took many forms. In Finland, trade in sexual services was not a separate and distinct social problem in its own right before the mid-nineteenth century, as all sex between unmarried men and women was viewed as fornication and a criminal act.[5] The word "prostitution" (Finnish: *prostituutio*; Swedish: *prostitution*), borrowed from French, was not known or used in Finland or in neighboring Sweden before the middle of the nineteenth century.[6] In Finland's Swedish-language newspapers, "prostitution" first started to appear as a loanword used to describe changing circumstances in the cities of continental Europe, where industrialization had led to the destruction of customs, the physical degeneration of children, the prostitution of women, and the immorality of the working men.[7] The word "prostitution" only became established in Finnish in the twentieth century. Likewise, "prostitute" was a new word popularized by the emergence of Finland's semiofficial brothels at the end of the nineteenth century.[8]

Swedish ethnologist Rebecka Lennartsson has found that it was not until the nineteenth century that a separate identity of the prostitute started to be distinguished in its own right from dissolute acts committed by the population in general. Any adult could be accused of fornication but not until at the end of the nineteenth century, prostitution was a label with which women who sold sex were specifically stigmatized.[9] In the harshest approach taken at the time, the "wicked nature" of the prostitute was even considered to be an innate characteristic and an indication of hereditary degeneration. Medical science in Europe in the Victorian period often saw prostitutes as a separate species of human, deviating from their fellow human beings in their morals and their habits, and as antisocial, lazy, bloated, and dirty nymphomaniacs.[10] French historian Alain Corbin links the official regulation of prostitution to major societal changes, such as industrialization, urbanization, and the rise of capitalism taking place in general in the late nineteenth century, in which everything could be traded and measured in monetary terms.[11] Similarly, the wide-ranging anthology *Selling Sex in the City: A Global History of Prostitution, 1600s–2000s* points out that the demonization of prostitution was linked to the major commercialization of sexual services in late nineteenth-century societies embracing capitalism.[12] As an early modern historian, I use the concept of "prostitution" when I describe and focus on the trade of sexual services in the beginning of nineteenth-century Finland. Instead of prostitution, sex work refers only to sexual transactions between adults, not to human trafficking or child prostitution.

In early nineteenth-century Finland or Sweden, a woman selling sex did not even have a name by which to refer to using sexual behavior as capital. In official documents, such women were usually females (Swedish: *kvinnspersoner*) who had given birth to illegitimate children and whose lifestyle was termed dissolute (Swedish: *liderlig*, *lösaktig*, *otuktig*), wicked (Swedish: *lastfull*, *vanartig*), indecent (Swedish: *oanständig*), depraved (Swedish: *lastbar*), or itinerant (Swedish: *kringstrykande*). These adjectives did not refer solely to having extramarital sex, or even to sex work, but to a broader loss of social respect. Prohibited sexual relations in the Nordic countries in the period before the mid-nineteenth century are in fact mainly studied as a combination of extramarital sex and wickedness, not as prostitution. Research has investigated individuals who committed fornication, men as well as women, and illicit sexual relations between unmarried people (Swedish: *lägersmål*), as well as adultery.[13]

In early nineteenth-century Finland, the sale of sex was not yet conspicuous or regulated and had not yet taken on an established form. The "dissolute women" of the day did not walk particular streets from one evening or night to the next in search of clients. The police did not arrest them for this kind of behavior, nor do the sources tell of their provoking passers-by with their shouts or by their dress. Nor did sex work yet have its own separate sphere along the lines of a brothel in the Finnish towns of the early nineteenth century. At this period, sex work was not yet tied to a specific place or location in which it was possible to offer sexual services and which clients would have had to know to go solely for the purpose of buying sex. Instead, the sale of sex was mobile and flexible, practiced in inns, outbuildings, saunas, and the small, rented rooms of the women themselves. Women also offered sexual services in places where many young, unmarried men were gathered: at fairs, in barracks or on the outskirts of garrisons and ports, and perhaps at public dances. Some of them also lived near inns, ports, or military outposts.[14]

The sale of sex is not even directly visible in contemporary sources. It is almost impossible to find unambiguous indications in Finnish or Swedish documents dating prior to the mid-nineteenth century. Before the end of the nineteenth century, Finnish, or Swedish courts in general, rarely dealt with crimes involving professional fornication.[15] In terms of the documents, the prior history of sex work in Finland and Sweden is intertwined with the history of sexually transmitted diseases and vagrancy. Entries were made in the records when sex workers suffering from venereal diseases were treated in hospitals or sent to a penal institution as female vagrants with no place of employment. From the nineteenth century, there are registers of legal sex workers obliged to regularly undergo medical examinations for venereal disease.

This chapter specifically studies the visits to fairs made by women subjected to the compulsory medical examinations of anyone suspected by the police in Turku of carrying venereal disease in 1838–1848. Who were these women, and what kind of social backgrounds did they have? What were the reasons for their mobile life, either at urban or at rural fairs? Geographically, the women studied visited fairs and traveled around the area of southern Finland. Turku had been Finland's largest and most important administrative city for centuries. In 1812, it lost its capital city status when this role was moved to Helsinki, but this did not diminish Turku's population until the 1840s. Finnish towns were centers of trade for merchant burghers and craftsmen, but the towns also held fairs several times a year. The largest fairs might bring together thousands of people from the local area and further afield for several days. Besides attending the fairs in Turku, people in the southern parts of Finland in the early nineteenth century were also drawn to the fairs in the towns of Tampere, Hämeenlinna, and Porvoo. The rural fair held in Salo (a center of rural commerce since at least the sixteenth century onwards), not far from Turku, and the fair further to the east in Heinola, which gained its town charter in 1839, were also popular.

Research on the history of prostitution in the Nordic countries has generally focused on the late nineteenth century onwards, in other words only during the period in which prostitution was officially regulated.[16] The history of prostitution in Finland, Sweden, Denmark, and Norway has solely concentrated on this period or the period that followed.[17] In the late nineteenth and early twentieth centuries, prostitution was regulated and prostitutes were monitored by strict legislation, which makes prostitution clearly visible in the sources and thus ostensibly easy to research. During this time period, prostitution is described as a subculture separate from the rest of society, in which women obtain income, directly or indirectly, from sexual relations.[18] Besides prostitutes and their customers, pimps, brothel-keepers, the police, and doctors revolved around the money and sexual services.[19] Researchers have found poverty and difficulties earning a living to be factors underlying prostitution, as well as a need on the part of society to control women who defied social norms.[20]

Women and Medical Examinations of Venereal Disease in Turku, 1838–1848

> Henrika Österlund, who had first caused hatred and discord between herself and Johan Hongois due to evilness and wickedness, then separated from Johan Hongois against his will and two years ago moved to the village of Pahaniemi where she is still living with her mother, farmwife Brita Alistalo, also known as Österlund, during which time Henrika Österlund has also become pregnant from an illicit union and given birth to a child.[21]

Henrika Österlund, who had left her husband, was one of the women ordered to undergo monthly medical examinations to ascertain her sexual health in 1830s' Turku. Entered into the Turku police station's records of medical examinations for venereal disease as number 27, Österlund had been married exceptionally young, when only 16. At the age of 22, she left her husband and as a consequence of several instances of adultery, a divorce was finally ordered in 1833. On her mother's death from cholera, the divorced Österlund was without close relatives. Towns offered earning opportunities and anonymity, and so Henrika Österlund moved to Turku, Finland's largest city, where she gave birth to two more illegitimate children. In 1838, she was one of the first batch of women in Turku ordered to attend the police station for a medical examination for venereal disease, which indicates that Österlund was obtaining income from selling sex.

In the 1830s, Finland was an autonomous part of the Russian Empire. The city of Turku had three different barracks, housing about a thousand Russian soldiers and their commanding officers. Cases of venereal disease were rising in the barracks, and therefore, in October 1838, on the orders of the commander of the Russian troops the Turku police started compulsory medical examinations of "the city's dissolute women" (See Fig. 7.1). At the national level, the background for this was an order issued by the Medical Board in April 1838, according to which towns that provided accommodations for Russian troops were to examine "the female population known to be immoral" to prevent syphilis.[22] The model was taken from Napoleonic France, where sex workers were regularly examined to prevent the spread of venereal disease. The system was later widely adopted in a Europe overrun with syphilis.

In Finland, a woman who underwent such a procedure was called an "examined woman" (Swedish: *besiktningskvinna*). At the Turku police station, a separate register or journal was kept of the examinations held every month, which contained each woman's personal details, place of residence, and the dates of the examinations.[23] When the examinations began, with its 13,000 inhabitants Turku was the largest city in Finland in terms of population.[24]

In total, 164 women living in Turku were suspected, for one reason or another, of actively spreading venereal disease. The group mainly comprised unmarried women aged 25–35 born in Turku or near the city. At least half of them had given birth to a child or more than one, and half of them were suffering from syphilis or infected with it during this period. The average period of the medical examinations spanned about five years, but some women were involved in examinations for seven or eight years. One in five of the women examined for venereal disease disappeared from the documents of the Turku police upon moving to another large city, such as Helsinki or Saint Petersburg. Of the women who remained in

Fig. 7.1 Women examined for venereal diseases in the early nineteenth-century capital of Turku, Finland, worked at inns, in private homes, visited fairs, and traveled to markets, consorting with sailors, journeymen, and soldiers. Adolf von Becker's (1831–1901) undated drawing features a young man and an unmarried woman socializing. (Photo by Hannu Pakarinen. Finnish National Gallery)

Turku, a third (39 women) married during the period, after which their medical examinations for venereal disease ceased. Fifteen of the women died of tuberculosis or various fevers during the period. Seventeen of the women examined for venereal disease ended up in prison serving extended terms for such crimes as repeated vagrancy or theft. The remainder were liberated from medical examinations either due to old age or when they gained permanent employment (e.g., as a servant).[25] Several researchers have considered these women, with entries in police records denoting their having undergone medical examination for venereal disease, to have been working prostitutes.[26]

It is clear that the officials suspected Österlund and other women entered in the medical examination register of spreading venereal disease. However, the fact that their names are in the register does not automatically mean that they were professional sex workers. Although all sexual relations outside marriage were a sin in the eyes of the Church and a crime in the eyes of the law, receiving payment for sex was not made a separate criminal offense in Finland until 1889. Under the Civil Code of 1734, only procurement and keeping a brothel were criminal.[27] At times, women were brought before the Turku police for practicing fornication and being caught in the act, but if they had a job or otherwise had the right to live in the city, they were released with a reprimand following a medical examination for syphilis. Neither the police nor the judges were interested in the source of the women's earnings, and therefore money is not mentioned in the archives of the Turku police or the courts.[28] However, it is probable that the women subjected to medical examinations were gaining at least part of their income from sex work.

Henrika Österlund is first entered in the Turku police station's register of medical examinations for venereal disease in October 1838 as a divorced woman aged 31. A year later, she was arrested at the Salo fair for pilfering and leading an immoral life. Gustava Förstling and Gustava Ilander, both of whom also underwent examinations for venereal disease, were in the same company. Henrika Österlund had her 12-year-old daughter and a three-week-old baby boy with her. She had probably become pregnant with the boy at an earlier fair in January, as the Turku city doctor had written a certificate declaring Henrika Österlund free of syphilis, enabling her to travel to fairs, in January 1839. Henrika Österlund became pregnant soon after receiving the certificate and gave birth to the boy in late September the same year. Förstling and Ilander were marginalized women like Österlund, orphaned in childhood and as adults sentenced for drunkenness, vagrancy, and theft. The trio had clearly gone to the fair for the purpose of earning money, although, according to the custom of the time, Henrika Österlund would have still been in her lying-in period.

The Dark Side of Fairs: Drinking, Theft, and Sexually Transmitted Diseases

The women examined for venereal disease in Turku traveled between all the fairs in the southern parts of Finland; besides Turku they visited Salo, Hämeenlinna, Tampere, Helsinki, Porvoo, and Heinola. Four times a year, the population of Turku almost doubled, when thousands of people and hundreds of vessels thronged to the St. Henry fairs in January and June, the Lenten fair in February–March and the autumn fair in September. The events were held in a fog of alcohol. In the view of people of the time, the whole city at fair time was simply an open tavern. Although public drunkenness was punishable by law and a drunk person whose movements, appearance, and confused state of mind revealed their drunkenness was liable to be arrested,[29] alcohol was sold without any restrictions.[30] After a couple days of revelry, the local paper was able to rejoice that "the drunken celebrations are over once more."[31]

Fifty kilometers south of Turku, the Salo autumn fair also attracted visitors in their thousands. By the bridge over the Uskela River, the main roads from Turku, Helsinki, and inland Finland converged, and the people from the archipelago sailed to the site along the coast. The fair was held at the rainiest time of the year and crowds of fairgoers shoved and jostled each other in the mud and puddles on the riverbank. Drunks yelled, bony horses were whipped left and right, and thieves were busy among the crowds.[32] Barrels of herring and grain changed hands and the servant population of neighboring parishes spent their annual salary, the men on drink and the maids on trinkets. Horses being driven at top speed, drinking, the sale of alcohol, fights, and pickpockets were a perennial nuisance. Arrests were frequent, especially of male drunks and female pickpockets working in pairs. One would steal a purse in the bustle and pass it on immediately to her partner in crime, who was keeping a lookout.[33]

For women wishing to travel to fairs, a certificate of health issued by the Turku police station was required, at least initially, to show they had been examined for venereal disease. Turku city doctor August Wilhelm Wallenius wrote ten such travel permits for the women he had examined in late 1838 and early 1839, when venereal disease examinations were carried out most frequently and assiduously in the city. These travel permits were most certainly written by the examiner even later, in accord with the imperial decree of 1811, but for some reason do not exist in the journal of the venereal examinations of the Turku police department after January 1839. Based on the different sources, a total of twelve women from Turku examined for venereal disease visited for different reasons the major fairs in the southern parts of Finland from October 1838 to October 1839.

Tavern Maids Traveling to Fairs

Tavern maids who worked in market stalls, taverns, and restaurants were often also labeled as sex workers. The keepers of Turku's taverns and restaurants employed several women who were subjected to medical examinations by the police for venereal disease. At least three restaurant owners, Lovisa Almgren and Anna Plaisant born in Sweden and Maria Sjöberg born in Turku, also sent their maids to sell alcohol at fairs in the southern parts of Finland. None of them were of particularly good repute. Both Plaisant and Sjöberg had been convicted of drunkenness in a public place. Lovisa Almgren, on the other hand, was an unmarried woman who had been found guilty of *lägersmål* (sex between two unmarried persons). After giving birth to two illegitimate sons, she had not been "churched" afterwards; in other words, as the mother of illegitimate children, she had not submitted to reproaches from the priest, and she had not attended church or taken communion in years.[34]

Anna Plaisant and Maria Sjöberg owned restaurants and inns in Turku's popular amusement area on the very edge of the city, close to the road to the new Finnish capital Helsinki.[35] Sjöberg had a total of four women in her employ, at different addresses, who underwent medical examinations by the police; Plaisant had three. Five of the women examined for venereal disease worked at Almgren's inn. Plaisant had originally inherited her late husband's inn, called Sibylla, which had a billiard hall and was a popular place of amusement among the gentry. It was located on the road to Turku's neighboring parish of Raisio, but she moved her business to Turku in 1835.[36]

While all three restaurant owners employed waitresses, who were subjected to medical examinations, Almgren's, Plaisant's, and Sjöberg's businesses could not, however, have been brothels as such; by law, procurement carried the threat of the pillory, whipping, and three years' forced labor. In their own way, the entries in the official documents also show this; for instance, Almgren first offered her guests food and a bed for the night. Thus, keeping an inn was not merely cover for a brothel. Similarly, in the winter of 1836, Maria Sjöberg and her maid Maria Lovisa Andersdotter traveled between fairs in the southern parts of Finland in Helsinki, Porvoo, and Heinola, selling spirits.[37] It was possible, however, that sex was also for sale, as Maria Lovisa Andersdotter, known by the ominous nickname Musta Maija (Black Maija), monthly visited the Turku police station for medical examinations for venereal disease in 1838–1845.[38]

In early January 1839, Johanna Hornberg, Catharina Handfast, and Eva Grönroos, who worked as maids for Maria Sjöberg, were granted travel permits by the Turku city doctor following medical examination for venereal disease. Anna Rosenlund, also employed by Sjöberg, had traveled to the Tampere winter fair a couple of weeks earlier, at the end of December 1838. In January, permits were also granted to Serafia Lindström who worked as a tavern maid for Lovisa Almgren, and the Sweden-born Beata Moberg in the service of Anna Plaisant. Of these, we have the most information about the lives of Hornberg, Grönroos, Rosenlund, and Lundström. Eva Grönroos gave birth to four illegitimate children, who died young, before marrying a Russian noncommissioned officer named Ivanoff in 1841. Johanna Hornberg, who died of pulmonary tuberculosis in 1840, had three illegitimate children, while Serafia Lindström had five. Anna Rosenlund had hidden a newborn baby, which died unbaptized in July 1830. Although there were no signs of violence on the small body, Rosenlund was found guilty of infanticide and sentenced to two years in the Lappeenranta workhouse for women. On her release, she worked in taverns in Turku.[39] Suffering from mental illness, Anna Rosenlund spent the last months of her life in the county hospital and the poorhouse, where she died of a fever in May 1843 at the age of 38.[40]

Visits to Fairs by Poor, Unemployed Women

The poorest of all the women examined for venereal disease traveled from one fair to the next without a job. They survived through petty crime and, apparently, sex work. This group included the women mentioned above, Henrika Österlund, Gustava Förstling, and Gustava Ilander, arrested at the Salo fair in October 1839. These three women were suspected of vagrancy and several petty thefts; three umbrellas were seized from them, presumed to have been stolen, one of which was dark brown with a yellow border and the other two of pale blue fabric edged with light grey. An umbrella was a valuable possession, and both lost and found umbrellas were often announced in local papers. The women claimed that they did not know to whom the umbrellas belonged. As there were no witnesses to the thefts, this aspect of the case was dropped.[41]

Besides the sale of foodstuffs, fabrics, spirits, hides, cattle, and trinkets, the fairs were renowned as places for intimate relations, and the visits to fairs of women examined for venereal disease show that sex was also sold there. Förstling, Ilander, and Österlund had also attracted the attention of the local authorities in this respect. They reported the women to the Turku police station for having behaved particularly immodestly and in a visibly dissolute and wicked manner at the fair. In the official documents of the time, these words were often used to describe sex work.[42] However, the information did not give rise to any action on the part of the police in Turku. The women lead dissolute lives did not, as such, entitle the authorities to exercise their administrative powers or impose a custodial sentence. Gustava Förstling's medical examinations for venereal disease and visits to fairs only ended when she was sentenced to several years in prison in 1842 for persistent vagrancy. Gustava Ilander was sentenced to two years in prison for theft in October 1843. Henrika Österlund's life ended in the Turku poorhouse in June 1856.[43]

Like Österlund, Förstling, and Ilander had been extremely disadvantaged women for years before being examined for venereal disease. Gustava Förstling, born in Turku as the illegitimate daughter of a maid, was orphaned at the age of nine. Her mother, Lovisa Förstling, died in childbirth, having previously given birth to four illegitimate children. The family had lived under the roof of Lovisa Förstling's elderly parents, but in January 1819 Gustava Förstling and her younger brother were the only living members of the family left.[44] Gustava Förstling first found herself in the police records ten years later, in 1829, as a female vagrant who had "lost her honor." In 1832, she received the severest corporal punishment penalty that existed for women: 90 strokes of the birch on bare skin. Over the years, Förstling had been convicted of drunkenness in a public place on four occasions.[45] Gustava Ilander was also orphaned in childhood; she was seven when her mother died, and her father died of cholera when Ilander was 12. Her older sister had died at the age of only five, so from 1831 onwards Ilander, too, was without close relatives and a recipient of

Turku's poor relief. As an adult, she was described as depraved, wicked, and indecent, and the court charged her with theft and vagrancy.[46]

As well as Henrika Österlund, unemployed women from Turku named Ulrika Sacklén, Fredrika Hornberg, and Eva Wessman received permits to travel to fairs around the new year of 1839. Of these, the illegitimate Ulrika Sacklén, who herself had three illegitimate children who died in infancy, was the most socially excluded and disadvantaged. She was first examined for venereal disease at the unusually young age of 16. In addition, she was illiterate and thus had not been confirmed. Under the law, this meant that she did not have the opportunity to marry. In a society in which marriage was an important means of survival for women, not being confirmed was comparable to a physical deformity, a disadvantage that caused severe social exclusion.[47] The Henrika Österlund suffered from a similar burden, because as a divorced woman she was unable to remarry; the innocent party in the divorce, her former husband Johan Hongois, never remarried. Being found guilty of adultery isolated a person from their previous circle and from a shared married life, which in the nineteenth century was the best guarantee of economic and social security for women and men alike.[48] For women examined for venereal disease—like Österlund, Förstling, Ilander, and Sacklén, who were among the poorest members of society—the social whirl of the fairs, gathering together a large, anonymous population, seems to have offered, besides fun and excitement, a socially reprehensible and even criminal means of earning income, incorporating the sale of sex, pickpocketing, and the illicit sale of alcohol.

The women arrested at the fair could, like Österlund, Förstling, and Ilander, also be suspected of vagrancy. In Finland at that time, those who had no approved work or place of abode were considered vagrants. Although the women examined had illegitimate children and had contracted venereal disease, they were not fundamentally vagrants if they were employed or if their children were young and needed their mother's care.[49] Prostitution itself only represented one manifestation of vagrancy and lacking means of support in the latter half of the nineteenth century. As late as the Vagrancy Act of 1937, "a person who habitually obtains income by means that are contrary to decent behavior and abhorrent to society" was by definition a vagrant. However, this was not yet the case in Finland in the early nineteenth century.

When the local police chief arrested Henrika Österlund, Gustava Förstling, and Gustava Ilander at the Salo fair, they were charged with vagrancy. The charge was dropped, however, since Förstling and Ilander had jobs as servants in the house of a certain burgher in Turku named Ekström, and Österlund was looking after her young children at home. However, Ekström said that his maids were at the fair without permission, and he no longer wanted such "disobedient" women in his house. The Turku police could do nothing other than order the women to seek new work and then release them.[50]

Conclusions

There was not a single mention of selling sex in the documents studied. In early nineteenth-century Finland, the sale of sex was not yet regulated and had not yet taken on an established form. An adult could be accused of fornication but not profiting from selling sex. Only the procuring of prostitutes was an illegal act. The patient records of Turku's hospital for venereal disease show that many of the women examined were prone to syphilis. At least half of them had been treated with mercury in hospitals, many of them several times. Sex work seems a natural explanation for contracting this disease, at least if the same person underwent the mercury cure several times from one year to the next. Similarly, at least half of the women examined for venereal disease had given birth to children outside wedlock, many of them several times, which indicates that they were practicing sex outside marriage, also over a long period of time. The director of the Medical Board and local doctors especially saw servant women working in inns ("inn nymphs") and women who sold beer and spirits at fairs and at rural court hearings in the courtyard ("fair women") as potential carriers of the disease. Another source of infection was seen in the largest towns, which had sailors, itinerant journeymen, soldiers, and, naturally, "wicked" women.[51] For the women examined for venereal disease in Turku, their way of life included work at inns, visits to fairs and consorting with sailors, journeymen, and soldiers. These were clearly the places and the circles in which they engaged in sex work.

Otherwise, the life of the women examined for venereal disease conformed to that of the majority poor population in Turku, especially the way of life of poor women. Turku in the 1830s and 1840s was largely a city of workers and the poor. A quarter of the population comprised poor women, maids, widows, and women without means of support. Almost a thousand people in Turku relied on poor relief, either entirely or partly. About 500 women had given birth to children out of wedlock. The 164 women entered in the Turku police register as having been medically examined had hundreds of non-examined peers among the city's unmarried mothers, patients with venereal disease, women without means of support, alcoholics, and petty criminals. Well-off families were in a clear minority in the city.[52]

In the sources, the difference between medically examined women and their non-examined fellows is often unclear and blurry. Through the documents, no unambiguous identity as sex workers can be attributed to the medically examined women, and their way of life or worldview cannot be reduced to a single format or into a "nutshell." Admittedly, some of the women examined for venereal disease were more visibly engaged in sex work at inns and fairs, during alcohol retail, and on the outskirts of ports and garrisons than others entered in the register of medical examinations for venereal disease, but by no means was this the case for all of them. The same picture is drawn in the recent research in *Selling Sex in the City. A Global History of Prostitution, 1600s–2000s*. One of its editors, the Dutch historian Elise van Nederveen Meerkerk, emphasizes that in preindustrial societies, sex work was performed along with poor women's other economic activities, low-paid industry or domestic service, or employment in bars and taverns.[53]

Based on the sources, we know that at least twelve women from Turku examined for venereal disease spent time at the major fairs in the southern parts of Finland from October 1838 to October 1839. Six of them traveled as tavern maids employed by tavern owners from Turku, while another six traveled with no such employment. If we compare these women with the 164 women examined for venereal disease, it is clear that the women who visited fairs were almost without exception the most disadvantaged and despised representatives of this group of women, who were already destitute. Only nine (or five percent) of the women examined for venereal disease had been orphans since childhood.[54] However, one in six of the women who sold sex at fairs was an orphan. Women who were sentenced to long imprisonments or died as sex workers were also in the minority, representing one fifth of all of those examined for venereal disease,[55] but clearly made up a higher proportion of those who visited fairs (a quarter of them). Those who visited fairs also included the only woman examined for venereal disease to be found guilty of infanticide, Anna Rosenlund. Of five unconfirmed and illiterate women examined for venereal disease, at least one, Ulrika Sacklén, turned to visiting fairs to survive; of three divorced women, this was also the case for one, Henrika Österlund.[56]

It is also worth noting that most women who went to the fairs no longer had adult family members or other relatives living in Turku. Their social support networks were thus sparse or had entirely disappeared. At least Henrika Österlund, Anna Rosenlund, Gustava Förstling, Gustava Ilander, Johanna Hornberg, Serafia Lindström, Beata Moberg, and Anna Lovisa Andersdotter were particularly isolated in this way. Henrika Österlund, who lacked close family, even had to take her child with her to the drink-fueled atmosphere of the Salo fair. Ultimate loneliness and haplessness seem to have been the attributes of women who visited fairs and were examined for venereal disease.

Notes

1. Kejserl. Bref till samtelige Landshöfdingarna, ang. Veneriska smittans hämmande; den 12. Februari 1811. In *Finlands medicinal-författningar* 1837; Svanström 2006, pp. 40–41.
2. Bergqvist 2015, p. 183; Rebecka Lennartsson. 2015. "Prostitutionens korta historia. Stockholmska kvinnoöden på Skuggsidan"; Lewis and Ellis 2015, p. 2.
3. Henderson 1999, pp. 45, 194.
4. Grönqvist 2000, pp. 312–314; Häkkinen 1995, pp. 25–35; Järvinen 1990, pp. 98–111; Lundquist 1982, pp. 75–76.
5. van Nederveen Meerkerk 2017, p. 805.
6. Johannisson 1994, p. 15; Svanström 2006, pp. 33–34.
7. *Finlands Allmänna Tidning* 9/13/1844; *Åbo Underrättelser* 2/8/1843.
8. Suominen 2015, p. 15.
9. Lennartsson 2001, p. 16; Rebecka Lennartsson. 2015. "Prostitutionens korta historia. Stockholmska kvinnoöden på Skuggsidan"; Svanström 2006, p. 34; see also Rodríguez García et al. 2017, p. 11.
10. Corbin 1990, pp. 3–9; Johannisson 1994, pp. 63–64.
11. Alain Corbin. 1990. *Women for Hire. Prostitution and Sexuality in France after 1850.*
12. Rodríguez García et al. 2017, p. 13.
13. Seppo Aalto. 1996. *Kirkko ja kruunu siveellisyyden vartijoina. Seksuaalirikollisuus, esivalta ja yhteisö Porvoon kihlakunnassa 1621–1700*; Hanna Kietäväinen-Sirén. 2015. *Erityinen ystävyys. Miehen ja naisen välinen rakkaus uuden ajan alun Suomessa (n. 1650–1700)*; Marie Lindstedt Cronberg. 1997. *Synd och skam. Ogifta mödrar på svensk landsbygd 1680–1880*; Mari Välimäki. 2009. "Vill du äkta denna kvinna? Universitetsstuderandes föräktenskapliga sexualrelationer och giftermål i 1600-talets Uppsala och Åbo."

14. Vilkuna 2015, pp. 264–271.
15. Häkkinen 1995, p. 163.
16. Marianne Grönqvist. 2000. "Glädjeflickor och bordeller. Den reglementerade prostitutionen i Åbo kring sekelskiftet 1900"; Tiia Hakanen. 2015. *Se tavallinen tarina? Ohjesääntöinen prostituutio Tampereella tarkastusnaisten elämäkertojen kautta tarkasteltuna*; Antti Häkkinen. 1994. "Maksettua rakkautta. Prostituutiokulttuuria Helsingissä 1860-luvulta nykypäivään"; Antti Häkkinen. 1995. *Rahasta – vaan ei rakkaudesta. Prostituutio Helsingissä 1867–1939*; Antti Häkkinen. 1996. "Rikkaiden pojat ja köyhien tyttäret. Helsingin vanha prostituutiokulttuuri"; Margareta Järvinen. 1990. *Prostitution i Helsingfors.En studie i kvinnokontroll*; Juha Lehtinen. 2012. *Laitakaupungin syntinen laulu. Ohjesääntöinen prostituutio Tampereella 1890–1905*; Pia Leminen. 1994. "Elämää prostituution jälkeen"; Pirjo Markkola. 2014. "Moraalin miehet. Mitä prostituution sääntely kertoo mieheydestä?"; Toivo Nygård. 1989. "Prostituutio 1800-luvun lopun ja 1900-luvun alun Suomessa"; Toivo Nygård. 1998. *Erilaisten historiaa. Marginaaliryhmät Suomessa 1800-luvulla ja 1900-luvun alussa*; Tiina Tuulasvaara-Kaleva. 1988. *Prostituoitujen valvonta ja rankaisusäädökset 1875–1939.*
17. Ida Blom. 2012. *Medicine, Morality, and Political Culture. Legislation on Venereal Disease in Five Northern European Countries, c. 1870–c. 1995*; Merete Bøge Pedersen. 2000. *Den reglementerede prostitution i København fra 1874 til 1906.En undersøgelse af prostitutionsmiljøet og de prostitueredes livsvilkår*; Anna Jansdotter. 2004. *Ansikte mot ansikte. Räddningsarbete bland prostituerade kvinnor i Sverige 1850–1920*; Anna Jansdotter, and Yvonne Svanström (eds.). 2007. *Sedligt, renligt, lagligt.Prostitution i Norden 1880–1940*; Rebecka Lennartsson. 2001. *Malaria urbana. Om byråflickan Anna Johannesdotter och prostitutionen i Stockholm kring 1900*; Tommie Lundquist. 1982. *Den disciplinerade dubbelmoralen. Studier i den reglementerade prostitutionens historia i Sverige 1859–1918*; Yvonne Svanström. 2006. *Offentliga kvinnor.Prostitution i Sverige 1812–1918*; Tomas Söderblom. 1992. *Horan och batongen. Prostitution och repression i folkhemmet.*
18. Häkkinen 1995, p. 74.
19. Hakanen 2015, p. 6.
20. Grönqvist 2000, pp. 287–288.
21. The Archive of the Chapter of Turku Archdiocese, File FIg 3b Divorce application 322/1833, National Archives of Finland, Turku.
22. See *Finlands medicinal-författningar*, 1846, and there "General-Directeurens för Medicinal-Verket Embetsskrifvelse till Divisions-Generalen för Ryska Militairen i landet, ang. besigtningar vid inqvartering till hämmande af Venerisk smitta, af den 26 April 1838."; Grönqvist 2000, p. 293; Soikkanen 2016, p. 141.

23. The Archive of Turku Police Department, Journal of the venereal examinations n.d. 1838–1848, National Archives of Finland, Turku.
24. Grönqvist 2000, p. 286; Nikula 1973, pp. 122, 217.
25. Vainio-Korhonen 2018, pp. 9, 167–226.
26. Grönqvist 2000, p. 290; Hakanen 2015, p. 1; Häkkinen 1995, pp. 21–22, 216.
27. See *Sweriges Rikes Lag Gillad och antagen på Riksdagen åhr 1734*, pp. Missgärningsbalken LVII Kapitel Om koppleri och skiörlefnad §§ 1–2.
28. Vainio-Korhonen 2018, p. 12.
29. See *Den Unge Juristen eller Juridisk Handbok för Medborgare af alla Klasser i Finland*, pp. 154–156.
30. Nikula 1973, pp. 274–275, 359.
31. *Åbo Underrättelser* 1/21/1869.
32. *Åbo Underrättelser* 10/19/1867.
33. *Åbo Underrättelser* 10/27/1863, 10/19/1867; Kallio 1940, pp. 82–100.
34. The Archive of Swedish Parish in Turku, Communion records IAa2:20 Kingelins villa and Communion records IAa2:22 Real property number 6.4.1; the Archive of Turku Police Department, Letter concept book 289/1839, n.d. National Archives of Finland, Turku.
35. Vainio-Korhonen 2018, pp. 50–51.
36. Heinricius 1914, p. 128; Perälä 1951, p. 42.
37. Vainio-Korhonen 2018, p. 162.
38. The Archive of Turku Police Pepartment, Journal of the venereal examinations, woman number 35, n.d. National Archives of Finland, Turku.
39. The Archive of Swedish Parish in Turku, Communion records IAa2:9 Norra 159 and Communion records IAa2:15 Kloster 166 and Sotalais Gammelgård, National Archives of Finland, Turku.
40. The Archive of Swedish Parish in Turku, Book of the dead 13.5.1843; The Archive of Turku Police Department, Letter concept book 1842/436 and 1843/12 and 1843/116, National Archives of Finland, Turku.
41. The Archive of Turku Police Department, Minutes and verdicts (Policekammarens i Åbo protokoll och utslag) 22.10.1839 § 16, National Archives of Finland, Turku.
42. The Archive of Turku Police Department, Minutes and verdicts (Policekammarens i Åbo protokoll och utslag) 22.10.1839 § 16.
43. Vainio-Korhonen 2018, pp. 181–192; The Archive of Turku Police Department, Minutes and verdicts (Policekammarens i Åbo protokoll och utslag) 21.2.1845 § 4, 5.5.1846 § 1 and 11.8.1848 § 1; Journal of the venereal examinations, women number 19 and 102, National Archives of Finland, Turku.
44. The Archive of Finnish Parish in Turku, Communion records IAa1:42 Östra 59 and Book of the dead 24.4.1815, National Archives of Finland, Turku.

45. The Archive of Turku Police Department, Journal of vagrants (Diarium över vid Poliskammaren i Åbo anmälda försvarslösa personer) 1829–1834, National Archives of Finland, Turku.
46. The Archive of Turku Police Department, Minutes and verdicts (Policekammarens i Åbo protokoll och utslag) 9.10.1838 § 3 and 22.10.1839 § 16, 3.10.1843 § 1 and 24.4.1846 § 2; The Archive of Finnish Parish in Turku, Communion records IAa1:43 Norra 172, National Archives of Finland, Turku.
47. Vainio-Korhonen 2018, p. 76.
48. Frigren 2016, pp. 165, 186.
49. Nygård 1985, p. 143.
50. The Archive of Turku Police Department, Minutes and verdicts (Policekammarens i Åbo protokoll och utslag) 22.10.1839 § 16, National Archives of Finland, Turku.
51. Nygård 1985, pp. 132–133.
52. The Archive of the Chapter of Turku Archdiocese, Population table of Turku 1845, National Archives of Finland, Turku; Nikula 1973, pp. 122, 217.
53. van Nederveen Meerkerk 2017, p. 809.
54. Vainio-Korhonen 2018, p. 75.
55. Vainio-Korhonen 2018, pp. 221–222.
56. Vainio-Korhonen 2018, p. 87.

Bibliography

Archival Sources

National Archives of Finland, Turku, Finland.

The Archive of the Chapter of Turku Archdiocese: Divorce applications and Population tables.

The Archive of Turku Police Department: Minutes and verdicts, Letter concept books, Journal of vagrants, and Journal of the venereal examinations.

The Archive of Swedish Parish in Turku: Communion records and Books of the dead.

The Archive of Finnish Parish in Turku: Communion records and Books of the dead.

Published Sources

Den Unge Jurister Eller Juridisk Handbok För Medborgare Af Alla Klasser I Finland; Ett Alfabetiskt Ordnadt Sammandrag Af Wigtigare Lagrum, Stadgar Och Författningar, Hwilkas Kännedom är Den Enskilte Medborgaren Nödig För Wårdandet Af Hans Juridiska Angelägenheter; Jemte Formulärer Till

Dithörande Akter Och Dokumenter. 3. tillökta uppl. Helsingfors: hos A. W. Gröndahl, 1846.

Finlands medicinal-författningar. Tredje delen 1836-1845. J. Simelii Arfvingar, Helsingfors 1846.

Sweriges Rikes Lag Gillad Och Antagen På Riksdagen Åhr 1734. Stockholm: Tryckt uti historiographi regni tryckerij af Hartwig Gercken, 1736.

Newpapers

Finlands Allmänna Tidning, 1844.

Åbo Underrättelser, 1843, 1863, 1867, 1869.

Literature

Aalto, Seppo. *Kirkko ja kruunu siveellisyyden vartijoina. Seksuaalirikollisuus, esivalta ja yhteisö Porvoon kihlakunnassa 1621–1700.* Helsinki: Suomen Historiallinen Seura, 1996.

Bergqvist, Johanne. "Making a Living by 'Indecency'. Life Stories of Prostitutes in Christiania, Norway." In *Prostitution and Eighteenth-Century Culture. Sex, Commerce and Morality*, edited by Ann Lewis and Markham Ellis, 171–184. London and New York: Routledge, 2015.

Blom, Ida. *Medicine, Morality, and Political Culture. Legislation on Venereal Disease in Five Northern European Countries, c. 1870–c. 1995.* Lund: Nordic Academic Press, 2012.

Bøge Pedersen, Merete. *Den reglementerede prostitution i København fra 1874 til 1906. En undersøgelse af prostitutionsmiljøet og de prostitueredes livsvilkår.* København: Museum Tusculanum, 2000.

Corbin, Alain. *Women for Hire. Prostitution and Sexuality in France after 1850.* London and Cambridge, MA: Harvard University Press, 1990.

Frigren, Pirita. *Kotisatamassa. Merimiesten vaimot, naisten toimijuus ja perheiden toimeentuloehdot 1800-luvun suomalaisessa rannikkokaupungissa.* Jyväskylä: Jyväskylän yliopisto, 2016.

Grönqvist, Marianne. "Glädjeflickor och bordeller. Den reglementerade prostitutionen i Åbo kring sekelskiftet 1900." In *Historiska och litteraturhistoriska studier 75*, edited by Pia Forssell and John Strömberg, 283–332. Helsingfors: Svenska litteratursällskapet i Finland, 2000.

Hakanen, Tiia. *Se tavallinen tarina? Ohjesääntöinen prostituutio Tampereella tarkastusnaisten elämäkertojen kautta tarkasteltuna.* MA Thesis in Finnish History. Tampere: University of Tampere, 2015.

Heinricius, G. *Från samhällslivet i Åbo 1809-1827. Kultur- och personhistoriska skildringar.* Helsingfors: Svenska litteratursällskapet i Finland, 1914.

Henderson, Tony. *Disorderly Women in Eighteenth-Century London. Prostitution and Control in the Metropolis, 1730-1830*. London: Longman, 1999.

Häkkinen, Antti. "Maksettua rakkautta. Prostituutiokulttuuria Helsingissä 1860-luvulta nykypäivään." In *Huono-osaisuus ja hyvinvointivaltion muutos*, edited by Matti Heikkilä and Kari Vähätalo, 90–127. Tampere: Gaudeamus, 1994.

Häkkinen, Antti. *Rahasta—vaan ei rakkaudesta. Prostituutio Helsingissä 1867–1939*. Helsinki: Otava, 1995.

Häkkinen, Antti. "Rikkaiden pojat ja köyhien tyttäret. Helsingin vanha prostituutiokulttuuri." In *Matkoja moderniin*, edited by Marjatta Rahikainen, 73–92. Helsinki: Suomen historiallinen seura, 1996.

Jansdotter, Anna. *Ansikte mot ansikte. Räddningsarbete bland prostituerade kvinnor i Sverige 1850–1920*. Eslöv: Symposion AB, 2004.

Jansdotter, Anna, and Yvonne Svanström (eds.). *Sedligt, renligt, lagligt. Prostitution i Norden 1880–1940*. Göteborg: Makadam, 2007.

Johannisson, Karin. *Den mörka kontinenten. Kvinnan, medicinen och fin-de-siècle*. Stockholm: Nordstedts, 1994.

Järvinen, Margareta. *Prostitution i Helsingfors.En studie i kvinnokontroll*. Åbo: Åbo Akademis förlag, 1990.

Kallio, V. J. *Salon historia*. Salo: Salon kauppala, 1940.

Kietäväinen-Sirén, Hanna. *Erityinen ystävyys. Miehen ja naisen välinen rakkaus uuden ajan alun Suomessa (n. 1650-1700)*. Jyväskylä: Jyväskylä University, 2015.

Lehtinen, Juha. *Laitakaupungin syntinen laulu. Ohjesääntöinen prostituutio Tampereella 1890–1905*. MA Thesis in Finnish History. Joensuu: University of Eastern Finland, 2012.

Leminen, Pia. "Elämää prostituution jälkeen." In *Huono-osaisuus ja hyvinvointivaltion muutos*, edited by Matti Heikkilä and Kari Vähätalo, 128–148. Tampere: Gaudeamus, 1994.

Lennartsson, Rebecka. *Malaria urbana. Om byråflickan Anna Johannesdotter och prostitutionen i Stockholm kring 1900*. Stockholm: Brutus Östlings bokförlag Symposion, 2001.

Lennartsson, Rebecka. "Prostitutionens korta historia. Stockholmska kvinnoöden på Skuggsidan." In *Från Skuggsidan. Folk och förbrytelser i Stockholms historia*, edited by Rebecka Lennartsson, 74–85. Stockholm: Stockholmia förlag, 2015.

Lewis, Ann, and Ellis Markham (eds). *Prostitution and Eighteenth-Century Culture. Sex, Commerce and Morality*. London and New York: Routledge Taylor & Francis Group, 2015.

Lindstedt Cronberg, Marie. *Synd och skam. Ogifta mödrar på svensk landsbygd 1680–1880*. Lund: Historiska institutionen, Lunds universitet, 1997.

Lundquist, Tommie. *Den disciplinerade dubbelmoralen. Studier i den reglementerade prostitutionens historia i Sverige 1859–1918*. Göteborg: Meddelanden från Historiska institutionen i Göteborg, 1982.

Markkola, Pirjo. "Moraalin miehet. Mitä prostituution sääntely kertoo mieheydestä?" In *Näkymätön sukupuoli. Mieheyden pitkä historia*, edited by Pirjo Markkola, Ann-Catrin Östman, and Marko Lamberg, 134–158. Tampere: Vastapaino, 2014.

Nederveen Meerkerk, Elise van. "A Gender Analysis of Global Sex Work." In *Selling Sex in the City. A Global History of Prostitution, 1600s–2000s*, edited by Magaly Rodríguez García, Lex Heerma van Voss, and Elise van Nederveen Meerkerk, 801–832. Leiden: Brill, 2017.

Nikula, Oscar. *Åbo stads historia 1809-1856*. Åbo: Åbo stad, 1973.

Nygård, Toivo. *Irtolaisuus ja sen kontrolli 1800-luvun alun Suomessa*. Jyväskylä: Jyväskylän yliopisto, 1985.

Nygård, Toivo. 'Prostituutio 1800-luvun lopun ja 1900-luvun alun Suomessa," in *Pysy lujana omalla maalla. Erkki Lehtiselle omistettu juhlakirja*, edited by Erkki Markkanen, 113–132. Studia historica Jyväskyltäensis. Jyväskylä: Jyväskylän yliopisto, 1989.

Nygård, Toivo. *Erilaisten historiaa. Marginaaliryhmät Suomessa 1800-luvulla ja 1900-luvun alussa*. Jyväskylä: Atena kustannus, 1998.

Perälä, Tauno. *Turun esikaupunkien historia. Turun esikaupungit ja niiden aiheuttamat probleemat ensimmäiseen maailmansotaan mennessä*. Turku: Uuden Auran Osakeyhtiön kirjapaino, 1951.

Rodríguez García, Magaly, van Voss, Lex Heerma, and Elise van Nederveen Meerkerk (eds.). *Selling Sex in the City. A Global History of Prostitution, 1600s–2000s*. Leiden: Brill, 2017.

Soikkanen, Timo. *Suomalaisen poliisin synty ja Turun poliisilaitos 1816-1918. Turun poliisi 200 vuotta osa I*. Turku, 2016.

Suominen, Sara. *Se on ollu vaan läppää, ei mitää vakavaa ollenkaan. Nuorten näkemyksiä huora-sanan merkityksistä*. MA Thesis in Finnish Language. Tampere: University of Tampere, 2015.

Svanström, Yvonne. *Offentliga kvinnor. Prostitution i Sverige 1812–1918*. Stockholm: Ordfront, 2006.

Söderblom, Tomas. *Horan och batongen. Prostitution och repression i folkhemmet*. Stockholm: Gidlunds förlag, 1992.

Tuulasvaara-Kaleva, Tiina. *Prostituoitujen valvonta ja rankaisusäädökset 1875–1939*. MA Thesis in Finnish History. Tampere: University of Tampere, 1988.

Vainio-Korhonen, Kirsi. *Musta-Maija ja Kirppu-Kaisa. Seksityöläiset 1800-luvun alun Suomessa*. Helsinki: Suomalaisen Kirjallisuuden Seura, 2018.

Vilkuna, Kustaa H. J. *Juomarien valtakunta 1500-1850. Suomalaisten känni ja kulttuuri*. Helsinki: Teos, 2015.

Välimäki, Mari. "Vill du äkta denna kvinna? Universitetsstuderandes föräktenskapliga sexualrelationer och giftermål i 1600-talets Uppsala och Åbo." *Historisk Tidskrift* 3 (2009): 381–395.

CHAPTER 8

Exhibiting the Extraordinary Body: Six Itinerant Performers and Their Livelihood in the Nordic Countries, 1864–1912

Maren Jonasson

Now the "little fellow" has started traveling around the country in order to show himself for money.
—"Nu har 'pysen' börjat resa landet rundt för att låta se sig för pengar" *Vimmerby Tidning* 6/13/1902

The "little fellow" in the quote above was not little by any standards. In fact, the Swede Gustaf Edman, of whom this was written in 1902, is still one of the tallest men ever. In 1902, he had just started his career as an extraordinary-bodied itinerant performer, and he was marketed as "The Giant of all Giants,"[1] "The Swedish Giant,"[2] and "The Giant from Gotland."[3] This chapter examines the livelihoods of six extraordinary-bodied itinerant artists, who performed and were exhibited in the Nordic countries ca. 1860s–1910s They all traveled extensively and were shown

M. Jonasson (✉)
Culture, History and Philosophy, Åbo Akademi, University, Turku, Finland
e-mail: maren.jonasson@abo.fi

J. Ahlbeck et al. (eds.), *Encounters and Practices of Petty Trade in Northern Europe, 1820–1960*,
https://doi.org/10.1007/978-3-030-98080-1_8

to varied audiences in Denmark, Norway, Sweden, and Finland, at town markets, in restaurants, at hotels, in connection to so-called museums, and at other locations and events where large crowds were expected to gather.

In this chapter, I examine the reasons why the performers—or their relatives in their stead—decided to go on tour. I also investigate their marketing strategies—that is, their advertisement practices, expenses, and ticket revenues—and which additional items were for sale, and what the role of the impresario was. The source material, mainly consisting of digitalized newspapers in Sweden, Denmark, Norway, and Finland, does not provide detailed information on ticket incomes and expenditures in each individual case, but some general remarks can be made, nonetheless. Judicial sources, such as an estate inventory (Swedish: *bouppteckning*), a declaration of an estate bankruptcy (Swedish: *urarvakonkurs*), and a series of title deeds (Swedish: *lagfarter*), have supplied some useful additional information on the prevalent economic terms and conditions of the performers to earn a living from showing their bodies to a paying audience. There is also circumstantial evidence suggesting relative success—but also a complete failure—of the exhibition tours.

The number of extraordinary-bodied artists touring in Europe and in the Nordic countries for longer or shorter periods between the 1860s and 1910s was immense, and therefore a careful selection had to be made for this study. The criteria for choosing the artists were the length of their careers and the geographical scope of their tours in the Nordic countries. I thus chose artists who had traveled and performed for over ten years and in at least three of the four Nordic countries.

Rather than choosing larger groups, so-called human caravans, or circus troupes,[4] I sought acts consisting of only one or two individuals. In studies on larger performing groups, such as human caravans, the individual and his or her economic prerequisites tend to fade out, as the overall economics of the tours are dealt with. After these aspects had been taken into consideration, I ended up analyzing more profoundly two single artists and two duos: (1) Anna Sofia Nilsson (1848–1922), a crofter's daughter from Blackstad parish in the county of Kalmar, Sweden, who was born without arms and had deformed legs[5]; (2) the sisters Aurora (1855–1905)[6] and Amalia Eklund (1858–1922),[7] born in Vimmerby, Sweden, and both suffering from albinism; (3) the exceptionally tall Gustaf Edman (1882–1912),[8] born in the parish of Burs on the island of Gotland, Sweden; and (4) Katie Stewart (ca. 1845–1893) and Alice Ruffen (ca. 1867–1897), two African-American women, possibly from the state of

Alabama. The last case is used to exemplify how the concept of "extraordinary bodies" is strongly connected to time and place. The two African-American women were, of course, not extraordinary in any sense in Alabama, but they were nevertheless able to support and promote themselves as extraordinary-bodied in the Nordic countries in the late nineteenth century, as there were very few other persons of African or African-American descent at the time in this part of the world. To my knowledge, almost no sources deriving from the extraordinary-bodied performers themselves have survived. I prefer to use the term "extraordinary-bodied" instead of the more derogatory "freaks," as none of the selected artists were labeled or described as a freak in the source material I have retrieved for this study.

Reasons to Go on Tour

There might be multiple concurrent, interlinked factors for an individual to decide to show his or her body for a paying audience. It is important to remember that a person born with a severely deformed body or a rare medical condition faced some challenges that were out of the ordinary towards the end of the nineteenth century. Paupers were a societal problem, worsening from time to time with bad harvests, famine and times of scarcity and war. A person who was physically or mentally unfit for work threatened to become an economic burden for both their family and the surrounding local community.[9]

Blind persons and injured war veterans who sang at the town markets were a common sight. They collected alms and lived off the charity of others, as they had few other means to make a living. In other words, there was a certain tradition of seeing and perhaps staring at persons with defective bodies or lacking some crucial senses, such as eyesight. Bearded ladies, obese men, women and children, dwarfs, conjoined (or Siamese) twins, and heliophobics (albinos or persons who were afraid of sunlight) were among some of the groups of individuals seen on stages in Europe and also in the Nordic countries.[10] As it was part of the experience for market-goers to see and experience something uncommon there, paying a small sum, a coin or two, to see something or somebody with an unusual appearance, an extraordinary-bodied person, could almost be called a tradition.

In Anna Sofia Nilsson's case, the narrative on how exhibitions of her as the armless embroideress first began was given by the impresario G. A. Hedman in 1866. He claimed he had discovered Nilsson's extraordinary skills, and he described how against all odds she had managed to become a very skillful seamstress and maker of needlepoint works (see Fig. 8.1). She had also acquired the skill of writing. Credit was given to Jenny Dahlström, the daughter of the local chaplain, who had spent endless hours in Nilsson's company, training her. The impresario Hedman claimed he had "rescued" Nilsson and her mother from a small room, where the daughter had done her handicraft in conditions resembling slavery. Thanks to Hedman, Nilsson and her mother now lived a comfortable life, traveling from town to town with performances of Nilsson showing her skills to an audience.[11] In his account, Hedman does not mention that he, in fact, was the one making the money, although he claimed he shared the income with Anna Sofia Nilsson and her mother. In other words, the two women saw a possibility to get a larger income than Nilsson would

Fig. 8.1 Picture of Anna Sofia Nilsson doing needlework with her feet. (Västergötland's Museum)

have been able to earn if she had remained in the working and living conditions she was in when Hedman "discovered" her.[12] Anna Sofia Nilsson was 17 years of age when she went on her first tour.

Aurora and Amalia Eklund's father Carl Edvard Eklund was a carpenter and mirror maker in the town of Vimmerby in Sweden. However, his business was not doing well at the end of the 1860s, and in a newspaper advertisement, he tried to sell his house and real estate connected to plot number 23 in the north quarter of the town.[13] Judging from later evidence, he was unable to sell the property at the time.[14] In 1870, he and his wife Hedvig Charlotta Carolina (*née* Ringström) started touring with their two albino daughters.

The economic distress of the family worsened considerably right at the beginning of the tour in Stockholm, when Aurora Eklund had an accident and burned herself severely. Due to an epileptic seizure, she had fallen over the stove. In the newspaper advertisements, their father had promised to show *two* albino girls,[15] but due to the accident he was now only able to show *one*. Of course, this threatened to lessen the public's interest in the show. Inexperienced as they were in show business and perhaps somewhat naïve, they had also agreed to pay exorbitant rent far above the normal price.[16] The family was in even deeper economic trouble than they had been before leaving Vimmerby. They reached out to a powerful man from the same region as them, Chamberlain Axel Fredrik Liljenstolpe, who had influential friends among the Stockholm elite. Liljenstolpe arranged a charity campaign for the poor family and managed to collect 181.25 riksdaler.[17] The family was able to pay off some of the debt they had accrued during their stay in Stockholm and cover the medical expenses of Aurora Eklund's injury. She recovered and the family was able to continue the tour and the shows. When the tour started in 1870, the Eklund sisters were 11 and 14 years old.

A year later, the economy of the family was still meagre. In 1871, the local authorities in Vimmerby arranged a judicial auction (*exekutiv auktion*) to sell two-thirds of the house and property holdings of the father to cover his debts. The property was valued at 666.67 riksdaler.[18] Therefore, it seems probable that the decision to show Aurora and Amalia Eklund for money was made due to economic distress.

Also, in Gustaf Edman's case, the underlying cause to go on tour seems to have been economically motivated. His father was a butcher, and from a young age, Edman worked as a farmhand. He was exceptionally strong, and when something heavy had to be moved or lifted, Edman was always called upon. It was said that a Danish circus director, Mr. Schröder, spotted Edman at a market in Hemse on Gotland and immediately signed a deal with him. Schröder promised to pay Edman six times the money he made as a farmhand if he joined Schröder on a tour in Sweden and some cities on the European mainland. During his first years on tour, Edman was shown both as an exceptionally strong man and as an exceptionally tall man (see Fig. 8.2). Toward the end of his career, his height attracted all the attention. Edman was described as a cheerful, funny, and kind person, which of course increased his popularity.[19] Like Anna Sofia Nilsson, but in contrast to the Eklund sisters, Gustaf Edman had an occupation and income before the decision to go on tour.

Fig. 8.2 Picture of Gustaf Edman with his wife Anna and their children. This photograph is taken ca. 1912 by Carl Lindblad in Oskarshamn, Sweden. (Pielinen Museum)

Edman experienced the negative sides of being dependent on an impresario. In March of 1903, newspapers in Århus, Denmark, reported an incident involving Edman and his impresario at the time, Mr. Køhn. Edman had signed a contract stipulating restrictions on how and when he could move freely in the streets. He was only allowed to show himself in the streets during the night, and Køhn would lock him up in his room during the day. Edman was paid only 40 kronor per month, whereas Køhn earned up to 3000–4000 kronor during their time in Copenhagen. While in Århus, Edman contacted a lawyer, who instructed him to immediately break the slave-like contract with Køhn and arrange his own shows without the help of an impresario.[20] In addition to economic reasons, the lure of adventure may have tempted Edman to leave his home and go on tour.

The reasons why Katie Stewart and her daughter/niece[21] Alice Ruffen left Alabama or some other southern state in the United States around 1874 are not easily determined. But it is clear that when they arrived in Malmö, Sweden, in 1874 they did not speak the local language or have any sort of social network or support. While it cannot be excluded that they made an independent decision to go to Europe to show themselves at markets and thereby make a living, it is also possible that they were tricked or conned into boarding the ship and then taken against their will to Malmö. A Danish impresario, O. Sørensen, started showing them at markets almost immediately after their arrival. It goes without saying that Stewart and Ruffen were in a very vulnerable position during their first year on tour in Denmark and Sweden. Once they learned to speak Swedish, Danish, or a mix of the two, they were able to communicate with people around them and thus acquire some agency of their own. Prior to this, their livelihood and fate were completely in the hands of whoever was their impresario at the time. An indication of how they were viewed right after their arrival as objects or animals rather than as human beings is found in in a Danish newspaper advert, which announced that a "negro slave" and her "negro daughter" would be shown at a market in Svendborg alongside parrots, apes, and mechanical devices.[22] The fact that their names were not mentioned in the ads during the first three years supports the assumption that they were only barely regarded as humans.[23] The names of their Swedish counterparts in this chapter were never left out in advertisements of their performances.

During their more than twenty-year career as itinerant performers in the Nordic countries, Stewart and Ruffen used several names, none of which were verified by reliable sources. Thus, it is almost impossible to find out who they really were and where they were born.[24] Katie Stewart used first and last names such as Katie, Katy, Ketty, Ketti, Kitte, Zitte, Senorella, Stewart, Stjordt, Johnson, Janson, Jansson, Jansen, and Negorosa, while Alice Ruffen's last name was spelled Ruffin, Ruffen, Rofin, Rosen, Rafen, and so on. Toward the end of her life, she also used the first names Alise, Topsy, and Toppsy and Jonsson as her last name. Their actual identities remain unsolved, as neither their names nor time and place of birth have been verified. Nevertheless, there are numerous sources on their lives in the Nordic countries. They both died in Sweden, Katie Stewart in 1893 and Alice Ruffen in 1897. When their life as itinerant performers started in 1874, Stewart was in her mid-twenties and Ruffen was still a small child, perhaps only six years old. For the two artists, the decision to sign a contract with an impresario and go on tour was a question of survival. As undocumented migrants, they had few other alternatives than to use their best asset—namely, exoticism—becoming "negro bush women" and showing their "brown-skinned" bodies to curious Nordic spectators.

Marketing Strategies

As both the single acts and the duos discussed in this chapter had fairly long careers, the marketing strategies changed somewhat over time and varied from case to case. In this section, I will specifically look at the way their bodies were portrayed in newspaper ads, articles, and news items.

Anna Sofia Nilsson's body was described in minute detail in newspaper advertisements and articles. The general tone is one of amazement, both in the ads and in the reactions of the audience described in articles and shorter news items following her performances. Nilsson did not have fully developed arms, just short stumps without fingers. "Born without hands and arms" was an oft-repeated description.[25] On her left foot, she had three toes, but the knee joint was missing; on her right leg she had a knee joint and four toes. Both her legs were shorter than normal legs and they were of different lengths. She used her right foot to do embroidery and needlepoint, but also to eat. She used a knife, a fork, and a spoon alternately.[26] She was also able to put thread on a needle by herself. To write, she pressed the pen between her cheek and her right shoulder. The emphasis in the marketing of Nilsson was put on her skill as an embroideress and the fact that she was able to do what she did *despite* her disability. During the first years, she was described as *underbarnet*, or the child prodigy, but later, since she was no longer a child, the description *fotkonstnärinnan* ("female foot artist") was used more commonly. Nilsson's career as a foot artist lasted at least until 1902, possibly 1908 and perhaps even longer. She died in 1922 at the age of 74 in Linneryd, near Växjö, in Sweden.[27]

The fact that Nilsson was rewarded for her work was mentioned several times in the ads and used as an additional marketing strategy. At the age of 14, she received an honorary award by the Economical Society in the County of North Kalmar, and at the age of 18, she was awarded a special honorary diploma at the Industrial Exposition in Stockholm.[28] The pedagogical aspects of her show were also emphasized. Both servants and young girls could learn from Anna Sofia Nilsson what could be gained through hard work and determination.[29] Nilsson was "displayed" in a black silk dress, sitting on top of a table doing her needlepoint, very much like a work demonstration at an expo or fair. All around her, needlepoint works and works of embroidery were likewise put on display, with Nilsson as the centerpiece.

The showing of the Eklund albino sisters did not include any other activity than the audience looking at the two individuals on stage. They themselves did not perform, speak to the audience, or act in any manner. Very much like in Anna Sofia Nilsson's case, the unusual looks of the Eklund sisters were described in detail. In adverts, much emphasis was placed on their physical appearance and whiteness. Their pale skin, red eyes, and completely white hair and eyebrows were described.

> They are recognized by their milky white, morbid skin color as well as white hair and red eyes. Their white skin and silvery white wool hair (similar to unspun silk), curly and ample like silver thread, gives them, although at such a young age, a serious and quite pleasant appearance, which often has aroused the greatest astonishment.[30]

They were also depicted as being afraid of light, always spending their time indoors and in dim candlelight; this added to the mysteriousness surrounding them. Another emphasized thing was the normality of their parents, who were described, in contrast to their daughters, as "normal Swedish parents," but also as "dark parents."[31]

Of the six performers portrayed in this chapter, the Eklund sisters were the only ones marketed as natural wonders, and their extraordinary medical condition was highlighted. The advertisements included testimonies from medical experts saying that the albino sisters were a rare phenomenon. Albinism is extremely uncommon, and for two sisters to have the same condition is even more unlikely. The Eklund sisters traveled extensively, and it was said that they had also been exhibited to the "royal families of Sweden and Norway."[32] This was a common way of marketing these kinds of performers. The connection to the royal families was mentioned to enhance the public's interest, but it was not always true.

In Gustaf Edman's case, his height, arm span, and weight are repeated in the advertisements. The measurements show some variation over the years, and it cannot be excluded that he in fact grew and gained weight during the ten years he toured. His height was reported to be 2.35 meters, his arm span 2.85 meters, and his weight 195–235 kilograms.[33] To Edman's dissatisfaction, the impresarios tended to exaggerate the measurements in the ads. Photographs of Edman, where he was shown next to a person of normal height, were also used in advertisements. In the photos, he was usually wearing a top hat, which emphasized his height even more. His parents were said to be of normal height, but the adverts claimed that his sister was exceptionally tall as well.[34] Repeated numerous times was the size of his wedding band, so large that he could easily pass a two-kronor coin through it. In ethnological material, Edman's large wedding band and the two-kronor coin are also mentioned.[35] An ethnological questionnaire sent out in 1944 also gives information on how Edman's impresario tried to sell the performance at markets. It is stated that the impresario in front of the tent showed Edman's exceptionally large shoe to the marketgoers and spoke in a loud voice to the passers-by:

> The Swedish Giant is shown here! The Giant Gustaf Edman from Gotland! Everyone ought to see and admire him! In here you can see him live! You can see his bed and his unusual attire! He will perform only one day at the market in Tierp! Everyone should see him and be astonished![36]

Of all the six performers analyzed in this chapter, Edman knew best how to deal with newspaper reporters. When he arrived in a new town, he oftentimes paid a surprise visit to the news desk of the local newspaper. The reporters were, of course, shocked by what they saw, as many found his physical appearance both intimidating and frightening. As a rule, the visits always resulted in a news piece in the following issue of the newspaper, thereby giving Gustaf Edman the publicity he needed without paying for an ad.[37]

In Katie Stewart and Alice Ruffen's case, the marketing strategies varied the most. In the beginning, in 1874–1877, they traveled in Denmark and Sweden and the tour was led by impresarios. The impresarios changed after 6–12 months and a new impresario modified the advertised characteristics of the women. Right at the beginning, the claimed fact that Stewart had been a slave earlier in her life was highlighted, but soon the attention shifted to their physical appearance. The color of their skin ("brown"), the texture of their hair ("curly like the wool of a black sheep"), their alleged lack of religion, and their alleged weakness for everything that glittered and sparkled were included in the description.[38] Various narratives about how Stewart and Ruffen had been kidnapped by a captain and later managed to escape from the ship that had taken them across the Atlantic were also common features in the adverts, being included to strengthen the fascination of the public and portray their lives as adventurous.

As the years went by, and probably at a point in time when Stewart and Ruffen were independent of any impresarios and therefore in greater control over what was written about them in the ads, factors such as their decent way of dressing and their skills as singers and dancers were given attention. Decency was used as a marketing strategy, because if the artists were decently dressed and had decent manners, also women could come and see their show.

In the last years of their almost twenty-year tour, the humor and comical qualities of the artists were of appeal to the audiences:

> Everybody, both old and young, please come and see these funny negro women! Everyone will laugh![39]

In their marketing, Stewart and Ruffen used their supposed geographical origin in varied forms over the years: "South America," South Africa, Brazil, and the city of Mobile in Alabama, by the Mississippi River, were among the locations they claimed they originally came from. "South America" in this context implied the southern states of the USA (see Fig. 8.3).

In addition to exotic locations, exotic foods were listed as Stewart and Ruffen's preferred diet. Among these were snakes, lobster, frogs, locusts, and French bread. However, eating exotic foods in front of the audience was not part of the show. Throughout the years, Stewart and Ruffen built their performance around song and dance, which they claimed were

Fig. 8.3 Newspaper advertisement of Katie Stewart and Alice Ruffen. Their performance and show were marketed as "Come and experience two Bush Negro Women". (*Borgåbladet* 11/26/1881)

"national." In the advertisements, their "national songs" and "national dances" were not defined or linked to any specific nation. Announcements that the upcoming performances were "the last chance" to see the artists were used repeatedly. It was not necessarily true, since many times the performances continued after "the last chance" had passed.[40]

Expenses and Ticket Prices

In order for the artists to make a living and have some income from the performances, the expenses could not exceed the amount of money they were able to gain through ticket sales. Constant traveling was expensive. A horse and cart, and trains to some extent, were probably the means of transportation and conveyance most used by the six performers. Katie Stewart's announcement in the local newspaper about two runaway horses in Skellefteå in 1880[41] and her job advertisement for a coachman in Vyborg in 1882[42] both suggest that Stewart and Ruffen owned horses and used them for transportation. Judging from the speed at which the same women traveled along the Norwegian coast in 1877, giving performances in several coastal towns, the steamships and sailboats operating along the coast must have been their primary form of transportation in that phase of their tour.[43] As opposed to the others, Stewart and Ruffen did not have a "home," hometown, or any other form of permanent place of residence, which meant that, in addition to their clothes, props, and possibly a tent, they had to carry everything they owned with them all the time. They probably transported their belongings in trunks, coffins, and sacks.[44] The others were originally from Sweden, and it can be assumed that they had some form of home, rented room, or relatives who could harbor their belongings while they were on tour.

Rent, accommodations, and food were three major expenses that had to be covered by ticket sales. The price for renting a room, an empty shop, or some other suitable location for the performances varied considerably depending on where the place was situated. An ideal location was close to the center of the town, the market square, or the main roads in the area. The fact that the artists sometimes changed the location for the performance and moved it to another part of the town, mostly from a finer location or hotel to a less fashionable part of the town or a tavern, after a few days or a week of performances suggests short leases and hesitation on whether they should keep performing in the current location or continue the tour to a new town or village. Attendance numbers and ticket sales had to exceed rent and other expenses; otherwise, it was smarter to move on. During market days, many towns charged a separate market fee for sellers, vendors, cheapjacks, artists, and others wanting to rent a market stall or erect a tent.[45]

It is not known with certainty where the itinerant performers ate their meals, but taverns, inns, and private homes rather than expensive restaurants were presumably locations where they could get a meal for a reasonable price. The estate inventory list written after Alice Ruffen's passing in 1897 does not contain any kitchen utensils or cooking equipment.[46] On the other hand, the *urarvakonkurs* documents after Gustaf Edman's unexpected death in 1912 do mention a portable stove (*primuskök*) and a can opener, which Edman had received in July 1912 but not paid for. The hardware store Ågrens Jernhandel was therefore demanding payment in the bankruptcy proceedings.[47] If Edman was in possession of a portable stove and a can opener, he probably prepared his food himself while on tour. As an extremely tall person, Edman needed more nutrition daily than a man of average height. It is likely that by preparing or heating his own food, he managed to save some money. However, itinerancy presumably hampered food storage and food preparation, both for him and for the other artists.

Printed posters and newspaper adverts were additional high-cost items, but crucial for the success of the performances. At least in Stewart and Ruffen's case, there is evidence that they had posters with "blanks" printed on them. The blanks could be filled in by hand with information on the performance dates, show times, locations, and ticket prices; the printed poster itself only carried information of them as artists and their pictures.[48] Some of the artists, or their impresarios, also arranged for postcards and photographs of the artists to be printed, all adding to the expenses.

The ticket prices were fairly constant over the years: 50 öre was usually the price for an adult, 25 öre for children and servants. In Norway, adults paid 12 skilling and children and servants half the price, or 6 skilling. Some minor variations can be found, but generally speaking, all members of the audience paid a relatively small price for the joy of watching an extraordinary-bodied performer in the Nordic countries from the 1860s to the 1910s. Factors that could temporarily lower the ticket prices were competition from other performing artists in town during the performance days, low expectations of attendance numbers, or a prolonged stay in the same town.

Gustaf Edman was shown to the Finnish audience "for free" at the itinerant Hartkopf's Museum in 1912. Edman performed in at least twelve Finnish towns.[49] The owner of the museum, the Dane Niels Nielsen, used Edman as an attraction to draw more spectators, and he probably had an agreement with Edman about a fixed weekly or monthly salary. Those paying the entrance fee to the museum—Nielsen offered a panopticon, a wax museum, and an anatomical cabinet—got to see "The Giant from Gotland" for no extra charge.[50]

It is difficult to calculate the exact number of spectators needed to cover the expenses in each individual case, but since the current expenditures were relatively high due to the factors listed above, it was of vital importance to pique and maintain the interest of the public. The curiosity of the onlookers was the propelling force that supported the performances, but once this had been sate, they were unwilling to pay for additional viewings. Therefore, new audiences and new potential customers had to be sought again and again. Consequently, an itinerant lifestyle was inevitable for the artists. It was also extremely burdensome and could affect their health. At least two of the six artists discussed in this chapter died while on tour, and one of the remaining four passed away due to an indirect cause related to the lifestyle.

The Role of the Impresarios

One very important person affecting the livelihood of the performers and the success of the tour was their impresario. Information is not comprehensive on whether the artists had an impresario for all their years on tour, but the source material allows for a fairly good estimate. In Anna Sofia Nilsson's case, the aforementioned impresario G. A. Hedman signed a deal with her and her mother in 1866. Thirty years later, in 1896, an impresario named Mr. Charles Jensen surfaced for a few of Nilsson's performances in Århus.[51] While Jensen disappeared quickly from the sources and probably also from Nilsson's life, Hedman's role was vital in the beginning of her career. He claimed that his pure intention was to help her and secure *her* financial situation, but naturally, he had an economic interest himself to make as much money as possible from showing her and her works of needlepoint and embroidery. Apart from Hedman and Jensen, Nilsson's advertisements did not reveal any other impresarios during her long career, but due to her physical limitations, her mother and possibly some other assistants must have traveled with her.

The Eklund sisters were initially shown by their parents, but after their mother's death in 1878 and their father's passing in 1880, the acrobat and leader of a family circus troupe, Theodor Pettersén, took over as their impresario. In Pettersén's company and under his auspices, the Eklund sisters toured Finland and Russia.[52] In Moscow, the two sisters were shown at a large industrial exposition as "natural wonders." The fact that they could not be exposed to sunlight or any other bright light complicated matters for them. Presumably, all traveling had to take place in the evenings or at night in order to protect their sensitive eyes from bright light. This also made them more dependent on others to arrange practicalities, such as booking locations and hanging posters for the upcoming shows. It seems unlikely that the albino sisters would have been able to tour without the help of others.

Upon their arrival in Malmö in 1874 and during their first years on tour, Katie Stewart and Alice Ruffen were completely dependent on their impresarios. O. Sørensen, who started showing them for money, transferred their charge to Josef Sidoli, an Italian immigrant. Shortly thereafter, Sidoli left them in the hands of A. Altenborg. In Norway, C. Schultz was in charge of the tour and the shows for a short period of time, but soon afterwards, perhaps in 1878 or 1879, Stewart assumed control. Their independence lasted for years, including the entire tour in Finland 1881–1883, but in October of 1883, a person involved in show business at the time, J. C. Jené, had signed Stewart and Ruffen's advert, but this was probably only a temporary arrangement. During the coming years, a few men were described as their impresarios, yet it is more likely that they were just somewhat questionable characters who joined the women for a while. A convicted criminal and former artilleryman, G. F. Larsson, was mentioned as their impresario in 1887, followed by a railroad worker named Linderoth in 1889.[53] Both Stewart and Ruffen developed a serious drinking problem over the years, and as Stewart's condition worsened to a point where she was no longer able to take care of the practical arrangements of the tour, Ruffen stepped in and took the lead.[54]

Of all the six artists, Stewart and Ruffen were independent of impresarios for years at a time. Anna Sofia Nilsson needed assistance in many other matters, but she seems to have arranged the tours herself after the initial years. Perhaps Gustaf Edman could have arranged his own tours, but for some reason he preferred to sign deals with impresarios, time after time. At first glance, using a middleman or intermediary might not seem a smart decision fiscally speaking, but as shown above, all extraordinary-bodied artists did not have the ability or will to arrange everything on their own. Often impresarios and their artists worked as an economic team. If productization had been a concept in use already in the late nineteenth century, Anna Sofia Nilsson and her impresario Hedman would have been masters at it. Early on, Hedman sold photographs of Nilsson with or without her signature. A wide range of articles with embroideries that Nilsson had done with her toes were also for sale: handbags, slippers, coat hangers, trays for candle scissors, small cushions for pocket watches, bookmarks, and paper bins. Lottery tickets and photographs of Nilsson's mother were also sold to the audience.[55]

Aurora and Amalia Eklund and Gustaf Edman sold photographs to members of the audience, Edman also sold postcards of himself, but Katie Stewart and Alice Ruffen did not sell anything directly connected to themselves as artists. In 1886, they were caught selling illicit alcohol in their tent outside the area of a military training camp[56]; although they probably earned a comfortable extra income selling moonshine, it cannot be regarded as additional merchandise equivalent to photographs or autographs.

Economic Success or Failure?

Life as an extraordinary-bodied itinerant performer took its toll. Katie Stewart had a stroke while she and Alice Ruffen were on tour in the county of Kopparberg, and Stewart passed away in 1893. Ruffen was hospitalized in the fall of 1897 and died of "acute alcoholism," probably liver failure, and intestinal catarrh, on December 4 that same year. Gustaf Edman died of dysentery while on tour in Finland in 1912.[57] Only Aurora and Amalia Eklund and Anna Sofia Nilsson survived their active years.

The information that Stewart had died did in fact reached her former homeland through an administrative procedure stipulated in Swedish law. If a foreigner died in Sweden, the parson or vicar in the parish where the death occurred was to send a letter to the county governor, who in turn informed the Department of Foreign Affairs in Stockholm. The ministry forwarded the information to the Swedish consulate in the homeland of the deceased person. In this case, the Swedish-Norwegian consulate in Washington, DC, in fact received a letter with the somewhat distorted information that the American citizen *Mr.* Senorella Jansson had died in the parish of Safsnäs in the county of Kopparberg. The announcement was then sent to the Secretary of State and published in the newspaper *The Evening Star*.[58] To my knowledge, no estate inventory was written after Stewart's death. If there were any assets to inherit, Ruffen inherited everything without any formal legal procedure. The formal estate inventory written after Ruffen's death in 1897 is a sad testimony on the poor, cold, and wet life of two African-American women. Wool clothing and underwear, wool hats, raincoats, scarves, hurricane lamps (or the like), and many broken and worthless items are listed as her belongings. Many of the listed possessions were probably things the two artists had owned jointly before Stewart died. When the costs for the funeral and other expenses were withdrawn from her assets, Alice Ruffen's life ended with an economic deficit of 6 kronor and 40 öre.[59]

Like Ruffen, Gustaf Edman was only 30 years of age when he died. He was married and had two children. Due to his debts and the creditors' unwillingness to settle them with his widow, the estate of Edman was declared bankrupt in December of 1912. The estate inventory showed a deficit of only 114 kronor and 97 öre, but the trustees referred to an unsuccessful real estate deal and poor economic sense in the household when they recommended that the bankruptcy of the estate assume legal force.[60]

After their active years on tour, the economic situation of Aurora and Amalia Eklund was satisfactory. A series of title deeds in 1902 shows that they were still the owners of real estate in Vimmerby, although they had sold smaller parts of the estate earlier.[61] There is also information of Amalia Eklund donating 3000 kronor in her testament to a fund for "three women in need" in 1922.[62]

Considering her prerequisites and the fact that Anna Sofia Nilsson spent the first 12 years of her life in a poorhouse, the rest was an economic success story. After her active years showing herself, her skills, and her works of embroidery and needlepoint to a paying audience, she was able to retire to a fairly comfortable and economically stable life. Already in 1871, she was able to buy a house in Västervik, and in the late 1870s, she donated a part of her property and some funds to the Methodist congregation there, thereby enabling the building of a church.[63] Anna Sofia Nilsson was not only economically successful during her active years, but she was also, it seems, able to manage her funds well later on and live off the revenue.

Conclusions

An important—and one might even say crucial—element of the town markets consisted of the various entertainers, artists, exhibitions and other shows, organ grinders, merry-go-rounds, exotic animals, tame bears, and lotteries offered to the marketgoers. In connection to the markets, but also as separate events outside the market season, extraordinary-bodied itinerant performers showed their bodies and skills to a paying audience.

In this chapter, I have examined the artists' reasons to go on tour, their marketing strategies, expenses and ticket revenues, the role of the impresarios, and the additional merchandise for sale, in order to determine whether or not it was possible to make a living in the Nordic countries as an extraordinary-bodied itinerant performer between 1864 and 1912. The answer is both yes and no.

The extraordinary-bodied performers selected for this chapter were all able to support themselves and their families for long periods of time by using their physical appearance as a type of merchandise. Additional income was gained from selling photographs, postcards, and, in the case of the woman without arms, the works of embroidery she had made using only the four toes on her right foot. The two African-American women were selling and serving illicit moonshine from time to time to get extra income.

The shows or performances of extraordinary-bodied persons were oftentimes popular and perhaps even profitable, but the expenses for the performers also tended to be considerably high. At the same time, the performances were sometimes heavily criticized in newspapers, and the impresarios were accused of exploiting the artists and taking advantage of their vulnerability. In the cases of the Eklund sisters and Anna Sofia Nilsson, their parents were involved in the shows as impresarios and assistants, revealing how these artists were in fact the "breadwinners" in their families. Exhibiting their extraordinary bodies was a means of support for these people, one of the few means available to them. Some were more successful in the long run, but during their active years, they were all able to earn a living, and even support others while enriching their impresarios. Yet, the unfortunate fate of Katie Stewart, Alice Ruffen, and Gustaf Edman goes to show how life as an itinerant performer was by no means a road to success for everyone.

Notes

1. Danish advert for *Kæmpernes Kæmpe* ("The Giant of All Giants"), *Fredericia Social-Demokrat* 6/6/1903.
2. Swedish advert for *Svenske Jätten* ("The Swedish Giant"), *Borås Tidning* 10/25/1904.
3. Finnish advert for *Gotlantilainen Jättiläinen* ("The Giant from Gotland"), *Helsingin Sanomat* 2/1/1906.

4. On human caravans in Denmark, see Rikke Andreassen and Anne Folke Henningsen. 2011. *Menneskeudstilling. Fremvisninger af eksotiske mennesker i Zoologisk Have og Tivoli*; on "freaks" in Finland, see Ville-Juhani Sutinen. 2019. *Kääpiöistä kolosseihin. Kummajaisten historia Suomessa*; on circus troupes in Finland, see Sven Hirn. 1982. *Sirkus kiertää Suomea 1800–1914*; on "freaks" in Norway, see Herman Berthelsen. 2002. *Skjeggete damer og siamesiske tvillinger. Fra Tivoli til Big Brother*; on visual representations of the colonial world in Sweden and exotic shows, exhibitions and attractions, see Åsa Bharathi Larsson. 2016. *Colonizing Fever: Race and Media Cultures in Late Nineteenth-Century Sweden*; on the world tour of a group of Australian Aborigines led by R. A. Cunningham, see Roslyn Poignant. 2004. *Professional Savages: Captive Lives and Western Spectacle*; for a Canadian perspective, see Jane Nicholas. 2018. *Canadian Carnival Freaks and the Extraordinary Body 1900–1970s.*
5. Anna Sofia Nilsson's (or Carlsdotter's/Nilsdotter's) birth record December 1, 1848, available online, Blackstads kyrkoarkiv, Födelse- och dopböcker, SE/VALA/00035/C/4 (1821–1849), p. 341: https://sok.riksarkivet.se/bildvisning/C0026758_00154#?c=&m=&s=&cv=153&xywh=2554%2C101%2C4725%2C2755. Below her name it is noted that she was "born a cripple."
6. Aurora Eklund's birth record November 27, 1855, available online, Vimmerby kyrkoarkiv, stadsförsamlingen, Huvudserien, Födelse- och dopböcker 1855, SE/VALA/00419/C1/7 (1846–1861): https://sok.riksarkivet.se/bildvisning/C0029042_00096#?c=&m=&s=&cv=95&xywh=349%2C1809%2C2974%2C1734
7. Amalia Eklund's birth record July 8, 1858, available online, Vimmerby kyrkoarkiv, stadsförsamlingen, Huvudserien, Födelse- och dopböcker 1858, SE/VALA/00419/C1/7 (1846–1861): https://sok.riksarkivet.se/bildvisning/C0029042_00121#?c=&m=&s=&cv=120&xywh=748%2C363%2C5139%2C2996
8. Carl Gustaf Emmerik Edman's birth record February 4, 1882, available online: Burs kyrkoarkiv, Födelse- och dopböcker, SE/ViLa/23019/C1/6 (1880–1894): https://sok.riksarkivet.se/bildvisning/00009382_00011#?c=&m=&s=&cv=10&xywh=-83%2C693%2C3399%2C1982
9. Nygård 2001, p. 80 ff.
10. A bearded lady advertised as *Skogskvinnan* ("The Forest Woman") toured in Finland in 1897; see *Åbo Tidning* 6/27/1897. On bearded women in Norway, see Berthelsen 2002, pp. 75–79. On obese persons exhibited in Norway, see Berthelsen 2002, pp. 100–103. *Fröken Minna* ("Miss Minna") was one of many obese women who toured in Sweden; see *Tidning för Wenersborgs Stad och Län* 5/23/1881. The dwarf *Fröken Viola* ("Miss Viola, also known as "Betty Viola") toured in both Sweden and Norway;

see *Helsingborgs Dagblad* 12/24/1895 and Norwegian *Aftenposten* 2/1/1896. On conjoined twins, see Berthelsen 2002, pp. 83–88, and an advertisement for the conjoined twins Rosa and Josepha Blazek in *Ny Tid* 4/9/1903 and in *Morgenbladet* 4/21/1903. A family consisting of four "heliophobics" (or albinos) toured Sweden in 1855–1856; see *Korrespondenten* 9/8/1855.

11. "Oscarshamn besökes för närwarande," *Jönköpingsposten* 10/23/1867, gives an account of Anna Sofia Nilsson and her mother's life when, due to the illness of Nilsson's father, they were forced to live in a poorhouse among other paupers. After her father's death, Anna Sofia Nilsson and her mother continued to live in the poorhouse, where the mother took a job as caretaker of the poor. She left the job when Nilsson was 12. Soon after this, Anna Sofia Nilsson seems to have been the one supporting the family by selling her handicraft and taking sewing assignments from a local retailer of women's clothing.
12. G. A. Hedman defended himself against accusations of fraud and trickery. *Åbo Underrättelser* 10/25/1866.
13. "Kom och köp!" *Wimmerby Weckotidning* 7/26/1867.
14. The heirs of Carl Edvard Eklund wanted to auction the same plot and property in March of 1881; see "Kungörelse," *Wimmerby Weckotidning* 3/11/1881.
15. *Stockholms Dagblad* 2/5/1870.
16. According to Axel Fredrik Liljenstolpe's account, the Eklund family had agreed to pay 180 riksdaler to rent two rooms for nine weeks. In Uppsala, they had agreed to pay 70 riksdaler for only one week's stay. *Aftonbladet* 4/28/1870.
17. *Aftonbladet* 4/4/1870; *Aftonbladet* 4/28/1870; *Aftonbladet* 5/27/1870.
18. "Magistratens kungörelser," *Wimmerby Weckotidning* 3/24/1871.
19. Backman 2008, pp. 91–95.
20. "Kæmpens Trængsler." *Demokraten* (Århus) 3/23/1903.
21. There is contradictory information about their relationship. Alice Ruffen is mentioned both as Katie Stewart's daughter and as her niece. Without sources on their origin, it is not possible to determine how they were related, if at all.
22. "Paa Pladsen bag Raadhuset," *Svendborg Avis* 7/20/1874.
23. *Negerbuskekvinder* or its Swedish equivalent *Buskeqvinnor* are the most-often used terms in the advertisements at this time. Their names are mentioned for the first time in *Bergens Tidende* 6/7/1877, almost three years after their life on tour started.
24. It is possible that Stewart and Ruffen consciously used different names at different times to cover their trail against the authorities. Both were

involved in illegal and shady activities from time to time. They were not in possession of and did not carry passports or other legal documents stating who they were and where they came from. Konseljakter E 1 A:638, dat. 13.4.1888, ärendenr 13, Justitiedepartementet, huvudarkivet, Riksarkivet (Sweden).

25. "Född utan händer och armar," *Göteborgs Handels- och Sjöfartstidning* 11/20/1866; "Tapisseri-sömmerska utan händer," *Borås Tidning* 8/2/1871; "Född utan händer," *Dagens Nyheter* 7/12/1875.
26. "Till Norrköpings museum," *Göteborgsposten* 7/20/1864. The news item also depicts a needlepoint work Nilsson donated to the museum in Norrköping.
27. *Dagens Nyheter* 3/21/1902; *Kalmar* 3/15/1908; Åkerman 1988, pp. 60–62.
28. "Länets norra hushållningssällskap," *Barometern* 2/7/1863; Åkerman 1988, p. 61; "Bland pristagarne," *Kalmar* 7/21/1866.
29. "...förevisningen är så långt utsatt på afton, så att tjenare skola få tillfälle äfven påse hvad en så vanlottad menniska genom fast vilja och ihärdighet kan åstadkomma," *Härnösandsposten* 8/29/1866; "Familjemödrar böra medtaga sina döttrar för att beundra denna qwinna och lära sina barn att inse hwad den som will arbeta kan uträtta här i werlden," *Tidning för Wenersborgs Stad och Län* 6/10/1870.
30. "De igenkännas på deras mjölkhvita, sjukliga hudfärg samt hvita hår och röda ögon. Deras hvita hud och silfverhvita ullhår (liknande ospunnet silke), lockigt och fylligt som silfvertråd, gifver dem, ehuru de äro vid så ung ålder, ett allvarligt och rätt så behagligt utseende, som ofta väckt den högsta förundran," *Stockholms Dagblad* 1/7/1874.
31. "Mörka föräldrar," *Stockholms Dagblad* 1/7/1874. The adjective "dark" probably referred to the hair color of the parents.
32. *Tampereen Sanomat* 9/3/1881. Norway did not have a "royal family" at this time, as Norway was in a union with Sweden and reigned over by the Swedish king.
33. The measurements were given in Finnish ads during the last months of his life. "Gottländska Jätten," *Jakobstad* 5/22/1912.
34. *Åbo Underrättelser* 1/9/1906; *Turun Lehti* 1/13/1906.
35. Nordiska museet, Stockholm, Etnologiska undersökningen, Frågelista 122: Marknadsnöjen och kringförda sevärdheter I, p. 521.
36. Ibid., p. 521. "Det var. här den svenska jätten förevisas! Jätten Gustaf Edman från Gotland! Alla måste se och beundra honom! Här inne får ni se honom livslevande! Ni får se hans säng, och hans onormala utstyrsel i kläder! Han uppträder endast en dag på Tierps marknad! Alla måste se och förvånas!"

37. *Helsingborgs Dagblad* 4/15/1904; *Turun Sanomat* 1/9/1906; *Holbæk Amts Venstreblad* 6/16/1907.
38. "Tvenne brunskinnade Buske-Kvinnor," *Alingsås Weckoblad* 4/22/1876.
39. "Se, läs och haf i minnet!" *Dagens Nyheter* 12/31/1891.
40. In Tromsø, Katie Stewart and Alice Ruffen announced that the performances at the end of May 1878 would be the last shows given there. The performances nevertheless continued in June with ticket prices for adults cut in half. *Tromsø Stiftstidende* 5/26/1878 ("Forevises for sidste Gang") and *Tromsø Stiftstidende* 6/2/1878.
41. "Bortsprungna hästar," *Skellefteå Nya Tidning* 7/7/1880.
42. "Palwelukseen halutaan," *Ilmarinen* 2/2/1882.
43. In May of 1877, Stewart and Ruffen performed in the southernmost part of Norway, in Grimstad and Flekkefjord, respectively, thereafter traveling all the way to Vadsø in the north. On the way, they stopped and performed at least in Bergen, Kristiansund, Trondheim, Bodø, and Tromsø before reaching Vadsø in August. Considering the Norwegian coastal terrain, travel by sea seems like the most probable form of transportation. See Berg 2003, pp. 18–24. Berg's article also mentions Anna Sofia Nilsson's performances in the northernmost part of Norway in June of 1877, less than three months before Katie Stewart and Alice Ruffen reached Vadsø.
44. In Finland, Stewart and Ruffen used rail freight to move their belongings and equipment but forgot to pay or did not have the money to pay for the carriage. A list of unclaimed goods transported on the Finnish railroads during the fourth quarter of 1881 (*Finlands Allmänna Tidning* 2/7/1882) states that Stewart had not claimed some trunks, boxes, and a sack weighing in total 380 *skålpund*, or 161.50 kilograms. Also, the estate inventory list for Ruffen in 1897 mentions the same or similar form of storage: trunks, coffins, and sacks.
45. Ehrnrooth 1915, pp. 127–169.
46. "Laga bouppteckning efter Negrinnan Toppsy eller Alise Jonsson från norra Amerika," 9.12.1897, Köpings rådhusrätt och magistrat, Bouppteckningar 1896–1900, F 2 A:36, Landsarkivet i Uppsala, Sweden.
47. Oskarshamns rådhusrätt och magistrats arkiv F IV 71, handlingar hörande till urarvakonkursen efter Karl Gustaf Emrik Edman 724/1912, Landsarkivet i Vadstena, Sweden.
48. Larsson 2016, p. 147.
49. According to newspaper advertisement, Edman performed at least in Kemi, Mikkeli, Iisalmi, Kajaani, Oulu, Pietarsaari, Lahti, Vaasa, Hanko, Joensuu, Turku, and Savonlinna before his sudden death in Savonlinna on the 3rd of October 1912. During 1912, Niels Nielsen toured in several other Finnish towns with Hartkopf's Museum, but Edman is not always explicitly mentioned in the ads. Edman had toured Finland also in 1906.

50. "Hartkopfs-Panoptikon och Anatomiska museum," *Hangö* 8/3/1912.
51. "Fodkunstnerinde Frk. Nilsson," *Århus Stiftstidende* 8/8/1896.
52. "Bland naturunder," *Dagens Nyheter* 7/17/1882.
53. "En negerimpressario," *Nerikes Allehanda* 8/12/1887; "Negressen och hennes dotter," *Jämtlandsposten* 10/28/1889.
54. "Tvenne Amerikanska Negresser," *Vestmanlands läns tidning* 3/19/1892. Advertisement signed by "Miss Toppsy," a name Alice used late in her career.
55. "Förewisning i Skrifning och Tapisseri-sömnad," *Stockholms Dagblad* 6/20/1866.
56. "Lönkrögeri och slagsmål," *Dagens Nyheter* 6/7/1886; the occurrence at Kronoberg heath also made the news in Finland; *Fredrikshamns Tidning* 6/26/1886.
57. On Stewart's death, see "Ett ovanligt dödsfall," *Dagens Nyheter* 2/10/1893. On Edman's death, see "Gustaf Edman on kuollut," *Keski-Savo* 10/3/1912. Alice Ruffen's death was not reported in newspapers, but records of her passing and the cause of her death are found in church archives, available online, Köpings stadsförsamlings kyrkoarkiv, Död- och begravningsböcker, SE/ULA/10695/F/8 (1895–1916): https://sok.riksarkivet.se/bildvisning/00181976_00029#?c=&m=&s=&cv=28&xywh=101%2C117%2C4482%2C2572
58. "Died abroad," *The Evening Star* 3/9/1893. The aforementioned church records on Ruffen's death suggest a similar flow of information as in Stewart's case, from the parish level to authorities in Stockholm and onwards, but the official correspondence has not been found, or has been lost.
59. "Laga bouppteckning efter Negrinnan Toppsy eller Alise Jonsson från norra Amerika," dated 12/9/1897, Köpings rådhusrätt och magistrat, Bouppteckningar 1896–1900, F 2 A:36, Landsarkivet i Uppsala, Sweden.
60. Oskarshamns rådhusrätt och magistrats arkiv F IV:71, Carl Gustaf Emmerik Edmans urarvakonkurs, godemänsberättelse, dated 3/3/1913. Landsarkivet i Vadstena, Sweden.
61. "Beviljade lagfarter," *Vimmerby Tidning* 9/19/1902.
62. Bäckman 2000, pp. 18–19; Nordmark 2005, pp. 88–89.
63. Åkerman 1988, pp. 60–62.

Bibliography

Archival Sources

Church Archives from Blackstad Parish, Regional Archive in Vadstena, Sweden.
Church Archives from Burs Parish, Regional Archive in Visby, Sweden.
Church Archives from Köping Townparish, Regional Archive in Uppsala, Sweden.

Church Archives from Vimmerby Townparish, Regional Archive in Vadstena, Sweden.
Köping Town Hall Court and Magistrate's Archive, Regional Archive in Uppsala, Sweden.
Oskarshamn Town Hall Court and Magistrate's Archive, Regional Archive in Vadstena, Sweden.
Department of Justice, National Archive, Stockholm, Sweden.
Nordiska Museet, Stockholm, Sweden.

PUBLISHED SOURCES

Newspapers

Aftenposten, 1896.
Aftonbladet, 1870.
Alingsås Weckoblad, 1876.
Barometern, 1863.
Bergens Tidende, 1877.
Borås Tidning, 1871, 1904.
Dagens Nyheter, 1875, 1882, 1886, 1893, 1902.
Demokraten (Århus), 1903.
Finlands Allmänna Tidning, 1882.
Fredericia Social-Demokrat, 1903.
Fredrikshamns Tidning, 1886.
Göteborgs Handels- och Sjöfartstidning, 1866.
Göteborgsposten, 1864.
Hangö, 1912.
Helsingborgs Dagblad, 1895, 1904.
Helsingin Sanomat, 1906.
Holbæk Amts Venstreblad, 1907.
Härnösandsposten, 1866.
Ilmarinen, 1882.
Jakobstad, 1922.
Jämtlandsposten, 1889.
Jönköpingsposten, 1867.
Kalmar, 1866, 1908.
Keski-Savo, 1905.
Korrespondenten, 1855.
Morgenbladet, 1903.
Nerikes Allehanda, 1887.
Ny Tid, 1903.
Skellefteå Nya Tidning, 1880.
Stockholms Dagblad, 1866, 1870, 1874.

Svendborg Avis, 1874.
Tampereen Sanomat, 1881.
Tidning för Wenersborgs Stad och Län, 1870, 1881.
The Evening Star, 1893.
Tromsø Stiftstidende, 1878.
Turun Lehti, 1906.
Turun Sanomat, 1906.
Vestmanlands läns tidning, 1892.
Vimmerby Tidning, 1902.
Wimmerby Weckotidning, 1867, 1871, 1881.
Åbo Tidning, 1897.
Åbo Underrättelser, 1866, 1906.
Århus Stiftstidende, 1896.

Literature

Andreassen, Rikke, and Anne Folke Henningsen. *Menneskeudstilling. Fremvisninger af eksotiske mennesker i Zoologisk Have og Tivoli.* København: Tiderne Skrifter Forlag, 2011.

Backman, Olle. "*Vi var starkare förr.*" *Svenska kraftkarlar i ord och bild.* Stockholm: Santérus förlag, 2008.

Berg, Thoralf. "Kulturliv i Vadsø på 1870-tallet", in *Varanger årbok 2003. Tema: Humor i Varanger,* 18–24. Vadsø: Sør-Varanger historielag, Vadsø historielag, Vardø historielag, 2003.

Berthelsen, Herman. *Skjeggete damer og siamesiske tvillinger. Fra Tivoli til Big Brother.* Oslo: Cappelen, 2002.

Bäckman, Magnus. "Albinosystrarna från Vimmerby." *Släkthistoriskt Forum* 4, 18–19. Stockholm: Sveriges släktforskarförbund, 2000.

Ehrnrooth, Leo. "Om afgifter till stat och kommun för offentliga nöjen i Finland." *Tidskrift, utgifven af Juridiska föreningen i Finland.* Tredje och fjärde häftet, 127–169. Helsingfors: Juridiska föreningen i Finland, 1915.

Hirn, Sven. *Sirkus kiertää Suomea 1800–1914.* Helsinki: Suomalaisen Kirjallisuuden Seura, 1982.

Larsson, Åsa Bharathi. *Colonizing Fever. Race and Media Cultures in Late Nineteenth-Century Sweden.* Mediehistoriskt arkiv 32. Lund: Lund University, 2016.

Nicholas, Jane. *Canadian Carnival Freaks and the Extraordinary Body, 1900–1970s.* Toronto, Buffalo and London: University of Toronto Press, 2018.

Nordmark, Håkan. "Aurora och Amalia Eklund. Två ovanliga Vimmerbysystrar", in *Karaktärerna i Wimmerby. En unik bok om personligheter i Vimmerby,* edited by Håkan Nordman, 88–89. Vimmerby: Björkbackens Karaktärshotell & Kalmar läns museum, 2005.

Nygård, Toivo. *Erilaisten historiaa. Marginaaliryhmät Suomessa 1800-luvulla ja 1900-luvun alussa.* Jyväskylä: Atena Kustannus Oy, 2001.
Poignant, Roslyn. *Professional Savages. Captive Lives and Western Spectacle.* New Haven and London: Yale University Press, 2004.
Sutinen, Ville-Juhani. *Kääpiöistä kolosseihin. Kummajaisten historia Suomessa.* Helsinki: Into, 2019.
Åkerman, Petter. *Sällsamheter i Småland. Del 2. Nordöstra delen.* Stockholm: Rabén & Sjögren, 1988.

CHAPTER 9

"The Whole World Had the Sound of the Barrel Organ": Representations of Fairs in Finnish Newspapers and Fiction from the 1870s to the 1910s

Anna Kuismin

> The fair—a celebration of drunkenness and mistreatment of animals—will take place next Thursday. All kinds of bagmen, most of whom are Russians and Tatars, have already arrived at our town. The merry-go-round, barrel organs and the like are already in full swing, and seem to make good money.
>
> —*Tampereen Sanomat* 9/2/1884

This extract, published in a local Tampere newspaper in 1884, is an example of the ways Finnish newspapers treated fairs or "market days" (Finnish: *markkinat*; Swedish: *marknader*). Apart from reporting on selling and buying, prices, and the number of people attending such events,

A. Kuismin (✉)
University of Helsinki, Helsinki, Finland
e-mail: anna.kuismin@kotikone.fi

J. Ahlbeck et al. (eds.), *Encounters and Practices of Petty Trade in Northern Europe, 1820–1960*,
https://doi.org/10.1007/978-3-030-98080-1_9

newspapers also used to describe the amusements offered there, often in disapproving or condemning tones. Such a negative attitude appears even in a piece of news on the fees decreed by the Tampere town council for vendors, merry-go-rounds, panoramas, barrel organs, street singers "and other rubbish."[1]

As a regular gathering of people for the purchase and sale of livestock and other commodities, the fair also figures in novels, poems, and plays. It is no wonder because Finnish literature has a strong tradition of portraying life at the grassroots level. Going to the fair was an important thing for ordinary country people, so it is natural that the topic appears in fiction. The fair provides a situation in which characters act in an environment different from their usual circles. As Diana O'Hara writes, the marketplace offered a place in which "the communication of ideas, gossip, news, and the experience of exceptional levels of noise and activity, might mediate changes in social relations and permit the negotiation of new relationships."[2]

The extraordinary character of the fair is apparent in the great number of compound words connected to the event, such as 'atmosphere,' 'amusement,' and 'noise' (Finnish: *markkinatunnelma*, *markkinahuvi*, *markkinamelu*). O'Hara argues that it is possible to imagine the marketplace "as a liminal zone within formally bounded areas, where people from different communities met together outside their normal, daily pattern of life. Although participants in the market were ostensibly engaged in economic exchange, the marketplace with its social ambience was also a territory where social transactions were conducted."[3] O'Hara writes about medieval fairs in England, but her observation concerns Finnish fairs in the nineteenth and early twentieth centuries, too. According to the Merriam-Webster Dictionary, *liminal* points to an intermediate state, phase, or condition, something that is "in-between, transitional." Folklorist Arnold van Gennep used the term *liminality* in his famous study of rites of passage in the early twentieth century, and anthropologist Victor Turner developed the concept further in his investigations of ritual processes.[4] In 1974, Turner coined the term *liminoid*, which refers to experiences that do not result in a change of status, like those in rites of passage. Play, playing and time of leisure characterizes the liminoid.[5] There have been studies of liminality in various disciplines and fields, the latest of which include Critical Event Studies. In investigating the fair, this approach to liminality is most fruitful, as fairs can be compared with sports events and other large gatherings. However, in some texts, the first trip to the fair figures as a kind of a rite of passage. In addition, the fact that the word *härkäpoika* ("bull boy") was used for young men who had not yet experienced the event points to this ritual aspect of the fair.

My aim in this chapter is to analyze the factors that contributed to the liminoid experience at the fair, mainly from the point of view of rural common people, who comprised most visitors. I use the term "common people" to refer to individuals who earned their living by means of physical labor and handicrafts. Rural inhabitants coming to the fair included landowning farmers and landless people, such as crofters, cottagers, craftsmen, and servants. My focus is on the representations of amusements, entertainers and petty traders in newspapers, magazines, and fiction. In this chapter, I ask what kinds of social practices were adopted at the fair? What type of information do the fictive and non-fictive texts offer on the producers and consumers of entertainment, as well as on traders and trading encounters? The third aim concerns the criticism of the fair, a recurring theme in many sorts of texts. For example, the governor of Häme sought to ban "all kinds of conjurers, rope dances and other tricksters" from the fair—so that only those who had something to sell or to buy would be allowed at the event.[6] What lies behind these negative attitudes toward entertainment?

Research Material and Source Criticism

The timeframe of my inquiry covers the period from the 1870s to the 1910s because the role of entertainment at fairs seems to have been at its high point at this time. The Gutenberg Project has been helpful in locating fictive texts that include depictions of fairs, but most of the material—reports of a fair as part of newsletters, including articles, columns, news items, letters to the editor, and advertisements—originates from the Digital Collections of the National Library of Finland. As the terms *markkinat* and *markkina* (leading to many compound words) appear more than 110,000 times in the database during this period, it is not possible to study every hit. The word *markkinat* appears in the metaphorical sense (cf. "vanity fair") or as part of the economic system, too. In addition to covering fairs in Finland, newspapers published travelogues with depictions of similar events abroad. To find information on fairs and amusements, in my searches I used compound words and terms indicating various types of entertainment. Due to the large quantity of material available, I concentrate on texts written in Finnish.

Self-taught farmers and rural craftsmen formed the majority of the so-called country correspondents, who sent newsletters to papers interested in covering local news.[7] In many cases, they were either unsigned or published with initials or under pseudonyms. Reports do not always include mentions of entertainment, but it is difficult to know if this was because there were no amusements at those fairs or if the writer did want to cover them in a short space. The disparaging voice in many of these texts belonged to advocates of ***kansanvalistus*** (literally "enlightenment of the common people"; Swedish: *folkupplysning*; German: *Volksaufklärung*). As country correspondents dealt with issues like the overuse of alcohol, it was not in their interest to depict the fairs in a positive or neutral light. It is likely that people like Lutheran clergymen sent letters to the editor in which the sinful life at the fair was criticized. Editors of papers, representing the urban middle classes, also wrote about fairs in the spirit of popular education.

Newspapers and magazines also published longer depictions and reminiscences of the fair as well as fictive stories. These texts, mostly published with initials or under pseudonyms, include information on the mores and customs related to the event. A critic commented on the popularity of the fair as a topic in his review of a collection of Kasimir Leino's short stories that included "Härmänmäkeläisten markkinamatka" ("The Härmänmäki Folks at the Fair"): "So much has been written on fairs that one knows these 'trips' thoroughly. There is nothing new in this story. People swarm at the marketplace and on the streets, things are bought and 'comedies' visited."[8] Although the story seems to be true to life, its value diminishes because of the commonness of the topic, or so goes the argument in the review. In his letter to the editor, the pseudonym P. A. criticized literary realism for its aim to record real life. With the shorthand method of writing and the phonograph becoming more widespread, it will be possible to know exactly what "farmhand Matti and maid Liisa talked at the fair," wrote the pseudonym in 1891.[9] In her article on the use of fiction in the study of history, Marja Vuorinen states that one can start from the assumption that writers had knowledge of the phenomena, customs, and social norms of their times.[10] Naturally, the information included in both newspapers and fictive texts cannot be taken at face value, but it is evident that depictions of the fair had their origin in the observations and experiences of authors. It is important to pay attention to the types of texts and their conventions. For example, stories that warn readers of the dangers of the fair emphasize different aspects than texts whose main function is to amuse readers.

Approaching the Liminoid

Everyday life in nineteenth- and early twentieth-century rural Finland was austere. For the majority, life consisted of hard physical work, simple food, and confinement to one's household and nearby surroundings. Especially in central, eastern, and northern Finland, distances between villages were great, and even going to church was a rare event. The fair was a welcome break in a monotonous life. "If youngsters have to stay at home during the fair, they feel like prisoners in Siberia," remarks a character in a story by Juho Reijonen.[11] When farmhands and maids negotiated their terms of employment with their masters, they tried to make sure that they would be allowed a trip to the fair at least once a year. Some servants would even accept smaller wages if they were granted that "golden journey."[12] In Kasimir Leino's story, mentioned above, a maid is willing to pay for a substitute so that she can leave for the fair.[13]

The fair was an important topic of conversation as the event came closer.[14] Preparations started with loading carriages with products to be sold as well as provisions needed during the trip. In Lapland, the northernmost part of Finland, the trip to Rovaniemi could even take a week for those who lived in the farthest villages. Depending on the season, the means of transportation included sleighs, boats, skiing, and walking.[15] The journey to the fair represented a pre-liminoid phase. Overnight stays offered opportunities for interacting with other people heading to the same event. In J. Krumberg's feuilleton, a young woman eagerly listens to the more experienced girls talk about amusements, anticipating the pleasures ahead.[16] In a story by Minna Canth, a young man called Antti travels to the fair for the first time in his life. His friend Matti sings a song about a boy who drinks rum there and has a girl sitting on his lap. Matti blames Antti for his lack of *markkinailo*, the proper spirit one has to adopt at the fair and forces him to take a slug from his bottle. Ritualistic behavior also appears in the following custom: whips cracking, horse racing, and men hollering a song about the fair when the town is in sight.[17]

Drinking and racing were part of male bonding and peer ranking.[18] Alcohol enabled men to act in ways that were different from their normal behavior. According to an individual writing under the pseudonym Tiitus Tuiretuinen, *raaka ilo* ("wild/raw joy") on the way to the fair manifested itself in screaming, swearing, and the flogging of horses.[19] It is strange to see how the Finnish peasant, "usually so quiet and mute like a fish, yells and makes noise at the fair," remarked an anonymous writer in 1873.[20]

The liminoid character of the fair supported the challenging of social boundaries, too: "Give way, masters (*herrat*) are coming," shout men driving to the fair in a novel by I. A. Vatanen.[21] A line in Larin-Kyösti's poem "Markkinoilla" ("At the Fair") captures the same feeling: "the tenant farmer is now a lord."[22] The anonymity of the fair made it possible for the underdog to shatter power relations governing social behavior, and the event allowed different rules regarding drinking. According to Satu Apo, households and communities controlled the practices of drinking in everyday life.[23] On one hand, men were expected to drink at fairs, but destructive behavior like squandering one's property was disapproved of.[24]

Arriving at the destination, the first thing was to find lodgings in households of merchants or other townspeople. According to a report published in *Savo*, the yards of houses were so full of sleighs that one had to zigzag around them to get in the building. The walls of the common room were full of bags and coffers, and coffee pots were brewing on the stove all day long. At night, straw on the floor served as a mattress for communal sleepers.[25] Naturally, this kind of situation differed from that at home, where the number of people in the household was much smaller and there were no strangers present. Richer visitors rented rooms of their own in order to have more comfort and privacy. Not much time was spent in one's lodgings, however; wearing their best clothes, visitors headed for the marketplace where they encountered a dense crowd. Writers compared the throng of people to a swaying cornfield, a human snake with a thousand heads and a restless beehive.[26] For people who were used to knowing most of the people present at a gathering, this kind of scene was extraordinary indeed.

The Fair as a Liminoid Experience

In addition to the density of the crowd, auditory experiences characterized the liminoid experience at the fair. "Wilho" begins his report by remarking that he can still hear the cries of horse dealers and the sounds of their whips, the tunes of barrel organs, and the songs of street singers.[27] In Juhani Aho's feuilleton, a young man loves the thundering sound of the crowd and the tinkles of jingle bells and cascabels.[28] In a story by an anonymous writer, two young people, Katri and Matti, go to the fair to buy engagement rings—a customary thing for the recently betrothed—and things for their future household. When they reach the marketplace, they are amazed at the sight: "What a racket and buzz! What a crowd of people! There were amusement makers at every corner, and the whole world had the sound of a barrel organ."[29] According to the pseudonym "Y," the experience of merging into the crowd, as well as seeing, hearing, smelling, and tasting things different than usual, makes one melt into "pure sensations."[30] Thanks to alcohol and the unwritten rules of the fair, young people embraced freer modes of behavior. Several writers mention that young people walked hand in hand and hugged in public.

Many texts point to the fact that drinking at the fair was a social practice or even a cultural norm. A man who is not intoxicated during the fair is "a useless poor thing, not fit to be in other men's company," wrote the pseudonymous Poskeinen: "You have to look drunk. You have to torture your horse as much as possible; you have to yell so that your neighbor's years are blocked, you even have to try the sharpness of your knife on other people."[31] The majority of visitors were men, and especially the scene at the horse market was an exaggeratedly masculine one. The behavior at the fair could include instances of boasting, brashness, and extravagance. In Johannes Linnankoski's novel, a wealthy farmer adopts something of the spirit of *potlatch*, the gift-giving practice involving giving away or destroying wealth or valuable items in order to demonstrate a leader's wealth and power. People heard tales of things that the farmer did in town: how he treated a crowd of people on the merry-go-round or drove straight into the restaurant with his horse and carriage. However, he did not touch drink: "A ferocious man of the fair who does not hit the bottle—what kind of a man was he?"[32]

The liminoid character of the fair had an effect on social distinctions, too. In his depiction, the pseudonymous Tiitus Tuiretuinen paid attention to the equality of people there: gentlemen and ladies, burghers and craftsmen, farmers and farmhands, Roma and Finns, Tatars and Russians go ahead "in one big flurry."[33] In his study on the fair in Mikkeli, Matti Varsta writes about the dissolution of boundaries. Things like creed, class and ethnicity were forgotten when "the spirits of commerce and entertainment" ruled.[34] These call to mind Victor Turner's concept of *spontaneous communitas*, the experience of togetherness.[35] Contrary to usual circumstances, equality and anonymity ruled at the fair, at least to a degree. In this way, the marketplace became a liminoid space in which social encounters that were different than usual ones could take place.

When the fair was over, memories lived on. In a poem by Joel Lehtonen, men returning from the town talk about merry-go-rounds, the prices of things, horses, the Roma people, and so on.[36] Young people who had made new friends started to look forward to the next journey to town. In Kauppis-Heikki's novel, a farmer's daughter received letters from boys she had met at the fair.[37] The journey was present in the stories people told, sometimes long afterwards. A man in Niilo Kivinen's novella brags about his exploits: "Once I was at the fair in Vaasa, somebody was trying to steal my pipe. I kicked his face so hard that he flew several yards and landed on his back."[38] In Maiju Lassila's novel *Tulitikkuja lainaamassa* ("Borrowing Matches"), the protagonists talk about a fellow who was so strong that the police had to get extra hands to take him to the drunk tank.[39] Stories of this kind have their counterparts in folktales in which strongmen perform extraordinary feats of strength.[40]

Amusements and Entertainers

In the following, my aim is to give a brief overview of the amusements that contributed to the proper atmosphere of the fair, leading to liminoid experiences. The merry-go-round (*karuselli, karusell*) was one of the most important ones; a round platform with seats often in the form of horses, lions, and other exotic animals, it revolved about a fixed center, first operated with the help of stallions and later with steam power. Decorations could include pearls, trinkets, shining bits of cloth, tussles, small mirrors, and lanterns. For a newcomer from the countryside, a sight of this kind was something new and wonderful. The pseudonymous Topias Toivovainen depicted "plump young people" riding on a wooden horse, legs astride, smiling more blissfully than at church, as well as boys sitting in a revolving sleigh, arms entwined around the waists of girls.[41] Young people usually appear in texts as the regular customers of the merry-go-round, but in a story by Juho Rauta, a boy attending the fair for the first time sees a grown man sitting on a crocodile.[42] Maiju Lassila's humorous novella *Kilpakosijat* ("Rival Suitors") includes an episode in which a middle-aged couple asks bystanders to hold their animals—a bull and a pig—while they take a ride.[43]

Barrel organs (*posetiivi, posetiv*) played a seminal role at the fair, too. Among other things, they contributed to the acoustic ambiance of the fair and provided background music for merry-go-rounds and other amusements. The barrel organ consisted of a small pipe organ played by turning a handle, which rotated a cylinder studded with pegs that opened the valves to produce a pre-set tune. Like in many other countries in Europe, during the period under investigation, the operators were mostly Italian or of Italian origin.[44] They earned their living by selling little pieces of paper called *onnenlehti* ("slips/leaflets of fortune") to the people who had gathered around them to listen to the tunes. When one placed a coin on top of the barrel organ, a bird or a monkey picked a piece of paper that told one's fortune (see Fig. 9.1). In the story about Katri and Matti mentioned above, the young couple buy a slip of fortune that promises them five sons and seven daughters "who flourish like the branches of olive trees and cedar trees on the mountain of Lebanon."[45]

The "revolving *panorama*" was a long strip of painted fabric wound between two vertical cylinders and unrolled before an audience. The intended effect was to make viewers feel as if they were standing amid images. Panoramas often included scenes of great wars and views of big cities. In 1875, there were four panoramas at the fair in Kajaani; barrel organs, violins, drums, and harps enhanced their attraction.[46] Tours of waxworks and anatomical museums sometimes coincided with the time of the fair. According to another anonymous writer, some of the things displayed were obscene.[47] Advertisements included the mention "for adult

Fig. 9.1 Amusement-maker with an organ grinder and a monkey in the Tampere marketplace in Finland, 1908. (Unknown photographer. The Finnish Heritage Agency)

males only."[48] No doubt this pointed to the sexual nature of some of the works, which acted as an extra attraction for some visitors. Very short or tall individuals, as well as people of color, were also exhibited at the fairs.[49]

Kometiia ("comedy") was a colloquial expression for various types of performances. In Joel Lehtonen's novel, a dark man dressed in leotards, decorated with red and silver stars, cries in broken Finnish: "Everybody come see this program. Big rope king. Ring of death. Magic tricks."[50] The entertainment included a show of gymnastics and a female snake charmer performing magic, among other things. There were occasional mentions of tightrope dancers, sword swallowers, ventriloquists, and clowns.[51] Fire-eating also figures as a form of *kometiia* in J. Krunberg's feuilleton.[52] In a reminiscence on a fair, the foreign artists have "pale and hungry faces" spoiled by maquillage, dressed in thin and dirty rags, trying to coax people to enter their tent, with their piercing cries in the cold autumn rain.[53] Performers at the "comedies" were often racialized. They looked different, they spoke differently, and they did things that did not belong to the ordinary lives of Finnish common people.

Itinerant menageries visited the fairs, too. For example, "Karamatti" exhibited dancing dogs and monkeys during the fair.[54] Bartolomeo Caramatti (1848–1920) toured Finland in 1879, 1882, and 1889–1892.[55] An advertisement signed by L. Bono boasts a sea lion and a lamb with five legs.[56] Elisabeth Bono, an Italian citizen, received a permit to exhibit a collection of live animals and a shooting gallery.[57] According to an anonymous writer, the audience saw a bear who danced and wrestled with a man, a camel who bowed politely, and a monkey dressed in a red hussar's uniform: "Young people looked at these animals like miracles. These beasts probably figured in their dreams and stayed as a lasting recollection from the famous Kuopio fairs."[58] This comment shows that menageries, like other "foreign" amusements, produced exciting experiences that were not possible in everyday life.

Vendors and Buyers

Town shopkeepers had stalls at the marketplace during the fair. For example, goldsmiths sold engagement rings, pocket watches, and jewelry.[59] Artisans and farmers offered their wares from their carriages or sleighs, while townspeople made money by feeding visitors and young boys by selling cigars. Sellers of chapbook songs (*arkkiveisut*, *skillingvisa*) were a regular sight at fairs. In addition to love and courting, the topics of songs included accidents, natural disasters, and crimes. Unlike barrel organists and most performers at the "comedies," chapbook vendors were Finnish. During the golden age of chapbook publishing from the 1870s to the early twentieth century, the production and distribution of popular songs were in the hands of the common people. However, the number of men who earned their living from this trade was rather small.[60] At the beginning of Juhani Aho's novella *Muuan markkinamies* ("A Man at the Fair"), the narrator is standing at the marketplace, observing the way "the old Leppänen, that ancient seller of songs, an ex-soldier" sings and interacts with his audience.[61] This character was not fictional: Aleksanteri Leppänen (1851–1886) earned his living by selling chapbooks.[62] Aho's story depicts an encounter between a chapbook vendor and his clients. According to the narrator, people who had gathered around Leppänen wanted to buy a particular song or demanded something new. The demeanor of the "Song Master" reflected the moods of his listeners: "He knew many songs and could choose the one that suited each customer. He sold a lot and was known at every fair."[63]

Another well-known producer and seller of chapbooks, Paavo Putkonen, figures in a memoir of Aleks Seppänen sent to the Finnish Literature Society in the 1930s. It highlights the interaction between the vendor and his audience, revealing both verbal and non-verbal modes of communication. When people asked about the prices of songs, Putkonen did not quit his performance but included his answers during singing. When he sang about love, boys and girls exchanged glances and those holding hands started swaying, and when the song was finished, they purchased the chapbook, wrote Seppänen.[64] It is apparent that the vendor skillfully took advantage of the amorous atmosphere when selling his wares. There is also an interesting depiction of a blind man and his family performing at the fair in Jyväskylä. Father and sons formed a small band consisting of violin, bass, and triangle, while the mother of the family sang with a basket of chapbooks hanging around her neck. The audience was captivated: "The hearts of women and girls melt into song. They, too, start to sing, and when the song is finished, they take 10 pennies and buy the text," wrote an anonymous reporter.[65] These examples demonstrate that encounters at the fair between sellers and buyers were multifaceted and involving interaction, among other things.

Vendors of manufactured clothes and accessories offered their wares at the fairs, too. There are several depictions in fictive texts of young men buying fashionable long scarves and sporting them during the fair. In a story by Juhani Aho, two young women, Liisa and Kaisa, shop for overcoats. Vendors eagerly served their clients, and onlookers took part in the encounter, too:

> Liisa was in a flurry: first, she was dressed as a fine lady, wearing an overcoat and a silk scarf, then she stood in her green dress, bareheaded, her hair all messed up. Some gentlemen were watching the event. They laughed, joked, and commented on the girls in a racy way, amused by their own words. They encouraged the girls to buy the coats and said that they fitted well. Another Jew had taken Kaisa's arm and soon she was in the grip of a similar spell as Liisa.[66]

The presence of various kinds of sellers of refreshments and trinkets was vital in creating the atmosphere at the fair. The liminoid worked in their favor, too. Special baked goods called *Viipurin rinkeli* were consumed and bought as gifts. There was even a special word (*markkinaiset*) for presents purchased for those who had to stay at home during the fair.[67] Boys invited girls to drink coffee or *varimakea*, a hot drink made out of water, treacle, and spices. Buying trinkets from vendors at the fair had a role in courting rituals, too. According to the pseudonymous Nyyrikki, every young couple sported a balloon and a red *markkinakukka*, a brooch in the form of a flower.[68] These kinds of accessories acted as tokens of belonging to a special group among the wider crowd.

Criticism of Fairs

Misuse of alcohol is a recurring feature in reports, letters to the editor, and fictive stories. Newspapers used to comment on the general drunkenness during the fair or mentioned the number of people detained. The pseudonymous Räty wrote that nearly everyone at the horse market in Oulu was drunk, and even those who were sober pretended to be intoxicated. A drunken man tried to climb into his carriage but failed, even with two men giving him a hand. Another man fell from his carriage, and a third man coaxed his horse, even though he was sitting in an empty wagon, wrote Räty.[69] According to Tiitus Tuiretuinen, screaming, swearing, lewd words, obscene manners, arguments, quarrels and fights, and the sounds of whips and rattling carriages constituted the auditory scene of the fair.[70] Criticism of the mistreatment of horses often figures in reports and letters to the editor.

Readers were repeatedly reminded about the misfortunes to which drinking could lead. For example, a young man had spent a lot of money on drink, but on his way home he fell asleep on a frozen pond, which resulted in the amputation of a leg.[71] In Minna Canth's cautionary story, Antti ends up in a drunk tank and his friend Matti dies after having taken part in a fight.[72] The pseudonymous Ville observes a group of young women who entered a restaurant with young men. The girls are a little hesitant when the first drink arrives, but the second and the third go down without effort. When port changes to brandy, lewd songs are sung, writes Ville.[73] In newspapers and magazines, criticism of fairs overlaps with criticism of popular songs. Like alcohol and amusements, they arouse desires in dangerous ways: songs of love and courtship result in immoral behavior, the writers argue, and those depicting famous criminals lead young men to imitate the conduct of these "heroes."[74]

The underlying argument in many texts is that drinking eased the visitors' engagement in various kinds of amusements that aroused, titillated, and excited the wrong sentiments. In a letter to the editor, an anonymous writer declares that the dangers of the fair include the loss of female innocence.[75] Country correspondents also frowned upon the dances that were sometimes organized during the fair. In Rovaniemi, they started in the morning and went on until late in the evening.[76] According to someone writing under the pseudonym Nyyrikki, some girls did twelve-hour shifts at a dance hall in Oulu without any trace of being tired.[77] Juxtaposed against the values of diligence and hard work widely espoused in Finnish rural society at the time, this kind of behavior was frivolous indeed. Marriages based on relationships established at fairs do not always end well, warned the pseudonymous Tiitus Tuiretuinen.[78] Newspapers did not openly write about prostitution, but it undoubtedly increased then. According to Jouko Heinonen, there were prostitutes who traveled to Rovaniemi for the fair. Professional pickpockets, thieves, and swindlers also took advantage of the fair.[79] In Joel Lehtonen's poem, a young lumberjack mourns for the pocket watch and wallet that he had lost after playing cards with two Russian horse dealers.[80] In a story by the pseudonymous Päiviö, two young men who take to drink lose their horse.[81] "How many people are killed or become crippled, how many thefts and fights are the results of the fun at the fair?" asked the pseudonymous Kansalainen in his letter to the editor.[82]

Insofar as there is no smoke without fire, it is true that excess drinking caused problems. On the other hand, it seems that writers felt that they had to cover the theme, no matter what. When there were no harmful occurrences, this fact was also included in reports. Middle-class journalists, who themselves were used to drinking in bars or among gatherings of friends, seem to have accepted the condemnation of alcohol as a necessary part of reports and news, as did the country correspondents. Naturally, not every fairgoer followed the expected modes of behavior. For example, supporters of revivalist movements could meet during the event, and there were numerous fairs at which nothing extraordinary happened: business was slow, the crowd was small, the weather was bad, and due to bans or restrictions on selling alcohol, there were few offenses.

Time after time, newspapers reproved people for spending their hard-earned money on amusements and trinkets. According to the pseudonymous Markkina-Matti, the slips of fortunes promising happy marriages, long lives, good-natured in-laws, and unexpected inheritances sold like hot cakes. In particular, it was noted, servants should not squander their wages on "nothing." Even worse, writers reminded their readers, the profits went into the pockets of foreigners. When you buy a slip of fortune from the barrel organist, "the dark-haired Italian laughs at the stupidity of our people," wrote the pseudonymous Markkina-Matti.[83] Both newspaper reports and fictional texts took a negative attitude toward "foreign" traders selling manufactured and used clothes. There are instances of racialization in texts depicting vendors, too. "Children of Israel" sell worthless rags, claimed the pseudonym "N – I."[84] In Minna Canth's story, mentioned above, Antti buys a jacket from a Jewish vendor. When it begins to rain, the cloth looks old and blotchy. Criticism of Jewish and Tatar vendors comes up in Juho Reijonen's story as well.[85]

The ideals of modesty and frugality, promoted by popular education, motivated the critique of spending money on ready-made clothes and showy accessories as well as amusements. Religious reasons were apparent, too: dressing in fancy clothes was a sign of worldliness. Criticism of the common people who wanted to buy "luxurious" products not suitable for their status was a recurring theme in newsletters of country correspondents in general.[86] In one piece of news, the merry-go-round is called *Riettaan mylly*, "the Devil's mill."[87] The underlying idea behind this designation is that the mill usually grinds grain, but at the fair, it robs frivolous people of their money. Newspaper reports and letters to the editor reminded their readers that the pleasure produced by amusements, sweets, and trinkets is a fleeting one, and so people should save their money or use it in a more sensible way.

Some writers also resented the shattering of social boundaries that took place at the fair. Fine restaurants turned into cabins filled with smoke; "now the (common) people have the power," stated an anonymous writer in his long depiction of the fair.[88] *Odi profanum wulgus* ("I hate throngs of commoners"), a quote from Horace, came to the mind of the pseudonymous Aapeli when he saw the "idle, drunken crowd at the fair, living like there's no tomorrow."[89] The debate surrounding universal suffrage in the early twentieth century is present in the report of the pseudonymous Juntta. He starts his depiction with the cacophony of barrel organs, various musical instruments, and the cries of entertainers, and ends it with the following question: "Does one really have to grant the right to vote for every man and woman in this noisy and surging bunch of people, and have a say in affairs of our country?"[90] This comment, given *from above*, exemplifies the fear that many in the middle or upper classes felt before the change that would shatter the old class society.

Conclusions

Considering both fictional and non-fictive texts dating from the 1870s to the 1910s, the fair was a secular feast in which economic exchange provided the ground for social activity. Sellers and buyers, entertainers and their audiences, townspeople and visitors formed a crowd that enabled liminoid happenings. At the fair, one could experience things that did not belong to one's quotidian life. In particular, the fair was important for young people as a scene of courting. The dizzying feeling of the merry-go-round, the loud tunes of barrel organs, the thrill of magic tricks and acrobatic shows, and the happy futures promised by fortune-telling—amusements of these kinds—transported people from the monotonous cycle of everyday life. Trading laid the ground for entertainment—and vice versa. Both activities contributed to the special character of the fair. However, the point of view of entertainers and petty traders is barely visible in the material analyzed in this article. More specifically, writers did not see the producers of amusements as subjects, nor were their activities considered as labor, unlike farming and craftsmanship. The emphasis of the texts is on consumers, representing the great majority of Finnish people from the 1870s to the 1910s.

The supporters of popular education and the temperance movement encouraged people to stop spending their money on drinks, amusements, fashionable clothes, trinkets, and chapbook songs. In particular, farmhands and maids were the targets of this kind of criticism. According to folklorist Satu Apo, some ethnographers have also depicted the landless people as carefree and prone to following their desires by spending their money.[91] The disdain for foreign entertainers and vendors representing ethnic minorities is present in many kinds of texts as well. This originated from the fear of the "Other" and from the nation-building project espoused by many kinds of writers.

The criticism of the amusements was part of the struggle between the "high" culture of the elite and the "low" culture of the common people, manifest in dichotomies like theater versus *kometiia*, concerts versus street singers, and poetry versus chapbook songs. Alternative forms of entertainment were organized to provide more elevating ways to spend evenings during the fair. For example, there were soirées with speeches and choral singing.[92] Interestingly, images of popular entertainers did not rouse opposition when there was a need to raise money for good causes. For example, a seller of chapbooks and a barrel organ grinder figured at a masquerade organized by university students for the benefit of ethnographic research.[93] Few people can resist the temptation of the fair, remarked an anonymous writer in 1897.[94] Many journalists who wrote about the entertainment of the marketplace in a critical way, undoubtedly enjoyed the buzz of the fair. Voices of understanding and sympathy appear in the stories and novels of Juhani Aho, Teuvo Pakkala, and Kasimir Leino, among others. It is no wonder, for the event offered a chance for courtship, humorous incidents, and misadventures.

Notes

1. *Aamulehti*, 9/5/1885.
2. O'Hara 2000, p. 139.
3. O'Hara 2000, p. 139.
4. Victor Turner. 1969. *The Ritual Process: Structure and Anti-structure.*
5. Turner 1974, pp. 66–69.
6. *Hämeen Sanomat* 1/27/1885.
7. Laura Stark. 2013. "Sanomalehtien maaseutukirjeet."
8. *Keski-Suomi* 10/2/1889.
9. *Aura* 7/17/1891.
10. Vuorinen 2014, p. 70.
11. Reijonen 1900, p. 665.
12. *Uusi Suometar* 2/9/1874.
13. Leino 1889, p. 10.

14. Heinonen 1984, p. 106.
15. Heinonen 1984, pp. 108–109.
16. *Kaiku* 6/14/1888.
17. Canth 1878, p. 5.
18. Apo 2001, p. 185.
19. *Laatokka* 9/23/1884.
20. *Hämäläinen* 1/30/1873.
21. Vatanen 1913, p. 68.
22. Larin-Kyösti 1913, p. 52.
23. Apo 2001, p. 108.
24. Apo 2001, p. 168.
25. *Savo* 1/19/1889.
26. *Savo* 2/5/1887; *Kaiku* 3/5/1913; Leino 1889, p. 17.
27. *Tapio* 1/24/1874.
28. *Keski-Suomi* 2/18/1886.
29. *Uusimaa* 10/8/1895.
30. *Keski-Suomi* 1/1/1894.
31. *Wiipuri* 3/3/1901.
32. Linnankoski 1907, p. 32.
33. *Laatokka* 9/23/1884.
34. Varsta 1946, p. 107.
35. Turner 1969, p. 132, pp. 134–140.
36. Lehtonen 1912, p. 26.
37. Kauppis-Heikki 1889, pp. 119–121.
38. Kivinen [1889] 1987, p. 12.
39. Lassila 1910, p. 115.
40. Simonsuuri 1963, pp. 503–505.
41. *Savo* 1/31/1914.
42. *Karjalatar* 6/6/1890.
43. Lassila 1913, p. 75.
44. Karvonen, 2020, pp. 26–55.
45. *Uusimaa* 10/8/1895.
46. *Uusi Suometar* 1/29/1875.
47. *Tampereen Sanomat* 9/12/1876.
48. *Ilmarinen* 2/18/1882.
49. Ville Sutinen. 2019. *Kääpiöistä kolosseihin. Kummajaisten historia Suomessa.* See also Maren Jonasson's article in this volume.
50. Lehtonen 1920, p. 155.
51. *Päijänne* 9/13/1878; *Aura* 19/21/1878; *Kansan Tahto* 9/29/1909.
52. *Kaiku*, 6/14/1888.
53. *MDS*, 2/1902, p. 53.
54. *Tampereen Sanomat* 9/12/1876.

55. Maren Jonasson, 2019. "Inte vilken 'karamatti' som helst: om hur en kringresande släkt slog rot i vårt språk."
56. *Savo-Karjala* 3/2/1898.
57. *Wiipuri* 8/19/1896.
58. *Savo-Karjala* 1/17/1890.
59. *Inkeri* 9/27/1891.
60. Kuismin 2020, pp. 47–48.
61. Aho 1884, p. 22.
62. Laurila 1956, p. 164.
63. Aho 1884, p. 21–22.
64. Laurila 1956, p. 167.
65. *Keski-Suomi* 9/20/1879.
66. *Keski-Suomi* 2/25/1886.
67. Vuorela 1979, p. 268.
68. *Kaleva* 9/26/1908.
69. *Kaiku* 10/2/1886.
70. *Laatokka* 7/22/1884.
71. *Savo* 3/9/1889.
72. Canth 1878, p. 57, pp. 12–13.
73. *Savo* 10/2/1888.
74. Hanna Karhu and Anna Kuismin, 2021. "'Rekiviisujen' halveksunta ja houkutus: Keskustelu arkkiviisuista ja rekilauluista 1870-luvulta 1910-luvulle."
75. *Kaiku* 10/8/1897.
76. Heinonen 1984, p. 217.
77. *Kaleva* 9/26/1908.
78. *Laatokka* 1/28/1884.
79. Heinonen 1984, pp. 131–133.
80. Lehtonen 1912, p. 26
81. *Laatokka* 1/28/1893.
82. *Oulun Lehti* 10/11/1884.
83. *Lahden Lehti* 11/13/1901.
84. *Uusi Suometar* 1/20/1875.
85. Reijonen 1900, p. 666; see also Wassholm and Östman 2017, pp. 24–25.
86. Kajander 2020, p. 57.
87. *Karjalatar* 11/8/1902.
88. *Savo* 1/19/1889.
89. *Kaiku* 3/5/1913.
90. *Keski-Savo* 9/23/1905.
91. Apo 2001, p. 170.
92. *Savo-Karjala* 1/17/1890.

93. Hanna Karhu and Anna Kuismin, 2021. "'Rekiviisujen' halveksunta ja houkutus: Keskustelu arkkiviisuista ja rekilauluista 1870-luvulta 1910-luvulle."
94. *Kaiku* 10/8/1897.

Bibliography

Fiction

Aho, Juhani. *Kievarin pihalla; Muudan markkinamies.* Porvoo: Werner Söderström, 1884.

Wilja [Canth, Minna]. "Ensimmäiset markkinat." *Novelleja ja kertomuksia* (1878): 3–15.

Kauppis-Heikki. *Viija. Kuvaus Savon kansan elämästä.* Porvoo: Werner Söderström, 1889.

Kivinen, Niilo. *Tuppelan Kalle ja Koturi-Heikki. Kuvaus "tukkipoikain" elämästä.* [1889] 1987. Project Gutenberg: https://onlinebooks.library.upenn.edu/webbin/gutbook/lookup?num=50233.

Larin-Kyösti. *Valittuja runoja.* Helsinki: Otava, 1913.

Lassila, Maiju. *Kilpakosijat. Kertomus.* Helsinki: Otava, 1913.

Lassila, Maiju. *Tulitikkuja lainaamassa. Kertomus.* Helsinki: Kansa, 1910.

Lehtonen, Joel. *Markkinoilta. ("Rakkaitten muistojen" sarjaa).* Helsinki: Otava, 1912.

Leino, Kasimir. *Elämästä. Pienempiä kertomuksia.* Porvoo: Werner Söderström, 1889.

Linnankoski, Johannes. *Taistelu Heikkilän talosta y.m. kertomuksia.* Porvoo: Werner Söderström, 1907.

Pakkala, Teuvo. *Oulua soutamassa.* Oulu: K. F. Kiwekäs, 1885.

Reijonen, Juho. *Kertoelmia ja kuvauksia.* Werner Söderström, Porvoo, 1900.

Vatanen, J. I. [Maiju Lassila], *Avuttomia.* Helsinki: Otava, 1913.

Texts in Newspapers and Magazines (in Chronological Order)

"Hameenlinnasta." *Hämäläinen* 1/30/1873.

"Wiipurista." *Uusi Suometar* 2/9/1874.

Wilho. "Kirje Kuopiosta." *Tapio* 1/24/1874.

N – I. "Maaseuduilta." *Uusi Suometar* 1/20/1875.

"Kajaanista." *Uusi Suometar* 1/29/1875.

"Tampere." *Tampereen Sanomat* 9/12/1876.

"Markkinoita." *Päijänne* 9/13/1878.

"Markkina-kuwia." *Keski-Suomi* 9/20/1879.
–yhä. "Wiipurin markkinat." *Ilmarinen* 2/5/1881, 2/6/1881.
Tiitus Tuiretuinen. "Markkinaksia." *Laatokka* 7/22/1884, 8/5/1884, 9/23/1884, 9/30/1884.
Kansalainen. "Mietteitä markkinoista." *Oulun Lehti* 10/11/1884.
"Pertun markkinat." *Tampereen Sanomat* 9/2/1884.
"Läänin Herra kuwernöörin wuosikertomuksessaan tekemiä toiwomuksia." *Hämeen Sanomat* 1/27/1885.
"Waltuusmiesten kokouksessa." *Aamulehti* 5/9/1885.
– ah – [Juhani Aho]. "Jywäskylän markkinoilla." *Keski-Suomi* 2/18/1886, 2/25/1886, 3/18/1886.
Räty. "Markkinoilta." *Kaiku* 10/2/1886.
Jussi [Juhani Aho]. "Muinoisista markkinoista." *Savo* 2/5/1887.
"Miten Mökin Matin käwi Waasan markkinoilla." *Waasan Lehti* 1/26/1889.
J. Krumberg. "Markkinamiehiä." *Kaiku* 6/14/1888.
"Torikertomus." *Aura* 9/21/1888.
Wille. "Naisten markkinatavoista." *Savo* 10/2/1888.
"Markkinat." *Savo* 1/19/1889.
"Jalka paleltunut." *Savo* 3/9/1889.
"Juhannusmarkkinoilla." *Tampereen Sanomat* 7/3/1889.
"Kirjallisuutta." *Keski-Suomi* 10/22/1889.
Juho Rauta. "Ensimmäinen markkinamatka." *Karjalatar* 6/6/1890.
"Markkinahuwituksista." *Savo-Karjala* 1/17/1890.
P. A., "Sananen yhteiskunnan parantajista erittäin meidän aikana." *Aura* 7/17/1891.
"Kirje Helsingistä." *Inkeri* 9/27/1891.
Ville. "Muistelmia ensimmäiseltä markkinaretkeltäni." *Uuden Suomen juttutupa* 1/1/1892.
Päiwiö. "Matti Neuwosen markkinamatka." *Laatokka* 1/28/1893.
Y. "Markkinat." *Keski-Suomi* 1/11/1894.
"Katri ja Matti." *Uusimaa* 10/8/1895.
"Kuopion uutisia." *Savo-Karjala* 1/15/1896.
Tiitus. "Kirje Kuopiosta." *Wuoksi* 2/8/1896.
"Eläinnäyttely." *Wiipuri* 8/19.1896.
Tampereelta ja lähiseudulta. *Tampereen Sanomat* 8/26/1897.
"Markkinain jälestä." *Kaiku* 10/8/1897.
"Jyväskylästä ja lähiseudulta. Markkinalystiksi." *Suomalainen* 1/7/1898.
M. P. "Mitä kansan karttuisa käsi auttaa?" *Uusi Savo* 14.03.1899.
Poskeinen. "Poskeisen pakinoita." *Wiipuri*, 3/3/1901.
Markkina-Matti. "Markkina-pakinaa." *Lahden Lehti* 11/13/1901.
"Riettaan mylly kukistui kokoon." *Karjalatar* 11/8/1902.
– A. – N. "Muuan markkinamuisto." *MDS* 2/1902.

Juntta. "Kirje Sawonlinnasta." *Keski-Savo* 9/23/1905.
Nyyrikki. "Oulun kirje." *Kaleva* 9/26/1908.
-O. "Markkinat." *Kansan Tahto* 9/21/1909.
Aapeli. "Rowaniemen kirje." *Kaiku* 3/5/1913.
Topias Toiwowainen. "Markkinapakinaa." *Savo.* 1/31/1914.

Literature

Apo, Satu. *Viinan voima: Näkökulmia suomalaisten kansanomaiseen alkoholiajatteluun ja -kulttuuriin.* Helsinki: SKS, 2001.

Heinonen, Jouko. *Rovaniemen markkinat.* Rovaniemi: Lapin maakuntamuseo, 1984.

Jonasson, Maren. "Inte vilken 'karamatti' som helst: om hur en kringresande släkt slog rot i vårt språk." 3/3/2019. https://blogs2.abo.fi/kommunicerandekonsumtion/tag/karamatti/.

Kajander, Kosta. *Talonpoika, herra, puoliherra. Etnologinen tutkimus puoliherrakategorioista ja talonpoikaisuuden kulttuurisista malleista suomalaisissa sanomalehdissä 1847–1870.* Jyväskylä: Jyväskylän yliopisto, 2020.

Karhu, Hanna, and Anna Kuismin. "Rekiviisujen' halveksunta ja houkutus: Keskustelu arkkiviisuista ja rekilauluista 1870-luvulta 1910-luvulle." *Kasvatus ja aika* 15, no. 1 (2021): 22–44. https://doi.org/10.33350/ka.95615

Kuismin, Anna. Rahvas ja kirjallisuuden rikkaruohot: Arkkiveisujen kauppiaat ja kuluttajat 1800-luvun Suomessa. *Ennen ja nyt* 21, no. 1 (2020): 44–62. https://doi.org/10.37449/ennenjanyt.90990

Laurila, Vihtori. *Suomen rahvaan runoniekat sääty-yhteiskunnan aikana. I osa: Yleiset näkökohdat.* Helsinki: SKS, 1956.

O'Hara, Diana. *Courtship and Constraint. Rethinking the Making of Marriage in Tudor England.* Manchester: Manchester University Press, 2000.

Simonsuuri, Lauri. "Historialliset ja paikallistarinat." In *Suomen kirjallisuus I: Kirjoittamaton kirjallisuus*, edited by Matti Kuusi, 499–508. Helsinki: SKS & Otava, 1963.

Stark, Laura. "Sanomalehtien maaseutukirjeet." In *Kynällä kyntäjät: Kansan kirjallistuminen 1800-luvun Suomessa*, edited by Lea Laitinen and Kati Mikkola, 145–177. Helsinki: SKS, 2013.

Turner, Victor. *The Ritual Process: Structure and Anti-structure.* New York: Cornell University Press, 1969.

Turner, Victor. "Liminal to Liminoid: In Play, Flow, and Ritual: An Essay in Comparative Symbology." Rice Institute Pamphlet. *Rice University Studies* 60, no. 3 (1974): 53–92. https://scholarship.rice.edu/bitstream/handle/1911/63159/article_RIP603_part4.pdf?sequence=1&isAllowed=y.

Varsta, Matti. *Mikkelin kaupungin markkinat loistokautenaan 1838–1867.* Taloushistoriallinen tutkielma. Mikkeli: Mikkelin kaupunki, 1946.

Vuorinen, Marja. "Kaunokirjallisuus historian tutkimusaineistona." *Avain* 2 (2014): 68–73.

Vuorela, Toivo. *Kansanperinteen sanakirja*. Porvoo, Helsinki, Juva: WSOY, 1979.

Wassholm, Johanna, and Ann-Catrin Östman. "Skillnader och hierarkierskapades i möten på marknader." *Tidskriften Ikaros* 2 (2017): 23–25. http://www.tidskriftenikaros.fi/wp-content/uploads/2017/09/%C3%B6stman.pdf.

CHAPTER 10

"Threatening Livelihoods": Nordic Enemy Images of Peddlers from the Russian Empire

Johanna Wassholm

In the late nineteenth-century Nordics, many people were temporarily or constantly on the move. Diverse mobile groups, such as peddlers, rag collectors, and seasonal workers, traveled around in search of a livelihood. Some originated outside the Nordics, connecting local communities in the region to transregional and transnational flows of people and goods. Many peddlers were from the multiethnic Russian Empire, and they differed from the sedentary population in terms of ethnicity, language, and religion. The most numerous of these groups were the so-called "Rucksack Russians" from Russian Karelia. Other groups included Muslim Tatars, mainly from the Nizhny Novgorod Governorate, Jews from the Pale of Settlement in the western part of the empire, and saw grinders from the Novgorod Governorate.

This chapter explores the ways in which the Nordic press portrayed "Rucksack Russians," Tatars, eastern European Jews, and Novgorodian saw grinders as a threat in the late nineteenth and early twentieth centuries. The analysis engages the following questions: In which contexts and

J. Wassholm (✉)
Culture, History and Philosophy, Åbo Akademi University, Turku, Finland
e-mail: johanna.wassholm@abo.fi

J. Ahlbeck et al. (eds.), *Encounters and Practices of Petty Trade in Northern Europe, 1820–1960*,
https://doi.org/10.1007/978-3-030-98080-1_10

concrete situations were peddlers from Russia perceived as a threat? What characterized the rhetoric that authors utilized to describe the threat? The interests of which groups in the local society did the attitudes voiced in the press represent? As it is a given point of departure that the press depictions were pejorative, I analyze the topic through the concept of *enemy image*. Following Spillman and Spillman's notion, an enemy image can be defined as a stereotypical negative evaluation of the "other." It originates in a perception of the unfamiliar or strange and is utilized with an aim to evoke negative emotions toward outsiders.[1] The "other," be it a nation, a group, or an individual, is condemned or denounced for unfriendliness and for refusing to respect the essential moral values of the "threatened" group, and at times is also accused of malicious and hostile intentions.[2]

Several concurrent factors contributed to the pejorative rhetoric. First, sedentary societies have commonly perceived people with mobile lifestyles as a threat. In a societal order where everyone ideally occupied a given role and position, people without a fixed place have been viewed as a potentially dangerous anomaly. This has been particularly evident in times of conflict or distress when diverse interest groups in the sedentary society have portrayed mobile people as "strangers," utilizing their "otherness" to create and sustain mechanisms of caution, aversion, and fear.[3] Second, such descriptions reflect a general derogatory attitude toward ethnicized petty trade and the consumption of the lower classes.[4] And third, attitudes have been affected by preconceived negative notions of the peddlers' ethnicity and confession, as well as of "the East" as uncivilized and Russia as a military aggressor.[5]

The sources consist of articles and short paragraphs dealing with mobile groups from Russia in Swedish and Finnish periodicals, accessed through newspaper databases.[6] Mobile petty trade has left few and fragmentary traces in historical records, due to its informal character and existence as a gray zone between the legal and illegal.[7] However, the searchable databases containing digitalized newspapers that have emerged in the past decades have opened up new possibilities for researchers to localize these fragmentary mentions.[8] A given point of departure is that the sources predominantly represent the views of the authorities, who aimed to control mobile trade, and of sedentary merchants, who viewed peddlers as unjust competitors, while the voices of the traders and their customers remain silent. However, this does not contradict the main aim of the chapter, which is to disclose the mechanisms through which the Nordic press constructed an image of mobile groups from the Russian Empire as a threat.

Newspapers played a central role in shaping public opinion in the late nineteenth century, and thus functioned as an important channel for disseminating enemy images to the broader public.[9]

Of the four groups explored in this chapter, the "Rucksack Russians" have drawn the most interest in previous research.[10] The Jewish and Tatar peddlers, who were less numerous and only emerged in the region in the 1860s, have been studied in a number of publications beginning in the 1990s.[11] Finally, the Novgorodian saw grinders have been examined in an article by Pia Karlsson, and they are also mentioned in works on Swedish military strategy and Swedish–Russian relations.[12] Despite the fact that mobile trade as a livelihood was strikingly transnational in character, peddlers from the Russian Empire have mainly been studied as separate groups within a specific national setting. I argue that transcending the national framework will offer both more general and nuanced insight into the preconditions that the diverse groups of mobile traders originating in Russia faced when seeking a livelihood in the Nordics.

Peddlers from the Russian Empire

Göran Rosander has described the late nineteenth century as the culmination point of mobile trade in the Nordic region in terms of both scope and ethnic diversity.[13] It was an era of modernization and growing consumption in which both the supply of and demand for consumer goods grew because of incipient industrialization and rising living standards. The growth also encompassed the lower strata of society, a segment of which for the first time had resources that enabled consumption beyond the most basic needs.[14] Peddlers played an important role in the distribution of the growing bulk of commodities in the geographically vast but sparsely populated Nordic region.[15]

Of the four groups studied in this chapter, "Rucksack Russians," who peddled all over Finland and in northern Scandinavia, had the longest history in the region. Most of them originated in White Sea Karelia in the Arkhangelsk Governorate or in the northern parts of the Olonets Governorate.[16] Although Finland was a Grand Duchy of the Russian Empire from 1809, the Russian Karelians' trade was formally illicit according to Finnish law, which included a citizenship right that legally differentiated its inhabitants from other imperial subjects. Despite this, both local customers and the Finnish authorities commonly looked at even evident illicit peddling through their fingers.[17]

Compared to the "Rucksack Russians," the Eastern European Jews and the Tatars were newcomers on the Nordic trading scene, emerging in the region only in the second half of the nineteenth century. The Jews originated in the Pale of Settlement in the western part of the Russian Empire and started to migrate to Sweden in the 1860s. They were part of a broad European migration movement from east to west, a result of many concurrent factors, such as a demographic crisis, harsh economic conjunctures, and pogroms.[18] Most Jews ultimately aimed to migrate to the United States, but some permanently settled in Western Europe, including Sweden. The Jewish population in Sweden grew from 1155 to 3912 persons between 1860 and 1900, with the growth mainly being ascribed to the immigration of Russian and Polish Jews.[19] In somewhat lesser numbers, Jews from the Russian Empire also migrated to Norway, where the majority initially earned their living by peddling. In a way that is typical for early transitional phases of migration, peddling offered a low-threshold livelihood to many newcomers, as it did not require investment.[20]

Jews from the Russian Empire also emerged in Finland, although for different reasons. Finnish legislation, building on eighteenth-century Swedish laws, prohibited Jews from migrating to the Grand Duchy. This changed in 1858, when an ordinance issued in Russia gave soldiers of the Russian military permission, after completing their service, to settle in the locations where they had served. As the ordinance was interpreted to include Jews, Jewish civil communities emerged in the garrison towns of Vyborg, Helsinki, and Turku from the 1860s. A Finnish ordinance issued in 1869 stipulated that the former soldiers and their families could earn their living exclusively by selling minor goods, such as bread, berries, fruit, cigars, matches, and second-hand clothes and shoes. The trade had to take place in spaces specifically intended for the purpose in the towns where Jews resided. Jews were formally forbidden to peddle in rural areas or visit fairs in other Finnish towns.[21]

The Tatars exclusively traded in Finland, migrating from the Russian Empire at the same time as the Jews. However, it was only from around 1880 that the Finnish press started to observe that a previously unknown group of "Orientals" was roaming the Grand Duchy, trading at urban fairs and peddling in rural regions.[22] The Tatars mostly originated in a few villages in the Sergach district southeast of Nizhny Novgorod, approximately 550 kilometers east of Moscow. Many had previously resided in Saint Petersburg, seasonally or permanently earning a living as petty traders.

Without citizenship rights in Finland, the Tatars were not formally allowed to peddle.[23]

The fourth group studied in this chapter, the saw grinders from the Novgorod Governorate, started to visit Sweden and Norway in the 1890s. Although their livelihood was based on offering a service, sharpening saws, and other utilities, rather than selling commodities, mobility was a prerequisite for their livelihood, like it was for the peddlers.[24]

Originating in the vast and multiethnic Russian Empire, all four groups to various degrees differed from the majority population of the Nordic societies regarding appearance, ethnicity, language, and religion. Although they were relatively few in absolute numbers, ranging from a few hundred to some thousands, the peddlers' mobile lifestyles, combined with their distinctive features, made the groups disproportionally conspicuous.[25] The "Rucksack Russians" were Orthodox Christians, a feature that separated them from their predominantly Lutheran customers. They also stood out with regard to some cultural attributes, such as clothing. However, they were also associated with Karelia, a transborder region that played a central role in nineteenth-century Finnish nation-building. In this respect, they were partly seen as related to the Finns, a trait that was strengthened by their knowledge of the Karelian language, at the time considered a dialect of Finnish.[26]

The Eastern European Jews and Tatars differed considerably more. The Tatars were the first Muslims that the inhabitants of the Nordic region had encountered in their everyday lives. In press portrayals, they were commonly described as "Orientals," with the use of stereotypes that represented Western European views of the "barbaric" traits of the "East."[27] Attitudes toward peddling Jews were in turn influenced by negatively charged anti-Semitic stereotypes that had been central in European thought for centuries.[28] Preexisting anti-Eastern and anti-Semite stereotypes, reflecting general contempt for people from Eastern Europe, were reinforced as a result of the vast migration movement to the West that was taking place. From a Western European viewpoint, the migrants were commonly described as strange people who spoke outlandish languages, wore bizarre clothes, and followed odd religious practices.[29]

The attitudes toward the mobile groups were further affected by preconceived derogatory notions of Russia as a repressive and expansionist power. Historical relations between the Nordics and Russia had given birth to an old tradition of animosity, reinforced by a Western European perception of Russia and the East as the "barbaric" antithesis of the "civilized" West.[30] In Finland, anti-Russian sentiments strengthened in the last decades of the nineteenth century, as rising Russian nationalism resulted in attempts to weaken Finnish autonomy and tie the Grand Duchy closer to the empire's core.[31] Russia's tightened grip on Finland was also reflected in Sweden, where in their ambitions to strengthen the country's defenses patriotic circles utilized portrayals of Russia as a military aggressor.[32]

Despite the diversity of geographical origin, ethnicity, and confession, some background factors were common to the groups. The "Rucksack Russians," the Tatars, and the Novgorodian saw grinders were all initially part-time farmers, who came from barren regions that could not offer subsistence for the whole year. This had made mobile trade or craftsmanship an important source of additional seasonal income in their respective home regions. The tradition, in turn, gave peddlers access to existing knowledge and a transnational network that they could exploit as a springboard to expand their business. Due to the seasonal character of their mobility, the peddlers' families did not accompany them to the Nordics. Consequently, the traders that the newspapers describe are almost exclusively men. Even after some of them permanently settled in the region, bringing their families along, female sellers are rarely mentioned, except for Jewish women in Finland. As Jewish trade was largely restricted to the towns in which Jews resided, Jewish women were engaged in the actual selling and thus noted in the press.

Another essential factor that explains the growing presence of mobile traders from Russia in the Nordics in the late nineteenth century is the development of modern transport technologies. Regular steamship routes and the continually expanding railway network made migration, travel, and the transport of commodities faster and more efficient. An important turning point was the connection of the Finnish railway network to that of Russia in 1870.[33] Peddlers could now utilize trading networks stretching from St. Petersburg and Moscow all the way to Kazan, an important market town 800 kilometers east of Moscow.[34]

Economic Threat

One major threat that the press claimed that mobile traders from Russia posed to Nordic societies was economic. Peddlers were commonly accused of causing economic loss to both local societies and the national economy. Such discussions often centered around the question of legality.

Throughout the nineteenth century, Finnish law formally forbade persons without citizenship rights in the Grand Duchy to peddle. This prohibition caused tensions between the Finnish and the Russian administration, which culminated in 1900 when a Russian ordinance made peddling in the Grand Duchy legal for all Russian subjects.[35] In Sweden as well, peddling was prohibited for foreigners, except for a period of liberal legislation between 1864 and 1887.[36] Tensions usually arose from the gray zone between legal and illegal, which characterized mobile petty trade. In addition to the uncertainties caused by this gray zone, at times laws and regulations were contradictory and applied inconsequently, while the authorities often tolerated even apparently illicit trade.[37]

In most cases, it was merchants, the segment of local society whose interests peddling was most likely to harm, who articulated the alleged economic threat. Following a general pattern in this period, the discourse centered around the argument that foreign peddlers utilized their position in the gray zone of legality in ways that made them unfair competitors to established local merchants. Peddlers were accused of evading taxes and other trading fees that merchants had to pay, as well as selling illegal or contraband commodities not regulated by customs.[38] The allegations were typically conveyed to the authorities and the public through associations that represented the merchants at the local or national level. Since the liberalization of trade legislation abolished guilds in the mid-nineteenth century, trade associations became the channel through which merchants could bring pressure to bear on the authorities and legislative bodies.

The associations usually became proactive when merchants felt that petty traders were expanding their trade to such an extent that it threatened their business. In Finland, initiatives made by merchants opposed both peddlers originating in Russia in general and Jews in particular. The Finnish Diet repeatedly debated whether peddling in the Grand Duchy should be legalized for foreigners, including Russian subjects. In her analysis of how the topic was discussed at the Diet of 1877–1878, Hanna Lindberg illustrates the transnational aspect of the Finnish debate. For instance, those who opposed legalization referred to the harm that Jewish peddlers allegedly caused to economic life, even though the right of Jews to reside in Finland was restricted and they were not allowed to peddle. Although opinions were divided, peddling remained heavily restricted for Finnish citizens and, in the otherwise liberal Trade Act of 1879, completely prohibited for persons without citizenship rights.[39]

In the early 1880s, the focus of the Finnish debate shifted from the "Rucksack Russians" to Jewish petty trade. At a national meeting of Finnish merchants in Vyborg in 1883, the local association of Tampere presented a memorandum containing explicitly anti-Semitic rhetoric and examples of countries in which Jewish trade had harmed the economy.[40] Two years later, in a similar initiative, a group of merchants in Turku summoned the public to discuss the "Jewish question."[41] They protested that a number of Jews had been granted permission to open shops in accordance with the Trade Act of 1879. Town magistrates had initially rejected the applications, expressing doubt as to whether the law could be applied to Jews. The Jewish applicants, in turn, appealed to the governors, who repealed the magistrates' decisions, stating that they lacked the authority to reject the applications.[42] This enraged some merchants, who accused the governors of interpreting the laws in an overly liberal way. The merchants behind the initiative claimed that a considerable segment of the public in Turku had met the decision with "repulsion."[43] They appealed the governors' decision to the Finnish Senate, which on many occasions was harsher toward the Jews than the regional authorities.[44]

In Sweden as well, merchants played an active role in attempts to alter national trade legislation in a more protectionist direction. Since the liberal Trade Act of 1864 allowed foreigners to peddle, merchants' associations repeatedly criticized it. While not denying the benefits that freedom of trade contributed, they drew attention to the "obvious" injustices and nuisances that peddling foreigners had caused; the merchants argued that the "flood of complaints" voiced all over Sweden proved that the overly liberal legislation had turned peddling into a "distorted picture" of what it had once been.[45] In 1886, Pehr Emanuel Lithander, a wholesale dealer from Gothenburg who was also a parliamentarian and president of the national merchants' association, made a motion to revise the Trade Act of 1864 with regard to peddling. Utilizing anti-Semitic stereotypes and emphasizing that he represented the interests of all Swedish merchants, Lithander's ambition was partially successful. In 1887, a revision of the law prohibited foreigners from peddling.[46]

As many Russian Jews lacked Swedish citizenship, the revision resulted in some of them leaving the country. For instance, in 1888, the lost opportunity to pursue peddling as a livelihood was mentioned as the reason behind the emigration to the United States of a group of Jews residing in Lund.[47] However, the revision did not end peddling altogether, as many continued—albeit illegally.[48] In the following years, many observers deemed the revision a failure. Instead of fulfilling its original aim to limit the nuisance caused by "wandering Jews and other loose people," it had merely made it more complicated for honest, hardworking people to pursue their trade.[49]

The contradictory regulation and its inconsistent application repeatedly raised questions regarding the legal status of petty traders from the Russian Empire. Such uncertainties are reflected in short notices in the newspapers, which contain inquiries about whether specific traders are allowed to peddle in specific situations.[50] Occasionally, newspapers also contained short paragraphs on peddlers who had been arrested on suspicion of illegal trade. For instance, a group of Polish Jews from Stockholm, Lund, and Malmö, three of whom were Russian subjects, were arrested near Uppsala in 1901.[51] Likewise, Finnish newspapers regularly reported on detainments of Russian Karelian and Tatar peddlers.[52] If they were found guilty of illicit trade, the penalty was usually confiscation of their commodities and a fine.[53] Jewish traders in Finland, whose mobility was restricted the most, took a severe risk if they visited a fair outside their town of residence. If caught, they could in the worst case be banished from the Grand Duchy.[54]

At times, those who wrote opinion pieces for the newspapers urged the general public to denounce peddlers to the police if they suspected that their trade was illicit.[55] However, it was more common that they called for the authorities to take action. In 1885, merchants in Turku forced the local and regional authorities to apply the restrictions that the ordinances of 1858 and 1869 placed on Jewish petty trade.[56] Likewise, merchants in Gothenburg in 1900 notified the governor that Polish Jews were conducting large-scale illegal ambulatory trade in the Bohuslän archipelago.[57] The authorities were commonly criticized for their lax attitude toward even clearly illicit peddling and for shirking their responsibilities as guardians of law and order. In the Finnish coastal town of Kotka, local merchants in the 1880s and 1890s repeatedly complained about the "gross injustice" they witnessed, as the town authorities failed to banish Tatar traders from town like their colleagues in neighboring Hamina had done.[58] Similar complaints were expressed in other towns; for example, in an editorial letter to the local newspaper in 1892, merchants in Tammisaari provocatively asked how long the town administration intended to allow Tatars to wander from house to house, selling their "Russian rags and cloths."[59]

Moral and Sanitary Threats

Another set of threats that peddlers from Russia were said to pose can be described as moral and sanitary. The alleged tendency of peddlers to undermine the morality of their customers and cause sanitary problems has been observed in previous research on mobile trade. Disadvantages commonly associated with peddling include violent and dishonest behavior, the sale of harmful substances such as drugs or poison, and the spread of venereal and other diseases.[60]

While the Nordic press voiced all these threats, two in particular rise to the fore. The first emanated from a stereotypical and pejorative perception of petty trade conducted by ethnic groups, combined with an equally derogatory attitude toward the consumption of the lower classes. This ideological construct portrayed peddlers as dishonest people who lured customers into unnecessary consumption that harmed both their economic situation and morals.[61] Depictions of the encounter between local customers and ethnic sellers follow a staid pattern. Usually, a "stranger"—the trader from the outside—approaches, using his "well-oiled" and "cunning" tongue to attract the attention of a potential customer.[62] While descriptions of the peddlers' enticing oral skills can contain a degree of admiration, their trading practices are generally portrayed as persuasive and deluding. They were commonly reprimanded for utilizing a "strange" and insolent tactic, an "importunacy that can only be described as audacious," to force their goods onto the customer.[63] Occasionally, Jews and Tatars were even accused of accosting customers physically, dragging them into their stalls, or giving them a box on the ear if they refused to buy.[64] Allegations of physical violations are largely absent regarding the "Rucksack Russians," however, indicating the existence of a difference in attitudes toward the various groups of peddlers.

Another practice commonly associated with petty trade, and ethnicized petty trade in particular, was haggling.[65] The Nordic press portrayed Russian, Jewish, and Tatar traders as the most aggressive hagglers, thus revealing a kind of ranking. In 1886, a journalist in the newspaper *Göteborgs Handels- och Sjöfartstidning*, a mouthpiece for Swedish merchants, claimed that the recently arrived Jews had far exceeded the infamous Swedish peddlers from Västergötland with regard to aggressive haggling.[66] In Finland, in turn, an author in the newspaper *Sanomia Turusta* in 1874 complained that common people seemed to have adopted the "deplorable custom of haggling" that the "Rucksack Russians" had introduced.[67]

However, with the arrival of the Jews and the Tatars, the Finnish press increasingly associated aggressive haggling with the newcomers.[68] The pejorative attitude toward the trading practices was further projected onto the Russian peddlers' commodities, which were claimed to be fake and consisting of "all sorts of worthless rubbish" of "foreign" origin.[69]

The alleged harmful consequence of the peddlers' persuasive and fraudulent trading practices was that customers paid excessive prices for certain items, up to ten times more than their worth.[70] The poor customers, especially in rural regions, were lured to part with their scarce money for low-quality commodities that they did not even need.[71] In 1909, an author in the Finnish newspaper *Wiborgs Nyheter* claimed that fairs had turned into nothing more than occasions for mobile Tatars, Jews, and other petty traders to "deceive honest people."[72] While newspaper writers accused peddlers of having contributed to this development, they did not get the blame alone.[73] Responsibility was equally laid on the customers, who were described with derogatory rhetoric dealing in stereotypes and reflecting both class and gender distinctions. In detailed portrayals, the customer is often a "naïve," "unexperienced," and "uneducated" poor male from the countryside, who gets swindled due to his inexperience with the petty traders' persuasive trading practices.[74] Depictions of female customers, in turn, reflected clichéd perceptions of women as vain consumers.[75] In both cases, the customers were deemed too inexperienced to act in their own best interest. Newspapers therefore commonly issued warnings of peddlers who were on the move in a specific region, offering detailed descriptions of their allegedly predatory methods.[76]

The sanitary threat that peddlers from Russia were associated with became increasingly topical toward the end of the nineteenth century. The development of transport technology, combined with increasing mobility, made the authorities aware of the risk that epidemics could be spread through peddlers and other mobile groups.[77] In 1902, for instance, a provincial doctor in the Kronoberg county of Sweden urged the authorities to investigate whether the recent outbreak of a smallpox epidemic in the region could be traced to Russian saw grinders.[78]

Most commonly, the perception of a sanitary threat occurred in conjunction with recurring cholera epidemics that spread westward from the Russian interior, provoking fears all around Western Europe. When news about cholera outbreaks in Russia reached Finland, the authorities took action to prevent potential carriers of the disease from crossing the border into the Grand Duchy.[79] One such action was to restrict or cancel fairs, as peddlers with contacts to the affected areas were seen as possible vectors. In 1892, the Finnish Senate canceled several fairs in Finland, but turned down a petition made by the health board of Turku to cancel the town's autumn fair. Consequently, the board published announcements in the local newspapers, advising the public to refrain from buying anything from Tatars, Russians, and other traders from cholera-infested regions of Russia. Russian traders were expected to arrive in large numbers as usual, bringing with them leather goods, furs, and textiles that could contain contagious agents. Common people writing to the newspapers demanded that the items should not be allowed into town, or at least not until they had been thoroughly disinfected[80] (See Fig. 10.1).

Throughout the 1890s, health boards in several Finnish towns published similar announcements when cholera epidemics hit Russia, urging the public to avoid contact with "strangers, especially mobile traders"; the public was also warned of letting peddlers from Russia into their homes, and to inform the police if they tried to enter.[81] In this context, the threat that peddlers from Russia posed was further connected with allegations of poor hygiene. In an announcement published in the newspaper *Turun Lehti* in 1894, readers were warned of a group of Tatars, "dressed in untidy kaftans, carrying their filthy bags," who were roaming Turku.[82] Dirt—real or imagined—was typically associated with "the Other" in the late nineteenth century, and commonly used to justify exclusionary practices and ethnic class distinctions.[83]

The negative characterizations of the moral and sanitary harm that mobile Russians allegedly posed promoted the image of them as a threat that the Nordic societies had to fend off. In this context, the enemy image was primarily created by the authorities, who aimed to uphold law and order and hinder the spread of diseases. However, the image was at the same time highly compatible with the local merchants' ambitions to keep competing peddlers out by representing them in a negative light.

Political Threat

The third perceived threat reflected in the sources is political. In Finland, the political threat was closely related to the irreconcilable conflict between the Grand Duchy and the imperial central administration that characterized the last decades of the nineteenth century. While the Finns strove to preserve the Grand Duchy's autonomy, strengthening sentiments of imperial nationalism required that the Russian Empire's eastern borderlands be

Fig. 10.1 A crowded Helsinki marketplace during the annual autumn fish market. This area of the harbor was called "the Cholera Basin." In the 1890s, recurring cholera epidemics hit the Russian interior, evoking fears about contagious agents spreading the disease to Finland with itinerant traders and their goods. To prevent the spread of the epidemics, the authorities restricted or canceled fairs and markets, urging the public to avoid contact with peddlers from cholera-infested regions in Russia. (Photo by Carl Lundström, 10/11891. Helsinki City Museum)

tied closer to its core. This resulted in several Russification measures, aimed to streamline the Grand Duchy's administration and legislation with that of the empire.[84] In this process, Russian peddlers in Finland became "political tools," utilized by both Finnish and Russian ideologues to enforce their strategic goals. This occurred as early as the 1860s, when Russian nationalist circles accused Finnish officials of mistreating and persecuting Russian peddlers.[85] The conflict culminated in 1899, when Russia's February Manifesto formally revoked the Finnish autonomy that had gradually evolved since 1809. The manifesto evoked huge discontent in the Grand Duchy, giving rise to strong anti-Russian sentiments. Within weeks, the press reported that mobile Russians with malicious intentions—peddlers, knife grinders, castrators, rag and bristle collectors, and ice cream sellers—had been observed around Finland.[86]

The Finnish press accused mobile Russians of two main offenses. First, they were said to spread unfounded and subversive rumors among the rural poor, claiming that land was to be confiscated from landowners and given to the landless. These ideas stemmed from the Russian *mir*- and *obshchina* institutions.[87] Rumors of land division had circulated around the Russian Empire already earlier, including Finland, where they emerged in conjunction with heated debates on crofters and land ownership.[88] Second, peddlers were accused of collecting signatures for some sort of address thought to be a countermeasure to the Great Petition collected in Finland in defense of autonomy.[89] The press claimed that this allegedly "false" counter-address was to be presented to high-ranking officials in the empire's machinery of power, with the aim of conveying an erroneous impression of the political sentiments in Finland.[90]

In the press campaign that followed the issuing of the February Manifesto, mobile Russians were portrayed as "suspect" figures engaging in a shady and hostile mission to divide and undermine the Finnish society.[91] Allegedly, they sought to agitate the lower classes to revolt against the elite through misleading information, distorting the sense of justice of the most "defenseless," namely, the uneducated and children.[92] The peddlers were said to be operating on behalf of a "subversive band" of "foreign nationality," led by K. P. Pobedonostsev, Procurator of the Holy Synod and ideologue of Russian autocracy, and supported by Governor-General N. I. Bobrikov and his anti-Finnish regime.[93] Supposedly acting on the orders of anti-Finnish forces, peddlers were accused of being agitators, instigators, and spies, while their activities were likened to "mole work," a metaphor commonly used to depict persons engaged in underground missions with hostile intentions.[94] With other negatively charged metaphors, they were portrayed as "wretched creatures," "pushy parasites," "harmful weeds" or, in conjunction with the cholera threat, a "filthy drain" of people aiming to "contaminate" the Finnish nation.[95]

While mobile Russians had already previously been associated with various threats, the growing political tensions around 1900 made the rhetoric more aggressive. As censorship hardened, from the summer of 1900 the agitation moved to the Finnish underground press, which, according to Duncan Huxley, reveals a "more or less fanatical concern" with Russian peddlers.[96] The underground press represented the Finnish constitutionalists' strategy of passive resistance, which propagated a boycott of "all things Russian." The boycott encompassed peddlers, who were now portrayed as being increasingly politically motivated to destroy "all things sacred to the Finns": religion, language, and the ancestral social order.[97] Resistance writers claimed that the Russians sought to take over Finland altogether by undermining the Lutheran Church and the local school system on behalf of the Orthodox faith and the Russian language. A parallel was drawn to the Baltic provinces, where a similar tactic had already succeeded. Supported by Russian nationalists, peddlers there had allegedly managed to drive local merchants out of business, consequently settling down as shopkeepers to prepare ground for other Russians. The goal in Finland was said to be the same: after establishing roots, Russian shopkeepers would bring their families and employ more people from their home region. Eventually, the Russians would be so numerous as to require that Orthodox churches and Russian language schools be established.[98]

The political tensions in Finland were soon reflected in Sweden. The conflicts were reported in the Swedish press, as well as in a book by publicist Valfrid Spångberg, who followed the events in Finland in person in the spring of 1899.[99] Russia's tightening grip on Finland had raised concerns in Sweden, where patriotic circles viewed Russia as an aggressive power that sought to expand westward as if by a law of nature. From a military perspective, the expansion of the railway network on the Finnish side of the border was seen as a concrete manifestation of the expansionist ambitions. The question about the Swedish military's potential to withstand a possible Russian offensive became even more acute when the railway network, in 1886 already in Oulu (130 kilometers from Sweden), reached the border at Tornio in 1903.[100]

Speculations and rumors about mobile Russians soon began to spread in the Swedish press, however, taking on a slightly different form. In Sweden, it was the small group of saw grinders from the Novgorod Governorate that was suspected of conducting military espionage (see Fig. 10.2). Göran Rosander has estimated that they numbered only about 50 around 1900, increasing to a maximum of 300 in 1913.[101] From 1900, Swedish newspapers suddenly started to report observations of saw grinders from around the country, purportedly engaged in some sort of military activity, and allegedly carrying with them maps of Sweden, Norway, and Denmark. They were also reported to be making maps and drawings of communications and defensive structures.[102] The local authorities were urged to rigorously supervise the saw grinders, and to detain them in case

Fig. 10.2 From 1899 to the First World War, the Swedish press occasionally portrayed Russian saw grinders from the Novgorod Governorate as military spies in disguise. Approximately 150 saw grinders were detained and interrogated by the police. Research has shown that the false allegations were part of a political campaign that aimed at strengthening the military defense of Sweden. (Photo taken at police interrogations in Stockholm, Sweden. Stockholm City Archives)

there was reason to believe that the motive for their presence in Sweden involved some sort of subversive activity. Pia Karlsson has found 178 protocols of such hearings in Swedish police archives.[103]

Suspecting peddlers or other mobile persons of being military spies or agents was by no means unique to the Nordics. Espionage was a highly topical matter in Europe in the decades preceding the First World War, to such an extent that one could speak of "spy fever."[104] Several works on espionage, such as V. N. Klembovsky's *L'espionnage militaire en temps de paix et en temps de guerre* (1895) and Hamil Grant's *Spies and Secret Service* (1915), featured peddlers. It was commonly thought that intelligence services sent out military officers disguised as mobile traders to spy in hostile countries. Citing Klembovsky's work, in 1902 a Swedish author noted that it included illustrations of an officer drawing by his table and a Russian peddler offering his goods for sale, obviously establishing a connection between the two. The significance of Klembovsky's work, the author claimed, hardly needed to be stressed in Sweden, which had the "questionable pleasure of being so much frequented by saw grinders and other Russian 'craftsmen.'"[105] While the Finnish press did not state as explicitly as the Swedish press that peddlers might have been military spies, such references are found in other contexts.[106]

Modern research has found no evidence of Russian peddlers or saw grinders being involved in any organized political agitation or military intelligence. The press campaigns against them are explained rather by political tensions, which made mobile persons suitable "tools" in the hands of political factions with specific political aims. In the Finnish case, the proponents of passive resistance tried to create an image of the peddlers as enemies to strengthen their proposed boycott against "all things Russian." In a situation where armed resistance was not an option, a boycott was the best strategy they could conceive in defense of Finnish autonomy.[107] In the Swedish case, it was patriots arguing for a strengthening of the Swedish army against Russian expansionist ambitions that lay behind the campaign against Novgorodian saw grinders. Although their ambitions did not succeed, and despite the fact that the Swedish government denied early on that there was any truth to the allegations, warnings of saw grinders being military spies in disguise occasionally resurfaced in Swedish press until the First World War.[108] In both Finland and Sweden, the propaganda campaigns responded to a central mechanism in the creation of enemy images: in order to attain certain political goals, political ideologues constructed and utilized a caricature of a group with malicious intents.[109]

Conclusions

In this chapter, I have explored Nordic press portrayals of peddlers from the Russian Empire in the late nineteenth and early twentieth centuries. I have examined in which contexts "Rucksack Russians," Eastern Jews, Tatars, and Novgorodian saw grinders were perceived as a threat, the rhetoric used in expressing those threats, and the motives behind such expressions. The aim has been to disclose an aspect of reality that mobile Russians seeking a livelihood in the Nordics faced, as well as to illustrate the mechanisms through which enemy images were created.

The analyzed groups differed from the Nordic societies in varying degrees regarding geographical origin, ethnicity, appearance, and confession. The "Rucksack Russians" who originated from Russian Karelia were Orthodox Christians but ethnically and linguistically perceived as related to the Finns. The Jews and Tatars were newcomers on the trading scene, appearing in the region only in the 1860s. Their geographic origin was more distant, and they differed more from the local communities than the

"Rucksack Russians." Finally, the Novgorodian saw grinders were ethnic Russians. All four groups faced preconceived negative notions that partly arose from a general negative attitude toward the "barbaric" East and the Russian state as a military aggressor. Furthermore, the peddlers encountered prejudices related to ethnicity and religion. The Jews were affected by stereotypical anti-Semitic attitudes, while the Tatars experienced negative attitudes toward "Orientals."

The analysis shows that peddlers from Russia were depicted as a threat in economic, moral, sanitary, and political respects. In the economic context, they were primarily perceived as unfair competitors to local merchants, who blamed them for evading taxes and trading fees that they themselves had to pay. Peddlers were also blamed for demoralizing their local customers by luring them into buying low-quality or fake commodities through fraudulent trading practices. The sanitary threat, in turn, emanated from fears that mobile people might spread infectious diseases such as cholera. In the political context, finally, the peddlers and saw grinders were used as tools in the political ideology of Finnish constitutionalists and Swedish patriots aiming to strengthen the country's defense against Russian military aggression. Viewing the portrayals through the lens of an enemy image, it becomes obvious that the peddlers are not depicted as individuals but rather as representatives of a collective accused of hostile intentions. The collective was burdened by negatively charged characteristics described in a stereotypical and derogatory rhetoric.

The threats and complaints that appear in the sources mainly represent voices beyond the traders and their customers. They primarily emanate from local merchants, who viewed the peddlers as unfair competitors, authorities who sought to maintain order and offer security, and political actors. Consequently, they reveal little or nothing about the actual encounters between the peddlers and the common people or about the meanings that customers may have ascribed to the commodities that the peddlers sold. However, the very fact that peddling persisted—despite the enemy image created around it—indicates that demand for the mobile Russians' goods and services did exist. Despite the fact that the images conveyed by the press were highly ideological and stereotypical, it is an indisputable fact that they comprised part of the reality that mobile people from the Russian Empire faced when seeking a livelihood in the Nordics. Considering the role that the press had in shaping public opinion, it is also reasonable to assume that the images created in the newspapers to some degree affected attitudes toward them.

Notes

1. Spillmann and Spillmann 1997, pp. 50–51.
2. Fiebig-von Hase 1997, pp. 2–3; Eckhart 1989, pp. 11–12.
3. Runefelt 2011, pp. 205–206; Häkkinen 2005, pp. 226–227.
4. Trentmann 2016, pp. 37–39; Ahlberger 1996, p. 59.
5. See, e.g., Hammarström 2016, pp. 38–42; Iver B. Neumann. 1999. *Uses of the Other: "The East" in European Identity Formation.*
6. Sweden: tidningar.kb.se; Finland: digi.kansallisarkisto.fi.
7. Wassholm and Sundelin 2018b, p. 202.
8. Wassholm and Sundelin 2020, pp. 119–120.
9. Stark 2011, pp. 40–42; Fiebig-von Hase 1997, p. 14.
10. Pekka Nevalainen. 2016. *Kulkukauppiaista kauppaneuvoksiin. Itäkarjalaisten liiketoimintaa Suomessa*; Mervi Naakka-Korhonen. 1988. *Halpa hinta, pitkä mitta. Vienankarjalainen laukkukauppa*; Nils Storå, 1989. "Ostkarelische Wanderhändler als Kulturvermittler in Finnland"; Nils Storå, 1991. "'Rucksack Russians' in Finland: Peddling and Culture Contact"; Johanna Wassholm and Anna Sundelin, 2018a. "Emotions, trading practices and communication in transnational itinerant trade: Encounters between 'Rucksack Russians' and their customers in late nineteenth- and early twentieth-century Finland."
11. Jacqueline Stare. 1996. *Judiska gårdfarihandlare i Sverige*; Carl Henrik Carlsson. 2004. *Medborgarskap och diskriminering. Östjudar och andra invandrare i Sverige 1860–1920*; Per Hammarström. 2007. *Nationens styvbarn. Judisk samhällsintegration i några Norrlandsstäder 1870–1940*; Per Hammarström, 2015. "'Judar öfwersvämma landet.' Den judiska gårdfarihandeln i Kungl. Maj:ts befallningshavandes femårsberättelser 1865–1905"; Laura Katarina Ekholm, 2019. "Jews, Second-Hand Trade and Upward Economic Mobility: Introducing the Ready-to-Wear Business in Industrializing Helsinki, 1880–1930"; Johanna Wassholm, 2017. "Handel i marginalen. Den judiska småhandeln och lokalsamhället i Åbo i slutet av 1800-talet"; Johanna Wassholm, 2018. "Liikkuva kauppa ja kulttuurien kohtaaminen. Tataarien kulku- ja markkinakauppa Suomessa vuosina 1870–1920"; Johanna Wassholm, 2020. "Tatar Pedlars in the Grand Duchy of Finland in the Late Nineteenth Century"; Ainur Elmgrén, 2020. "Visual Stereotypes of Tatars in the Finnish Press from the 1890s to the 1910s."
12. Pia Karlsson 1998. "En officer och gentleman? De ryska sågfilarna och spionanklagelserna"; Åselius 1994, p. 72; Rodell 2008, pp. 93–94; Nerman 1946, pp. 216–219; Nilsson 1990, pp. 141–144.
13. Rosander 1980, pp. 21–22.
14. Hjerppe 1989, pp. 41–42; Honningdal Grytten and Minde 1997, p. 61.

15. Lundqvist 2008, pp. 19–20.
16. Nevalainen 2016, pp. 28–30; Rosander 1980, p. 66.
17. Nevalainen 2016, p. 84–85; Wassholm 2020, p. 16.
18. Brinkmann 2013, pp. 3–5; Lüthi 2013, p. 29.
19. Bredefeldt 1997, pp. 34–35.
20. Gjernes 2012, p. 148.
21. Ekholm 2019, pp. 77–79; Wassholm 2017, pp. 593–596.
22. *Åbo Tidning* 9/23/1885, p. 3. See also *Tammerfors Aftonblad* 9/8/1882, p. 2; *Kaiku* 7/28/1883, p. 2; *Satakunta* 9/12/1883, p. 3.
23. Baibulat 2004, p. 14; Leitzinger 1999, p. 25; Wassholm 2020, p. 14.
24. Rodell 2008, pp. 93–94.
25. Gjernes 2012, p. 147; Wassholm 2020, p. 14.
26. Storå 1989, p. 34.
27. Elmgrén 2020, pp. 27–29.
28. Carlsson 2004, pp. 141–142; Andersson 2000, pp. 256–259.
29. Lüthi 2013, pp. 29–31.
30. Kari Tarkiainen. 2017. *Moskoviten. Sverige och Ryssland 1478–1721*; Iver B. Neumann. 1999. *Uses of the Other: "The East" in European Identity Formation.*
31. Thaden 1981, pp. 76–88.
32. Åselius 1994, p. 72.
33. Brinkmann 2013, p. 6; Hjerppe 1989, pp. 81–82; Rodell 2008, pp. 93–94.
34. Wassholm 2020, pp. 13–14.
35. Jussila 2004, pp. 453–458; Polvinen 1995, p. 171; Tommila 1999, pp. 255–256.
36. Carlsson 2013, pp. 57–58.
37. Lindberg 2018, pp. 207–209; Wassholm and Sundelin 2018b, p. 199.
38. *Smålandsposten* 2/16/1886, p. 2; *Höganäs Tidning* 1/17/1899, p. 2; *Ny Tid* 12/14/1900, p. 3; *Östgöten* 1/11/1902, p. 4.
39. Lindberg 2018, pp. 215–218.
40. Jakobsson 1951, pp. 197–199.
41. *Aura* 1/17/1885, p. 1.
42. Jakobsson 1951, p. 202; Seela 2005, pp. 10–11.
43. *Aura* 1/20/1885, p. 2; 5/28/1885, p. 2.
44. The question was connected to national politics and reflected the anti-Semitic rhetoric expressed in the recurring parliamentary debates regarding Jewish citizenship rights. Jews could not acquire citizenship in Finland until 1918. Torvinen 1989, pp. 50–51; Jakobsson 1951, pp. 197–200.
45. *Smålandsposten* 2/16/1886, p. 2; *Helsingborgs Dagblad* 6/8/1886, p. 2.
46. Carlsson 2004, pp. 134–144.
47. *Korrespondenten* 5/3/1888, p. 2; *Trelleborgstidningen* 8/21/1897, p. 2.

48. Hammarström 2007, p. 111.
49. *Granskaren* 6/14/1890, p. 1.
50. Wassholm 2020, p. 16.
51. *Tidning för Skaraborgs Län* 1/18/1901, p. 3.
52. *Hämeen Sanomat* 12/7/1886, p. 2; *Päivälehti* 5/4/1898, p. 4; *Kotka* 4/14/1898, p. 3.
53. *Jämtlandsposten* 8/1/1902, p. 4; *Wasa Tidning* 4/7/1898, p. 2; *Wiipuri* 1/1/1911, p. 3.
54. Petterberg-Möntti 2001, p. 86.
55. *Fäderneslandet* 8/22/1860, p. 2; *Figaro* 6/2/1888, p. 2.
56. *Aura* 1/20/1885, p. 2; 5/28/1885, p. 2.
57. *Ny Tid* 12/14/1900, p. 3; *Sydsvenska Dagbladet Snällposten* 12/17/1900, p. 2.
58. *Kotka* 7/25/1885, p. 3; 4/24/1886, p. 3; 12/1/1892, p. 2; *Kotkan Sanomat* 11/29/1892, p. 2. For similar complaints in other towns, see *Åbo Underrättelser* 12/10/1898, p. 2; *Perä-Pohjolainen* 8/20/1898, p. 4.
59. *Vestra Nyland* 9/23/1892, p. 3.
60. Lindberg 2018, pp. 224–226; Runefelt 2011, pp. 207–209.
61. Trentmann 2016, pp. 27–39; Ahlberger 1996, p. 59.
62. *Wasa Tidning* 3/22/1885, p. 2; *Helsingborgs Dagblad* 6/8/1886, p. 2; *Figaro* 6/2/1888, p. 2; *Åbo Underrättelser* 10/3/1893, p. 2.
63. *Hufvudstadsbladet* 10/1/1886, p. 2. See also *Kotka* 7/25/1885, p. 3; *Åbo Underrättelser* 10/2/1892, p. 2; *Höganäs Tidning* 1/17/1899, p. 2.
64. *Borgåbladet* 1/26/1884, pp. 1–2; *Tampere* 9/6/1884, p. 3.
65. Geertz 1963, pp. 32–33; Ekholm 2013, p. 91.
66. *Göteborgs Handels- och Sjöfartstidning* 4/30/1886.
67. *Sanomia Turusta* 9/11/1874, p. 1. See also *Turun Lehti* 9/22/1888, p. 2.
68. *Helsingfors* 6/16/1882, p. 2; *Turun Lehti* 9/22/1888, p. 2; *Björneborgs Tidning* 10/13/1888, p. 2.
69. *Fäderneslandet* 8/22/1860, p. 2; *Aura* 11/10/1885, p. 3. *Smålandsposten* 2/16/1886, p. 2; *Helsingborgs Dagblad* 6/8/1886, p. 2; *Figaro* 6/2/1888, p. 2; *Avesta Tidning* 10/17/1884, p. 3; *Granskaren* 6/14/1890, p. 1.
70. *Folkwännen* 7/2/1883, pp. 2–3; *Norra Posten* 10/31/1888, p. 3; *Turun Lehti* 9/22/1888, p. 2.
71. *Höganäs Tidning* 1/17/1899, p. 2.
72. *Wiborgs Nyheter* 3/6/1909, p. 2.
73. *Fäderneslandet* 8/22/1860, p. 2; *Avesta Tidning* 10/17/1884, p. 3; *Kotka* 7/25/1885, p. 3; 4/24/1886, p. 3; *Helsingborgs Dagblad* 6/8/1866, p. 2; *Figaro* 6/2/1888, p. 2.
74. *Tampere* 9/6/1884, p. 3.
75. Trentmann 2016, pp. 37–39.

76. *Fyris* 1/22/1883, p. 2; *Åbo Underrättelser* 12/10/1896, p. 1; *Vestra Nyland* 10/15/1897, p. 3.
77. Lüthi 2013, pp. 37–39.
78. *Hultfreds Tidning* 4/8/1902, p. 2.
79. Pesonen 1980, pp. 382–383; Nygård 2004, pp. 214–216; Wassholm 2018, pp. 225–227.
80. *Åbo Underrättelser* 9/14/1892, p. 2; *Turun Lehti* 8/25/1894, pp. 2–3.
81. *Hämäläinen* 9/23/1893, p. 1; 9/27/1893, p. 3; *Vestra Nyland* 10/3/1893, p. 2; *Ekenäs Tidning* 10/7/1893, p. 2; *Turun Lehti* 8/25/1894, pp. 2–3.
82. *Turun Lehti* 8/25/1894, pp. 2–3. For an association with dirt, see also *Östra Finland* 9/7/1892, p. 3.
83. Masquelier 2005, pp. 6–7; Häkkinen 2005, pp. 226–227.
84. Thaden 1981, pp. 76–88.
85. Jussila 2004, pp. 453–458.
86. Wassholm and Sundelin 2018a, p. 133; Tommila 1999, pp. 248–250; Naakka-Korhonen 1988, pp. 177–181.
87. *Laatokka* 4/5/1899, p. 2; Spångberg 1899, pp. 122–124.
88. Suodenjoki 2010, p. 97.
89. Tommila 1999, pp. 247–249.
90. *Västra Finland* 3/15/1899, p. 1; *Wasa Nyheter* 5/7/1899, p. 3; *Wasabladet* 4/11/1899, p. 2.
91. See f.ex. *Wasa Nyheter* 5/7/1899, p. 3; *Wasabladet* 4/11/1899, p. 2; *Vestra Nyland* 4/21/1899, p. 2; *Kristinestads Tidning* 9/29/1900, p. 2.
92. *Vestra Nyland* 4/21/1899, p. 2. See also *Tampereen Sanomat* 4/11/1899, p. 3; *Wiborgs Nyheter* 4/22/1899, p. 3.
93. See, e.g., *Åbo Tidning* 3/14/1899, p. 1; *Kotka Nyheter* 3/18/1899, p. 3; *Laatokka* 4/5/1899, p. 2; *Upprop till fosterlandets försvar*, p. 6; *Aftonbladet* 8/18/1900, p. 2.
94. *Västra Finland* 3/15/1899, p. 1; *Laatokka* 4/5/1899, p. 2; *Kristinestads Tidning* 9/29/1900, p. 2.
95. *Laatokka* 4/5/1899, p. 2; *Västra Finland* 3/15/1899, p. 1; *Kotkan Uutiset* 4/23/1899, p. 1.
96. Huxley 1990, p. 169.
97. *Upprop till fosterlandets försvar*, p. 2.
98. *Aftonbladet* 8/18/1900, p. 2; Homén 1906, pp. 11–12. On Russification measures in the Baltic provinces, see Thaden 1981, pp. 33–75.
99. Valfrid Spångberg. 1899. *Statskuppen i Finland 1899.*
100. Åselius 1994, pp. 70–71.
101. Rosander 1980, p. 66.

102. *Folkets Tidning* 1/13/1900, p. 3; *Fäderneslandet* 1/20/1900, p. 2; *Engelholms Tidning* 7/5/1900, p. 2; *Hudiksvalls Nyheter* 11/5/1900, p. 2.
103. Karlsson 1998, p. 145.
104. David French, 1978. "Spy Fever in Britain, 1900–1915."
105. *Göteborgs Aftonblad* 4/12/1902, p. 2. See also *Göteborgs Aftonblad* 3/3/1900, p. 1.
106. Gripenberg 1922, pp. 81–82; Parmanen 1936, p. 266.
107. Polvinen 1995, p. 170.
108. *Dalpilen* 4/22/1913, p. 2; *Provinstidningen Dalsland* 5/10/1913, p. 3; *Söderhamns Tidning* 8/27/1913, p. 4; *Östgötaposten* 3/13/1914, p. 2; *Trelleborgstidningen* 5/4/1914, p. 3.
109. Eckhart 1989, pp. 11–12; Fiebig-von Hase 1997, pp. 2–3.

Bibliography

Archival Sources

The Archives of the Swedish Literature Society, Helsinki.
Upprop till fosterlandets försvar.

Published Sources

Newspapers

Aftonbladet, 1900.
Aura, 1885.
Avesta Tidning, 1884.
Björneborgs Tidning, 1888.
Borgåbladet, 1884.
Dalpilen, 1913.
Engelholms Tidning, 1900.
Figaro, 1888.
Folkets Tidning, 1900.
Folkwännen, 1883.
Fyris, 1882.
Fäderneslandet, 1860, 1900.
Granskaren, 1890.
Göteborgs Aftonblad, 1900, 1902.

Göteborgs Handels- och Sjöfartstidning, 1886.
Helsingborgs Dagblad, 1866, 1886.
Helsingfors, 1882.
Hufvudstadsbladet, 1886.
Hudiksvalls Nyheter, 1900.
Hultfreds Tidning, 1902.
Hämeen Sanomat, 1886.
Höganäs Tidning, 1899.
Jämtlandsposten, 1902.
Kaiku, 1883.
Korrespondenten, 1888.
Kotka, 1885, 1898.
Kotkan Sanomat, 1892.
Kotka Nyheter, 1899.
Kotkan Uutiset, 1899.
Kristinestads Tidning, 1900.
Laatokka, 1899.
Norra Posten,1888.
Ny Tid, 1900.
Provinstidningen Dalsland, 1913.
Päivälehti, 1898.
Sanomia Turusta, 1874.
Satakunta, 1883.
Smålandsposten, 1886.
Sydsvenska Dagbladet Snällposten, 1900.
Tammerfors Aftonblad, 1882.
Tampere, 1884.
Tampereen Sanomat, 1884, 1899.
Tidning för Skaraborgs Län, 1901.
Trelleborgstidningen, 1897, 1914.
Turun Lehti, 1894, 1888, 1906.
Vestra Nyland, 1892, 1893, 1897, 1899.
Västra Finland, 1899.
Wasabladet, 1899.
Wasa Nyheter, 1899.
Wasa Tidning, 1885, 1898.
Wiipuri, 1911.
Wiborgs Nyheter, 1899, 1909.
Åbo Tidning, 1885, 1899.
Åbo Underrättelser, 1892, 1893, 1896.
Östgötaposten, 1914.
Östgöten, 1902.

Literature

Ahlberger, Christer. *Konsumtionsrevolutionen. Om det moderna konsumtionssamhällets framväxt 1750–1900.* Göteborg: Göteborgs universitet, 1996.

Andersson, Lars M. *En jude är en jude är en jude ... Representationer av 'juden' i svensk skämtpress omkring 1900–1930.* Lund: Nordic Academic Press, 2000.

Åselius, Gunnar. *The "Russian Menace" to Sweden: The Belief System of a Small Power Security Élite in the Age of Imperialism.* Stockholm Studies in History 51. Stockholm: Almqvist & Wiksell International, 1994.

Baibulat, Muazzez. *Tampereen Islamilainen Seurakunta: juuret ja historia.* Tampere: Tampereen Islamilainen Seurakunta, 2004.

Bredefeldt, Rita. "Ekonomi och identitet: de svenska judarnas ekonomiska verksamheter och självbild från 1800-talets andra hälft till 1930." *Nordisk judaistik/Scandinavian Jewish Studies* 18, no. 1–2 (1997): 22–49. https://doi.org/10.30752/nj.6953.

Brinkmann, Tobias. "Points of Passage: Reexamining Jewish Migrations from Eastern Europe after 1880." In *Points of Passage: Jewish Migrants from Eastern Europe in Scandinavia, Germany, and Britain 1880–1914*, edited by Tobias Brinkmann, 1–23. New York: Berghahn Books, 2013.

Carlsson, Carl Henrik. *Medborgarskap och diskriminering. Östjudar och andra invandrare i Sverige 1860–1920.* Studia Historica Upsaliensia 215. Uppsala: Uppsala universitet, 2004.

Carlsson, Carl Henrik. "Immigrants or Transmigrants? Eastern European Jews in Sweden, 1860–1914." In *Points of Passage. Jewish Migrants from Eastern Europe in Scandinavia, Germany, and Britain 1880–1914*, edited by Tobias Brinkmann, 47–62. New York: Berghahn Books, 2013.

Eckhart, William. "Making and Breaking Enemy Images." *Peace Research* 21, no. 4 (1989): 11–16.

Ekholm, Laura. *Boundaries of an Urban Minority: The Helsinki Jewish Community from the End of Imperial Russia until the 1970s.* Helsinki: Helsinki University, 2013.

Ekholm, Laura Katarina. "Jews, Second-Hand Trade and Upward Economic Mobility: Introducing the Ready-to-Wear Business in Industrializing Helsinki, 1880–1930." *Business History* 61, no. 1 (2019): 73–92. DOI: 10.1080/00076791.2018.1546694.

Elmgrén, Ainur. "Visual Stereotypes of Tatars in the Finnish Press from the 1890s to the 1910s." *Studia Orientalia Electronica* 8, no. 2 (2020): 25–39. https://doi.org/10.23993/store.82942.

Fiebig-von Hase, Ragnhild. "Introduction." In *Enemy Images in American History*, edited by Ragnhild Fiebig-von Hase and Ursula Lehmkuhl, 1–40. Providence: Berghahn, 1997.

French, David. "Spy Fever in Britain, 1900–1915." *The Historical Journal* 21, no. 2 (1978): 355–370.

Geertz, Clifford. *Peddlers and Princes: Social Development and Economic Change in Two Indonesian Towns*. Chicago: University of Chicago Press, 1963.

Gjernes, Marta. "Uldjøder, tøyjøder og klesjøder. Jødar i norsk varehandel 1851–1940." *Heimen* 49 (2012): 146–162.

Grant, Hamil. *Spies and Secret Service: The Story of Espionage, Its Main Systems and Chief Exponents*. London: Grant Richards Ltd., 1915.

Gripenberg, Lennart. *Ur mina levnadsminnen*. Helsingfors: Söderström, 1922.

Hammarström, Per. *Nationens styvbarn. Judisk samhällsintegration i några Norrlandsstäder 1870–1940*. Stockholm: Carlsson, 2007.

Hammarström, Per. "'Judar öfwersvämma landet.' Den judiska gårdfarihandeln i Kungl. Maj:ts befallningshavandes femårsberättelser 1865–1905." In *Den nya staten: ideologi och samhällsförändring kring sekelskiftet 1900*, edited by Erik Nydahl and Jonas Harvard, 25–50. Lund: Nordic Academic Press, 2016.

Hjerppe, Riitta. *The Finnish Economy 1860–1985: Growth and Structural Change*. Helsinki: Bank of Finland, 1989.

Homén, Theodor. *Passiivinen vastarintamme: politillisia kirjoituksia 1899–1904*. Helsinki: Otava, 1906.

Honningdal Grytten, Ola, and Kjell Bjørn Minde. "Konsum og levestandard under industrialiseringen i Norge. Endringer i kjøpekraft og privat konsum 1850–1920." In *Kultur och konsumtion i Norden 1750–1950*, edited by Johan Söderberg and Lars Magnusson, 71–81. Helsingfors: Finska Historiska samfundet, 1997.

Huxley, Steven Duncan. *Constitutionalist Insurgency in Finland: Finnish "Passive Resistance" against Russification as a Case of Nonmilitary Struggle in the European Resistance Tradition*. Helsinki: Suomen Historiallinen Seura, 1990.

Häkkinen, Antti. "Kiertäminen, kulkeminen ja muukalaisuuden kohtaaminen 1800-luvun lopun ja 1900-luvun alun maalaisyhteisössä." In *Vieraat kulkijat – tutut talot. Näkökulmia etnisyyden ja köyhyyden historiaan Suomessa*, eds. Antti Häkkinen, Panu Pulma and Miika Tervonen, 225–262. Helsinki: SKS, 2005.

Jakobsson, Santeri. *Taistelu ihmisoikeuksista. Yhteiskunnallis-historiallinen tutkimus Ruotsin ja Suomen juutalaiskysymyksen vaiheista*. Jyväskylä: Gummerus, 1951.

Jussila, Osmo. *Suomen suuriruhtinaskunta 1809–1917*. Helsinki: WSOY, 2004.

Karlsson, Pia. "En officer och gentleman? De ryska sågfilarna och spionanklagelserna." In *Bröd och salt. Svenska kulturkontakter med öst*, edited by Roger Gyllin, Ingvar Svanberg and Ingmar Söhrman, 144–165. Uppsala: Uppsala universitet, 1998.

Leitzinger, Antero. "Tataarit Suomessa." In *Muslimit Suomessa*, edited by Tuula Sakaranaho and Heikki Pesonen, 25–58. Helsinki: Helsinki University Press, 1999.

Lindberg, Hanna. "'I händerna på arkangeliter, judar och andra schackrare.' Debatten om gårdfarihandel på Finlands lantdag 1877–1878." *Historisk Tidskrift för Finland* 103, no. 2 (2018): 205–230. https://journal.fi/htf/article/view/69230.

Lundqvist, Pia. *Marknad på väg. Den västgötska gårdfarihandeln 1790–1864.* Avhandlingar från historiska institutionen i Göteborg 52. Göteborg: Göteborgs universitet, 2008.

Lüthi, Barbara. "Germs of Anarchy, Crime, Disease and Degeneracy: Jewish Migration to the United States and the Medicalization of European Borders around 1900." In *Points of Passage: Jewish Migrants from Eastern Europe in Scandinavia, Germany, and Britain 1880–1914*, edited by Tobias Brinkmann, 27–44. New York: Berghahn Books, 2013.

Masquelier, Adeline. "Dirt, Undress, and Difference: An Introduction." In *Dirt, Undress, and Difference: Critical Perspectives on the Body's Surface*, edited by Adeline Masquelier, 1–34. Bloomington and Indianapolis: Indiana University Press, 2005.

Mikkola, Kati, and Laura Stark. "Himotut ja halveksitut kulutustarvikkeet: uusien kulutustottumusten vaikutukset suomalaisiin maalaisyhteisöihin 1800-luvun loppupuolella ja 1900-luvun alussa." *Historiallinen Aikakauskirja* 107, no. 1 (2009): 4–17.

Naakka-Korhonen, Mervi. *Halpa hinta, pitkä mitta. Vienankarjalainen laukkukauppa.* Helsinki: SKS, 1988.

Nerman, Ture. *Svensk och ryss. Ett umgänge i krig och handel.* Stockholm: Saxon & Lindströms Förlag, 1946.

Neumann, Iver B. *Uses of the Other: "The East" in European Identity Formation.* Minneapolis: Minnesota University Press, 1999.

Nevalainen, Pekka. *Kulkukauppiaista kauppaneuvoksiin. Itäkarjalaisten liiketoimintaa Suomessa.* Helsinki: SKS, 2016.

Nilsson, Sture. *Rysskräcken i Sverige. Fördomar och verklighet.* Örebro: Samspråk, 1990.

Nygård, Henry. *Bara ett ringa obehag? Avfall och renhållning i de finländska städernas profylaktiska strategier 1830–1930.* Åbo: Åbo Akademis förlag, 2004.

Parmanen, Eino I. *Taistelujen kirja: kuvauksia itsenäisyystaistelumme vaiheista sortovuosina. I Osa: Routakauden puhkeaminen ja sen ensimmäiset vuodet.* Porvoo et al.: Werner Söderström Osakeyhtiö, 1936.

Pesonen, Niilo. *Terveyden puolesta – sairautta vastaan. Terveyden- ja sairaanhoito Suomessa 1800- ja 1900-luvulla.* Porvoo Helsinki Juva: Werner Söderström Osakeyhtiö, 1980.

Petterberg-Möntti, Teija. "'Vieraita' Viipurin kaupungissa: saksalaiset ja juutalaiset." Viipurin Suomalaisen Kirjallisuusseuran Toimitteita 13, 78–90. Helsinki: VSKS, 2001.

Polvinen, Tuomo. *Imperial Borderland. Bobrikov and the Attempted Russification of Finland 1898–1904.* Durham, NC: Duke University Press, 1995.

Rodell, Magnus. "Fallna svenskar och fortifikationer i vildmarken – om det ryska hotet och medielandskapet kring 1900." In *Berättande i olika medier*, edited by Leif Dahlberg and Pelle Snickars, 79–115. Stockholm: Statens ljud och bildarkiv, 2008.

Rosander, Göran. *Gårdfarihandel i Norden. En översikt av en gammal handelsform*, Stockholm: LT Förlag, 1980.

Runefelt, Leif. *En idyll försvarad. Ortsbeskrivningar, herrgårdskultur och den gamla samhällsordningen 1800–1860.* Stockholm: Sekel Bokförlag, 2011.

Seela, Jacob. "Juutalaisia kaupustelijoita ja kauppiaita 1800-luvun Turussa." *HaKehila* 2 (2005): 9–12.

Spillmann, Kurt R., and Kati Spillmann. "Some Sociobiological and Psychological Aspects of 'Images of the Enemy.'" In *Enemy Images in American History*, edited by Ragnhild Fiebig-von Hase and Ursula Lehmkuhl, 43–63. Providence, RI: Berghahn, 1997.

Spångberg, Valfrid. *Statskuppen i Finland 1899.* Ur det moderna samhällslifvet 19. Stockholm: Albert Bonniers Förlag, 1899.

Stare, Jacqueline (ed.). 1996. *Judiska gårdfarihandlare i Sverige.* Stockholm: Judiska museet, 1996.

Stark, Laura. *The Limits of Patriarchy: How Female Networks of Pilfering and Gossip sparked the First Debates on Rural Gender Rights in the 19th-Century Finnish-Language Press.* Helsinki: Finnish Literature Society, 2011.

Storå, Nils. "Ostkarelische Wanderhändler als Kulturvermittler in Finnland." *Jahrbuch für Volkskunde und Kulturgeschichte* 32 (1989): 34–43.

Storå, Nils. "'Rucksack Russians' in Finland: Peddling and Culture Contact." *Ethnologia Scandinavica* 21 (1991): 74–96.

Suodenjoki, Sami. *Kuriton suutari ja kiistämisen rajat. Työväenliikkeen läpimurto hämäläisessä maalaisyhteisössä 1899–1909.* Helsinki: Suomalaisen Kirjallisuuden Seura, 2010.

Söderberg, Johan, and Lars Magnusson. "Inledning." In *Kultur och konsumtion i Norden 1750–1950*, edited by Johan Söderberg and Lars Magnusson, 7–18. Helsingfors: Finska Historiska Samfundet, 1997.

Tarkiainen, Kari. *Moskoviten. Sverige och Ryssland 1478–1721.* SSLS 818. Helsingfors: Svenska litteratursällskapet i Finland, 2017.

Thaden, Edward C. "The Russian Government." In *Russification in the Baltic Provinces and Finland, 1855–1914*, edited by Edward C. Thaden, 15–108. Princeton, NJ: Princeton University Press, 1981.

Tommila, Päiviö. *Suuri adressi.* Porvoo: WSOY, 1999.

Torvinen, Taimi. *Kadimah. Suomen juutalaisten historia.* Helsinki: Otava, 1989.

Trentmann, Frank. *Empire of Things: How We Became a World of Consumers, from the Fifteenth Century to the Twenty-First.* London: Allen Lane, 2016.

Wassholm, Johanna. "Handel i marginalen. Den judiska småhandeln och lokalsamhället i Åbo i slutet av 1800-talet." *Historisk Tidskrift för Finland* 102, no. 4 (2017): 589–617. https://journal.fi/htf/article/view/70363.

Wassholm, Johanna. "Liikkuva kauppa ja kulttuurien kohtaaminen. Tataarien kulku- ja markkinakauppa Suomessa vuosina 1870–1920." In *Sattumalta Suomessa*, edited by Marko Lamberg, Ulla Piela and Hanna Snellman. Kalevalaseuran vuosikirja 97, 215–232. Helsinki: Suomalaisen Kirjallisuuden Seura, 2018.

Wassholm, Johanna. "Tatar Pedlars in the Grand Duchy of Finland in the Late Nineteenth Century." *Studia Orientalia Electronica* 8, no. 2 (2020): 8–24. DOI: 10.23993/store.83460.

Wassholm, Johanna, and Anna Sundelin. "Emotions, trading practices and communication in transnational itinerant trade: encounters between 'Rucksack Russians' and their customers in late nineteenth- and early twentieth-century Finland." *Scandinavian Economic History Review* 66, no. 2 (2018a): 132–152. https://doi.org/10.1080/03585522.2018.1466725.

Wassholm, Johanna, and Anna Sundelin. "Småskalig handel på glidande skalor." *Historisk Tidskrift för Finland* 103, no. 2 (2018b): 191–204. https://journal.fi/htf/article/view/74542.

Wassholm, Johanna, and Anna Sundelin. "Gendered encounters in mobile trade: human hair as a commodity in the Nordics, 1870–1914." *History of Retailing and Consumption* 6, no. 2 (2020): 118–136. https://doi.org/10.1080/2373518X.2020.1859927.

CHAPTER 11

Respectable and Masculine Livelihoods: Roma Stories of Horse Trading

Jutta Ahlbeck

This chapter examines the livelihoods of Finnish Roma/"Gypsies" (Finnish Kaale[1]) by looking at strategies of survival and economic practices at a time when Roma primarily supported themselves through itinerant trade. In so doing, I analyze interviews with Roma from the late 1990s that deal with memories of market trade and peddling from the 1920s and onwards. Although research on Roma in the social sciences and the humanities is extensive, often addressing the negative and racist views held by the majority population, Roma's means of subsistence, particularly from the viewpoint of the people themselves, have received little attention.[2] This dilemma of not finding Roma voices pertains especially to historical explorations, which can be partly explained by the oral tradition of Romani people, but also by the majority's seeming disinterest in Roma's narratives. However, anthropological research has explored contemporary settings, Roma livelihoods and experiences, offering important themes,

J. Ahlbeck (✉)
Culture, History and Philosophy, Åbo Akademi University, Turku, Finland
e-mail: jutta.ahlbeck@abo.fi

J. Ahlbeck et al. (eds.), *Encounters and Practices of Petty Trade in Northern Europe, 1820–1960*,
https://doi.org/10.1007/978-3-030-98080-1_11

and underlining Roma's innovative trading strategies and specialized skills.[3]

I will focus on how Roma's itinerant trade, especially horse trading practiced by men, has been recollected and narrated. I underline performativity in economic practices when investigating how gender and notions of respectability operated in narratives of horse trading, and how the construction of a masculine (Roma) self was taking place in certain spatial realms, like the marketplace. This chapter follows Michel de Certeau's conceptualization of space and tactics in two ways.[4] First, I look at how a particular space and economic practices were narrated ("spatial stories"); second, I highlight performative tactics in Roma livelihoods as forms of resistance. These livelihoods were discredited by society, the majority population, and not regarded as decent livelihoods—or rather as not even livelihoods at all. I argue that stories of successful and honest horse trading reflect struggles for those in disfavored social positions to gain respect and value. Drawing on Beverley Skegg's notion of gender and respectability,[5] I suggest that Roma masculinity is constructed in relation to respectability and, concomitantly, respectability is gendered as masculine.

Since the Roma as an ethnic group[6] have been marginalized and often stigmatized, I will address issues of power and agency in relation to Roma livelihoods. Considering the subjugated position of Roma in Finnish society, it is relevant to trace the economic strategies Roma have employed to make a living, and to explore how the Roma minority mobilized social, cultural, and economic resources in a context of vulnerability, dependence, and financial insecurity. I suggest that Roma voices and experiences can be understood as subjugated knowledges and counter-narratives, enacting creative resistance to structures upholding their subordination.

Dishonest Livelihoods: A Problematic Master Narrative

The Finnish Kaale are a Roma population living in Finland and officially recognized as a traditional minority in the country.[7] The Kaale community in Finland dates to the beginning of the sixteenth century, when Finland was part of Sweden.[8] At present, there are approximately 10,000 Kaale living in Finland, and 3000 more in Sweden. Today, the Finnish Roma comprise a sedentary population, living mainly in cities in southern Finland. Unlike many of the Roma communities in Eastern Europe, who speak a variant of the Romani language, most Finnish Roma speak Finnish as their mother tongue. The use of the Finnish Romani language among the Kaale (henceforth Roma) has deteriorated greatly over centuries of forced assimilation attempts and interventions by the Finnish state.[9]

Scholars in the field have demonstrated how industrialization, rural migration, urbanization, the wars, and later assimilation and housing policies led the Finnish Roma to abandon their itinerant lives and livelihoods from the 1940s onwards.[10] As a consequence of major societal changes, traditional Roma livelihoods, like itinerant trade, slowly came to an end in the 1950s–1960s. Still in the 1950s, after the Second World War, horses were needed in the reconstruction, particularly in forestry in eastern and northern Finland. However, cars, tractors, and buses were slowly replacing horses as means of transportation and in agricultural work. The mechanization of agriculture and modernization of transportation resulted in a diminishing need for work horses (for both the peasantry and Roma). This drastically affected Roma livelihoods, as horse trading was one of the most important means of sustenance. In the 1960s–1970s, the state initiated so-called "Roma social policies," with the aim of assimilating and integrating Roma into mainstream society. Housing and educational policies were seen as crucial in integrating Roma and urging them to abandon their mobile lifestyle.[11] Today, Finnish Roma continue to practice what is recognized (by the Roma community and the majority) as age-old customs, purity rituals, and community norms that differ from those of contemporary Finnish society, such as specific dress codes (especially for women), age, kinship and gender hierarchies, and particular sexual taboos. All these elements have been argued to constitute reasons for continued marginalization by mainstream Finnish society.[12]

When tracing Roma livelihoods in the late nineteenth century and the first half of the twentieth century, there are two interconnected research-related and ethical problems. First, it is difficult to find sources that explicitly deal with Roma livelihoods, and second, the sources and materials are very biased and produced by the majority population, not by Roma themselves. As I turned to public writings at the turn of the nineteenth century, it became quite clear that the majority did not regard the trade and commerce that Roma families pursued as legitimate livelihoods or "normal" work, but as shenanigans and disguised begging. Late nineteenth-century newspaper articles identified "the Gypsy" as devious, lazy, and incompetent, as seen in the following (1895):

> In the villages, women acquire money by fortune-telling, stealing, etc. The men do mostly nothing, but they always take care of the money earned. In horse trading, exchange and theft, the gypsies have achieved surprising skills. To make their horses beautiful, they give them arsenic and alum. At times, someone may pursue farming, yet it always leads to bad results. Some gypsy women do needlework, whereby they exhibit laces and ribbons as proofs. Generally, gypsies foster great contempt toward any systematic work.[13]

Besides ethnic otherness, one of the biggest concerns surrounding Roma involved their mobile lifestyle, which was related to assumed criminality and dishonesty. The discourse on "the Gypsy" as a criminal and vagrant, avoiding "decent work" at any cost, can be traced back to the vagrancy legislation in the nineteenth century and the so-called "Gypsy Question." During this period, Finland, like other European countries, initiated various vagrancy laws, particularly targeting itinerant gypsies, equating all gypsies with vagrants. In addition, "gypsy clauses" led gypsies to be punished more severely than other vagrants.[14]

The condescending view regarding Roma and their economic activities correspond with Anton Blok's notion of "infamous" or "pariah occupations,"[15] or even worse, as Roma livelihoods were not regarded as "occupations." A deeply embedded master narrative, the view of "the Gypsy" as unreliable and not cut out for regular (agricultural) work recurred in newspaper texts. To paraphrase Stuart Hall, this narrative unfolded the "Spectacle of the Other",[16] in which the majority population had the prerogative and power to define the "spectacle." Postcolonial scholars and critical race theorists have defined a master narrative, like the one of "the Gypsy," as "an all-encompassing and authoritative account of some aspect of social reality that is widely accepted and endorsed by the larger society."[17] The discourse on "the Gypsy" had gained societal authority by its cultural acceptance through mechanisms of social, political, and institutional structures of power.[18] Thus, these sources were problematic, as they were prejudiced, and Roma's own interpretations and narratives were missing.

Interviews and Nostalgic Narration

To find Roma narratives of livelihoods, I turned to a collection of interviews with Finnish Roma, conducted by Roma activists and collected by the Finnish Literature Society (Suomalaisen Kirjallisuuden Seura/SKS) in 1998–2000. These interviews are part of a larger collection, consisting of approximately 200 interviews, transcribed, and archived in the SKS archives. In the 1960s, interviews with Roma were first initiated by Finnish folklorists, ethnologists, and anthropologists, and in the late 1990s by Roma themselves as part of the extensive ROM-SF interview project. In the ROM-SF project, the interviewers were Roma laypersons. In this project, 107 Roma (born in 1907–1980) were interviewed. The interview questions are organized around Roma's lives and experiences, with the overall aim of charting and surveying the Finnish Roma culture(s) and customs in the way Roma themselves have experienced it. A recurrent interview question pertains to *encounters* between the majority population of "the whites" (*kaajeet*) and Roma (*mustalaiset/kaaleet*).

In the 92 interviews I reviewed, I looked for questions pertaining to "the old days," "the Kaale way of life," "market days," "peddling", and "trade," where itinerant trade and livelihoods were discussed. These narratives unfold a bygone era, depicting childhood and adolescent memories of market days in the past, with the oldest ones reflecting the 1920s–1940s. The informants recall how families until the 1960s were in constant movement (being non-residents) and practicing itinerant trade, both peddling (visiting private homes) and trading at marketplaces and fairs (public spaces). These interviews convey experiential aspects and meanings behind varied economic practices, as well as give information on how the Roma community was socially reproduced.[19] I look at how the informants narrate and (re)construct their experiences by tracing particular narratives and discourses. In line with Michel de Certeau, I approach the interviews as "treatments of space".[20] They are "travel stories," a spatial practice. These spatial stories travel like buses or trains; "they traverse and organize places; they select and link them together; they make sentences and itineraries out of them. They are spatial trajectories."[21] In this way, stories transform "places into spaces or spaces into places."[22] This everyday practice of telling stories maps a geographical structure in which places are linked together. Hence, narration—the interview in this case—is not only a description of something but a practice or act that connects the present with the past and the future.

Memory, writes de Certeau, is part of storytelling, and a story changes the real by making "detours" as it travels in time.[23] The interview questions call for memories and experiences of the market ("How were the market days in the old days?" "Do you remember market trade and peddling?" "How did the Kaale make a living back in the day?"). Although not all Roma families were engaged in peddling and itinerant trade, as some were stationary and working on farms, for example, the interviewees present the past in nostalgic terms as an itinerant "Gypsy life," traveling around by horse and cart. By the time of the ROM-SF interviews in 1998–2000, itinerant trade—such as market trade—was a distant phenomenon, yet memories thereof remained, or at least were narrated. Spatial aspects of Roma livelihoods turned out to be important; the marketplace in particular was narrated as a space that encompassed different meanings for Roma. Stories like these interviews can be understood as comprising part of that space; according to de Certeau, "there are as many spaces as there are distinct spatial experiences."[24]

Not all informants had their own memories of market trade or "itinerant Gypsy lives," yet this fact did not hinder them from retelling stories and memories that their parents or older generations had told them. Thus, these nostalgic narratives are not only individual memories but also based on the stories and emotions of older Roma generations; that is, informants retell, take over, and reconstruct experiences of the past. The former market days are depicted as "a joyous time,"[25] a festivity. The nostalgic feelings are both personal and collective, stretching over generations—and time.

One male informant[26] details three major meanings of the marketplace, which aptly represents how many other interviewees presented this space. First, the market offered a venue for meeting relatives and old acquaintances, but also for making new Roma friends. Second, the market was a space for business, that is, selling and swapping horses. The third aspect of the marketplace was consumption; the market offered an opportunity to acquire commodities and necessities, such as clothes and shoes. In other words, the informant stressed the social (e.g., relationships, networks) and economic meanings (livelihood and consumption) of the market, and these meanings were connected. In the narratives, the marketplace as a distinct space is presented as an important gathering venue and a fixed space for families, who normally were scattered around the country. While finding overnight accommodations was usually a constant battle for survival, during market days it seemed to be effortless. According to the informants, Roma families worked together and helped each other find overnight shelter.

Gendered and Specialized Livelihoods

In her pioneering work on British Roma, Judith Okely describes Roma as nomadic service providers and entertainers who exploit opportunities that are not covered by the mainstream, formal provision of goods and services.[27] Okely, as well as the comparative collection *Gypsy Economy: Romani Livelihoods and Notions of Worth in the 21st Century*, edited by Micol Brazzabeni, Manuela Ivone Cunha, and Martin Fotta, underline performativity in economic practices.[28]

The division of labor, trade practices, and commodities were strictly gendered. Roma women and men followed a clear distribution of work, with different tasks being associated with shared understandings of femininity and masculinity. Roma's most important commodities and barter goods included horses, horse-related gear, and the equipment that men manufactured. Additionally, needlework—particularly the laces that women knitted—was sold and swapped. Laces could be traded for a piece of bread and fortune-telling for an overnight stay. Roma women also provided their customers with entertainment, doing palm reading or reading cards, providing gossip, telling stories, singing, and so forth. Leo Lucassen et al. refer to these practices as "emotional services"; Roma women talked about the joys and sorrows of life, and about future fortunes (like marriage) and misfortunes.[29]

With the help of trade and barter goods, Roma families could secure food for their families. The strategy of "walking" and "asking" for food—begging—was a female task. Women's versatile work tasks (e.g., securing food for the family, palm reading, selling needlework, entertaining customers, domestic services) required trust and assistance from the local residents. Women's work guaranteed the continuity of Roma society, ensuring that members of the family had enough to eat, while male labor maintained the place of the household in society. In particular, horse trading created and developed relationships with the domestic majority group. It was of great importance that both horse trading and women's handicraft barter trade succeeded, as it was easier the next time around if good relations with potential customers were already established. Such relations were critical both in peddling (i.e., door-to-door activities) and in market trade and fairs (see Fig. 11.1).

Although peddling was the most common form of livelihood for Roma, being practiced all year round, market trade was an essential source of income, particularly when it came to horses. The informants remember

Fig. 11.1 A peddling Roma family in Muhos, Finland, 1945. (Photo by Antti Miikkulainen, 1945. The Finnish Literature Society)

their fathers coming home with delicacies and money after successful horse deals. Income and livelihood were thus gendered, and horse trading was conducted solely by men.

> Well, my father always visited the marketplaces [...] was there and swapped horses. Did business and always got some money from there... Yes, those marketplaces were such, where you did business.[30]

> The men went to the market to swap horses and normally women did lace business and palm reading. It was a form of livelihood.[31]

> Interviewer: Well, how did the gypsy get his bread besides horse swapping?
> Informant: Women used to do fortune telling.[32]

> Women talked with women, and men with men, men usually talked about horse trading and gave each other advice, and there was no envy involved.

> Women talked amongst themselves. Whatever they talked about, they did not talk about rags or aprons, they had much more important things to talk about—there was less talk about what kind of cloth you had bought.[33]

The livelihood narratives expressed and shaped gendered social relations and practices. Gendered networks were established between the minority and majority populations, the Roma and the "whites." Male networks were organized around horse trading, both amongst Roma men and between Roma men and white men. Female networks seem to have been wider and their livelihood practices largely depended on good social relations with the majority population.

As opposed to public writings with the racist master narrative, Roma informants described their encounters and experiences with the majority population in (surprisingly) positive terms.

> Interviewer: What were the whites like in those days if you compare to how they are today?
>
> Informant: Well, in those days, back in the day, they were good, because they helped us and gave to gypsies when gypsies were begging, and they were much more understanding than they are today, and the help did come from the whites, similarly as today. Well, in the past, they gave whenever somebody asked. There was nothing to it. The whites did give in the past. Quite honestly.[34]

The *kaajeet* offered help in many ways, and they treated Roma well, giving them food and shelter. Roma accentuated that they themselves had been behaving courteously and had been honest in their commerce activities. Some informants openly admitted, however, that the Roma were completely dependent upon help from the whites.

> Interviewer: Were whites better, back in the day?
>
> Informant: Whites were better to the gypsy back then. If you think about it, quite truthfully, gypsies lived at the expense of the whites. Gypsies did not understand anything about work at that time.[35]

In contrast to scholars who have emphasized reciprocity in interethnic relations and mutual dependencies between the majority population and Roma (or other itinerant groups) in the late nineteenth and early twentieth centuries,[36] I maintain that the dependence was clearly one-sided: Roma needed the customers, food and shelter provided by peasant families. The relations between the white majority and ethnic minority cannot be regarded as "equal," not even reciprocal. It is undebatable that without the help from the peasantry, the survival of Roma families would have been compromised.

The Horseman

While Roma women were handcrafters, palm readers, "askers", and fortune-tellers, the "Gypsy man" was a horse trader and/or horse swapper. Horse trading was one of the traditional "Gypsy" forms of trade, being a form of livelihood often associated with Roma, and thus it was an ethnicized practice. Horse trading, as well as the handling of animals and veterinarian-related activities that the Roma practiced, demanded specialized knowledge. Traditional know-how passed from father to son enabled Roma to establish themselves as skillful horse traders, sometimes giving them a monopoly. In their comparative study of Roma livelihoods, Brazzabeni et al. address the notion of "Gypsy specialization" as a "Simmelian social form," which arises "through the replication, standardisation or repetition of activities and through the production of conceptual apparatuses related to this specialisation."[37] Horse trading was a specialization, exclusively a male form of entrepreneurship, and regarded as the most lucrative and important source of income.

If we look at the actual commodities, goods, or "things" for sale, two artifacts—the horse and lace—were associated with and understood in relation to Roma. Lace was obviously regarded as a female artifact, crafted, sold, exchanged, or bartered by women, and thus marked as "feminine." The horse was intimately linked to Roma men. While a living horse may not be a "thing" or artifact in the traditional sense, it still functioned as a commodity. Donna Haraway understands the dog as a hybrid (figure): humans have shaped the dog throughout history, but the dog has also shaped humans.[38] The same applies to the horse, and its meanings for the Roma were multifaceted. The horse was a vehicle, commodity, status symbol, and companion. The horse enabled itinerant trade and the livelihoods of Roma. The horse cart not only carried Roma families, but also all the daily necessities (clothes, pans and pots, tents to sleep in, horse tools and gear, and so on) that the family needed for its survival, as well as the goods for sale.

In Roma culture, the horse and its harness, gear, reins, and water container belonged to a symbolically pure category, which further manifested the importance of the horse. Naturally, the horse was also important to the majority population in a rural society. Up until the Second World War, horses were used in agricultural work, forestry, industries, and for transportation. For the peasantry, horses were a crucial asset all year round. In addition, farmers needed horse gear, for workhorses needed regular maintenance, care, and attendance. After the war, however, the need for workhorses declined as an effect of agricultural mechanization, something that greatly affected Roma livelihoods.

The horse was gendered, as it was associated with masculinity. The Roma man did not own land but owned one or more horses. In Finnish, there is an expression, "Hevonen on mustalaisen pelto" ("The horse is the Gypsy's field"), which dates back to the eighteenth century.[39] The horse was a man's property, and his status was measured on the basis of his horse(s) and his skills as a horseman. The horse cart was also a status symbol. Roma carts were different from those of the majority population, being lower and painted in vibrant colors. The majority population referred to these as "Gypsy carts."[40] When Roma families gathered, the horses and carts were critically evaluated in relation to the status of the Roma man, including his economic position and his "commercial talent and status."[41] Hence, the symbolic value of the horse cannot be overstated. By means of horse selling, swapping, and bartering, male networks were established both among Roma and between Roma men and white men. Such horse trading was of particular importance for minority–majority relations. Both male and female informants regarded horse trading as decisive in terms of conducting successful business, but also for good relations with the majority population (see Fig. 11.2).

> Informant: I do remember the markets and fairs, because my father had the best horses of all Finnish Gypsies. And my father looked a lot like a white [Finn], a white Gypsy, so he helped other Gypsies. [Sometimes] other Gypsies could not sell or swap a horse by themselves, so they had to give the horse to my father [who then could sell it].
>
> Interviewer: So, he was, like, better at it [horse trading]?
>
> Informant: Yes.[42]

In these encounters, Roma men who resembled the majority population—like the father in the quote above, called a "white Gypsy"—could sometimes assume a special position and higher status because of their appearance. This fact made him a more successful horse trader, as he did

Fig. 11.2 A Finnish Roma (Kaale) man selling and swapping horses in 1958. Horse trading was one of the traditional Roma livelihoods and was practiced by men only. Competent salesmanship, knowledge of the local communities, bargaining and social skills, allowed Roma to become successful in their economic activities. (Photo by Erkki Voutilainen: Horse market on the Hyrylä racetrack in Tuusula, Finland. The Finnish Heritage Agency)

not look like a "typical" Roma man, and this appearance could help other Roma horse traders, who needed the white Gypsy's assistance in selling horses. In postcolonial research, this has been referred to as "passing" (i.e., when a non-white person can "pass as" white).[43] Through this "racial transformation," the person "passing" can gain privileges belonging to whites. It seems obvious that the "white Gypsy," resembling the majority population, was more easily accepted and trusted by the majority, because of his appearance. This in turn entailed that he had the upper hand in horse trade with the majority population, compared to Roma who did not have such a complexion. In this way, the "whiter" Roma man became more economically successful and was depicted as a "more skilled" horseman.

Michael Stewart's analysis of the Vlach Rom horse trade in socialist Hungary looks at how Roma men framed and understood selling, swapping, and bartering horses. For instance, Roma distinguished "selling" to Gázos from "swapping" with other Roma, thereby also maintaining ethnic boundaries. Horses were treated as commodities, and it was through Roma men's skills of speech and the ability to hustle that they were able to convince and "dominate" the Gázos ("whites") in trading encounters. A deal was regarded as successful when Roma achieved a price that was good enough, which in turn implied that the seller was "lucky," a criterion for success. Moreover, a Roma man was considered "lucky" if he constantly reconstructed himself as a true Gypsy.[44]

In the Finnish case, however, the interviews underlined honesty and decency as characterizing men's horse trade, rather than themes of "dominating," "convincing," or "deceiving" the customers. Even when poor, the means of livelihood was considered decent. Roma masculinity was again established in relation to successful horse trading.

> I had my own true he-man. He traveled around to markets and fairs and did horse business, and he earned a living out of it.[45]

The female informant's husband was depicted as a "he-man" for earning money from horse trading when on the road. Some Roma horsemen were famous all around the country as the best horse sellers, and they were respected both in the Roma community and by white men. Indeed, this form of livelihood was considered respectable and was highly appreciated. Both women and men emphasized the worth of the *masculine* form of livelihood. Although Roma informants emphasized decency and respectability almost as "innate" characteristics, trading encounters and practices can be seen as involving various strategic performances, such as passing for non-Roma (role-playing), impression management, knowing the local economy and the local people, establishing good contacts with resident communities, and having extraordinary social skills. Such techniques were fundamental in allowing Roma to master and become successful in their economic activities. Judith Okely points to the importance of "manual dexterity; mechanical ingenuity; highly developed memory; salesmanship and bargaining skills."[46] She also addresses role-playing, through which Roma related to Gorgios (the British Roma term for non-Gypsies) in different ways in economic interactions. Depending upon the context and situation, Roma variously hid or promoted their "Gypsyness," sometimes adapting, fitting into or even internalizing stereotypes produced by non-Gypsies. It seems plausible that Finnish Roma also manipulated "ethnic," non-Roma, stereotypes, tactically, according to the occasion and their needs. Okely sees a discontinuity between, on the one hand, Gypsies' representation of themselves to non-Gypsies through manipulating attributes of "ethnicity" and, on the other hand, the "real" Roma way of being and living in a consistent way with their "ethnic identity."[47]

Honest Livelihoods and Subjugated Knowledges

The nostalgic narration of the "good old days" depicted Roma livelihoods of the past as upstanding, the relations between *kaajeet* and *kaaleet* as friendly and respectable, and economic activities as professional and honest. Compared to sources produced by the majority population, these interviews tell a quite different story. While Roma believed they conducted respectable professional trade, the majority population did not regard it as proper work or business but as involving trickeries and disguised begging.[48] Following Richard Jenkin's notion of ethnicity, it is clear that the minority's self-perception (identification) was related to—and constructed in relation to—the racialized derogatory view of the majority and the public space (the external categorization).[49]

Roma as an ethnic minority and a collective identity have been portrayed as unworthy in relation to the majority population since their arrival in Finland in the sixteenth century. The "Gypsy Question" of the late nineteenth century established a persistent image of Roma as vagrants, beggars, criminals, and immoral in general.[50] Although politically speaking, the "Gypsy Question" slowly faded over time, the discourse itself prevailed. The itinerant life of Roma and their economic activities were regarded with suspicion and the notion of the "Gypsy" as incapable of (agricultural) work had been established. Thus, Roma broke established social norms and ideals according to which work not only served as a sign of decency, dignity, and decorum, but also normative citizenship.[51] This seemingly static representation of Roma as non-respectable with regard to the white majority population (with the power to define diligence, honesty, citizenship, etc.) reveals the racialized boundaries of citizenship that may have been inclusive—or in this case exclusive, depending on the context.

In his introductory lecture *Il faut défendre la société* ("Society Must be Defended"), Michel Foucault describes genealogy as "the insurrection of subjugated knowledges." According to Foucault, genealogy can offer the history of the struggle of one knowledge against others, showing how certain knowledges (*épistémès*) gain dominance in certain periods and how certain other knowledges ("subjugated knowledges") are suppressed. As with master narratives, certain knowledges "win" over others. Therefore, when we discuss "knowledge," we mean "the victorious knowledge," "the knowledge that defeated and subjugated other knowledges."[52]

Subjugated knowledges are not only forms of knowledge that are hidden or deliberately corrupted, but also knowledges that have been dismissed and disqualified, as in the case of Roma's own perspectives and accounts. By bringing back those subjugated knowledges, other possibilities of knowledge open up, and new thinking can recommence. Still, herein lies a challenge. For the scholar, it may be appealing to fall back on statements of the subjugated subjects and to regard these as more "true" or more reliable than the ones given by the majority population (the *épistémè*). However, the narratives of marginalized individuals are also constricted; hence, genealogy does not strive to replace authoritative histories with more "authentic" or absolute historical truths. Rather, the aim is to demonstrate how all truths and knowledges are situated in specific social and historical contexts. Genealogies are biased and partial as much as authoritative histories; they are also written and produced from a particular position. Interviews are shaped by context, discourses, expectations, and conventions. Thus, I do not claim to convey Roma's *realities*, instead, my aim is to make visible how the informants revoke and understand their experiences by identifying different narratives and by taking them seriously.

If the materials produced by the majority represent a powerful *épistémè*, or a master narrative, would it be possible to regard the Roma narratives as an insurrection, a mutiny against the image that the majority population has forced upon them?

Respectable Masculine Livelihoods as Resistance

According to Beverley Skeggs, social groups are differentiated by their possibilities to exhibit respectability.[53] Respectability contains judgments of class, race, gender, and sexuality, and different groups have varying degrees of access to the mechanisms for generating, resisting, and displaying respectability. For Skeggs, respectability is foremost a marker of social class and can be used as a means of "othering" deviant codes of individuals and behaviors. Respectability is a desirable symbol of dignity and morality, a type of cultural capital which historically has been granted the upper social classes. Therefore, striving for respectability has been stronger among social groups that have *not* been seen as respectable: working-class and black women, ethnic minorities, and other subjugated groups. Roma have repeatedly been portrayed as unreliable, unfit for work, dirty, uncivilized, anti-social and dangerous; in other words, as the *opposite* of propriety and respectability—the cultural capital defined by—and given to—the whites by themselves.[54] Postcolonial scholarship has demonstrated how the colonized person always carries the image of the Other as a part of themself and has to respond and relate to that representation.[55] Still today, a lack of respect is something that many Finnish Roma experience and have to manage in their daily lives. Camilla Nordberg discusses how Roma regard their citizenship and belonging *from below*: they perceive themselves as an underclass in Finnish society, particularly regarding schooling but also employment.[56]

> My dad pursued horse trading and supported us by honest horse trading, and he was not chased by gypsies or whites for doing something wrong or for having been sneaky or lying. So, in that way it felt good that we were poor, but honest. [...] Dad swapped horses and he always had good horses, and he swapped better horses, and then we were begging at places where people gave us food. But no violence anywhere. People gave of their own goodwill, and nobody was afraid of us. They welcomed us with open arms. We lived honestly and did nothing wrong.[57]

For Skeggs, the working class aims to become respectable by aspiring for middle-class social status and cultural capital. Roma, however, did not wish to become like the majority; rather, they wanted to be respected *as Roma*. Patrick Williams, in his analysis of French Roma, Manus, maintains that they live "in the world of the Gadzos" (non-Gypsies) but not "in the same world as the Gadzos," and that, while co-existing with the Gadzos, the Manus detach themselves from them, "which precisely cause them to become Manus and the Gadzos to become Gadzo."[58] So, while Finnish Roma mirrored themselves against the whites, they took pride in being Roma. Nevertheless, they actively resisted negative stereotypes of Roma. While Skeggs' focus is on women—namely, working-class women—and respectability, in the case of Roma, women remained in the shadows; thus, men were the ones striving for respectability *and* presented as respectable.

For the non-respectable to become respectable, they need to distance themselves from the unrespectable position and emphasize—and even exaggerate—respectable agency. Skeggs writes that working-class women set themselves in opposition to class-based accounts that present them as poor, deprived, depriving, or dangerous, thus defining themselves in terms of what they are *not*, as opposed to "who they are."[59] For the Roma, dis-identification entailed disassociation from racialized stereotypes as "non-workers," "unreliable," "lazy," and "aggressive," while instead maintaining their diligence, honesty, worthiness, and dignity. Also of importance was to stress inclusion, not exclusion and otherness. These can be regarded as tactics employed by Roma who were subjugated in the public space and othered by powerful discourses. For de Certeau, tactics are by nature defensive, used and seized momentarily within spaces that are both physical and psychological. Hence, interviews as counter-narratives resist "stories of domination," and Roma stories of successful horse trading seem to be defying "an oppressive identity and attempt to replace it with one that commands respect."[60] These performative accounts and tactics are critical for understanding subjugated groups, and they have particular significance for the Roma, marginalized within dominant discourses.

In their nostalgic narration, Roma emphasized respectability, inclusion, and belonging in terms of livelihood, thus defying the persistent view of "Gypsies" as beggars and swindlers rather than legitimate traders. In the context of Roma patriarchal culture, emphasis was placed on men and masculinity in relation to worth and work. Although Roma women's contributions to the family household were crucial, women's labor was presented in modest terms (by both men and women), whereas the masculine form of livelihood was underlined, being the one that gave respectability not only to the Roma man but the whole family. Hence, respectability was strongly gendered and related to horse trading. In spatial stories,[61] horse trading was seen as symbolizing male "Gypsyness," which was something to be continuously performed and embodied. The construction of Roma masculinity often took place in a certain spatial realm, like the marketplace. Masculine respectability was constructed in relation to successful horse trading and social relations with the majority population. Successful trade and its underlying strategies were often narrated with respect to male non-gypsies, such as when Roma men were able through their skills of speech and sometimes appearance (e.g., looking "white") to sell horses or swap them with whites.

Analysis of Roma livelihoods raises an important ethical question pertaining to notions of agency, subjugation, and power. How does an exploration of economic practices recognize the position of individual Roma communities in the societies they live in, a position that includes racism and poverty, while leaving the possibility for acknowledging, as Brazzabeni et al. so aptly formulate the dilemma, "a self-defining capacity to determine for oneself a posture vis-à-vis the workings of states, markets, money and so on?"[62] While social deterministic analyses have rightly been criticized for overlooking people's capacities to shape their own lives, the unproblematized stress on agency has also come under fire for its tendency to individualize action and overstate the range of choices people have at their disposal, something which is particularly problematic when it comes to marginalized social groups.[63] I believe that both power (domination, master narratives) and resistance (subjugated knowledge, counter-narratives, tactics) should be addressed without falling back on individualizing accounts of agency. According to de Certeau, stories can be regarded as spaces of resistance, meaning resistance to the narratives of instituted power.[64] Genealogical readings and counter-narratives open up and acknowledge the lives and livelihoods of marginalized individuals without disregarding the social structures upholding their subordination. James Staples notes that "people embody elements of the social structures that simultaneously oppress and enable them, their actions undertaken in the context of that embodiment."[65] The researcher's and genealogist's task is to question and deconstruct truths that are taken for granted, to offer alternative understandings, and to analyze excluded knowledges that have been ruled out. The aim is to trace how certain knowledges emerge and are legitimized, while at the same time listening to the voices that have been marginalized. The interviews and stories examined in this chapter can be understood as both counter-narratives and subjugated knowledges that actively resist the master narrative (the *épistémè*) and its negative representations of Roma. This becomes apparent in the way Roma informants underline the worth of livelihoods, encounters, and relations with the majority population. I suggest that this agency can be understood as resistance of the collective monolithic identity imposed upon Roma. Herein lies a possibility to alter or even reverse the majority view of Roma.

In conclusion, this chapter has tried to understand, analyze, and interpret economic activities of Finnish Roma at a time when they primarily supported themselves by itinerant trade. Using Roma's own narratives, I have approached the interviews as "spatial" and "travel" stories (per de Certeau), looking at how Roma recalled their livelihoods in the past. The marketplace (and its trade practices) is constructed as a particular space with different meanings (e.g., economic, social, nostalgic). The market was a pivotal social place in the public sphere, to which Roma had legitimate access and where Roma families could come together and interact amongst themselves. Thus, spatial aspects shaped feelings of belonging and worth. Through memories, emotions, interpretations, and associations that travel across generations, honest livelihoods—but also financial insecurities and dependencies—are disclosed in the narratives. It is obvious that the economic arrangements and strategies of Roma were complex and embedded in local social positions, as well as being historically specific. My intention has been to explore gendered and specialized trading practices, focusing on horse trading (swapping and selling) as a traditional Roma livelihood. In a subversive way, Roma performed respectability by maintaining honest livelihood practices, successful horse trading and good relations with the majority. Respectability was nevertheless strictly gendered, as it was linked to masculinity and to a form of sustenance which had been pivotal and was still important in the early postwar period, that is, after the Second World War. In addition, Roma trading practices demonstrated different meanings of work, informal economies, ethnic relations, performative tactics, and ways of economic strategizing. Although it cannot be denied that the Roma minority largely remained dependent upon help and goodwill from the majority population, this chapter suggests that the economic practices of Finnish Roma did not involve passive adaptation but active responses to wider socio-economic structures.

Notes

1. Given the complex history of the word "Gypsy," including negative images, there has been a tendency to replace the latter with "Roma" in most academic works and social policies. While I will mostly use the word "Roma," both "Kaale" and "Gypsy" also appear in my chapter, since Finnish Roma often refer to themselves with those terms. The word kaalo (Romani: kaale in plural; Finnish: kaaleet) comes from the word kalo/kaalo in Romani, meaning "black." In Finnish, the term is mustalainen (mustalaiset in plural), meaning "black people": musta means "black" and the suffix -lainen denotes belonging to a group. When it comes to kaajo (Romani: kaaje in

plural; Finnish: kaajeet), some scholars, such as Panu Pulma says that it means "white" (see Pulma 2015, p. 10). Others argue that it has no meaning other than non-Kaale (see Roman 2016, p. 9). In the interviews, Finnish Roma often spoke of non-Roma, that is, majority Finns, either as Kaaje or as valkolaiset ("white people"). Whenever reviewing scholarly literature on Roma, I will adopt the terms used by the authors of those texts to refer to the specific groups they have studied.

2. For exceptions, see Leo Lucassen, Wim Willems, and Annemarie Cottaar. 1998. *Gypsies and Other Itinerant Groups. A Socio-Historical Approach*; Miika Tervonen. 2010. *"Gypsies", "Travellers" and "Peasants". A Study on Ethnic Boundary Drawing in Finland and Sweden, c. 1860–1925*. For contemporary Roma economies, see Micol Brazzabeni, Manuela Ivone Cunha, and Martin Fotta. 2015. *Gypsy Economy. Romani Livelihoods and Notions of Worth in the 21st Century*.
3. E.g., Okely 1979, p. 23; Michael Stewart. 1997. *The Time of the Gypsies*.
4. Michel de Certeau. 1984. *The Practice of Everyday Life*.
5. Beverley Skeggs. 1997. *Formations of Class and Gender. Becoming Respectable*.
6. Scholarship on ethnicity and identity politics, including those of Roma, is extensive and cannot be elaborated within the scope of this chapter. My work builds on the insights of scholars who have addressed the problematic definition of Roma as an ethnic group, instead opting for an understanding of Roma/Gypsy lives as contextualized constructions of community belonging. See, Roman 2014, pp. 794–795; Raluca B. Roman. 2016. *Kaale Belongings and Evanceligal Becomings. Faith, Commitment and Social Outreach among the Finnish Kaale (Finnish Roma)*; Tatiana Podolinská. 2017. "'Roma' Label: The Deconstructed and Reconceptualized Category within the Pentecostal and Charismatic Pastoral Discourse in Contemporary Slovakia."; Seminal works include Paloma Gay y Blasco. 1999. *Gypsies in Madrid. Sex, Gender and the Performance of Identity*; Paloma Gay y Blasco. 2002. "Gypsy/Roma Diasporas: Introducing a Comparative Perspective"; Leo Lucassen, Wim Willems, and Annemarie Cottaar. 1998. *Gypsies and Other Itinerant Groups. A Socio-Historical Approach;* Judith Okely. 1983. *The Traveller-Gypsies*; Judith Okely. 2011. "Constructing Culture through Shared Location, Bricolage and Exchange. The Case of Gypsies and Roma"; Michael Stewart. 1997. *The Time of the Gypsies*.
7. Finland does not officially have national minorities, but Finnish Roma, as well as the Sámi, are recognized as traditional minorities. Finnish Roma are Finnish citizens and benefit from equal access to social services, education and employment opportunities, as the rest of the population The Romani language is also recognized as a non-territorial minority language. Päivi

Hernesniemi and Lauri Hannikainen. 2000. *Roma Minorities in the Nordic and Baltic Countries. Are their Rights Realized?*

8. E.g., Panu Pulma. 2012. *Suomen romanien historia.*
9. Roman 2015, p. 208; Tervonen 2010, p. 60; Hedman 2009, p. 30.
10. E.g., Pulma 2009, pp. 89–91.
11. Ibid.; Martti Grönfors. 1981. *Suomen mustalaiskansa.*
12. Roman 2015, pp. 208–209; see also, Camilla Nordberg. 2005. "Integrating a Traditional Minority into a Nordic Society. Elite Discourse on the Finnish Roma."
13. *Kotka* 10/31/1895, no. 42.
14. Tervonen 2010, p. 40.
15. Blok 2001, pp. 44–68.
16. Hall 1997a, b, pp. 225–239.
17. Acevedo et al. 2010, p. 125.
18. See, Halverson et al. 2011, p. 4.
19. See, Brazzabeni et al. 2015, p. 18.
20. De Certeau 1984, p. 122.
21. De Certeau 1984, p. 115.
22. De Certeau 1984, p. 23.
23. De Certeau 1984, p. 86.
24. De Certeau 1984, 118.
25. Man, 77 years old, 4/14/1998.
26. Man, 59 years old, 4/26/1998.
27. Judith Okely. 1979. "Trading Stereotypes. The Case of English Gypsies"; Judith Okely. 1983. *The Traveller-Gypsies.*
28. Micol Brazzabeni, Manuela Ivone Cunha, and Martin Fotta. 2015. *Gypsy Economy. Romani Livelihoods and Notions of Worth in the 21st Century.*
29. Lucassen et al. 1998, p. 168.
30. Woman, 63 years old, 4/24/1998.
31. Woman, 63 years old, 5/13/1999.
32. Woman, 72 years old, 3/13/1998.
33. Woman, 59 years old, 5/11/1998.
34. Man, 77 years old, 8/17/1999.
35. Man, 41 years old, 2/14/1999.
36. E.g., Leo Lucassen, Wim Willems, and Annemarie Cottaar. 1998. *Gypsies and Other Itinerant Groups. A Socio-Historical Approach*; Miika Tervonen. 2010. *"Gypsies," "Travellers," "Peasants."*
37. Brazzabeni et al. 2015, p. 16.
38. Donna Haraway. 2007. *When Species Meet.*
39. Pulma 2009, p. 82.
40. Blomster and Lindberg 2015, pp. 140–141.
41. Blomster and Lindberg 2015, p. 140.

42. Man, 57 years old, 5/14/1998.
43. See, e.g., Sarah Ahmed. 2007. "A Phenomenology of Whiteness"; Adrian Piper. 1992. "Passing for White, Passing for Black."
44. Michael Stewart. 1997. *The Time of the Gypsies.*
45. Woman, 80 years old, 6/12/1998.
46. Okely 1979, p. 23.
47. E.g., Okely 1979, p. 33.
48. Ahlbeck 2018, p. 293.
49. Jenkins 1997, pp. 198–201.
50. Tervonen 2012, p. 94.
51. Ahlbeck 2018, p. 268.
52. The lecture was given on January 7, 1976. Foucault 2003/1976, p. 182.
53. In her now classic work, Beverley Skeggs argues that "respectability is one of the most ubiquitous signifiers of class" (1997, p. 1). She examines the relations between gender, class and sexuality, and identifies the struggle for respectability—a middle-class signifier and form of cultural capital—among British working-class women (black and white), who distance themselves from the negative values (poor, deprived and degraded) associated with the working class. This struggle for respectability is understood in the context of the barriers placed on working-class women through their positions as classed, gendered and sexualized beings.
54. Eija Stark. 2018. "Cultural Intimacy and Othering through Narrative Culture. Folktales about the Finnish Roma."
55. E.g., Stuart Hall. 1997. *Representation. Cultural Representations and Signifying Practices.*
56. Nordberg 2006, p. 530; see also Charles Tilly. 1999. *Durable Inequality.*
57. Woman 41 år 3/27/1999.
58. Williams 2003, p. 29.
59. Skeggs 1997, p. 76.
60. Lindemann-Nelson 2001, p. 6; see, also Tommy Ender. 2019. "Counter-Narratives as Resistance. Creating Critical Social Studies Spaces with Communities."
61. De Certeau 1984, p. 115.
62. Brazzabeni et al. 2015, p. 2.
63. See, James Staples. 2007. *Livelihoods at the Margins. Surviving the City.*
64. De Certeau 1984, p. 23.
65. Staples 2007, p. 18.

Bibliography

Archival Sources

Suomalaisen kirjallisuuden seura (The Finnish Literature Society), Helsinki.
ROM-SF-interviews, 1998–2000.

Literature

Acevedo, Gabriel A., James Ordner, and Miriam Thompson. "Narrative Inversion as a Tactical Framing Device. The Ideological Origins of the Nation of Islam." *Narrative Inquiry* 20, no. 1 (2010): 124–152.

Ahlbeck, Jutta. "Tingens paria. Romers gårdfarihandel och artefakters betydelse under första hälften av 1900-talet." *Historisk Tidskrift för Finland* 103, no. 2 (2018): 262–294.

Ahmed, Sarah. "A Phenomenology of Whiteness." *Feminist Theory* 8, no. 2 (2007):149–168.

Blomberg, Michael and Molly Andrews (eds.). *Considering Counter Narratives. Narrating, Resisting, Making Sense.* Amsterdam: John Benjamins Publishing Company, 2004.

Blok, Anton. *Honour and Violence.* Cambridge: Polity Press, 2001.

Blomster, Risto and Väinö Lindberg. "Romernas hästar och vagnar", in *De finska romernas historia från svenska tiden till 2000-talet,* edited by Panu Pulma, 140–145. Helsingfors: Svenska litteratursällskapet i Finland, 2015.

Brazzabeni, Micol, Manuela Ivone Cunha, and Martin Fotta (eds.). *Gypsy Economy. Romani Livelihoods and Notions of Worth in the 21st Century.* Oxford: Berghahn Books, 2015.

De Certeau, Michel. *The Practice of Everyday Life.* Berkeley: University of California Press, 1984.

Ender, Tommy. "Counter-Narratives as Resistance. Creating Critical Social Studies Spaces with Communities." *The Journal of Social Studies Research* 42, no. 2 (2019): 133–143.

Foucault, Michel. "Il faut défendre la société." Lecture given on January 7, 1976). *Society Must be Defended. Lectures at the Collège de France, 1975–1976,* trans. David Macey. New York: Picador, 2003.

Gay y Blasco, Paloma. *Gypsies in Madrid. Sex, Gender and the Performance of Identity.* Oxford: Berg Publishers, 1999.

Gay y Blasco, Paloma. "Gypsy/Roma Diasporas. Introducing a Comparative Perspective." *Social Anthropology* 10 (2002): 173–188.

Grönfors, Martti. *Suomen mustalaiskansa.* WSOY: Helsinki, 1981.

Hall, Stuart. "The Spectacle of the 'Other'", in *Representation. Cultural Representations and Signifying Practices,* edited by Stuart Hall, 225–239. London: Sage, 1997a.

Hall, Stuart (ed.). *Representation. Cultural Representations and Signifying Practices.* London: Sage, 1997b.

Halverson, Jeffry, H.L. Goodall Junior, and Steven R. Corman. *Master Narratives of Islamist Extremism.* New York: Palgrave Macmillan, 2011.

Haraway, Donna. *When Species Meet.* Minneapolis: University of Minnesota Press, 2007.

Hedman, Henry. *Suomen romanikieli. Sen asema yhteisössään, käyttö ja romanien kieliasenteet.* Helsinki: Kotimaisten kielten tutkimuskeskuksen verkkojulkaisuja, Kotimaisten kielten tutkimuskeskus, 2009.

Hernesniemi, Päivi and Lauri Hannikainen. *Roma Minorities in the Nordic and Baltic Countries. Are their Rights Realized?* Rovaniemi: Lapland University Press, 2000.

Jenkins, Richard. *Rethinking Ethnicity. Arguments and Explorations.* London: Sage, 1997.

Kotka 10/31/1895, no. 42.

Lindemann-Nelson, Hilde. *Damaged Identities. Narrative Repair.* Ithaca, NY: Cornell University Press, 2001.

Lucassen, Leo, Wim Willems, and Annemarie Cottaar, (eds.). *Gypsies and Other Itinerant Groups. A Socio-Historical Approach.* London: Palgrave Macmillan, 1998.

Nordberg, Camilla. "Claiming Citizenship. Marginalised Voices on Identity and Belonging." *Citizenship Studies* 10, no. 5 (2006): 523–539.

Nordberg, Camilla. "Integrating a Traditional Minority into a Nordic Society. Elite Discourse on the Finnish Roma". *Social Work & Society 2*, no. 2 (2005): 158–173.

Okely, Judith. "Trading Stereotypes. The Case of English Gypsies", in *Ethnicity at Work*, edited by Sandra Wallman, 16–33. London: Macmillan, 1979.

Okely, Judith. *The Traveller-Gyspies.* Cambridge: Cambridge University Press, 1983.

Okely, Judith. "Constructing Culture through Shared Location, Bricolage and Exchange. The Case of Gypsies and Roma, in *Multi-Disciplinary Approaches to Romani Studies,* edited by Michael Stewart et al., 35–54. Budapest: Central European University Press, 2011.

Piper, Adrian. "Passing for White, Passing for Black." *Transition* 58, (1992): 4–32.

Podolinská, Tatiana. "'Roma' Label. The Deconstructed and Reconceptualized Category within the Pentecostal and Charismatic Pastoral Discourse in Contemporary Slovakia. *Journal of Nationalism, Memory & Language Politics* 11, no. 2 (2017): 146–180.

Pulma, Panu. "Kerjäläisyys, irtolaisuus, 'mustalaisuus'. Historiallisia yhteyksiä", in *Kerjääminen eilen ja tänään. Historiallisia, oikeudellisia ja sosiaalipoliittisia näkökulmia kerjäämiseen,* edited by Virpi Mäkinen and Anne Birgitta Pessi, 71–96. Tampere: Vastapaino, 2009.

Pulma, Panu, (ed.). *Suomen romanien historia.* Helsinki: Suomalaisen Kirjallisuuden Seura, 2012.

Pulma, Panu, (ed.). *De finska romernas historia från svenska tiden till 2000-talet.* Helsingfors: Svenska Litteratursällskapet i Finland, 2015.

Roman, Raluca B. "Trans-National Migration and the Issue of 'Ethnic' Solidarity. Finnish Roma Elite and Eastern European Roma Migrants in Finland." *Ethnicities* 14, no. 6 (2014): 793–810.

Roman, Raluca B. "Religion and Transnational Mobilization. From Local Religious Participation to Transnational Social Activism in the Case of the Finnish Roma, in *Is God Back? Reconsidering the New Visibility of Religion,* edited by Titus Hjelm, 205–216. London: Bloomsbury, 2015.

Roman, Raluca B. *Kaale Belongings and Evanceligal Becomings. Faith, Commitment and Social Outreach among the Finnish Kaale (Finnish Roma).* PhD Thesis, St Andrews: University of St Andrews, 2016.

Roman, Raluca B. "'Neither Here, nor There'. Belonging, Ambiguity, and the Struggle for Recognition among 'in-between' Finnish Kaale. *Romani Studies* 28, no. 2 (2018): 239–262.

Skeggs, Beverley. *Formations of Class and Gender. Becoming Respectable.* London: Sage, 1997.

Staples, James. *Livelihoods at the Margins. Surviving the City.* London: Routledge, 2007.

Stark, Eija. "Cultural Intimacy and Othering through Narrative Culture. Folktales about the Finnish Roma." *Narrative Culture* 5, no. 1 (2018): 70–94.

Stewart, Michael. *The Time of the Gypsies.* Bolder, CO: Westview Press, 1997.

Tervonen, Miika. *'Gypsies', 'Travellers' and 'Peasants'. A Study on Ethnic Boundary Drawing in Finland and Sweden, c. 1860–1925,* Florence: European University Institute, 2010.

Tervonen, Miika. "Kiertolaisia, silmätikkuja ja rajojen ylittäjiä", In *Suomen Romanien historia,* edited by Panu Pulma, 84–142. Helsinki: Suomalaisen Kirjallisuuden Seura, 2012.

Tilly, Charles. *Durable Inequality.* Oakland: University of California Press, 1999.

Williams, Patrick. *Gypsy World. The Silence of the Living and the Voices of the Dead.* Chicago: University of Chicago Press, 2003.

CHAPTER 12

Forced into Trade Out of Necessity: Working-Class Narratives on Petty Trade

Eija Stark

The peasant and the proletarian have been key concepts in studies of social change and modernization.[1] Peasants, farming a small piece of land with the aid of household labor and mainly for their own consumption, have been the enduring basis of agricultural production throughout history. Contrary to this, the proletarian has worked for wages with little or no control over the means of production. In terms of class position, collective action, and orientation regarding traditional values, these two groups have traditionally been distinguished from one another.[2] From the late nineteenth century onward, however, both the peasant and proletariat economies were increasingly based on multiple sources of income. The division between rural and urban work was not large, since the youth of the rural families worked seasonally in factories or industrial labor, whereas those in town often supplemented their daily wages by keeping cows and pigs for personal use at home.

The cultural experience of workers throughout Europe differed greatly from the master narrative of the Industrial Revolution, in large part due to

E. Stark (✉)
The Finnish Literature Society, Helsinki, Finland
e-mail: eija.stark@finlit.fi

J. Ahlbeck et al. (eds.), *Encounters and Practices of Petty Trade in Northern Europe, 1820–1960*,
https://doi.org/10.1007/978-3-030-98080-1_12

the triumph of the socialist movement. Compared to the United Kingdom or continental Western Europe, Finland's industrial development took place rather late, only in the late nineteenth century. Despite the exploitation of forests for timber and paper products, small-scale farming continued to be an important—if not the most important—source of livelihood. Rural livelihoods were fundamentally seasonal, and it was typical to combine factory work with farm work and small-scale trade of farm products that cut across urban and rural communities.[3] This casual labor was an economic category that consisted of a complex and fluid combination of unskilled labor, the regular influx of the seasonally unemployed, seasonal farm servants and those brought up without any industrial skill or training.[4] It goes without saying that the families involved in casual labor more and more commonly resorted to petty trade.

When casual workers resorted to petty trade or street vending, what kinds of livelihood strategies did they then employ? This chapter introduces three working-class individuals and their multiple sources of income, presented in their life stories, and seeks to trace the ways in which the casual laborers who likewise performed agricultural chores interacted with rising capitalist power structures.[5] Due to the scarcity of resources, the everyday struggle for one's livelihood had a central role in the lives of the poor working class, and because of rapid economic development and liberalization, a quick expansion of goods offered new income opportunities. The focus is thus on the life stories and the narratives therein on financial struggles. From the perspective of "the new history from below," combined with narrative analysis, this chapter sheds light on the agency of working-class individuals and their understanding of small-scale trade as a form of livelihood. It also points to the multifaceted "folk" as economic actors and discusses vernacular narratives as a critical discourse vis-à-vis the rise of capitalism.

The Casual Workers and Their Life Stories

Struggles over livelihoods are analyzed from the life stories of Ida (b. 1900), Anto (b. 1914) and Jouko (b. 1926), all of whom had direct insight into the destitute and rural lifeways in Finland. In addition, they belonged to the generations that witnessed the poor peasant state of Finland transforming into a modern and technologically advanced welfare state. However, telling one's life is not the same as living life. Human life is incoherent; it consists of confusion, contradictions, and ironies, as well as indecisiveness, repetition, and reversions. Narrating a life story is the process of organizing experience and making sense of life.[6] By definition, a story is a structured narrative. It has a beginning, middle and end. Some incidents and phases of life are emphasized more than others. A life story is thus an artifact, and the construction of this artifact occurs by transforming the chaos of lived, everyday life into straightforward, one-dimensional prose.

Following oral historian Alessandro Portelli, Ken Plummer argues that "life stories are not and cannot be objective: they are always 'artificial, variable and partial'. But, at the same time [...] this does not weaken them. We may even know that some statements are factually wrong: and yet such 'wrong' statements may still be psychologically 'true': 'this truth may be equally as important as factually reliable accounts.'"[7] As cultural performances, personal narratives are more traditional than innovative. They rely on some individual resources, but most of these are influenced to some degree by collective models, and all are within the range of "safe creation."[8] Certain types of stories conventionally tend to have extended reportability. These include, for example, stories about career milestones, marriage, and major illnesses. For example, one such kind in Ida's, Anto's and Jouko's life stories is their first "real job" and the paycheck received from it. Such matters are relevant and reportable over a major segment of one's life, and, indeed, involve just those events that must be communicated in order that one other event may be known.[9]

Life stories construct a relationship between childhood and adolescence in the past and the elderly narrator in the present. In the context of contemporary material wellbeing and food security, stories of economic hardships and the absolute poverty of the past represent experiences that needed to be told. Poverty, lack of food and the urgent need for work are the narrative events that mark phases in the narrators' life.[10] In the course of Ida's, Anto's and Jouko's lifetimes, social identity has been a matter of negotiating the differing group identities that they have maintained. Individuals are constructed by their past, but at the same time they reconstruct, reinterpret and re-remember the past based on present-situation categories that they use to structure their identities and their worldview.[11] From the researcher's point of view, the life-story method focuses on the individual, conforming to dominant Western psychological models that emphasize the private nature of self-knowledge, with the result that people remember their past as if it was a drama in which the protagonist is the focus of the plot and determines the storyline.[12]

The life stories of Ida, Anto and Jouko represent the source type that researchers have specifically gathered with a wider, usually literary, or social-scientific goal in mind. Anto's and Jouko's life stories originate from an autobiographical writing contest for Finnish men organized by the Finnish Literature Society's Archives together with the Council for Gender Equality in 1992. According to the call, ordinary people were encouraged to write about their lives in their own style, describing "frankly and openly" what it is like to be a Finnish man. The life-writing contest was thus a method targeting so-called ordinary people, as opposed to celebrities and professional writers, to write about their lives. The guidelines encouraged authors to start with their childhood and their family background, and then their later adult life up until the time of writing.

In contrast to those of Anto and Jouko, Ida's life story belongs to the Finnish Labor Archives' oral history collections, which contains oral histories and ethnographic questionnaires of Finnish working-class communities and individual members. Throughout the decades, Ida was one of the most active respondents regarding the questionnaires that the Labor Archives' oral history and labor tradition commission organized. The common feature for Ida, Jouko and Anto is that, although lacking a formal education, they had been interested in literature and history, and they actively read both prose literature and newspaper. Often, as the authors mentioned, their life story was written with careful thought and awareness of an audience reading the archives. The ability to read and write has become central to modern living as signifying the normality of our culture. Yet it is with the arrival of print, the rise of leisure time and the slow emergence of a culture of individualism putting more emphasis on one's individual life that the written tale of a self has become more common.

In addition to specific genre features, from rags to riches, is the most prevalent theme in the life stories of the generation born in the beginning of the twentieth century. People found it appropriate to narrate their experiences of "behind the scenes" strategies for coping with poverty. Life as a singular narrative unit can also be considered as *the history from below*, which reevaluates individual experience and considers ordinary common people as active agents in shaping their own history and culture.[13] Compared to traditional labor history studies, study of "the history from below" is more interested in shared expressions and vernacular culture than the actual organizations of the working class.[14] Working-class people may challenge middle-class accounts of their lives that presume to know their needs and worldviews. It is important to note how individuals consider themselves and what they are, and how they envision themselves as persons and type of workers.

The point of departure in this chapter is the assumption that the three casual workers use narrative resources to construct and negotiate their understanding of their economic position. The authors authentically represent the working class in the sense that not one of them had a profound connection to land. Therefore, the concept of "working class" is not a top-down concept but is perceived here as the narrators describe their lives and the choices they made. Although people sought livelihoods from various sources, such as smallholding farm works, industries, and petty trade, at the same time they became aware of new understandings of economic opportunities and consumption.

The first part focuses on petty trade as the example of marginal expedients for earning a living, and it discusses the entwined nature of working-class livelihoods and the rise of capitalist behavior. The second part focuses on the gendered culture of making and selling self-made goods door-to-door. A broad unskilled segment of society was accustomed to doing farm work, such as milking, animal care and plowing, but not to manufacture and sell goods. This made sporadic petty trade difficult, if not impossible. The gendered division of labor was related to spatial differences, and the male spheres of work were usually outside the farm or the dwelling place. The latter part of this chapter discusses how petty trade was organized in terms of items and selling habits at the time that this geography of gender divisions of labor was maintained.

Petty Trade as the Last Resort

The oldest of the narrators was Ida, born in 1900 in a textile industry town in South Finland. She was one of the most active respondents in the oral history and labor tradition ethnographic collections of the Finnish Labor Archives. Not only did she write memoirs and respond at length to various questionnaires, but the archivists also interviewed her. Ida was an ideal informant: she took seriously her role of giving cultural insights into the so-called working-class ways of life and mentalities. During her later years, she became the author of a fictional book based on her life. In her written life story, preserved in the archives, Ida talks about her background. Her father was a poor crofter whose first wife died, leaving him a widower with five children, four of whom later passed away as well. Her father ended up as an itinerant petty trader and at the age of fifty, he met

Ida's mother, who was a factory worker 26 years younger than he was. This was around 1890, during the time when young women played a significant role among migrants in the textile industry.[15]

The act of telling is a performance that positions the narrator and the audience. Ida is narrating to the reader, in other words, intending her life story to be read by someone, stating: "I have told you about my father, although he was not touched upon the labor movement. I wanted to tell you about my father because he was the previous generation of the actual political labor movement. Now I tell you about my mother, even though she did not belong to the labor movement either." Compared to history as a reconstruction of the past in the present, stories such as Ida's reflect this complexity and possibilities more freely. The concept of narrative includes the idea of interaction. The concept of story ownership refers to a relationship between a teller and a listener or a reader, and between a narrative and event.[16] Ida is highly aware of being the agent of her life story and identifies the addressee in making her narration dialogic. She explains why her parents were important in the rise of working-class consciousness, something that she herself had.

Ida's childhood was "extremely poor" and her parents barely coped with their meager living. Her father got a house loan, with which he was able to build a house for his family. He worked as a garbage-collecting driver, a job where he could collect other people's cast outs and put them to good use at his construction site. Besides job flexibility, as Sigrid Wadauer has argued, geographic mobility was a basic feature of earning one's bread.[17] Within the family unit, there used to be social roles that the family members took on and which were assigned to everyone, depending on their birth order and sex (see Fig. 12.1). The mother sent Ida's older siblings door to door to beg for food for the rest of the family. Ida, as the youngest child, was lucky to avoid begging. Later, when they were old enough, the older siblings were expected to leave the home croft. Although the family kept hens that offered some support in livelihoods, the mother also sewed *siro* skirts for sale at home. "Siros" were the end bits of rolls of fabric and textiles, which were given away almost for free from the stores held by factories. These end bits were exploited, especially among the poor factory workers if they could sew. By selling their family pig, Ida's mother took out a loan to buy a sewing machine. After selling some skirts, Ida's mother was able to pay down the loan and put some bread on the table. This kind of economic activity benefited household producers, who

Fig. 12.1 A peddler boy in the northern coastal town of Oulu, Finland, in 1932. Working-class oral histories often disclose how parents occasionally had to send their children to peddle in order to secure the livelihood of the family. Children evoked more sympathy and managed thus to sell hand-made goods, such as cruets. (Photo by Samuli Paulaharju. Finnish Heritage Agency)

could only compete with factory production by accepting less pay for more work.[18]

Besides the bulk of daily work, the perspective on life may have been different between the family members. Whereas Ida's mother could read and write, and she was a serious Christian, her father, who was not religious and did not want to attend the Sunday services, was barely literate. It is possible that orientation toward novelties or ideologies related to other forms of mentalities, too. In Ida's case, literacy and being open to heterogeneous economic opportunities probably went hand in hand for her mother, who was significantly younger than Ida's father.

The second narrator, Anto, was born in West Finland in 1914. The oldest of three children, at the age of six he lost his father. Just before his accidental death in the port of Mäntyluoto, Anto's father had bought a little house for the family, where they would continue to live. In addition to his mother and the three young children, Anto's maternal grandmother lived in the same dwelling. His father had done odd jobs, such as being as a sailor, working in the port and using a small schooner to organize boat transportation services on the local sea. After his father's death, due to no one having the required skills, Anto's mother sold the schooner. For her livelihood, Anto's mother bought a used loom, with which she started to make woollen shirts, coats, socks and "all kinds of stuff." She got the materials, such as wool and yarn, from their neighbors. In this way, she was able to provide for and nurture the family of five.

Anto contributed to provide livelihood in many ways: working in a seine fishing group as a helping hand (earning three shovels of herring for his daily salary), knitting fishnets and woollen socks (a skill taught by his grandmother), and selling newspapers and religious magazines on a street corner. Evidently, the livelihood strategies of the early twentieth-century working-class family were manifold; they reflected a combination of rural and urban possibilities. The boundary between the spheres was not absolute or rigid, but flexible and complementary. Migrating from the country to towns did not involve a major recasting of the ordinary people's worldview or ways of life. Furthermore, the labor-intensive and often unmechanized nature of work in towns made it relatively easy for people with a rural background to adjust to the new working patterns.[19] If the opportunity to earn one's own living in rural livelihoods was limited, then factory communities—that is, a larger population in a relatively small area and the commerce there—offered odd jobs as well as chances for a small business.

Life nevertheless entailed constant struggling since nothing seemed secure or permanent. The importance of social capital helped people to cope with poverty, and sometimes mere luck enabled new livelihood practices. This was the case when Anto received a little saw as a Christmas present from his friend. He started to prepare items, such as cruets and photo frames, from veneer plywood. He made these at home at the end of the kitchen table. After making two boxes of these, he went selling his products by going door to door in the nearby villages. Anto explains his decision to sell elsewhere than his community: "It was a kind of shyness that prevented me to sell my items in my local village." The marketplace usually required social interaction that was formulaic and traditional.[20] Places of trade provided both literal and metaphoric space for performances, and the role of a seller was unknown to the rural working-class people, who were more accustomed to labor as farmhands and servants. Although Anto succeeded in selling his products, he had no desire to do it again: "It was such an experience that I did not want to go to the same place anymore." Therefore, he ended his short career in itinerant door-to-door sales but continued making veneer plywood items that he sold to his mother's customers every now and then.

In every instance or narrative setting, identity is determined by contrast and contact with others. In his story, Anto constructed himself as a self-reliant, middle-class man, who, through careful planning and goal orientation, aimed at a good education and entrepreneurship. He positioned himself in a meritocracy and monetary economy. At the age of eleven, Anto found employment at the local lumber mill; he worked there regularly during the summers and earned his first own money. With this help, the family was able to repair their house, which had always remained unfinished. And with his very first cash salary, Anto was also able to buy a bicycle from the local parish village. He could still remember the exact price of the bike. In the countryside, it was still common to pay in kind, and for the poorest strata of society—such as Ida, Anto and Jouko—money transactions were rare. In addition to the increase of wealth in his family, Anto made plans for further education, which were supported by his mother. He applied to a cooking school in Helsinki, where he was accepted. As the case of Anto shows, odd jobs and variable life events were not merely a reflection of a changing society or a society in transition. On the individual level, they were sudden and unanticipated opportunities from which one was able to benefit.

The third narrator is Jouko, who was born in 1926 in North Finland. There were five members in his family. His father worked at the timber mill and did odd jobs, while his mother took care of the family's rural dwelling place, was responsible for the home chores and rented rooms to itinerant workers. The family moved frequently due to bad economic times, however. On the eve of the Great Depression of the 1930s, Jouko's father lost his job on a tugboat and became unemployed. He started making small wooden handiwork from veneer plywood—cruets, towel racks and shelves—that he sold in nearby areas. When those places became saturated, new destinations for trade had to be found. This was the impetus for investing in a small stall, where all that the family owned was packed. They attempted to squeeze a meagre profit from selling self-made products. Because Jouko's family did not have a long-term fixed abode, they were dependent on the goodwill of locals to accommodate them. Compared to the itinerant Finnish Roma, the begging practiced by ethnic Finns found overnight shelter more easily at farmhouses.[21] Jouko, who was but a young boy at the time of the Great Depression, says that his family acted more like beggars than petty traders.

Illegal Trade as the Source of Humorous Tales

Livelihood narratives within the life stories contain elements of social crime. They resemble social banditry, a phenomenon where individuals living on the edges of rural society, doing petty crime or other illegal acts to survive, were often seen by ordinary people as heroes.[22] Found usually in semi-industrial peasant societies or frontier societies, social banditry not only motivated certain forms of political resistance against oppressive regimes and social hierarchies, but also functioned as a channel of upward social mobility. According to Eric Hobsbawn, who introduced the concept, banditry was a form of self-help and means of escaping the exploitation that existed between the rural working class and the ruling elite.[23]

Unlike folktale tradition, where outlaw heroes such as Robin Hood or Pancho Villa display some level of wit or style, or evoke sympathy that distinguishes them from the common criminal or simply from the crowd,[24] in the life story a bandit is the narrator or someone from their family. Stories of banditry provide an accessible way to understand the social context of livelihood struggles, sometimes consisting of unlawful acts, which took place at home and in community settings. For example, Jouko's parents found a house to rent in the town where his father got a job at the timber mill, and his mother was hired as a mixer and carrier of mortar for bricks. Soon, however, his father became unemployed, and ended up stealing from the shops and granaries; for example, he stole a sack of grain and then the next morning sold it to a local shop. Displays of sudden wealth in Jouko's family were manifold; at Christmas, they all got presents and delicious food to eat. He explains: "Although this happened during the Great Depression and the poorest people in the countryside really suffered, my family succeeded in moving to a better house. The new house had a kitchen and a living room, and it was located just next to the rich, big-bellied Pihlgren's house." Even though the family was wealthier than ever, due to his father's thefts, Jouko and his mother continued working as farmhands in the bigger farmhouses.

In the spring, when Jouko's father stole a bicycle, he was caught and sent to prison for three months. Along with the rest of his family, Jouko had to move out of their nice house to a sauna building. He remembers: "The family was dependent on mother's small income as well as poor relief. Often, we ate potatoes in herring water which I had asked for from the local workers' cooperative store. It did not cost anything. If I happened to find some bread, mice often had gnawed it and it smelled bad.

But if you cut the mice's bite off, it was edible." Unlike Anto, who kept living together with his mother and grandmother in the same parish village and was able to cultivate his social contacts, the constant moving of Jouko's family prevented them from forming close and lasting relationships that might provide support in times of dearth. In this manner, Jouko's story is more proletarian than Anto's, since in Jouko's household the tie between property and family was broken and weakening family bonds promoted greater geographical mobility.[25]

In all three life stories, experiences with petty trade represent hardships in life that are worth sharing. For example, Jouko's mother dealt alcohol on the black market. Peddling, even the illegal type, was part of a makeshift economy. Its forbidden aspect provides the story with narrative value, that is, *tellability*.[26] In school, Jouko was bullied for his parish clothing given as poor relief. He occasionally skipped class and went begging instead: "I begged after my school days. I often got a whole rucksack full of food, which I could carry home. Every time I was hungry, begging was my only option. Once, during Christmas time, I got my sledge full of food and a big pile of clothes for my little sister." Besides begging, Jouko went door to door and sold homemade soap. People usually bought it, because he was so little and brutally honest when asked about his family's economic problems. At the same time, he was rewarded for telling private details—that is, gossiping—which was a powerful tool of social control in the small communities.

Through increased uncertainty and poverty, survivalist and opportunist strategies were developed.[27] For example, the extent of informal door-to-door or street trading increased in times of economic decline.[28] Ways of petty crime were shared as the uttermost livelihood strategy. The three narrators did not see their illegal acts as serious crime. Selling alcohol on the black market was one way to make do, as Jouko explains: "It was during the Prohibition [1919–1932] when intense transportation of rectified spirit from the sea to inland occurred. Although dangerous, my father got excited about this business." In the narratives, resorting to informal economic activities to earn one's livelihood was considered a sign of wits and great ability to get through hardships. In this manner, the outlaw hero served as the construction of oneself as being able to cope with hard times.

Interestingly, those who resorted to the illegal economy implicitly agreed that these economic activities were not morally acceptable, but because of poverty and due to the moral values of the narrative moment, illegal trade could not be considered serious. One such story is the following: "At night, father and Kalle went to the nearby forest where they collected broken dry branches from fallen trees. The local farm master had given permission to collect twigs and sticks, but those branches that my father and Kalle carried on their shoulder were more logs than sticks." As part of narrating the self, the criminal behavior of the past is not apologized for, underestimated, or exaggerated. The ways in which livelihoods were provided reflect the flexibility in social and economic change. Alternative employment possibilities were frequently sought after, and this kind of economic behavior sought not to maximize income but to ensure that all family members were adequately fed and employed.[29]

Gendered Space and Materials

Much like the self-sufficiency of the peasant, forms of economic behavior and petty trade were culturally constitutive. In the peasant economy based on patriarchal and patrilineal systems, work was delineated in gender-specific terms and self-made products were denoted as the responsibility of women as opposed to men.[30] Usually, men oversaw grain and animal meat, whereas women had control over dairy products as well as growing vegetables and roots and picking berries. The "feminine foodstuff" was bartered and sold at the market by women.[31] Hence, in terms of gender, items of economic exchange were differentiated. Although economic behavior represented a modern phenomenon and widened the traditional female sphere especially, it nevertheless continued to pass down age-old gendering practices that were often linked to materiality. Women sold the products they could prepare due to their upbringing and learning of history in home chores. Small-scale trade was often a last resort for Ida, Jouko and Anto, perhaps due to their strong cultural pattern of peasant self-sufficiency or, alternatively, of factory worker paternalism. However, when small-scale economic activity was carried out, it was gendered. Thus, due to the importance of material conditions, exchanges and productions for identity processes, forms of social formations such as households and social hierarchies occurred simultaneously according to traditions.[32]

What, then, was the gendered boundary within working-class petty trade? According to the narrators, men (or boys) purchased manufactured fabrics, trinkets and small items, whereas women sold homemade products. Ida narrates at length about her drunken husband, who desperately tried to find a suitable livelihood for the family. Ida was a factory worker, and her husband did odd jobs that, in terms of the labor hierarchy, were considered low status. Another time he was again sacked from his job, and with his last salary, he wanted to invest in goods that he could then sell as an itinerant trader. He was inspired by his brother-in-law, Ida's brother, who occasionally visited them on his trading tours. After seeing the brother-in-law counting his money, Ida's husband wanted to become an itinerant trader: "Now this fella [the husband] aspired to become rich doing the same thing. But he was not a salesman. With our sons, he only made one trading trip. He carried the sack but made our boys sell in the houses. There was neither big money when they returned nor fewer yarn skeins and combs. Late in the autumn, the boys still were selling these items after their schooldays. Hubby himself [that is, Ida's husband] found a new job making a road somewhere in the near area." Describing her marriage as an unbalanced relationship, Ida uses the euphemisms "hubby" and "fella" when referring to her husband. Without doubt, narratives in the form of half-public self-reflection serve as a performance act in reflecting on unsatisfactory conditions inside the family.

In addition to Ida's life-story collection, which contains several documents written over the years, there are newspaper and journal articles on Ida in the archive collections. She gained local fame after getting her autobiographical writings published as a novel. The book merged her autobiographical accounts with fictional elements. Besides her handwritten life-story, the archives have files of interviews with and media presentations about Ida. In one of the interviews, she tells how her husband's alcohol use was the hardest experience in her life. Hence, Ida was the provider of the family: "The family economy was upheld by Ida and for the sake of her imaginativeness. At the worst moments she even did some paintings that she asked her sons to sell door to door." Again, men and boys, not women, sold ready-made items when going door to door.

It is interesting how in her life story Ida tells how she was the head of the family, the de facto breadwinner, because her husband was obsessed with alcohol and weak in decision-making. However, in the media interview, the journalist—a male—describes their family according to the patriarchal ideal, with the man being the breadwinner and decision-maker of the household. "Laughing easily, sweet Ida is slightly tense in her first interview ever, but Lauri [the husband] just keeps smoking calmly. As a retired bricklayer, Lauri obviously leads the family. When Ida gets confused, he jumps into the talk and helps her forward." Unlike the life-story narratives, the interview gives a different view of the dynamics of the couple. Moreover, Ida's published book is presented as the result of the husband's strong will and fearless nature: "Obviously the book would not have existed without Lauri's intervention, because Ida was losing her courage many times." In addition to marriage, small-scale trading activities with the help of their sons were depicted differently in the life-story and in the magazine interview.

Without doubt, gender shaped practices of petty trade. The men's sphere was not only geographically wider but also provided multiple possibilities to purchase items. Soon after the Second World War, Jouko got a job in a textile factory. The factory had its own store for the workers, where they could buy items freely without wartime ration stamps. Jouko bought some fabric and then had it made into his first tailor-made suit. Soon he met a man selling old Finnish army tents, who mentioned that they were good material for overalls, that is, working clothes: "Instead of asking where he had got these tents, I bought one tent which I thought was cheap. I started to sell this tent fabric by the meter from house to another. Due to the wartime shortage of clothes, I was successful in my trade. I traveled around the country and money came in. I stayed in hotels and lived like a master." As in Jouko's case, narratives on petty trade might sometimes describe events, the details of people, and the dialogues with them very precisely. This occurs especially when something successful has been achieved. Although based at times on stretching the laws and uncertain times, success needed to be included in the narrative because it is part of the narrator's present self. Therefore, narratives work as a technique in self-production.

In time, Jouko became so rich that he could afford his father's funeral. His father had spent the rest of his life in prison. Soon thereafter, Jouko changed careers and started to work as a driver and then, after the war, at odd jobs like in the army, in the plywood industry and as a bricklayer at a construction site. Just as petty trade represented a sudden chance, Jouko's entire life seemed to be individual and "free." His career choices were probably not so much about explicit decisions and goal-oriented actions, but rather seizing the moment without concern for the future. Compared to Ida, Jouko's petty trade included social encounters and the ability to manage his work in sales. Moreover, small-scale trade demanded wit. More profoundly, the stories of petty trade reflect the condition of a society where men had more freedom and, unlike women, they were able to be independent early on.

Conclusions

Working-class livelihoods consisted of manifold sources, depending on the season and geographical location. Ida, Anto and Jouko were self-employed workers in terms of making and selling things, although they all worked occasionally at factories or on farms. From the early twentieth century onward, many kinds of odd jobs increased, along with the rise of capitalism and wage earning. Despite their rural background, Ida, Jouko and Anto as self-employed workers had little control over production. They were all dependent wage earners, or "disguised proletarians."[33]

One strategy for survival among the poorest people was petty trade. However, this was a last resort rather than a livelihood activity that was sought after. The items that were sold by people who were not skilled in craftsmanship included small wood products and self-made dresses. Not only were the items gendered—that is, men prepared things cut out of wood and women made dresses and clothes out of fabric—but the selling activities were as well. Sales took place outside the home and, as both male authors stressed, often outside one's own village. While petty trade was practiced by both genders, mobile petty trade was reserved for men. Undoubtedly, women were much more likely than men to be the victims of sexual harassment and sexual assault and, therefore, geographically mobile selling was not a viable option for women. Moreover, common views on what was considered a respectable livelihood did not encourage people to become a petty trader, since that was an occupation practiced by the stigmatized groups of the Finnish society, that is, Roma, Russians, or Jews (see Wassholm in this volume).

Another narrative theme within the life-stories regarding petty trade is social banditry. Originally, the term was introduced to describe those persons regarded by official society and the authorities as outlaws, but who remained within the bounds of the moral order of the peasant communities. Although banditry was illegal, locals usually viewed bandits as heroes. In the working-class livelihood narratives, the elements of social banditry appear in the form of petty theft by a person acting alone, not in a group. In this sense, social banditry was neither violent nor revolutionary. Moreover, the hero of the story tended to be the narrator or a close relative, such as either of one's parents. Tolerant and partly humorous attitudes toward crimes in the past can be explained by the own narrator's position as poor; even necessitating committing illegal acts at times, struggling for one's livelihood and surviving in a destitute state-required wits.

The original idea of social banditry by Hobsbawn suggested certain conditions of existence for the mode of primitive rebellion, primary among these being the presence of a traditional peasant environment and the absence of industrial capitalism. In their life stories, Ida, Jouko and Anto describe the period of social and economic change that transformed Finland from a rural peasant society into an industrial one. Therefore, it may be presumed that social banditry as the narrative theme had already merged with the stereotypical character of a trickster, who appears in mythology and folklore.

Notes

1. See, for example, Charles Tilly. 1984. "Demographic origins of the European proletariat"; Pertti Haapala. 1986. *Tehtaan valossa. Teollistuminen ja työväestön muodostuminen Tampereella 1820–1920.*
2. Roberts 1990, pp. 353–354.
3. Heikkinen 1997, p. 38.
4. E.g., Jankiewicz 2012, p. 395.
5. A Marxist approach to folklore is relatively rare among folklorists and ethnologists. There are a few who do engage it, however, such as José Limón. 1983. "Western Marxism and Folklore: A Critical Introduction" and Willow G. Mullins and Puja Batra-Wells (eds.). 2019. *The Folklorist in the Marketplace. Conversations at the Crossroads of Vernacular Culture and Economics.*
6. Schely-Newman 2009, p. 2.
7. Plummer 2001, p. 401; see also Portelli 1998, pp. 72, 68.
8. Stahl Dolby 1989, pp. 17–19.
9. Linde 1993, p. 23.
10. E.g., Charlotte Linde. 2015. "Memory in Narrative."
11. Andrews 1991, p. 65; Saltzman 1994, p. 107.
12. Andrews 2007, p. 53.
13. Lyons 2013, p. 16.
14. Anna Kuismin and M. J. Driscoll. 2013. *White Field, Black Seeds—Nordic Literacy Practices in the Long Nineteenth Century.*
15. Haapala 1986, p. 215.
16. Shuman 2015, p. 42.
17. Wadauer 2012, p. 225.
18. Dawley and Faler 1977, p. 471.
19. E.g., Magnússon 2011, p. 193.
20. Mullins and Batra-Wells 2019, p. 13.

21. Eija Stark. 2020. "Stories on the food-begging Roma: Boundary making in the Finnish peasant homes."
22. Eric Hobsbawn first introduced these concepts. See Eric Hobsbawn. 1959. *Primitive Rebels: Studies in Archaic Forms of Social Movement in the 19th and 20th Centuries*; Eric Hobsbawn. 1969. *Bandits.*
23. Hobsbawn 1969, p. 19.
24. Seal 2009, p. 74.
25. E.g., Roberts 1990, p. 363.
26. Ochs and Capps 2001, pp. 33–34.
27. E.g., Little 2014, p. 47.
28. Van den Heuvel 2012, p. 136.
29. E.g., Roberts 1990, p. 356
30. Worobec 2008, pp. 85–87.
31. E.g., Ann-Catrin Östman. 2000. *Mjölk och jord. Om kvinnlighet, manlighet och arbete i ett österbottniskt jordbrukssamhälle ca 1870–1940*; Pirjo Markkola. 1989. "Maaseudun työläisvaimot."
32. Van Gent and Toivo 2016, p. 263; Eirinn Larsen and Vibeke Kieding Banik, 2016. "Mixed feelings: Women, Jews, and business around 1900."
33. See, e.g., Roberts 1990, p. 364.

Bibliography

Archival Sources

Finnish Literature Society Archives, Materials on Traditional and Contemporary Culture, Autobiography collections of Satasärmäinen nainen and Eläköön mies.

The Labour Archives, the narrative collection of the Commission of Finnish Labour Tradition.

Literature

Andrews, Molly. *Lifetimes of Commitment: Ageing, Politics, Psychology*. Cambridge, UK: Cambridge University Press, 1991.

Andrews, Molly. *Shaping History: Narratives of Political Change*. Cambridge, UK: Cambridge University Press, 2007.

Ashton, William A. "What would Hermes do? A Jungian perspective on the trickster and business ethics." In *The Folklorist in the Marketplace: Conversations at the Crossroads of Vernacular Culture and Economics*, edited by Willow G. Mullins and Puja Batra-Wells, 234–251. Logan, UT: Utah State University Press, 2019.

Dawley, Alan, and Paul Faler. "Working-Class Culture and Politics in the Industrial Revolution: Sources of Loyalism and Rebellion." *Journal of Social History* 9, no. 4 (1977): 466–480.

Haapala, Pertti. *Tehtaan valossa. Teollistuminen ja työväestön muodostuminen Tampereella 1820–1920.* Tampere: Vastapaino, 1986.

Heikkinen, Sakari. *Labour and the Market: Workers, Wages and Living Standards in Finland 1850–1913.* Helsinki: Academia Scientiarum Fennica, 1997.

Heuvel van Den, Danielle. "Selling in the shadows: peddlers and hawkers in early modern Europe." In *Working on Labor: Essays in Honor of Jan Lucassen*, edited by Marcel van der Linden, Leo Lucassen and Jan Lucassen, 123–151. Leiden: Brill, 2012.

Hobsbawn, Eric. *Primitive Rebels: Studies in Archaic Forms of Social Movement in the 19th and 20th Centuries.* Manchester: Manchester University Press, 1959.

Hobsbawn, Eric. *Bandits.* London: Weidenfeld & Nicholson, 1969.

Jankiewicz, Stephen. "A dangerous Class: The Street Sellers of Nineteenth-Century London." *Journal of Social History* 46, no. 2 (2012): 391–414.

Kuismin, Anna and M. J. Driscoll (eds.). *White Field, Black Seeds — Nordic Literacy Practices in the Long Nineteenth Century.* Helsinki: Finnish Literature Society, 2013.

Larsen, Eirinn and Vibeke Kieding Banik. "Mixed feelings: Women, Jews, and business around 1900." *Scandinavian Journal of History* 41, no. 3 (2016): 350–368.

Limón, José. "Western Marxism and Folklore: A Critical Introduction." *Journal of American Folklore* 96, no. 379 (1983): 34–52.

Linde, Charlotte. *Life Stories: The Creation of Coherence.* New York and Oxford: Oxford University Press, 1993.

Linde, Charlotte. "Memory in Narrative." *The International Encyclopedia of Language and Social Interaction.* Hoboken, NJ: Wiley & Blackwell, 2015.

Little, Peter D. *Economic and Political Reform in Africa: Anthropological Perspectives.* Bloomington: Indiana University Press, 2014.

Lyons, Martin. *The Writing Culture of Ordinary People in Europe, c.1860–1920.* Cambridge: Cambridge University Press, 2013.

Magnússon, Sigurður Gylfi. "The Life of a Working-Class Woman: selective modernization and microhistory in early 20th-century Iceland." *Scandinavian Journal of History* 36, no. 2 (2011): 186–205.

Markkola, Pirjo. "Maaseudun työläisvaimot." In *Tuntematon työläisnainen*, edited by Leena Laine and Pirjo Markkola, 39–60. Tampere: Vastapaino, 1989.

Mullins, Willow G., and Puja Batra-Wells (eds.). *The Folklorist in the Marketplace: Conversations at the Crossroads of Vernacular Culture and Economics.* Logan, UT: Utah State University Press, 2019.

Ochs, Elinor, and Lisa Capps. *Living Narrative.* Cambridge, MA: Harvard University Press, 2001.

Plummer, Ken. "The Call of Life Stories in Ethnographic Research." In *Handbook of Ethnography*, edited by Paul Atkinson, Amanda Coffey, Sara Delamont, John Lofland and Lyn Lofland, 395–406. London: SAGE, 2001.

Portelli, Alessandro. "What makes oral history different." In *Oral History, Oral Culture, and Italian Americans*, edited by Luisa Del Giudice, 21–30. New York: Palgrave Macmillan, 1998.

Roberts, B. R. "Peasants and proletarians." *Annual Review of Sociology* 16 (1990): 353–377.

Saltzman, Rachelle H. "Folklore as Politics in Great Britain: Working-class Critiques of Upper-Class Strike Breakers in the 1926 General Strike." *Anthropological Quarterly* 67, no. 3 (1994): 105–121.

Schely-Newman, Esther. "To break down the wall: Constructing a literate self." *Narrative Inquiry* 19, no. 1 (2009): 1–17.

Seal, Graham. "The Robin Hood Principle: Folklore, History, and the Social Bandit." *Journal of Folklore Research* 46, no. 1 (2009): 67–89.

Shuman, Amy. "Story Ownership and Entitlement." In *The Handbook of Narrative Analysis, First Edition*, edited by Anna De Vina and Alexandra Georgakopoulou, 38–56. Chichester, UK: John Wiley & Sons, Ltd.., 2015.

Stahl Dolby, Sandra. *Literary Folkloristics and the Personal Narrative*. Bloomington: Indiana University Press, 1989.

Stark, Eija. "Stories on the food-begging Roma: Boundary making in the Finnish peasant homes." In *Food Identities at Home and on the Move: Explorations at the Intersection of Food, Belonging and Dwelling*, edited by Raúl Matta, Charles-Édouard Suremain and Chantal Crenn, 160–173. London: Routledge, 2020.

Teubner, Melina. "Street food, urban space, and gender: Working on the streets of nineteenth-century Rio de Janeiro (1830–1870)." *International Review of Social History* 64 (2019): 229–254.

Tilly, Charles. "Demographic origins of the European proletariat." In *Proletarianization and Family History*, edited by D. C. Levine, 1–85. Orlando, FL: Academic Press, 1984.

Van Gent, Jacqueline, and Raisa Maria Toivo. "Introduction. Gender, material culture and emotions in Scandinavian history." *Scandinavian Journal of History* 41, no. 3 (2016): 263–270.

Wadauer, Sigrid. "Asking for the privilege to work: Applications for a peddling license (Austria in the 1920s and 1930s)." In *Poverty and Sickness in Modern Europe: Narratives of the Sick Poor, 1780–1938*, edited by Andreas Gestrich, Elizabeth Hurren and Steven King, 225–246. London and New York: Continuum, 2012.

Worobec, Christine. "Peasantry." *The Oxford Encyclopedia of Women in World History*, 85–88. Oxford: Oxford University Press, 2008.

Östman, Ann-Catrin. *Mjölk och jord. Om kvinnlighet, manlighet och arbete i ett österbottniskt jordbrukssamhälle ca 1870–1940*. Åbo: Åbo Akademis förlag, 2000.

CHAPTER 13

Settling Down and Setting Up: Itinerant Peddlers from Russian Karelia as Shopkeepers in Late Nineteenth- and Early Twentieth-Century Finland

Anna Sundelin

Treats in a Wine Cellar

On November 12, 1927, the Ostrobothnian newspaper *Wasabladet* printed an obituary recounting the life of a locally well-known shopkeeper, Kiril Lipkin. Lipkin was born in 1855 in Vuokkiniemi in East Karelia and started out as an itinerant peddler, making his first trip to Finland when he was only twelve years old. In the 1880s, he settled down in the village of Vörå (Finnish: Vöyri) on the west coast of Finland. Soon he became a successful shopkeeper, but he was also active in numerous other types of businesses. He married a local woman, converted to the Lutheran faith and became a Finnish citizen. At the time of his death, he was described as "a good son of the place that became his second home, generally well liked for his good and cheerful nature."[1]

A. Sundelin (✉)
Culture, History and Philosophy, Åbo Akademi University, Turku, Finland
e-mail: anna.sundelin@abo.fi

J. Ahlbeck et al. (eds.), *Encounters and Practices of Petty Trade in Northern Europe, 1820–1960*,
https://doi.org/10.1007/978-3-030-98080-1_13

In many ways, Kiril Lipkin was typical of the itinerant peddlers from Russian Karelia who settled down in Finland at the end of the nineteenth and the beginning of the twentieth centuries. He had begun his career as an ambulatory trader at a young age, making numerous trips throughout the years between his home in Russian Karelia and his Finnish customers. And he was not the only one. According to the Finnish historian Pekka Nevalainen, some 300 to 400 men from the region of Vuokkiniemi annually earned a living as itinerant peddlers in Finland at the end of the nineteenth century. Including traders from other areas of Russian Karelia, an estimated 1400–1500 peddlers sold their goods yearly in Finland during the latter part of the nineteenth century, a number that grew to almost 2000 during the first decade of the twentieth century.[2] However, in other ways Kiril Lipkin was extraordinary. Far from all the itinerant peddlers of Russian Karelian origin who peddled their wares in Finland abandoned their itinerant way of life and settled down. And of those who did, not all became successful businessmen. At the time of his death, Lipkin not only owned several rural shops, he also had shares in ventures that were important for the running of daily life in the Finnish countryside: a bakery, a dairy, and a sawmill.[3] Furthermore, he had been involved in a project to modernize his new home region and connect it to the outside world. This venture brought the first telephone line to the people of Vörå. With his earnings, Lipkin had provided himself and his family with a large house, in the basement of which he had a wine cellar where his best customers were entertained after successful business deals. According to one anecdote, Kiril Lipkin, who spoke Swedish with an accent, would ask his customers in a broken tongue if they would prefer a small or a big glass while serving them drinks.[4] All in all, being a respected member of the community and entertaining guests in his own wine cellar was a huge advancement from the days when he had traversed the countryside on foot, carrying his supply of goods in a large pack on his back.

As exemplified by the case of Kiril Lipkin, some of the itinerant peddlers in time abandoned their itinerant way of life and settled down in the Finnish countryside, and a percentage of these chose to earn their living through shopkeeping. In this chapter, I examine the reception of the itinerant peddlers from Russian Karelia, with a focus on those who settled down in the Swedish-speaking parts of Finland. The aim is to demonstrate how these men made the transfer from peddling, considered to be the lowest level of retail trade, to being shop-based traders, and to examine how they managed, both socially and financially.

Peddlers Settling Down

Finland had transformed from an integral part of the Swedish realm into an autonomous Grand Duchy of the Russian Empire in 1809. In the nineteenth and early twentieth centuries, numerous traders from the Arkhangelsk Governorate and the Olonets Governorate in Russia proper roamed the Finnish countryside. Based on the way that they transported their goods, the Finnish locals commonly referred to these peddlers as "Rucksack Russians" (Swedish: *laukku-ryss*, *arkangelit*; Finnish: *laukku-ryssä*). The peddlers differed from their local customers in Finland through their Orthodox faith and some cultural attributes, such as language and the way that they dressed (see Fig. 13.1).[5] Due to a separate citizenship right that had developed in the Grand Duchy, the Russian Karelian peddlers were considered "foreigners" in Finland, and their trade was officially illegal.[6]

However, the peddlers' main customers, the people living in the Finnish countryside, were usually unbothered by this fact. With the improvement in the standard of living in Finland in the end of the nineteenth century, they could spend a larger part of their income on consumer items and occasional luxuries. The itinerant peddlers with their large backpacks or bundles with necessities and novelties were therefore awaited guests in many homes. A visit from an itinerant peddler was also appreciated for the amusement that the tradesman provided. The haggling over prices often turned into a spectacle, and in the evenings the peddlers would entertain their hosts with news and exciting stories from other places that they had visited.[7] Like other mobile groups in Finland at the time, such as the Roma,[8] the peddlers from Russian Karelia were dependent on the locals for accommodations and food during their journeys. Over time, they established closer connections with specific families and always returned to these houses. In some cases where the peddlers returned frequently to the same village, a friendship formed between the locals and the peddlers. This was important, as the need for a safe place to stay the night was a necessity for the traders so far away from home.[9]

In contrast to peddling, keeping a shop has been described as a form of small-scale commercial activity that holds the promise of a steady livelihood. Shopkeeping is potentially a means of upward social mobility. By definition, it involves ownership of a shop and is consequently a much more advanced form of entrepreneurship than street peddling. Keeping a shop does require some initial investment and a relatively stable enterprise,

Fig. 13.1 Two "Rucksack Russians" in a Finnish atelier, 1917. (Photo by Erik Hägglund. The Society of Swedish Literature in Finlan)

as well as an extended network of credit and customers. In addition, previous studies have highlighted that keeping a shop is one of the few legitimate sources of advancement for those who have fewer options, for example, due to a lack of education, discrimination against minorities, or language difficulties.[10]

During the decades following the famine years of the late 1860s, Finnish society began developing swiftly. A lower mortality rate gave rise to rapid population growth, affecting the rural inhabitants, who more often than before had to resort to working for money instead of working in their own fields. This caused some to leave the countryside, to look for work in the nearest town, while others emigrated. However, despite this movement, Finland was still an agrarian society at the beginning of the twentieth century.[11]

In the latter part of the nineteenth century, Finland also experienced a dramatic rise in consumption. The popularity and success of itinerant trade in this process can partly be explained by the fact that it offered rural consumers a practical way to make necessary purchases.[12] One alternative was to visit the nearest town or a country fair, but such journeys were rarely made, due to long distances. While town trips did bring some variety to everyday life, they were generally considered tiring, time-consuming, and economically unrewarding.[13]

Another alternative was to visit a rural shop. The shop network was relatively weakly developed in comparison to most Western European countries.[14] Furthermore, it seems that many peddlers could still offer a more diverse range of goods for sale than the local shops, and they often brought the latest novelties to their customers.[15] This put the peddlers who turned to shopkeeping in an interesting position that is worthy of scrutiny. On the one hand, they were skilled traders, with contacts to suppliers of novelties and consumer durables. On the other, they lacked an education and the knowledge that was necessary for the more stable livelihood offered by keeping a shop. Despite these challenges, however, some men were willing to take the risk.

During the past decade, historians have stressed the need for examining emotion. A focus on emotions in history will lead to a better understanding of the past as well as insight into how and why emotions have changed over time.[16] The itinerant peddlers evoked various and sometimes contradictory emotions among the people who were affected by their trade.[17] In general, their customers saw a visit from itinerant peddlers as something positive; the visit offered a welcome break from daily routines. Negative views were expressed by the authorities who had an interest in restraining illicit trade and depicting the itinerant peddlers as unjust competitors of honest Finnish merchants. An interest in the success or failure of the peddlers who turned into shopkeepers is part of a line of historical research that has examined the establishment of shops in the Finnish countryside. The most comprehensive study on rural trade has been done by Aulis J. Alanen, whose overview reveals that up until the late 1850s, shops were only allowed in towns. In 1859, however, an act permitted the opening of country shops if the distance to the nearest town was further than 50 km.

In addition, the potential shopkeeper had to meet several requirements: in order to set up a shop, one had to be a Finnish citizen with a good reputation, know how to read and write, and be skilled at bookkeeping. The supplies of the first shops were also limited by law.[18]

Despite these restrictions, there were already more than 400 country shops three years later, most of them in eastern Finland. According to Alanen, many of these were kept by former peddlers—in other words, men who were accustomed to trade. Furthermore, some of these applicants may have already had some experience of actual shopkeeping, as they had kept some form of illegal shops in farm storehouses prior to 1859. In 1889, the Act of Freedom of Trade had liberated things even more and many new country shops were set up. In his work, Alanen underlines that the opening of a shop was not a simple matter and that many who became involved in retail trade in this way failed. Yet, when the shopkeeper succeeded, the shop could be an important center in the village.[19] The shops not only provided the customers with better access to consumer goods, but they were also generally seen as the cultural outpost of towns in the countryside. The country shops represented places of retail and consumption, as well as places of gathering and recreation for the village residents.[20]

In general, the retail trade and the interaction between traders and buyers have grown more complex over time.[21] This chapter focuses on the years 1870–1910. This is roughly the time period covered by the sources, but the decades around 1900 are also interesting when considering the development of consumption in Finnish history. In addition to growth in the number of opportunities for consumption and trade, there was an increase in the amount of goods on the market, as well as their variety. Among the new consumer items, for example, were oil lamps, bicycles and other objects that changed people's everyday lives and made new activities possible. The increase in consumption was not least visible in the number of writings in the contemporary newspapers, where critical voices were raised against the superfluous and unnecessary consumption in society, especially among the lower classes.[22]

Accounts About Rural Consumption

By examining the reception of the traders and the commercial exchanges between them and their customers, I wish to broaden our understanding of the social significance of the peddlers. In this chapter, I will explore the following three questions: (1) how are the peddlers-turned-shopkeepers described in the examined sources, (2) what role did their shops seem to play for the local community, and (3) what was the relationship between the shopkeepers and the surrounding community like?

The analysis is based on a large array of sources, stretching from newspaper writings to court records and bankruptcy documents. The main sources for understanding the reception of the peddlers by the local communities are two ethnographic questionnaires sent out by the Department of Cultural History at Åbo Akademi University in the 1950s and 1960s. The first questionnaire focuses on the country shops in Finland in general, while the other examines the itinerant traders from Russian Karelia and their trade in Finland more specifically.

Ethnographic questionnaires became an important method for gathering data within ethnology in the mid-twentieth century. The ethnographic archives of Åbo Akademi University were founded in 1952 with the aim of acquiring knowledge about the Swedish-speaking culture in Finland. The questionnaire on Russian itinerant peddlers was sent out in 1957, and again in 1968 in a slightly modified version. The collection contains 178 responses from the Swedish-speaking regions of Finland. The other questionnaire, some of which took the form of interviews, was called "Shopkeeping in the countryside." Conducted in 1953, it received about 200 responses. At times it is difficult to identify specific questions and responses that relate specifically to the topic discussed in this chapter. The respondents have often written a coherent account without distinguishing between the various questions. In the responses to the questionnaire about the itinerant peddlers, the focus is mostly on the peddling itself; however, in some cases, the respondent mentions that the peddler also opened a shop and describes how it fared. It has been a significant discovery that some of the peddlers mentioned by name in the answers to the questionnaire about itinerant peddling reappear as shopkeepers later on.

In this chapter, I try to see the itinerant peddlers as part of a community, focusing on their ambitions and social networks and the practices that surrounded their trade both as peddlers and as shopkeepers. Previous studies have underlined how stories about itinerant traders, despite often being anecdotal, offer insights into the development of consumer society and the people who shaped it. An examination of the ethnographic sources studied in this chapter can illuminate elements of the relationships between retailers and consumers that are invisible in other sources. However, there are a few source-critical aspects to consider. The answers to the questionnaires were written down a long time after the actual events and may have been colored by nostalgia (see also Huldén in this volume Chap. 6). It is also evident that in some cases the accounts were not personally experienced but represent a compilation of interviews made with one or several other persons. This may further affect the reliability of the answers.[23]

Setting Up Shop

Those who are not good enough to do anything else might as well become keepers of a country shop. That was the situation in Finland during the 1880s, at least in the mind of a grumpy contemporary commentator writing for the newspaper *Åbo Tidning*. According to the commentator, numerous country stores had been set up since the liberation of trade; however, many of the shopkeepers seemed to lack the necessary skills and qualifications.[24]

Previous studies have shown that those who set up a shop in the countryside after the liberation of trade were a diverse group. Some were local farmers who kept a small supply of goods in their homes or a storehouse in the courtyard. Others were educated, including those who had moved to the area with the strict intent to set up a shop.[25] After the Act of Freedom of Trade in 1879, those desirous of shopkeeping still had to apply to the governor for permission. Yet, in order to make such an application, one needed permission from the local county sheriff and the city council, saying that they wanted the shop in the first place. By denying this permission, the local council could thus hinder unwanted peddlers from setting up a business. This is something that they often did, for local merchants were often part of the council and saw potentially competing shops as a threat to their own business. Therefore, some peddlers resorted to applying for the permit in the name of a local resident whom they had befriended. Another option was that the peddler became the keeper of a branch shop, while a native Finnish resident had applied for the permit for the main shop.[26]

As itinerant traders, peddlers from Russian Karelia visited most parts of Finland, and they also settled down all over the country.[27] Some spread into the Swedish-speaking areas on the Finnish west coast, venturing as far as the Åland Islands in the Baltic Sea (see Fig. 13.2).[28] One of these was Nikolai Rugojeff (1876–1914), whose family originated in Kostamus in Russian Karelia. Rugojeff started out as an itinerant peddler in the Åland Islands, selling mostly textiles of various sorts. After venturing into

Fig. 13.2 Göran Lipkin, a former "Rucksack Russian", established himself professionally as a storekeeper in Vörå, Finland. Here he is posing in his store in the early 1900s. (Photo by Erik Hägglund. The Society of Swedish Literature in Finland)

shopkeeping, he kept stores in numerous places, including Eckerö, Jomala, Hammarland and Saltvik.[29] The reason for these several attempts was probably the fierce competition among the shopkeepers in the Åland Islands at the time, as there were more traders than could support themselves.[30] One respondent reminisced that Nikolai Rugojeff had a quite substantial and varied supply in his shop: mostly fabrics, ready-made suits, a few types of underwear, pins, thread and the like. However, Rugojeff seems to have been a man of many trades. Besides shopkeeping, he also worked as a butcher, and despite owning a building stocked with merchandise, it seems that he still locked up his shop from time to time and went back to itinerant trade.[31]

Many of the Russian Karelian peddlers traveled with friends or relatives. When they settled down, they did so together. When Kiril Lipkin settled down in Vörå, he had help from his brother and nephew, who saw to the franchise shops.[32] Nikolai Rugojeff also had a brother, who peddled in the

Åland Islands and traded horses when possible.[33] There are also other examples of former peddlers who tried to open up a shop, but still from time to time went back to peddling or gained a livelihood in other ways.[34] In addition to all the practical skills needed by a shopkeeper, it was necessary to know if it would be profitable to open up a shop in a specific area.[35] As the itinerant peddlers in many cases had a long history of peddling in a specific area before they settled down, they knew their customers quite well. However, that was not enough to be a successful shopkeeper.

Kellery Graham has noted that shopkeepers in Britain changed their way of doing business during the nineteenth century. The shops became larger and brighter, and the prices of items were set instead of being based on haggling. Furthermore, the goods were placed on shelves, out in the open, so that customers could examine them by themselves.[36] A similar development was also experienced in the rural shops in Finland, albeit there were variations among the various establishments. According to Aulis Alanen, it was rare for a new shopkeeper to begin by building a specific house for the shop. However, as time went by and business was successful, buildings grew bigger and were purposely built for the needs of the shopkeeper, with room for storage and so on.[37] In the answers to the ethnographic questionnaire about country shops, one respondent describes Nikolai Rugojeff's shop in the following way:

> It was a quite small room and then there was a sales counter, and the walls were filled with hooks, where they had all kinds of goods, and the space where the customers could be was about 2 × 2 meters, no more than that, I think. [...] He kept his supply in a storehouse. But he had a large supply. They had glass on one part of the counter, and the rest was without glass, and then they lined up their supply on the counter so that the customers could see what was sold; but the part that was covered by glass, there the goods were kept under the glass and then the customer had to point at the desired item.[38]

Pekka Nevalainen has argued that the Russian Karelian peddlers who became shopkeepers often did so because they were "big players," men with the necessary resources and networks. Furthermore, many of them married local women, which further integrated them into the local community.[39]

From the sources that I have studied, it seems that many of these peddlers-turned-shopkeepers started out on a quite small scale and with modest means. One respondent mentions that the itinerant peddlers usually turned first from ambulatory trade to selling goods in the market square; thereafter, if they were successful, they moved on to opening a shop.[40] In the case of Nikolai Rugojeff, like many other peddlers settling down, he lacked an education in shopkeeping and no form of bookkeeping seems to have existed in his store. However, the room described above, with glass covering the sales desk, suggests that he was successful, as such displays were not found in every country store at that time. From some of the other respondents' descriptions of shops, it is clear that the peddlers-turned-shopkeepers could start out on a quite small scale. A respondent from the village of Jungsund in the region of Ostrobothnia remembers that the first shop there, opened in the 1860s, was much more modest than the one kept by Nikolai Rugojeff. The shopkeeper, a former peddler named Filippus, rented a room in one of the local farmhouses. He had a quite modest supply of goods: fabrics and various sorts of pieces of clothing, boots, gloves, Russian tobacco, coffee and sugar for those who could afford it. The shop operated for some years but closed after the shopkeeper died in the 1870s.[41]

Daily Necessities and Consumer Durables

The increase in consumer items on the market and the changes in people's consumption habits at the end of the nineteenth century gave rise to a widespread debate. In the contemporary newspapers, many critics complained that especially the poor people in the countryside spent what little money they had on unnecessary items.[42] The itinerant peddlers from Russian Karelia were often accused of spreading luxuries in the countryside. Now, the country shopkeepers as well were blamed for the same practice.[43]

The range of consumer items for sale in country shops was naturally of great interest to the customers. However, the supply of goods was not always that rich and varied. Especially in recently opened shops, the supply could be limited until the business got up and running properly.[44] Itinerant peddlers from Russian Karelia primarily sold consumer durables, such as ready-made clothes and textiles, rather than daily necessities like food. However, a considerable part of their supply can also be described as necessities, a concept that was changing and becoming wider in late nineteenth-century Finland.[45] For example, cotton, a fabric that previously had been considered a luxury, came to be used by people from all ranks of society in the furnishing of homes and as part of modern attire by the end of the nineteenth century.[46]

Itinerant peddlers in the best of times carried a surprisingly wide assortment of goods; in addition to textiles, these included small and light items such as ribbons, needles, buttons, medicines, prints and eyeglasses. Sometimes they also carried foodstuffs and later also factory-made clothes. The range in the quality of these items was as wide as the assortment. Much of it was of poor quality, but there were also new and modern items, as many of the traders were well connected.[47] The ambulatory traders brought their supplies of goods with them from major towns in Russia, such as Petrozavodsk, St. Petersburg or Nizhny Novgorod, while others had their own storages in Finland.[48] When the peddlers settled down, they naturally could continue to sell all the goods that they had previously carried, but they were no longer limited by the need to transport the goods on their backs. That said, the transport of merchandise was at times an issue even for country stores. Since much of the transport at the time was done via sailing ships, the shopkeepers had to build up a good stock of goods during the part of the year when sailing was possible.[49]

Some shopkeepers did quite well and had a wide and varied supply of goods. For instance, the shop of former peddler Ivan Schitinsky near Lovisa in Uusimaa seems to have been well stocked. Schitinsky mostly got his supply of goods from St. Petersburg, where he traveled by his own ship, by exchanging firewood for consumer items such as flour, grain, coffee, sugar, sweets, fabric, rope, boots, petroleum, porcelain, lamps, gunpowder, arsenic and so on. The shop had a good location, next to the main road, and displayed a sign that said *Olutkauppa* ("Beer store"). The shop was of medium size with two rooms and a hallway. While he was away, the shop was tended to by his wife and her mother. His wife was a Russian woman, but she had studied in a Swedish-speaking school in Finland and could therefore accommodate customers in their language (KIVA 4 M196).

The previously mentioned shopkeeper Nikolai Rugojeff made several attempts at keeping a shop in various places in the Åland Islands, but he unfortunately died during an appendectomy in Turku in August 1914 at the age of 38.[50] His sudden death left his businesses unsorted, and his wife and three underaged children had to file for bankruptcy. The documents reveal interesting details about his network and possessions, including the goods that were sold at his shop, at the time of his death. Among the goods are listed numerous foodstuffs but also soap, iron and nails. The list also mentions rags, skins and wool, items that commonly featured in barter with the Russian Karelian peddlers.[51]

As itinerant traders, the peddlers from Russian Karelia preferred to get paid in cash, but in some cases, barter was also an option. One special item that they bartered was human hair; poor women in the countryside would exchange a piece of their hair for a new headscarf. The peddlers, in turn, sold the hair to wigmakers or other parties who turned the hair into jewelry, false braids and so on.[52] In country shops, some shopkeepers offered their customers credit, but cash was preferred, and haggling was common. Kiril Lipkin seems not to have been the only one to treat his customers with small gifts. Especially during Christmas time, the shopkeepers added something extra to the purchases.[53]

In the Center of the Village

Street peddling is at best a temporary solution, allowing people from marginalized groups to earn a living.[54] For the peddler who managed to abandon their itinerant trade and establish a store, the choice of location was important. Villages and otherwise densely populated areas were often preferred.[55] In general, late nineteenth-century country stores placed in the middle of the village had an important role as gathering places for the people living in the surrounding areas.[56] In the shops established by the former peddlers, opening hours seem to have been quite late or not even defined; if there was a customer around, the shop was open.[57] Consequently, people passing by would know that they could meet others in the shop, even if they did not need to make any purchases. If the store was big enough, it soon became a place to gather in the evening to discuss and hear the latest news.[58]

The supply of the first country stores in Finland was regulated by law. Beer—but nothing stronger—was allowed.[59] The fact that Ivan Schitinsky sold beer in his store does not seem to have been appreciated by everyone, but the store was popular and especially on Sunday evenings people from several villages would gather there to socialize. This would sometimes result in fights in the store, fueled by the consumption of alcoholic beverages.[60] In other stores as well, people would gather to drink or socialize.[61] Kiril Lipkin even had revival meetings and sewing meetings arranged in his store.[62] One respondent underlined that the storekeeper was a central figure in the village, the only one in contact with the outer world, who could tell them about what was happening there.[63] The shopkeeper could also introduce novelties to his customers. As previously mentioned, Kiril Lipkin was involved in introducing the first phone line in his village, while the shopkeeper in Granboda in the Åland Islands was the first one to own a bicycle.[64]

Previous studies have underlined the link between shopkeeping and specific sets of knowledge. Those who wanted to be successful in shopkeeping needed to have certain skills, such as being aware of how to keep costs down, control stocks and display the goods in a proper way.[65] Furthermore, communication is a self-evident element in the relationship between sellers and consumers, and it played a key role in the interaction between local customers and itinerant peddlers. Several of the respondents mentioned that for the former itinerant peddlers, the Swedish language posed a challenge.[66] Indeed, the question of language was sometimes an obstacle in the Swedish-speaking regions of Finland already when the shopkeepers were still peddlers. The traders from Russian Karelia spoke Karelian or Russian as their mother tongue. Karelian was a dialect of the Finnish language, and the variety spoken in the border regions between Russia proper and the Grand Duchy of Finland was so close to standard Finnish that it did not constitute a communicative barrier in the Finnish-speaking regions.[67] By contrast, since Swedish is a Germanic language unrelated to Finnish, it posed a different kind of challenge. The ethnologist Nils Storå has maintained that the language of the itinerant peddlers from Russian Karelia was "completely incomprehensible" to customers in Swedish-speaking regions, and Nevalainen offers the linguistic challenge as an explanation for why the Swedish-speaking regions were the last in the Grand Duchy where they established their trade.[68] Nevertheless, language was not an insurmountable barrier. While the traders may have experienced initial language barriers in Swedish-speaking regions, most rather quickly learned the necessary words to communicate.[69]

One way to help communication with the customers was to employ a clerk or maid as a helper in the shop. It seems that some peddlers brought their whole families from Russian Karelia to Finland to work for them, while others hired local youngsters. When engaging local help, an important qualification was that they could count. To work in a shop seems to have been a desired job, albeit not one that was well paid. As the shop was open from early in the morning until late in the evening, many of the clerks slept above the store and could therefore always be of service. However, in addition to the pay and the place being a hub of activity, it seems that the people employed in the store were considered by their peers to have a little better social standing.[70] One reason for choosing a familiar helper may have been the need to trust the people minding the store. There was cash on hand and novelties for sale, and sometimes the temptation to take some might grow too strong. In a case from Jomala in the Åland Islands, a woman hired as a maid in the store of two former peddlers stole a number of goods, ranging from various textiles to buttons, candy and other foodstuffs.[71] However, the local county sheriff soon found out about the theft and she and her helper were given a fine.[72]

Peddlers and Fairytale Princes

One of the questions posed in the introduction to this chapter had to do with the way in which the former peddlers were received in the local communities, not as storekeepers but as potential sons-in-law and husbands. Due to the many tasks involved in shopkeeping, it was easier to keep a shop if someone was there to help, such as a wife.[73] In the answers to the questionnaires that I have examined, the peddlers—and especially the young ones—are often described as good-looking, fairy-tale princes. One of the respondents from the Åland Islands noted that around the year 1870, four itinerant peddlers came to the village and rented a small cottage where they kept their supply and slept when trading in the villages nearby:

> Their names were Pavel, Konstantin and Probus—these were all already older men. But Probus also had his son Elias with him, who was supposed to learn how the trade was done. The four traders became very popular. They were happy and lively—playing instruments and singing, and all four of them knew how to speak Swedish quite well [...] During the summer Elias made good friends with the younger people in the village. He even got to spend the evenings at the place where they gathered in the evenings, even if outsiders usually were beaten if they came there. Elias was like a fairy-tale prince. His clothes were different, he danced with soft, high, shiny boots, he sang and was happy. Everybody liked him. When autumn came and the traders were about to leave, he stayed as a son-in-law in one of the houses in the village.[74]

It is evident that romantic relationships did from time to time develop between the itinerant peddlers and the local women, and that this was a reason for the former to stay in the Finnish countryside, often supporting their family by keeping a country store or engaging in some other type of business.[75] There are also a few mentions of a peddler marrying a local woman and taking her with him back to Russian Karelia.[76] As was stated earlier, the itinerant peddlers evoked various feelings in the local communities. On the one hand, these relationships were sometimes frowned upon, as the peddlers occasionally provoked suspicion and anger. They were suspected, for example, of being especially friendly toward women and girls, as they thought that it was easier to lure these into buying low-quality goods.[77]

On the topic of marriage, one respondent mentions that weddings between a peddler and a local woman were not considered proper, and that the parties involved were ridiculed. In the contemporary newspapers, often representing the views of the government, local merchants and priests, the relationships were more often described in a negative manner.[78] In the case of the fairy-tale prince Elias, after a while he was forced by the local priest to convert and change his last name to a more Swedish-sounding one.[79] Similar accounts are also given by other respondents.[80] The former peddler Lipkin, mentioned in the introduction, also converted, perhaps as a form of adaption to the local community. However, a number of respondents described the peddlers as wealthy men or acknowledged that they at least had more money than the poor country dwellers did, and therefore these kinds of marriages were seen as something positive.[81]

One respondent from Lapinjärvi in Uusimaa remembered that one of the itinerant peddlers who frequented the area later settled down there. The name of the peddler was Ivan Semenoff (1830–1891), and he was born in Repola in Olonets. He married a local woman and changed his name to a Swedish one, Malmberg. He and his wife built their own place close to her childhood home and opened the first store in the area. After the death of his first wife, Malmberg married another local woman and built a new stylish home with a room for his shop and separate storage buildings for his merchandise. The commodities were brought from St. Petersburg and transported by boat and horse to the shop. According to the respondent's description, the store was spacious and had a large staircase leading directly from the road. The shopkeeper himself or his wife or her sister stood behind the counter, and the sister also worked as a cook and housemaid. There was also a farmhand who took care of the house and the horses and at times helped with the transport of goods. Without many skills—he seems, for example, to have lacked knowledge of bookkeeping—the former peddler Malmberg had managed to become a successful businessman and gain a large fortune through shopkeeping.[82]

Peddlers Settling Down

In this chapter I have discussed the reception of Russian Karelian peddlers who abandoned their itinerant way of life and settled down in the Finnish countryside at the end of the nineteenth and beginning of the twentieth centuries. My point of departure was that the transition from peddler to a shopkeeper in late nineteenth-century Finland posed several challenges but also possibilities. I was interested in finding out what the accounts about peddlers and shopkeepers would reveal about the setting up of a country shop, as well as the reception of the former peddlers by the local community. I have analyzed several responses to two ethnographic questionnaires dealing with peddling and shopkeeping as well as other sources.

For marginalized groups such as Russian Karelian peddlers, self-employment was often a necessity. However, in the sources examined, the peddlers-turned-shopkeepers are often mentioned by name, suggesting that they made something more than a fleeting impression. At least in the memories of the respondents to the questionnaires, they enjoyed similar or even better social standing than the locals. The outlay and appearance of the shops kept by former peddlers seem to have varied, but if the building or room stocked with goods was large enough, it soon became the center of the village. Then the shops had several purposes; they were not only places of consumption, but also places where people would go to hear the latest news or spend the evening in company.

Some of the former peddlers brought their wives with them to their new home, while others married local women. Based on the examined accounts, the responses of the local community to these marriages seem to have been twofold. On the one hand, they were seen as something positive, for the shopkeepers were considered to be wealthy men who could provide for their families. On the other hand, some former peddlers were still seen as outsiders and their marriages were questioned.

The stories about peddlers and shopkeepers examined in this chapter are also stories about consumption. Some of the peddlers who settled down could not offer their customers a larger variety of goods than they had done as peddlers, while others managed to build up a large and varied supply of merchandise. Taken together, these stories give us broader insight into the Finnish retail history of the late nineteenth and early twentieth centuries.

Notes

1. *Vasabladet* 11/12/1927, p. 2.
2. Nevalainen 2016, pp. 49, 52.
3. *Vasabladet* 11/12/1927, p. 2.
4. Holmström 2005, pp. 61, 66.
5. Storå 1989, p. 4.
6. Nevalainen 2016, pp. 95–96.
7. Wassholm and Sundelin 2018a, p. 144.
8. Miika Tervonen. 2005. "Elämää veitsen terällä: Kiertävien romanien ja maanviljeliöiden väliset suhteet muistelukerronnassa, 1920–1960"; Panu Pulma. 2012. *Suomen romanien historia.*
9. Nevalainen 2016, pp. 122–124.
10. Boyd 2010, pp. 318–319.
11. Haapala 2007, pp. 47–50.
12. Mikkola and Stark 2009, p. 6.
13. Aulis J. Alanen. 1957. *Suomen maakaupan historia*; Kati Mikkola and Laura Stark. 2009. "Himotut ja halveksitut kulutustarvikkeet: uusien kulutustottumusten vaikutukset suomalaisiin maalaisyhteisöihin 1800–luvun loppupuolella ja 1900-luvun alussa"; Viljo Rasila. 1982. "Kauppa ja rahaliikenne."
14. Nevalainen 2016, pp. 141–142; Naakka-Korhonen 1988, p. 131.
15. Wassholm and Sundelin 2018a, p. 147.
16. Barbara H. Rosenwein. 2002. *Worrying About Emotions in History*; see also Ute Frevert. 2011. *Emotions in History—Lost and Found*; Raisa Maria Toivo and Jacqueline Van Gent. 2016. "Introduction. Gender, material culture and emotions in Scandinavian history."
17. Naakka-Korhonen 1988, pp. 210–236.
18. Alanen 1957, pp. 213–214.
19. Alanen 1957, pp. 311–312.
20. Hedin 1955, pp. 106, 114; on country shopkeepers in more recent times, see Liisa Kurkinen. 2020. *Tiskin takana. Kauppiaselämänkerrat maaseudun elämän kuvaajina.*
21. The economic challenges posed by the keeping of a shop has been discussed by Kim Kaarniranta in his work on early shopkeepers and debt in the North Karelian countryside. His study shows that it was quite a diverse group of people who entered into the business; see Kaarniranta 2001, p. 9. When it comes specifically to the itinerant peddlers from Russian Karelia, Pekka Nevalainen has also made an important contribution. According to Nevalainen, it is impossible to give any exact numbers of the failed attempts at shopkeeping by former peddlers; however, many started out with modest means, making them more prone to bankruptcies and other financial problems. This makes an examination of the reception of the peddlers-turned-shopkeepers even more necessary if we wish to under-

stand the complexities of Finnish retail trade at the end of the nineteenth and the beginning of the twentieth centuries. Previous studies do also include work by Nils Storå and on specific shopkeepers of Russian Karelian origin. The specific case of Kiril Lipkin has been covered by John Holmström in a popular account.

22. Mikkola and Stark 2009, p. 4; Kuusanmäki 1936, p. 101.
23. Korkiakangas et al. 2016, pp. 20–21; Hagström and Marander-Eklund 2005, pp. 16–21.
24. *Åbo Tidning* 6/23/1889, p. 2.
25. Alanen 1957, p. 304; Kaarniranta 2001, pp. 70–71.
26. Nevalainen 2016, pp. 147–148.
27. Cultural sciences archive *Cultura* at Åbo Akademi University (KIVA) Questionnaire *9. Kringvandrande ryska handelsmän* (1957, 1968), M641:3, M688:1,M696, M697:1, M709:2, M711, M712:2, M721:1, M766:1, M778, M782, M2082, M2056, M2076, M2140, M675:1, M678:2.
28. Nevalainen 2016, pp. 57–68.
29. Nevalainen 2016, p. 70.
30. Sjöblom 1911, p. 154.
31. KIVA 9, 699:2.
32. Holmström 2005, p. 60.
33. KIVA 9, M702:1.
34. KIVA 9, M187, M2053.
35. Kaarniranta 2001, p. 67.
36. Graham 2008, p. 6.
37. Alanen 1957, p. 310.
38. Cultural sciences archive Cultura at Åbo Akademi University (KIVA) Questionnaire 4 Butikshandel på landsbygden (1954) KIVA 4 M1617.
39. Nevalainen 2016, p. 145.
40. KIVA 4, M1699.
41. KIVA 4, M395.
42. Kuusanmäki 1936, p. 101; Mikkola and Stark 2009, p. 4.
43. Alanen 1957, p. 315.
44. Alanen 1957, p. 309.
45. Stark 2011, p. 108.
46. Jonsson and Runefelt 2006, pp. 321–323.
47. Nevalainen 2016, pp. 23, 27.
48. Nevalainen 2016, p. 159; Rasila 1982, p. 89.
49. Kaarniranta 2001, p. 83.
50. *Åbo Underättelser* 9/1/1914, p. 4.
51. Judicial District of Åland, Bankrupties, 31, Provincial Archives of Åland.
52. Wassholm and Sundelin 2018b, p. 249.
53. KIVA 4, M193, M395, M399, M408.
54. Boyd 2010, p. 318; Alanen 1957, p. 178; Mitchell 2016, p. 6; Wassholm 2017, pp. 609–615.

55. Kaarniranta 2001, p. 64.
56. Alanen 1957, p. 312; Hedin 1965, p. 195.
57. KIVA 4, M196, M374, M399.
58. KIVA 4, M193, M1671.
59. Kaarniranta 2001, p. 14; Alanen 1957, pp. 327–328.
60. KIVA 4, M196.
61. KIVA 4, M354.
62. Holmström 2005, p. 64.
63. KIVA 4, M394.
64. KIVA 4, M374.
65. Phillips and Alexander 2005, p. 287–288, Kaarniranta 2001, pp. 72–76.
66. KIVA 4, M1671.
67. Wassholm and Sundelin 2018a, pp. 145–147.
68. Nils Storå. 1995. "Vad hade Ontrus i sin ränsel?"; Pekka Nevalainen. 2016. *Kulkukauppiaista kauppaneuvoksiin. Itäkarjalaisten liiketoimintaa Suomessa.*
69. Wassholm and Sundelin 2018a, p. 147.
70. KIVA 4, M374, M193.
71. Judicial district of Åland, Provincial Archives of Åland.
72. *Åland* 10/29/1910, p. 2.
73. Diner 2015, p. 15.
74. KIVA 9, M2165:1.
75. KIVA 9, M680:2, M688:1, M691:3, M699:2, M718:2, M2056, M2140.
76. KIVA 9, M680:2, M114:2, M2019.
77. KIVA 9, M704:2.
78. Wassholm and Sundelin 2018a, pp. 139–140.
79. KIVA 9, 2165:2.
80. KIVA 9, M2075:2, M2091.
81. KIVA 9, M746:6, M711:3.
82. KIVA 4, M2076.

Bibliography

Archival Sources

Cultural studies archive Cultura at Åbo Akademi University, Turku (KIVA).

Questionnaire KIVÅ 4: Frågelista nr. 4. Butikshandeln på landsbygden ("Shopkeeping in the countryside"), 1954.

Questionnaire KIVÅ 9: Kringvandrande ryska handelsmän ("Itinerant Russian peddlers"), 1957 and 1968.

Provincial Archives of Åland
Judicial District of Åland, Court records.
Judicial District of Åland, Bankruptcies, 31.

Newspapers

Wasabladet, 1927.
Åbo Underrättelser, 1914.
Åbo Tidning, 1889.

Literature

Alanen, Aulis J. *Suomen maakaupan historia*. Helsinki: Kauppiaitten kustannus, 1957.
Boyd, Robert L. "Ethnic shopkeepers in U.S. Cities in the Late Nineteenth Century." *Sociological Spectrum* 30 (2010): 317–337.
Diner, Hasia. *Roads Taken: The Great Jewish Migrations to the New World and the Peddlers who Forget the Way*. London: Yale University Press, 2015.
Frevert, Ute. *Emotions in History: Lost and Found*. Budapest: Central European University Press, 2011.
Graham, Kelley. *Gone to the Shops: Shopping in Victorian England*. London: Praeger, 2008.
Haapala, Pertti. "Kun kaikki alkoi liikkua." In *Suomalaisen arjen historia 2. Modernin Suomen synty*, edited by Kai Häggman and Ilkka Huhta, 47–63. Helsinki: Weilin + Göös, 2007.
Hagström, Charlotte, and Lena Marander-Eklund. "Att arbeta med frågelistor. En introduktion." In *Frågelistan som källa och metod*, edited by Charlotte Hagström and Lena Marander-Eklund, 9–30. Lund: Studentlitteratur, 2005.
Hedin, Nathan. "Lanthandeln under näringsfriheten". Ejdestam, Julius, Hedin, Nathan & Nygren, Erik, *Bilder ur lanthandelns historia*, Västerås: ICA-Förlaget, 1965, 127–311.
Holmström, John. "Bröderna Lipkins omfattande affärsverksamhet i Vörå med omnejd -viktga inslag i näringslivets utveckling åren 1880–1930." *I rågens rike* (2005): 60–73.
Häkkinen, Antti, Panu Pulma, and Miika Tervonen (eds.). *Vieraat kulkijat—tutut talot. Näkökulmia etnisyyden ja köyhyyden historiaan Suomessa*. Historiallinen arkisto 120. Helsinki: Suomalaisen Kirjallisuuden Seura, 2005.
Kaarniranta, Kim. *Elämää rahaa käärien ja velkoen. Pohjois-Karjalan maaseudun sekatavarakauppiaat ja heidän velallisensa 1860- ja 1870-luvulla*. Bibliotheca Historica 70, Helsinki, SKS, 2001.
Korkiakangas, Pirjo, Pia Olsson, Helena Ruotsala, and Anna-Maria Åström. "Kirjoittamalla kerrottua." In *Kirjoittamalla kerrotut. Kansantieteelliset kyselyt tiedon lähteinä*, edited by Pirjo Korkiakangas, Pia Olsson, Helena Ruotsala and Anna-Maria Åström, 7–39. Helsinki: Ethnos, 2016.

Jonsson, Pernilla, and Leif Runefelt. "Konsumtion: identitet, makt och livets nödtorft." *Sverige. En social och ekonomisk historia*, edited by Susanna Hedenborg and Mats Morell, 319–343. Lund: Studentlitteratur, 2006.

Kurkinen, Liisa. "Tiskin takana. Kauppiaselämänkerrat maaseudun elämän kuvaajina." *Kansantieteellinen Arkisto 60.* Helsinki, 2020.

Kuusanmäki, Lauri. "Kulutustavarain leviäminen maalaisväestön keskuuteen." In *Suomen kulttuurihistoria* IV. *Industrialismin ja kansallisen nousun aika*, edited by Gunnar Suolahti, Esko Aaltonen, Lauri Kuusanmäki, Väinö Voionmaa, Pentti Renvall, Heikki Varis and Eino Jutikkala, 96–119. Jyväskylä: K.J. Gummerus Osakeyhtiö, 1936.

Lahelma, Ville. *Tanner & Manner: Laihia–Vaasa–Orismala: vienalaista laukkukauppaa, tukkukauppaa, vaateteollisuutta, pakolaishistoriaa.* Helsinki, 1990.

Löfgren, Orvar. "Vad kan konsumtion vara?" In *Konsumtionskultur. Innebörder och praktiker*, edited by edited by Magdalena Petersson McIntyre, Barbro Johansson and Niklas Sörum, 259–274. Göteborg and Stockholm: Makadam, 2019.

Mikkola, Kati, and Laura Stark. "Himotut ja halveksitut kulutustarvikkeet: uusien kulutustottumusten vaikutukset suomalaisiin maalaisyhteisöihin 1800-luvun loppupuolella ja 1900-luvun alussa." *Historiallinen Aikakausikirja* 107, no. 1 (2009): 4–17.

Mitchell, Ian. *Tradition and Innovation in English Retailing, 1700 to 1850.* Farnham, UK: Routledge, 2016.

Mitro, A. *Mitro 1876–1939.* Jyväskylä: Unknown publisher, 1936.

Naakka-Korhonen, Mervi. *Halpa hinta, pitkä mitta: Vienankarjalainen laukkukauppa.* Helsinki: Suomalaisen Kirjallisuuden Seura, 1988.

Nevalainen, Pekka. *Kulkukauppiaista kauppaneuvoksiin. Itäkarjalaisten liiketoimintaa Suomessa.* Helsinki: Suomalaisen Kirjallisuuden Seura, 2016.

Phillips, Simon, and Andrew Alexander. "An Efficient Pursuit? Independent Shopkeeping in 1930s Britain." *Enterprise & Society* 6 (2005): 278–304.

Pulma, Panu (ed.). *Suomen romanien historia.* Helsinki: Suomalaisen Kirjallisuuden Seura, 2012.

Rasila, Viljo. "Kauppa ja rahaliikenne." In *Suomen taloushistoria 2: Teollistuva Suomi*, edited by J. Ahvenainen, E. Pihkala and V. Rasila, 89–113. Helsinki: Tammi, 1982.

Rosenwein, Barbara H. "Worrying about emotions in history." *The American Historical Review* 107, no. 3 (2002): 821–845.

Sjöblom, Walter. *Mariehamns stads historia*, 1861–1911, Mariehamn: Ålands tidningstryckeri, 1911.

Stark, Laura. "The limits of patriarchy. How female networks of pilfering and gossip sparked the first debates on rural gender rights in the 19th-century Finnish-language press". *Studia Fennica Ethnologica* 13, Helsinki: SKS, 2011.

Storå, Nils. "Från Östkarelen till Åland: gårdfarihandel och kulturkontakt." *Bottnisk kontakt II: Maritimhistorisk konferens*, 31–35. Mariehamn: Mariehamns kultursamfund, 1984.

Storå, Nils. „Ostkarelische Wanderhändler als Kulturvermittler in Finnland.“ *Jahrbuch für Volkskunde und Kulturgeschichte* 32 (1989): 34–43.

Storå, Nils. "'Rucksack Russians' in Finland: Peddling and culture contact." *Ethnologia Scandinavica* 21 (1991): 74–96.

Storå, Nils. "Vad hade Ontrus i sin ränsel?" *Historiska och Litteraturhistoriska Studier* (HLS) 70 (1995): 221–232.

Tervonen, Miika. "Elämää veitsen terällä: Kiertävien romanien ja maanviljeliöiden väliset suhteet muistelukerronnassa, 1920–1960." In Antti Häkkinen, Panu Pulma and Miika Tervonen (eds.), 263–295. *Vieraat kulkijat—tutut talot: Näkökulmia etnisyyden ja köyhyyden historiaan Suomessa*. Helsinki: Suomalaisen Kirjallisuuden Seura, 2005.

Toivo, Raisa Maria, and Jacqueline Van Gent. "Introduction. Gender, material culture and emotions in Scandinavian history." *Scandinavian Journal of History* 41, no. 2 (2016): 289–305.

Wassholm, Johanna. "Handel i marginalen: Den judiska småhandeln och lokalsamhället i Åbo i slutet av 1800-talet." *Historisk Tidskrift för Finland* 102, no. 4 (2017): 589–617.

Wassholm, Johanna, and Anna Sundelin. "'Emotions, trading practices and communication in transnational itinerant trade: encounters between 'Rucksack Russians' and their customers in the late nineteenth- and early twentieth century Finland." *Scandinavian Economic History Review* 66, no. 2 (2018a): 132–152.

Wassholm, Johanna, and Anna Sundelin, "'Det hänger på ett hår.' Praktiker, moral och varuflöden i handeln med människohår i Finland 1870–1900." *Historisk Tidskrift för Finland* 103, no. 2 (2018b): 231–261.

CHAPTER 14

Conclusions: Dealing with Difference

Jutta Ahlbeck, Ann-Catrin Östman, and Eija Stark

Focusing on the margins of retail, our volume has demonstrated the increasing flow of people and commodities in Northern Europe during the long nineteenth century, and it has examined exchanges between manifold locations and societies. Networks of petty trade extended through economically diverse regions, communities, and countries. From Russia to Finland, from Finland to Sweden, and so forth, itinerant traders traveled, sometimes quite long distances, along with their goods. The language used in these trading practices was often mixed. Russian sellers, for instance, quickly learned Finnish and Swedish, or at least enough to make themselves understood when trading.

The chapters in *Forgotten Livelihoods* have investigated significant and heterogeneous yet relatively underexplored groups of traders. For many marginalized groups, such as the rural and urban poor, as well as Roma, Tatar, and Russian Karelian peddlers, self-employment was often an

J. Ahlbeck (✉) • A.-C. Östman
Culture, History and Philosophy, Åbo Akademi University, Turku, Finland
e-mail: jutta.ahlbeck@abo.fi; aostman@abo.fi

E. Stark
The Finnish Literature Society, Helsinki, Finland
e-mail: eija.stark@finlit.fi

J. Ahlbeck et al. (eds.), *Encounters and Practices of Petty Trade in Northern Europe, 1820–1960*,
https://doi.org/10.1007/978-3-030-98080-1_14

inevitability. Although countries in the Nordics and municipalities imposed various decrees on peddling and petty trade in the nineteenth century, peasants and other traders defied such restrictions and continued selling and bartering various commodities at fairs in small towns. In the Nordic context, like elsewhere, minority groups often relied on petty trade to earn a living.

Applying interdisciplinary approaches, the authors have made detailed and empirically rich historical, sociological, and ethnologic analyses of petty trade. Due to its informal character, peddling as well as market trade have left few and fragmented historical records. Through informed investigations of various empirical materials and sources, the chapters make a range of livelihoods visible.

In a methodologically and theoretically rich chapter, Otso Kortekangas addressed the economic importance of Sámi trade in marketplaces in the subarctic regions. Looking at how a seemingly simple product such as shoe-hay was prepared by the fishing Sámi and then sold to reindeer herders in exchange for reindeer meat, he revealed the existence of a high degree of specialization in production and supply. Though the sale of sex is seldom visible in contemporary sources, Kirsi Vainio-Korhonen demonstrated how the poorest of the sex workers—in this case, women examined for venereal disease—utilized markets to make a living. Travelling from one fair to the next, these women survived by means of petty crime and, seemingly, sex work. In a similar vein, women of color and extraordinary-bodied itinerant female performers displayed and "sold" their bodies and skills at fairs and markets. Utilizing searchable newspaper databases as well as other historical documents, Maren Jonasson provided a rare contribution to studies on petty trade and livelihoods by tracing African-American entertainers who traveled across the Nordic countries.

These cases exemplify how individuals living under poor and uncertain conditions utilized marketplaces in different ways to earn a living (see Fig. 14.1). While Roma women were supporting themselves and their families by trading their handcrafted laces, Roma men were engaged in trading horses. Moreover, Niklas Huldén demonstrated how Finnish and Estonian families participated in the seasonal expeditions across the Gulf of Finland, and women, too, took part in markets on the other side of the gulf. Although several chapters dealt with male ambulatory traders, women were also engaged in petty trade, as Ella Johansson and Eija Stark highlighted in their chapters on rural and working-class women.

Fig. 14.1 Fish was a product coveted by customers of all social classes. The fish market in Helsinki at the turn of the twentieth century was a space of many encounters and practices. (Photo by unknown. The Finnish Heritage Agency)

As the chapters in *Forgotten Livelihoods* have demonstrated, petty trade was practiced full time, part-time, seasonally, or occasionally, during a period when multiple forms of employment were common or during times of unemployment. As petty trade was often informal, sellers operated in a grey zone between legal and illegal practices. By studying informal economic activities, we shed light on the conditions of uncertainty and poverty under which survivalist and opportunist livelihood strategies were widely used. To make a living, most people had many sources of income, and workers often had to resort to petty trade to sustain themselves. During periods of social or economic crises, such as famine or years of bad crops, widowhood, wars, and economic depression, many commoners took to petty trade to survive. Eija Stark analyzed experiences of petty trade and how the rural poor regarded petty trading as a "last resort," as a strategy to cope with poverty. In the past, trade and small-scale business seldom offered a way to success. On the contrary, they were a form of livelihood for those who were unable to afford the heavy costs of renting a shop or setting up their own farm. Similarly, rural small-scale farmers and urban laborers, who were seasonally unemployed from factory work, took up selling practices for lack of a better alternative.

Such a lack of alternative sources of livelihood was usually the prime reason for practicing petty trade, especially among certain ethnic minorities in the Nordic region who had difficulties finding employment and did not own land or were not even allowed to rent land. For the Roma, people of color and other ethnicized groups, for example, petty trade can be regarded as an effect of their marginalized status in their everyday struggles for survival, in addition to facing racism and discrimination. Over time, some ethnicities specialized in selling or exchanging certain kinds of goods and items. These business practices relied strongly on internal ties and relations among members of the ethnic community, and on particular trading traditions. There is evidence that these groups were able to hand down their knowledge and traditions from one generation to the next within one ethnicity.[1] In Finland, for instance, Jews, Russians, and Roma practiced petty trade proportionally more often than members of the majority society, that is, the Finnish- and Swedish-speaking populations who were sedentary and engaged in farming, hunting, and fishing economies. Moreover, ethnic traders did not usually sell self-produced commodities; instead, they purchased goods wholesale or from producers, which they then resold in retail to rural consumers. Roma women, however, were skilled handcrafters, and sold and bartered laces, while Roma men manufactured horse-related gear.

As a form of livelihood, petty trade and retail were characterized by class, gender, and ethnic segregation. Petty trade belonged to the informal economy, and the majority of those who were engaged in peddling or market trade, rather than selling goods from stores, seem to have been very poor. As a result of more liberal legislation concerning retailing in the late nineteenth century, new shops and stores were able to be established, including in the countryside. Although economic life was increasingly deregulated and modernized at the turn of the century, traditional and informal modes of trading were practiced up until the Second World War, and in the early postwar period.

Petty Trade in Society, Culture, and Memory

Drawing on a broad range of cross-disciplinary evidence, the chapters in our volume highlighted the societal meanings of trading activities as well as the cultural meanings connected to petty trade. The authors demonstrated how petty traders and peddlers became visible figures, both in public spaces as well as in the homes of their customers. Various forms of selling, exchanges, and informal trade practices laid the foundation for a variety of encounters in the Nordic region during the decades around the turn of the twentieth century.

Historically, popular knowledge about peddlers and itinerant traders was produced and distributed in folklore, oral history, and fiction. In the Nordics, male peddlers from Karelia ("Rucksack Russians") and female peddlers (*Dalkullor*) from Dalarna, for example, became famous, romanticized characters in folklore and cultural imagination. The fame of these traders partly reflected the importance of these two regions, Dalarna in Sweden, and Karelia in Finland, in the making of the nation-states of the two countries. Both Dalarna and Karelia were regarded as being the most culturally "authentic" areas of the countries, representing the origins of "Swedishness" and "Finnishness." Karelia, a historic province situated between Finland and Russia proper, and thus an area belonging to both Finland and Russia, was similarly presented in relation to "the origins" of Finland in terms of cultural traditions, language, and folklore.

Ella Johansson and Anna Sundelin explored how peddlers from these two regions were often saddled with stereotypical attributes, but their chapters also uncovered how the peddlers actively *used* the reputation of their home districts to their advantage in their economic practices. Sundelin investigated male peddlers from Karelia, the so-called "Rucksack Russians," who became famous peddlers in Finland. Their trade was geographically broad, reaching many customers across the country. The commodities they brought to rural customers were highly desirable and appreciated, as the rural poor rarely had the opportunity or means to acquire the consumption goods most often sold in cities. Johansson looked at the representations, strategies, and practices of female peddlers, the Dalkullor from Dalarna. The Dalkullor practiced petty trade in Stockholm, the capital of Sweden, and became visible in the city landscape by wearing traditional costumes with peaked hats. The Dalkullor thus utilized and profited from the romanticized fame of the region by dressing in local costumes. While many chapters in *Forgotten Livelihoods* addressed negative views of petty traders, particularly ethnicized sellers, the chapters discussed above, along with Niklas Huldén's contribution, also pointed to elements of nostalgia. Examining the trade between peasants in Finland and Estonia, Huldén showed how archival as well as published accounts presented trading encounters between Finnish peasants and their Estonian counterparts in a favorable light.

Although some peddlers have left traces in the archives, folklore, and collective memory—and in a favorable way, the lack of scholarly and archival interest in traders outside the mainstream—are rather striking. Ethnicized, racialized, classed, and gendered traders have seldom found their way into the archives, which can partly be explained by matters of national commemoration processes. When focusing on the peasantry, archives of folklore and ethnographic sources have in general aimed at creating a white, "homogeneous," nationalist past—an idealized and "polished" picture of the "history" of the nation. In doing so, the archives have participated in erasure, or at least in minimizing conflicts, such as "forgetting" about racial hierarchies, marginalization, and poverty.[2] This construction of a nationalist past becomes evident when looking at how trading activities of ethnic, linguistic, and religious minorities have been documented—or, rather, not documented—in archival institutions. Thus, it seems safe to argue that these livelihoods have been forgotten both in the archives and in research. The economic activities of Sámi and Roma have been made invisible or recollected in biased, racialized ways. Kortekangas demonstrated how the educated elite used tropes of classical literature to describe the "strangeness" and otherness of Sámi groups, whereas Ahlbeck discussed how Roma livelihoods were not regarded as proper economic actives *whatsoever* but as disguised begging and unlawful trickeries, reflecting the majority's condescending and racialized view of the Roma minority.

Despite relatively few sources on trading activities, the authors in our volume have "dug deep" to find miscellaneous archival collections and data. Oral history interviews, written life-stories, ethnographic questionnaires, court records, fiction, interrogation documents, and collected folklore memories mirror everyday struggles for survival. They are stories of coping with poverty, sorrow, and happiness, as well as successes and failures. By drawing upon this variety of sources, the chapters unfolded important traces of grassroots economic activities and practices of selling and buying, while uncovering changing consumption patterns.

Meanings of petty trade were negotiated as customers and traders encountered one another, and stories and experiences of exciting, "exotic" or dangerous traders were published in the newspapers. This is where common people could read about traders, what they sold and how they moved from one town, village, or municipality to another. Much like the historical records of the public authorities, newspapers in the nineteenth and early twentieth centuries wrote frequently on issues of petty trade, marketplace vending, and the (often unlawful) behavior of traders. For Nordic scholars of history, searchable databases of digitized newspapers, a major archival project which has been pursued in the Nordic countries in the past decade, have opened new opportunities for research. Many of the chapters in this volume have utilized these databases to find newspaper writings or rather short press items on petty trade and peddling. In this way, they have made visible fragments of stories, tracing how they are linked together and analyzing the complex puzzle to better understand the discourses and understandings of petty trade.

Anna Kuismin located and explored fiction and newspaper texts discussing fairs. Using the concept of "liminal space," Kuismin examined the subversive practices of commoners as represented in these texts. Newspapers mostly presented pejorative attitudes toward ethnicized traders as well as the consumption of commoners. The trading activities of peddlers were affected by how they were viewed as members of specific groups and to a growing extent were ascribed the role of the "other," which pushed them to the margins of society. These groups could be difficult to place in hierarchies of rural and urban communities, and to some degree they remained in inferior positions, performing economic activities that "respectable" subjects and citizens tended to avoid.

Peddlers from groups regarded as "ethnic others" seem to have awakened anxieties about the social order as well as class and gender among established groups. In general, during this period, people with mobile lifestyles were considered threatening and illegal, due to vagrancy legislation. Using the concept of "enemy image," Johanna Wassholm examined how preconceived negative notions of Russian Jewish traders regarding both ethnicity and religion echoed major social fears in the Finnish press. Hostile accounts of these peddlers must be understood in the context of Finland involuntarily being a Grand Duchy and part of Russia. Hence, it is fair to say that Russian Jewish traders were used as political figures in public discourses in Finland and Sweden to construct "the East" as uncivilized and threatening, presenting Russia as a military aggressor.

Newspaper writers often took the authorities' view on marketplace activities and had similar interests in condemning illicit trade. Both newspapers and authorities resisted the ever-growing consumption of the lower classes, whom those in power regarded as jeopardizing the traditional regime and social hierarchies. Overstepping class boundaries, for instance, was condemned; the habits of consumption of the poor were in general depicted as immoral, conspicuous, and unnecessary. Such biased sources illustrate the need to not rely too much on normative, prejudiced, and deceptive accounts. Instead, as discussed above, scholars determined to study marginalized economies have a responsibility to be innovative and find alternative sources, perhaps found in archives that do not necessarily deal with trade in an explicit way.

The sources analyzed in the chapters convey an array of collective memories, emotions, nostalgia, and popular stereotypes. Ann-Catrin Östman discussed how the elite depicted common people and traders in homogenizing and monolithic ways. However, in more personal accounts, like memories, ethnographic questionnaires and oral histories, customers recollected peddlers, mentioning them by name and giving them a kind of integrity. In her chapter, Sundelin suggested that Russian Karelian peddlers made an impact on local communities in the countryside, being more than impersonal passersby. Some peddlers became successful local businessmen, opening stores and becoming integrated into these communities. Sundelin underlined these traders' extraordinary social skills, wide networks, and economic know-how. In small rural communities, customers often came to know the peddlers personally, befriending them, and some of the traders even married local women.

On Gendered, Classed, and Ethnicized Practices

For a long time, scholars of gender have called for explorations of the ways in which the meanings and knowledge of gendered differences are constructed and used to signify power relations. In her classic account of gender, Joan Scott defines gender as an inseparable part of the reproduction of social order.[3] Influenced by this approach, we show how notions of gender structured interpretations of petty trade as well as constructed potential problems. In late nineteenth-century Europe and the Western world, social Darwinist understandings of gender, class, and ethnicity were flourishing in science and culture. The social Darwinist discourse was built upon the idea of difference and evolution. The lower social classes, not to mention non-white individuals, were regarded as less "developed," less "evolved," and more "animal-like" compared to the middle, upper, and educated classes, who were more "evolved" and "civilized"—following Darwin's notions but applied to humans. It is in this sociohistorical context that petty traders worked; thus, it should come as no surprise that both traders and their customers, often belonging to either the poor and/or ethnic minorities, were depicted as "others," as less civilized and unrespectable.

Scholars informed by postcolonial thought address the intersections between gender, ethnicity/race, and class. Gender is pivotal here, as it functioned as a catalyst for understanding "civilization," "development," and ethnicity. American historian Gail Bederman discusses how women and men were placed at different stages of cultural and evolutionary progress, to be endowed with different gendered moral qualities and characteristics in the late nineteenth century.[4] Informed by feminist scholars, including Judith Butler's notion of performative gender,[5] we take seriously Michel de Certeau's playful investigations when we are looking into routine everyday practices. In the Introduction, we discussed how de Certeau makes a distinction between "strategies" and "tactics," where "strategies" are linked with structures of power ("producers"); while individuals not included in the power apparatus, "common people", are described as "consumers." However, common people are not powerless, and de Certeau emphasizes the significance of the "practices of the weak" or the subaltern.[6] Groups such as migrants, workers, migrants, and subaltern ethnic minorities can utilize "tactics" as resistance stemming from daily life practices, for instance, in different forms of consumption.[7] Thus, despite repressive actions by those in power, ordinary people can enact creative resistance to power structures, which is in line with Michel Foucault's idea of power as productive, and resistance as inherent in all power relations.[8] The chapters in our volume disclose how traders could employ, re-employ, and sometimes alter existing social orders by the use of different performative tactics. Naturally, traders' actions and behavior were constrained by social structures and cultural expectations, but they were not, however, completely determined by these circumstances. Gender, for instance, could be enacted differently depending upon the context, and by bending or strengthening gendered norms, both female and male traders tactically encountered their consumers.

To adjust to changing and precarious situations and contexts, traders employed a multiplicity of tactics, such as sometimes using prejudices and cultural notions to their benefit. Traders could, for instance, *emphasize* their difference or uniqueness by dressing in specific clothes as a tactic to secure their livelihoods. Alternatively, African-American entertainers in the white Nordics used their black bodies to display both difference and exotism as a livelihood practice. Others were probably forced to downplay their otherness, instead of aiming at "melting in," behaving respectfully and, more importantly, looking like the majority population.

Trade practices, commodities, exchanges, and encounters, as well as sellers, were frequently depicted in gendered terms. As itinerant selling often took place outdoors at fairs and in marketplaces, spatial aspects impacted patterns of trading, including how women and men utilized space in different ways. Married women were more often trading in marketplaces, a fixed location, whereas unmarried women often worked in groups, traveling, and peddling together, as in the case of the maids (Dalkullor) from central Sweden. These women wore traditional local costumes to "brand" their economic activities and perform respectable femininity.[9] Female sellers were thus gendered in terms of both economic practices and materiality. When peddling in the public space, they dressed and performed in ways that the customers would consider respectable.

Stories of male traders interacting with female customers sometimes fed anxieties. The fact that many peddlers and other traders belonged to ethnic minorities contributed to the gendered stereotyping discourses on "foreign men coming to take our women" or "deceiving our innocent women." In such accounts, mobility in relation to trade played a part in constructing fears and perceived dangers. Vagrancy laws and restrictions contributed to the negative view of itinerant trade, particularly practiced by "other" men, so understandings of masculinities were often an issue.

Similarly, as trade, consumption was gendered, classed, and ethnicized in historical records. The consumption among the poor and lower social classes was constructed as conspicuous, but women's consumption especially was seen as harmful. Thus, the habits of women and notions of femininity were at stake.

Sellers could also introduce new practices of trading, which in some cases clashed with deep-rooted local customs and traditions. In addition to this, cultural clashes occurred as traders belonged to minorities, sometimes being foreigners or of working class. In some cases, male traders were ascribed ambiguous gendered qualities. From time to time, newspapers depicted them as "too loud," and their language and conduct "too dramatic." Male sellers could be regarded as "unmanly," practicing trade in a childish, ungentlemanly, or unrespectable manner. Their conduct toward women was discussed in certain cases, and traders could be accused of attempting to "lure" and "deceive" women and other groups considered to be vulnerable. While some of the traders were ascribed special charisma, being handsome, sometimes this was a problem as they were "too masculine" and charming, thus threatening local masculinities. It seems clear that many traders were aware of potential negative reactions toward their economic activities and themselves, and they accentuated respectable behavior. Naturally, it was important to be considered trustworthy and upstanding when it came to relations with potential customers (see Fig. 14.2).

Both female and male petty traders could be depicted as humble, poor, and fringe figures. One could say that they *sometimes* passed as almost

Fig. 14.2 A male peddler with his horse and commodities, surrounded by female middle-class customers in the Finnish eastern countryside at the border of Russia and Finland in the 1910s. (Photo by Edith Södergran. The Society of Swedish Literature in Finland)

genderless. Earlier, practices of petty trade were at times considered informal social welfare or poor relief, and town licenses for street vending were often given to the widowed, elderly, and disabled (i.e., to those who had few other possibilities for supporting themselves).[10] Implicitly, these informal entitlements characterized understandings of petty trade, as some traders remained dependent on the goodwill of others. Impoverished women and the elderly could invoke understandings of petty trade as a form of social rights provided for the deserving poor. Femininity was often associated with powerlessness, but the poverty-stricken could also allude to perceptions of petty trade as an entitlement.

Commodities and Trading Encounters

The chapters in *Forgotten Livelihoods* suggested that commodities were also important to the lower social strata (subjugated groups), and thus they made visible the possibilities of vernacular consumption in the rural North. Commodities as *things* were not only pivotal in both enabling and shaping trading encounters between different social groups, but they also had value in their own right. Culturally significant commodities could be empowering, allowing a more respectable status for traders as well as consumers. Historical records reveal little or nothing about the meanings that customers may have ascribed to the commodities purchased from petty traders. Yet, the very fact that these trading activities continued and persisted over a long period of time indicates that there was a real demand for consumer goods and that the commodities had significance.

Studying trading practices where sellers often belonged to minority groups and customers to the majority population, we see commodities—things—as important actors in the shaping of these relationships and in the perceptions of individuals who did not belong to the resident local communities. In this respect, the volume is aligned with international studies on materiality. Political philosopher Jane Bennett has introduced the concept of "thing-power": "so-called inanimate things have a life of their own, that deep within them is an inexplicable vitality or energy, a moment of independence from and resistance to us and to other things".[11] Consequently, things have power or things can be used as tools of power. According to Bennett, types of inorganic matter, such as consumer goods, are not passive and inert but play a decisive role in trading encounters. As things affect other bodies, they have the power of enhancing or weakening them.[12]

Furthermore, this volume has aimed to trace what Lorraine Daston calls "things that talk,"[13] or what Arjun Appudaraj identifies as the "social life of things" or the "cultural biography of things" (i.e., how objects circulate and become redefined as consumer goods in different ways depending on the cultural context).[14] Anna Sundelin and Johanna Wassholm followed how rags traveled and circulated across local and regional boundaries. From being worthless items for the individual, they transformed into necessities, as rags were used and needed in the manufacturing of paper. Commodities could sometimes take the shape of *gifts* in economic exchanges, as Niklas Huldén demonstrated in his chapter on Finnish-Estonian barter trade.

However, despite our wide array of sources, the commodities are difficult to discover, and they often remain invisible, even in sources that expressly deal with petty trade. It seems as if not only the subordinate livelihoods of petty traders have been forgotten, but the consumer goods have been as well. Commodities, such as agricultural produce needed for survival in the cities, were described positively, whereas conspicuous consumption, particularly among the poor, was depicted as redundant, even immoral. Conspicuous goods were "luxury" items, "unnecessary" goods such as shawls, and "nicer" clothes (i.e., often products targeted to women customers). Thus, goods were criticized when consumed by certain segments of the community, such as by women or buyers from lower social strata.[15]

Trading Encounters as *Third Space*

We have examined the dynamics and entanglements between social practices, the materiality of commodities, norms, and the discursive meanings attached to trading practices. Petty traders in Northern Europe often operated in informal ways, sometimes illegally, and they not only encountered different communities but also existing traditions, norms, and legal cultures. Although many traders lacked citizenship rights and the right to pursue trade, and they did not belong to the communities they visited, they managed to establish a position in local communities or at least some of them.

People involved in trading used, practiced, and created spaces. Michel de Certeau's notion of "space as a practiced place",[16] in which "place" transforms into "space," addresses the different meanings (the different spaces) a specific geographical place can have. Trading encounters took place in different spaces, both tangible and "imaginary." In a fascinating manner, Kuismin, in her chapter, approached the fair as a "liminal space;" Jonasson understood the marketplace as a "show space"; and Ahlbeck regarded the marketplace as a "narrated nostalgic space."

The overall increase in consumption in the long nineteenth century had broad cultural and social consequences that greatly affected social, ethnic, and language relations in the Nordics. In highlighting the specific dynamics of trading, we would propose that Homi K. Bhabha's theory of the "third space"—or "in-between space"—clarifies these encounters as "cultural encounters."[17] Following scholars who have studied cross-cultural mobile trade in an era of nation-building, globalization, and modernization with new forms of racism, we recognize power relations in trading. The "third space" emerges out of a tension between cultures and can be understood as a cross-cultural exchange. Bhabha introduces his concept of "hybridity" as the idea that no culture is authentic without influences from elsewhere, as it is always in contact with other cultures. As cultures come together, interact, and intersect, they form something "new," such as new identities, new practices, or new versions of historic memory.

The ideals of cultural homogeneity tend to be stronger in peripheral small-scale societies, like the Nordic countries. Approaching trading encounters as the "third space" challenges our understanding of the existing historical categories once employed in local communities. Moments of encounters in trade involved local, regional, global, and transnational entanglements in spaces, where newcomers and/or strangers interacted with local sedentary groups, both rural and urban, women and men. The following postcolonial statement by Bhabha invites us to think beyond binaries and unitary cultures: "These 'in-between' spaces provide the terrain for elaborating strategies of selfhood—singular or communal—that initiate new sights of identity, and innovative sites of collaboration, and contestation, in the act of defining the idea of society itself."[18]

As both itinerant traders and resident consumers often belonged to subordinate groups, it was a space where marginalities converged. These encounters involved both human subjects and different materialities and commodities. Bhabha suggests that something new can emerge from a social encounter.[19] Social encounters in trade seemed to generate not only confusion and tension but also creative misunderstandings that changed the structuration of the social. Peddling, consumption, and the growth of trade had the capacity to simultaneously increase and decrease the gap between social groups, thus functioning as a laboratory of social contact.

Both traders and consumers benefited from the mutual exchange that trading entailed. Transnational alliances and interregional relations enhanced the traders' possibilities, and they communicated new forms of consumption to rural groups. The chapters here have suggested that trading with peddlers was especially appealing to women, young people, laborers, and servants. Thus, lower-class customers gained social and cultural resources by means of petty trade, yet the livelihood was for the poor.

Trading encounters in the third space functioned both as an opportunity and as a site of struggle. As the chapters in *Forgotten Livelihoods* have demonstrated, encounters between sellers and buyers were not always harmonious and unproblematic. On the contrary, deals were complex and hierarchical, embedded in power relations, often resulting in tensions and upheaval. The users of these spaces had to adapt to different situations, and the same deployments did not always produce equal effects. The livelihoods of petty traders were affected by how they were viewed as members of particular groups, which were often ethnicized or otherwise subordinate. People were highly aware of social roles, their own and those of others, even within class boundaries. These boundaries were complex and open to multiple interpretations.

To the customers of the lower social strata for whom new commodities were important, traders brought a sense of luxury and modernity as well as the consumer goods needed for inclusion in modernizing societies. Among other things, petty traders offered clothes, shoes, and other items that empowered and facilitated social activities. Commodities (for instance, new clothes) gave customers possibilities to perform respectability and worth in a culturally acceptable way. The contradiction here is that the consumer goods offered by scorned traders brought modernity and respectability, as well as a touch of cultivation, to the popular classes.

The history of small-scale trade in Northern Europe is a story of change, as all histories are, but also of persistent continuities in terms of socioeconomic inequalities. Even if petty trade, peddling, and other forms of itinerant trade are no longer as visible or common as they once were in today's welfare states of Northern Europe and elsewhere, Roma and migrants are still found engaged in petty trading or begging in the streets. Some inequalities seem to be persistent, particularly when it comes to ethnicized groups and minorities.

Forgotten Livelihoods seeks to bridge the research gap in the interdisciplinary field of marginalized livelihoods, informal economies, minorities, and petty trade. Offering comprehensive historical research on trade practices among different minority groups, our volume sheds light on the diversity of Northern Europe, particularly the Nordics, a region that is often interpreted in terms of homogeneity. Here, the history of petty trade is manifold and contradictory. A hundred years ago, itinerant traders brought longstanding public concerns about mobility to the fore, but they also created new apprehensions. Yet, petty trade could be empowering for subjugated groups, both traders and their customers. The scholarly and societal significance of our research lies not only in its socially and ethically relevant topic, or in its ability to trace historical reasons and discourses on anxieties and fears connected to ambulatory groups, but also in that it helps to make sense of challenges that today's ethnic minorities are confronted with.

Notes

1. E.g., Laura Ekholm. 2019. "Jews, Second-Hand Trade and Upward Economic Mobility. Introducing the Ready-to-Wear Business in Industrializing Helsinki, 1880–1930"; Miika Tervonen. 2010. *"Gypsies", "Travellers" and "Peasants". A Study on Ethnic Boundary Drawing in Finland and Sweden, c.1860–1925*; Raluca Bianca Roman. 2016. *Kaale Belongings and Evanceligal Becomings. Faith, Commitment and Social Outreach among the Finnish Kaale (Finnish Roma)*.
2. Skott 2008, p. 21; Miika Tervonen. 2014. "Historiankirjoitus ja myytti yhden kulttuurin Suomesta"; Kati Mikkola, Pia Olsson, and Eija Stark. 2019. "Minority Cultures and the Making of Cultural Heritage Archives in Finland".
3. Joan Scott's leading statement on gender as an analytical tool involves two parts: "gender is a constitutive element of social relationships based on perceived differences between the sexes, and gender is a way of signifying relations of power." See Scott 1988, p. 42.
4. Gail Bederman. 1995. *Manliness and Civilization. A Cultural History of Gender and Race in the United States, 1880–1917*.
5. Judith Butler. 1990. *Gender Trouble. Feminism and the Subversion of Identity*; Judith Butler. 1993. *Bodies That Matter. On the Discursive Limits of Sex*.
6. De Certeau 1984, p. 37.
7. See de Certeau 1984, p. 17.
8. Michel Foucault. 1978. *The History of Sexuality. An Introduction, Vol. I.*; Michel Foucault. 1984. "Truth and Power".
9. See Beverley Skeggs. 1997. *Formations of Class and Gender. Becoming Respectable*.

10. E.g., Sigrid Wadauer. 2012. "Asking for the Privilege to Work: Applications for a Peddling License (Austria in the 1920s and 1930s)".
11. Bennett 2004, p. 358.
12. Bennett 2004, p. 122.
13. Daston 2004, p. 9.
14. Arjun Appadurai. 1986. *The Social Life of Things. Commodities in Cultural Perspective*; see, also Ivan Gaskell. 2018. "History of Things."
15. See e.g., Daniel Miller. 2002. "Artefacts and the Meaning of Things".
16. De Certeau 1984, p. 117.
17. Homi K. Bhabha. 1994. *The Location of Culture*.
18. Bhabha 1994, p. 2.
19. Bhabha 2004, pp. 56, 296–312.

Bibliography

Appadurai, Arjun. *The Social Life of Things. Commodities in Cultural Perspective*. Cambridge: Cambridge University Press, 1986.

Bederman, Gail. *Manliness and Civilization. A Cultural History of Gender and Race in the United States, 1880–1917*. Chicago, London: University of Chicago Press, 1995.

Bennett, Jane. "The Force of Things. Steps toward an Ecology of Matter." *Political Theory* 32, no. 3 (2004): 347–372. https://doi.org/10.1177/0090591703260853.

Bhabha, Homi K. *The Location of Culture*. London: Routledge, 1994.

Bhabha, Homi K. *The Location of Culture*. London: Routledge, 2004.

Butler, Judith. *Gender Trouble. Feminism and the Subversion of Identity*. New York, London: Routledge, 1990.

Butler, Judith. *Bodies That Matter. On the Discursive Limits of Sex*. New York, London: Routledge, 1993.

Daston, Lorraine (ed.). *Things That Talk. Object Lessons from Art and Science*. New York: Zone Books, 2004.

De Certeau, Michel. *The Practice of Everyday Life*. Berkeley: University of California Press, 1984.

Ekholm, Laura Katarina. "Jews, Second-Hand Trade and Upward Economic Mobility. Introducing the Ready-to-Wear Business in Industrializing Helsinki, 1880–1930." *Business History* 61, no. 1 (2019): 73–92. https://doi.org/10.1080/00076791.2018.1546694.

Foucault, Michel. *The History of Sexuality. An Introduction, Vol. I*. New York: Vintage Books, 1978.

Foucault, Michel. "Truth and Power", in *The Foucault Reader*, edited by Paul Rabinow, 51–75. New York: Penguin Books, 1984.

Gaskell, Ivan. "History of Things", in *Debating New Approaches in History*, edited by Marek Tamm and Peter Burke, 217–246. Bloomsbury: Bloomsbury Academic, 2018.

Mikkola, Kati, Olsson, Pia, and Stark, Eija. "Minority Cultures and the Making of Cultural Heritage Archives in Finland." *Ethnologia Europaea* 49, no. 1 (2019): 58–73. https://doi.org/10.16995/ee.818.

Miller, Daniel. "Artefacts and the Meaning of Things,' in *Companion Encyclopedia of Anthropology*, edited by Tim Ingold, 396–419. London: Routledge, 2002.

Roman, Raluca Bianca. *Kaale Belongings and Evanceligal Becomings. Faith, Commitment and Social Outreach among the Finnish Kaale (Finnish Roma).* PhD Thesis. St Andrews: University of St Andrews, 2016.

Scott, Joan. *Gender and the Politics of History.* New York: Columbia University Press, 1988.

Skeggs, Beverley. *Formations of Class and Gender. Becoming Respectable.* London: Sage, 1997.

Skott, Fredrik. *Folkets minnen. Traditionsinsamling i idé och praktik 1919–1964.* Göteborg: Institutet för språk och folkminnen & Göteborgs universitet, 2008.

Tervonen, Miika. *"Gypsies", "Travellers" and "Peasants." A Study on Ethnic Boundary Drawing in Finland and Sweden, c.1860-1925.* PhD Thesis. Florence: European University Institute, 2010.

Tervonen, Miika. "Historiankirjoitus ja myytti yhden kulttuurin Suomesta", in *Kotiseutu ja kansakunta. Miten suomalaista historiaa on rakennettu*, edited by Pirjo Markkola, Hanna Snellman and Ann-Catrin Östman, 137–162. Helsinki: Suomalaisen Kirjallisuuden Seura, 2014.

Wadauer, Sigrid. "Asking for the Privilege to Work: Applications for a Peddling License (Austria in the 1920s and 1930s)", in *Poverty and Sickness in Modern Europe. Narratives of the Sick Poor, 1780–1938*, edited by Andreas Gestrich, Elizabeth Hurren, and Steven King, 225–246. London, New York: Continuum, 2012.

Index[1]

[1] Note: Page numbers followed by 'n' refer to notes.

J. Ahlbeck et al. (eds.), *Encounters and Practices of Petty Trade in Northern Europe, 1820–1960*,
https://doi.org/10.1007/978-3-030-98080-1

Q

R

T

U

V

FSC
www.fsc.org
MIX
Papier | Fördert
gute Waldnutzung
FSC® C083411

Kolibri 360 GmbH
Ferdinand-Jühlke-Straße 7
99095 Erfurt, Deutschland
produktsicherheit@kolibri360.de